THE CAMBRIDGE (
TO THE ESS...

MW00810549

The Cambridge Companion to the Essay considers the history, theory, and aesthetics of the essay from the moment it's named in the late sixteenth century to the present. What is an essay? What can the essay do or think or reveal or know that other literary forms cannot? What makes a piece of writing essayistic? How can essays bring about change? Over the course of seventeen chapters by a diverse group of scholars, *The Companion* reads the essay in relation to poetry, fiction, natural science, philosophy, critical theory, postcolonial and decolonial thinking, studies in race and gender, queer theory, and the history of literary criticism. This book studies the essay in its written, photographic, cinematic, and digital forms, with a special emphasis on how the essay is being reshaped and reimagined in the twenty-first century, making it a crucial resource for scholars, students, and essayists.

Kara Wittman is Assistant Professor of English and Director of College Writing at Pomona College, where she also directs the Center for Speaking, Writing, and the Image. In addition to her work on the essay, she has published on wonder, originality, clarity, and small forms of communication: phatic utterances, marginalia, talking birds.

Evan Kindley is Visiting Assistant Professor of English at Pomona College. He is the author of *Poet-Critics and the Administration of Culture* (2017) and *Questionnaire* (2016) and a founding editor of the *Los Angeles Review of Books*.

THE CAMBRIDGE
COMPANION TO
THE ESSAY

EDITED BY

KARA WITTMAN
Pomona College

EVAN KINDLEY
Pomona College

CAMBRIDGE
UNIVERSITY PRESS

University Printing House, Cambridge CB2 8BS, United Kingdom

One Liberty Plaza, 20th Floor, New York, NY 10006, USA

477 Williamstown Road, Port Melbourne, VIC 3207, Australia

314–321, 3rd Floor, Plot 3, Splendor Forum, Jasola District Centre,
New Delhi – 110025, India

103 Penang Road, #05–06/07, Visioncrest Commercial, Singapore 238467

Cambridge University Press is part of the University of Cambridge.

It furthers the University's mission by disseminating knowledge in the pursuit of
education, learning, and research at the highest international levels of excellence.

www.cambridge.org
Information on this title: www.cambridge.org/9781316519776
DOI: 10.1017/9781009022255

© Cambridge University Press 2023

First published 2023

A catalogue record for this publication is available from the British Library.

Library of Congress Cataloging-in-Publication Data
NAMES: Wittman, Kara, editor. | Kindley, Evan, editor.
TITLE: The Cambridge companion to the essay / edited by Kara Wittman,
Evan Kindley.
DESCRIPTION: Cambridge ; New York, NY : Cambridge University Press, 2023. |
Includes bibliographical references and index.
IDENTIFIERS: LCCN 2022016872 | ISBN 9781316519776 (hardback) |
ISBN 9781009022255 (ebook)
SUBJECTS: LCSH: Essay – History and criticism. | BISAC: LITERARY CRITICISM /
Semiotics & Theory
Classification: LCC PN4500 .C364 2023 | DDC 808.4–DC23/eng/20220708
LC record available at https://lccn.loc.gov/2022016872

ISBN 978-1-316-51977-6 Hardback
ISBN 978-1-009-01114-3 Paperback

CONTENTS

Contents

FIGURES

CONTRIBUTORS

NORA M. ALTER is Professor of Film and Media Arts at Temple University. She is author of several books including *Vietnam Protest Theatre: The Television War on Stage* (Indiana University Press, 1996), *Sound Matters: Essays on the Acoustics of German Culture* (Berghahn Books, 2004), *Chris Marker* (University of Illinois Press, 2006), *Essays on the Essay Film* (Columbia University Press, 2017), and *The Essay Film after Fact and Fiction* (Columbia University Press, 2018). Future publications include a monograph on Harun Farocki.

KEVIN ADONIS BROWNE is a Caribbean–American photographer and essayist. He has authored two books: *Tropic Tendencies: Rhetoric, Popular Culture, and the Anglophone Caribbean* (University of Pittsburgh Press, 2013) and *HIGH MAS: Carnival and the Poetics of Caribbean Culture* (University Press of Mississippi, 2018). He is Associate Professor of Writing Studies, Rhetoric, and Composition at Syracuse University.

JASON CHILDS is an independent scholar and essayist living in Berlin, Germany. He has contributed chapters to *The Essay at the Limits* (Bloomsbury, 2021) and *The Edinburgh Companion to the Essay* (Edinburgh University Press, 2022). He is the editor, with Denise Gigante, of *The Cambridge History of the British Essay* and, with Christy Wampole, of *The Cambridge History of the American Essay*, both forthcoming in 2023.

JEFF DOLVEN teaches poetics at Princeton University and has written essays on prosody, handles, Shakespeare's reading, milk, Fairfield Porter, and player pianos, as well as essay-books on paraphrase and animal testing. He is also a poet and an editor-at-large at *Cabinet* magazine and was founding director of Princeton's Interdisciplinary Doctoral Program in the Humanities.

MERVE EMRE is Associate Professor of English at the University of Oxford. She is the author and editor of several books, including *Post-Discipline: Literature, Professionalism, and the Crisis of the Humanities*, forthcoming in 2022. She is a regular contributor to the *New Yorker* and *New York Review of Books*.

FRANCES FERGUSON is Mabel Greene Myers Distinguished Service Professor at the University of Chicago. She works on the rise of mass education in the late eighteenth century and has published on various topics including aesthetics and legal thought in the eighteenth and nineteenth centuries.

CLAIRE GROSSMAN is a PhD candidate in English literature at Stanford University. Her research focuses on literary and economic discourses of race in the postwar US. Her recent writing with Juliana Spahr and Stephanie Young appears in American Literary History and Public Books.

JANE HU is a writer with a PhD in English and Film & Media at the University of California, Berkeley. Her work has been published in venues such as *Textual Practice*, *Modernism/modernity Print+*, *Modern Fiction Studies*, *Verge: Studies in Global Asia*, *Victorian Studies*, as well as the *New Yorker*, *New York Times*, *Bookforum*, *Harper's*, and the *Nation*, among others.

EVAN KINDLEY is Visiting Assistant Professor of English at Pomona College. He is the author of *Poet-Critics and the Administration of Culture* (Harvard University Press, 2017) and *Questionnaire* (Bloomsbury, 2016) and a founding editor of the *Los Angeles Review of Books*. His scholarship has appeared in *Critical Inquiry* and *English Literary History* and he is a regular contributor to the *Nation*, *New York Review of Books*, and the *New Republic*.

GRACE LAVERY is Associate Professor in the Department of English at the University of California, Berkeley and general editor of *Transgender Studies Quarterly*. She is the author of *Quaint, Exquisite: Victorian Aesthetics and the Idea of Japan* (Princeton University Press, 2020), which won the NAVSA Best Book of the Year prize, and of *Please Miss*, an experimental memoir (Seal Press, 2022). Her essays have appeared in *Critical Inquiry*, *Foreign Policy*, *Differences: A Journal of Feminist Cultural Studies*, and *English Literary History*.

SAIKAT MAJUMDAR is Professor of English and Creative Writing at Ashoka University. He has published several books of fiction and criticism, including *Prose of the World: Modernism and the Banality of Empire* (Columbia University Press, 2013), *The Firebird/Play House* (Hachette India Local, 2015/Permanent Press, 2015), and *The Critic as Amateur* (Bloomsbury, 2019), a collection of essays coedited with Aarthi Vadde. He writes a column for the *Los Angeles Review of Books*, "Another Look at India's Books."

JESSE MCCARTHY is Assistant Professor of English and of African and African American Studies at Harvard University. He is the author of *Who Will Pay Reparations on My Soul? Essays* (Liveright, 2021) and a novel, *The Fugitivities* (Melville House, 2021), and winner of a 2022 Whiting Award. He edited the Norton Library edition of W. E. B. Du Bois's The Souls of Black Folk (2022) and is co-editor with Joshua Bennett of the Penguin anthology of African American poetry, Minor Notes. His essays and reviews have appeared in The Nation, Dissent, n+1, and The Point, where he is also a contributing editor.

DAEGAN MILLER is an essayist and critic whose first book, *This Radical Land: A Natural History of American Dissent* (University of Chicago Press, 2018), was chosen by both the *Guardian* and *Literary Hub* as a best of 2018.

ANAHID NERSESSIAN is Professor of English at the University of California. She is the author of *Utopia, Limited: Romanticism and Adjustment* (Harvard University Press, 2015), *The Calamity Form: On Poetry and Social Life* (University of Chicago Press, 2020), and *Keats's Odes: A Lover's Discourse* (University of Chicago Press, 2021). She edited the Broadview Press edition of Percy Bysshe Shelley's *Laon and Cythna; or, the Revolution of the Golden City* (2016) and founded and coedits the Thinking Literature series, published by the University of Chicago Press.

DAVID RUSSELL is Associate Professor of English at the University of Oxford, where he is a Fellow of Corpus Christi College. His most recent book is *Tact: Aesthetic Liberalism and the Essay Form in Nineteenth-Century Britain* (Princeton University Press, 2018). He is currently writing books about John Ruskin and Marion Milner.

IGNACIO M. SÁNCHEZ PRADO is the Jarvis Thurston and Mona van Duyn Professor in the Humanities at Washington University in St. Louis. He is the author of several books, including *Strategic Occidentalism: On Mexican Fiction, the Neoliberal Book Market and the Question of World Literature* (Northwestern University Press, 2018). He also writes essays about and is editor of various collections on Mexican and Latin American literature, film, and theory.

JULIANA SPAHR is Professor of Literature and Languages and Dean of Graduate Studies at Mills College. Her research focuses on literature's complicated relationship to nation-state politics, with a special interest in its relationship to resistance movements. Her most recently scholarly book is *Du Bois's Telegram* (Harvard University Press, 2018).

JULIANNE WERLIN is Assistant Professor of Early Modern English Literature at Duke University. She is the author of *Writing at the Origin of Capitalism: Literary Circulation and Social Change in Early Modern England* (Oxford University Press, 2021). Her current project is a prosopography of English writers born between 1480 and 1680.

KARA WITTMAN is Assistant Professor of English and Director of College Writing at Pomona College. She also directs the Center for Speaking, Writing, and the Image at Pomona. In addition to her work on the essay, she has published on wonder, originality, clarity, and small forms of communication: phatic utterances, marginalia, talking birds.

STEPHANIE YOUNG is Director of the Creative Writing Program at Mills College. Her recent books of poetry include *Pet Sounds* (Nightboat Books, 2019) and *It's No Good Everything's Bad* (Double Cross Press, 2018).

ACKNOWLEDGMENTS

We want first to thank Ray Ryan at Cambridge University Press for helping us imagine this *Companion* and for his enthusiasm for the project throughout. We owe our deepest thanks to the eighteen writers in this volume, who gave to it their time, their insight, and their unstinting brilliance. Thank you also to Sarah Allison, Anne Dwyer, Joanne Nucho, and Friederike von Schwerin-High for their contributions to our "440 Years of Essays" chronology. This has been a collaborative project throughout, and we are fortunate to have had two of the finest collaborators we could imagine as we put this book together: Our warmest thanks to Ahana Ganguly and Victor Solórzano-Gringeri, both gifted essayists themselves, who assisted with so many aspects of preparing and editing this book. Thank you also to the students in our spring 2020 "Essay and Experiment" seminar at Pomona College, all of whom, in the true adventurous spirit of the essay, persevered in writing and thinking with us even when campus was evacuated at the onset of the Covid-19 pandemic. Thanks to Andrew Ascherl for his careful indexing and proofreading; any mistakes are strictly our own. Eric Bulson's advice on assembling a collection of this scope was invaluable. We also want to thank each other for the pleasure of teaching, writing, editing, and thinking together. Thank you to Robert Wittman for his Montaignean spirit, his unfading inspiration. Thank you to our partners, Kent Puckett and Emily Ryan Lerner, who were unflaggingly generous and supportive throughout. And finally, to remind us every day of the curiosity, wonder, and joy that live in the essay form, we have Agnes Kindley and Harry Puckett: This book is for them.

We have selected the following texts to indicate the linguistic, cultural, and aesthetic range of essays published between 1580, the year Michel de Montaigne first published his *Essais*, and 2020, the year we began assembling this book. Texts were selected according to one or more of several criteria: 1) they were referred to, by their authors or others, as "essays" at the time of their publication; 2) they were identified as (or re-titled) "essays" at some later point in their publication, translation, or reception history; or 3) they display in their form and their content what Claire de Obaldia calls "the essayistic spirit," whatever their original generic designation.[1] We have tried to represent a wide range of literary modes and traditions in different countries and languages; our hope is that this chronology allows the reader to become familiar with the broadest possible range of notable essayists writing and publishing in the centuries after Montaigne. With few exceptions, texts are listed are in the language of their original publication (with English translation, where applicable) and according to the date of their first appearance. We note most exceptions, which include some literary journals (published over intermittent years) and a few essays for which the exact publication date is unknown.

1580	Michel Eyquem de Montaigne, *Essais* [*Essays*], Books I-II (France)
1581	Francisco Sanches, *Quod nihil scitur* [*Nothing is Known*] (Portugal)
1582	Richard Hakluyt, *Divers Voyages Touching the Discoverie of America* (England)
1583	Justus Lipsius, *De constantia* [*On Constancy*] (Belgium)
1584	James VI/I, *Essayes of a Prentice, in the Diuine Art of Poesy* (England); Leon of Modena, *Sur MeRa* [*A Philosophical Dialogue on Gambling*] (Italy, date appx.)
1585	John Calvin, *Institutes*, English trans. (France)
1586	William Paulet, *The Lord Marquess Idleness* (England)

1614	Thomas Tuke, *New Essayes: Meditations and Vowes* (England)
1615	Ahmad Baba al-Timbukti, *Miraj al-Suud ila nayl Majlub al-Sudan* [*Ahmad Baba Answers a Moroccan's Questions about Slavery*] (Western Sudan, date appx.)
1616	John Deacon, *Tobacco tortured, or, The filthie fume of tobacco refined shewing ... that the inward taking of tobacco fumes, is very pernicious vnto their bodies [...]* (England)
1617	Inca Garcilaso de la Vega, *Comentarios Reales de los Incas* [Royal Commentaries of the Incas], vol. 2 (Viceroyalty of Perú)
1618	*Newes from Italie* (news journal): *or, A prodigious, and most lamentable accident, latelie befallen concerning the swallowing up of the whole citie of Pleurs: belonging unto the Signorie of Venice* (Italy)
1619	Samuel Purchas, *Microcosmus, or The historie of man: relating the wonders of his generation, vanities in his generation, necessity of his regeneration* (England)
1620	Richard Braithwaite, *Essaies upon the fiue senses* (England)
1621	Robert Burton, *The Anatomy of Melancholy* (England)
1622	Henry Peacham, *The Complete Gentleman and the Truth of Our Times, Revealed out of One Man's Experience, by Way of Essay* (England)
1623	Owen Feltham, *Resolves, Divine, Moral, and Political* (England)
1624	Jakob Böhme, *177 Theosophic Questions, with Answers to Thirteen of Them*, English trans. 1691 (Germany)
1625	Francis Bacon, *Essays or Counsels, Civil and Morall...Newly Enlarged* (England)
1626	Jonatan de Sainct-Sernin, *Essais et obseruations sur les essais du Seigneur de Montaigne par le Sieur Jonatan de Sainst [sic] Sernin* [*Essays and Observations on Montaigne's Essays*] (France)
1627	Francis Bacon, posthumous release of *The New Atlantis* (England)
1628	Anrakuan Sakuden, *Seisuishō* [*Laughs to Keep You Awake*] (Japan); John Earle, *Microcosmography, or A Piece of the World Discovered in Essays and Characters* (England)
1629	Arthur Blake, *Sermons with Religious and Divine Meditations* (England)
1630	Koçi Bey, *Risale* (Ottoman Turkey)

1631	Shen Kuo, reprint of *Mengxi Bitan* [*The Dream Pool Essays*] (appx. 1088 CE) (China)
1632	William Cornwallis, *Essays* (reprint) (England)
1633	Thomas James, *The Strange and Dangerous Voyage of Captaine Thomas James* (Wales)
1634	Alonso Jerónimo de Salas Barbadillo, *El Curioso y fabulo Alexandro* (Spain)
1635	William Scott, *An Essay of Drapery, or The Compleate Citizen* (England)
1636	Edward Dacres, trans. Niccolò Machiavelli's *Discourses upon the Decade of T. Livius* (England)
1637	René Descartes, *Discours de la méthode* [*Discourse on Method*] (France); William Austin, *Haec Homo, Wherein the excellency of the Creation of Woman is described, By Way of an Essay* (England)
1638	John Robinson, *Essayes; or Observations Divine and Morall* (England)
1639	Stephen Daye, pub. *The Freeman's Oath* (England/USA)
1640	Kinoshita Chōshōshi, *On Ōhara* (Japan)
1641	Ben Jonson, *Timber: or Discoveries Made upon Men and Matters: As They Have Flowed out of his Daily Reading ...* (England); Jin Shengtan, "How to Read the Fifth Work of Genius, *Shuihu Zhuan* [*Water Margin*]" (China)
1642	Baltasar Gracián, *Arte de ingenio* [*The Mind's Art*] (Spain)
1643	Giuseppi Aromatari, *Autori del Bel Parlare* (Italy)
1644	John Milton, *Areopagitica* (England)
1645	Edward Herbert, *On the Causes of Errors* (England)
1646	John Hall, *Horae vacivae, or Essays* (England); Sir Thomas Browne, *Pseudodoxia Epidemica* (England)
1647	John Cotton, *The Bloudy Tenent, wash'd and made white in the bloud of the Lambe* (Colonial America)
1648	Walter Montagu, *Miscellania Spiritualia: or, Devout Essayes* (England)
1649	Georg Phillip Harsdörffer, *Frauenzimmer-Gesprächspiele* [*Garrulous Games for Women*] (Germany)
1650	Gerrard Winstanley, *Fire in the Bush* (England)
1651	John Donne, *Meditations* (England); Mao Xiang, *Reminiscences of the Plum Shadows Convent* (China, composition appx.)
1652	Seth Ward, *A philosophicall essay toward an eviction of the being and attributes of God* (England)

1653	Izaak Walton, *The Compleat Angler* (England); Henry Harflete, *A Banquet of Essayes* (England); Huang Zongxi, *Ming Yi Dai Fang Lu* [*Waiting for the Dawn*] (China)
1654	Richard Whitlock, *Zootomia, Or, Observations on Present Manners of the English* (England)
1655	Thomas Culpepper, *Morall discourses and essayes* (England)
1656	Abraham Cheare, *Sighs for Sion: or, Faith and Love ... In Way of Essay* (England)
1657	Jean-Louis Guez de Balzac, *Dissertations critiques* (France)
1658	Sir Thomas Browne, *Hydriotaphia, Urn Burial, Or A Brief Discourse of the Sepulchral Urns Lately Found in Norfolk* (England)
1659	John Uffley, *Wit's Fancies: or, Choice Observations and Essayes* (England)
1660	Thieleman Janszoon van Braght, *Het bloedig tooneel* [*The Martyrs Mirror, or the Bloody Theatre*] (The Netherlands)
1661	Robert Boyle, "Proemial Essay ... with considerations touching Experimental Essays in General" (England)
1662	Margaret Cavendish, *Orations of Divers Sorts* (England)
1663	Evliya Çelebi, *Seyâhatnâme* [*Book of Travel*] vol. 6–7 of 10 vols. 1630–1672 (Ottoman Turkey)
1664	La Rochefoucauld, *Sentences et maximes de morale* [*Sentences and Moral Maxims*] (France)
1665	Denis de Sallo, ed. *Journal des sçavans* (France)
1666	John Willis, "An Essay of Dr. John Willis, exhibiting his Hypothesis about the Flux and Reflux of the Sea" (England)
1667	Eirenaeus Philalethes (George Starkey), *Introitus apertus ad occlusum regis palatium* [*Secrets reveal'd; or, An open entrance to the shut-palace of the King*] (Bermuda)
1668	John Dryden, *Essay of Dramatick Poesy* (England)
1669	John Wagstaffe, *The Question of Witchcraft, debated* (England)
1670	Blaise Pascal, *Pensées de M. Pascal sur la religion et sur quelques autres sujets* [*Pascal's Pensées; or, Thoughts on Religion and some Other Subjects*] (France)
1671	Li Yu, *Pleasant Diversions* (China)
1672	William Ramesey, *The Gentlemans Companion: or, A Character of True Nobility and Gentility, In the Way of an Essay* (England)
1673	Robert Boyle, *Essays of Effluviums* (England)

1674   René Rapin, *Reflexions sur la Poétique d'Aristotle* [*Reflections on Aristotle's Poetics*] (France)

1675   J. Carel de Sainte-Garde, *La défense des beaux esprits de ce temps contre un satyrique* (France)

1676   Joseph Glanvill, *Essays on Several Important Subjects in Philosophy and Religion* (England)

1677   Pierre Nicole, *Essais de morale* [*Essays on Morality*] (France)

1678   Abraham Cowley, *Collected Works* (England)

1679   Charles Blount (as anon.), *Anima Mundi* (England)

1680   Li Yu, "On Having a Stomach" (= date of author's death; essay comp. unknown, China)

1681   *Several Weighty Queries Concerning Heraclitus and the Observator, in a Dialogue Betwixt Timothy the Corn-cutter and Mr. Semple* (England)

1682   William Penn, *Some Fruits of Solitude in Maxims and Reflections* (Colonial America)

1683   Pierre Bayle, *Pensées diverses sur l'Occasion de la Comète* (orig. 1682, exp. 1683) [*Various Thoughts on the Occasion of the Comet of 1680*] (France)

1684   Increase Mather, *An Essay for the Recording of Illustrious Providences* (Colonial America)

1685   Montaigne, *Essays*, trans. Charles Cotton (England)

1686   Bernard de Fontenelle, *Entretiens sur la pluralité des mondes* [*Conversations on the Plurality of Worlds*] (France)

1687   Isaac Newton, "Of the First Gate" (England, date appx.)

1688   Jean de la Bruyère, *Les Caractères ou les Moeurs de ce siècle* [*The Characters or the Manners of this Century*] (France)

1689   John Locke, *An Essay concerning Human Understanding* (England)

1690   Sor Juana Inés de la Cruz, *Carta Atenagórica y Respuesta a Sor Filotea* [*Letter Worthy of Athena and Response to Sor Filotea*] (Mexico/New Spain)

1691   John Dunton, *Athenian Mercury* (England)

1692   Saint-Évremond, *Miscellaneous Essays*, trans. John Dryden (France)

1693   Stephen Skynner, *Christian Practice described by way of essay upon the Life of our Savior* (England)

1694   Matsuo Bashō, *Oku no Hosomichi* [*Narrow Road to the Interior*] (Japan)

1695   W. C., *A discourse (By way of Essay) Humbly Offer'd to the Consideration of the Honorable House of Commons Toward the raising Moneys by an Excise* (England)

1696   Judith Drake, *An Essay in Defence of the Female Sex* (England)

1697   John Savage, trans. *Spanish Letters, Historical, Satyrical and Moral of the famous Don Antonion de Guevara, Bishop of Mondonedo ... written by way of essay on different subjects* (England/Spain)

1698   Jeremy Collier, *A Short View of the Immorality and Profaneness of the English Stage* (England)

1699   Ned Ward, *The Weekly Comedy* (England)

1700   Gombaud de Méré, *Oeuvres posthumes* [*Posthumous Works*] (France)

1701   William Anstruther, *Essays, Moral and Divine* (England)

1702   Samuel Parker, *Essays on Divers Weighty and Curious Subjects* (England)

1703   Daniel Defoe, *The Review* (England)

1704   John Dennis, *The Grounds of Criticism in Poetry* (England)

1705   James Clerk, *The practice of discipline [...] In way of essay.* (England); Robert Beverly, *An Essay Upon the Government of English Plantations Upon the Continent of America* (Colonial America)

1706   Fr. Manuel Bernardes, *Nova floresta* [*New Forest*] (Portugal)

1707   Anthony Collins, *Essay Concerning the Use of Reason* (England); Zhang Chao, *Quiet Dream Shadows* (= date of author's death, exact comp. date unknown, China)

1708   Anthony Ashley Cooper, 3rd Earl of Shaftesbury, *A Letter Concerning Enthusiasm* (England)

1709   Richard Steele, *The Tatler* (England)

1710   Cotton Mather, *Bonifacius, or Essays to Do Good* (Colonial America); Mary Chudleigh, *Essays Upon Several Subjects* (England)

1711   Joseph Addison and Richard Steele, *The Spectator* (England)

1712   Jonathan Swift, ed. *The Examiner* (Ireland)

1713   Thomas Parnell, *An Essay on the Different Stiles of Poetry* (Ireland)

1714   Anne Le Févre Dacier, *Des Causes de la Corruption du Goust* [*Of the Causes of the Corruption of Taste*] (France)

1715   Jonathan Richardson, *An Essay on the Theory of Painting* (England)

1716   Richard Blackmore, "Of Essays" (England)

1717   Ogyū Sorai, *Bendō* and *Benmai* [*Distinguishing the Way* and *Distinguishing Names*] (Japan)

1718   Ambrose Phillips, ed. *The Free-thinker* (England)

1719   Richard Steele, *The Plebeian* (England)

1720   Count Johan Oxenstierna, *Recueil de pensies du Comte J. O. sur divers sujets* [*Thoughts of the Count J.O. on Various Subjects*] (Sweden)

1721   Marivaux, *Le Spectateur Français* [*The French Spectator*] (France)

1722   Mary Astell, *An Enquiry After Wit* (England)

1723   John Trenchard and Thomas Gordon, *Cato's Letters (essays)* (England, pub. 1720–23)

1724   Matsuzaki Kanran, *Mado no Susami* [*Window Musings*] (Japan)

1725   Benito Jerónimo Feijóo y Montenegro, *Teatro crítico universal* [*Universal critical theater*] (Spain)

1726   Marquise de Sévigné, *Lettres de Marie Rabutin-Chantal,* (France)

1727   Matthew Byles, *Proteus Echo* (Colonial America)

1728   Francis Hutcheson, *An Essay on the Nature and Conduct of the Passions and Affections, with Illustrations on the Moral Sense* (Scotland)

1729   Jonathan Swift, *A Modest Proposal For Preventing the Children of Poor People From being a Burthen to Their Parents or Country, and For making them Beneficial to the Publick* (Ireland)

1730   Carl and Edvard Carleson, *Sedolärande Mercurius* [*Didactic Mercury*] (Sweden)

1731   Christian Falster, *Amoenitates philologicae* (Denmark, 1729–1732)

1732   Muro Kyūsō, *Shundai Zatsuwa* [*A Japanese Philosopher*] (Japan)

1733   Isaac Watts, *Philosophical Essays* (England)

1734   Alexander Pope, *An Essay on Man* (England)

1735   Nicolas Charles Joseph Trublet, *Essais sur divers sujets de littérature et de morale* [*Essays on Various Subjects, Literary and Moral*] (France)

1736   Fang Bao, *Imperial Anthology of Essays on the Four Books* (China)

1737   La Père Guillame-Hyacinthe Bougeant, *Amusement*

philosophique sur langage des bêtes [*A Philosophical Amusement on the Language of Beasts*] (date written, France)

1738   Benjamin Stillingfleet, *An Essay on Conversation* (England)

1739   Jean-Pierre de Crousaz, *An Examination of Mr. Pope's* Essay on Man (Switzerland)

1740   Johann Jakob Bodmer, *Critische Abhandlung Von dem Wunderbaren in der Poesie* [*Critical Treatise on the Wonderful in Poetry*] (Switzerland)

1741   Jonathan Edwards, *Sinners in the Hands of an Angry God* (Colonial America)

1742   Jacobus Capitein, *The Agony of Asar: A Thesis on Slavery by the Former Slave [...]* (Ghana)

1743   William Whitehead, *An Essay on Ridicule* (England)

1744   Eliza Haywood, *The Female Spectator* (England)

1745   Denis Diderot, *Essai sur le mérite et la vertu* [French trans. and annotation of the 3rd Earl of Shaftesbury's *Inquiry concerning Virtue*] (France)

1746   John Upton, *Critical Observations on Shakespeare* (England)

1747   Dazai Sundai, *Dokugo* [*Chats with Myself*] (Japan, date appx.)

1748   Montesquieu, *De l'esprit des lois* [*The Spirit of the Laws*] (France)

1749   J. Morin, *A Short Account of the Sufferings of Elias Neau*, English trans. John Jacobi (France)

1750   Samuel Johnson, *The Rambler* (England)

1751   Henry Fielding, *An Enquiry into the Late Increase of Robbers and Related Writings* (England)

1752   John Payne, pub. *The Adventurer* (England)

1753   The Humourist, *South Carolina Gazette* (Colonial America)

1754   George Colman and Bonnell Thornton, *The Connoisseur* (England)

1755   Benjamin Franklin, "Observations Concerning the Increase of Mankind, Peopling of Countries, etc." (Colonial America)

1756   Frances Brooke, *The Old Maid* (England)

1757   Yirmisekiz Mehmed Çelebi, *Sefâretnâme* [*Book of Embassies*], French trans. (Ottoman Turkey)

1758   David Hume, *Essays, Moral, Political, and Literary* (Scotland)

1759   Oliver Goldsmith, ed. *The Bee: Being Essays on the Most Interesting Subjects* (Ireland); Edward Young, *Conjectures on Original Composition* (England)

1760   Charlotte Lennox, *The Lady's Museum* (England)

1761   Oliver Goldsmith, *The mystery revealed; containing a series of transactions and authentic testimonials, respecting the supposed Cock-Lane ghost; which have hitherto been concealed from the public* (Ireland)

1762   Henry Home, Lord Kames, *Elements of Criticism* (Scotland)

1763   Voltaire, *Traité sur la tolérance* [*Treatise on Tolerance*] (France); Hanna Diyab, *Evliya Çelebi – The Book of Travels* (Syria)

1764   Samuel Ashwick, *An enquiry (by way of essay) into the origin of feudal tenures* (England)

1765   Carl Christoffer Gjörwell, ed. *Den svenska Mercurius* [*The Swedish Mercury*] (Sweden)

1766   Franz Mesmer, *De planetarum influxu in corpus humanum* [*On the Influence of the Planets on the Human Body*] (Germany)

1767   Nathaniel Appleton, *Considerations on Slavery* (Colonial America)

1768   J. Priestly, *An Essay Upon the First Principles of Government* (England)

1769   Nikolai Novikov, *Truten* [*The drone*] (Russia)

1770   John Trumbull, "The Correspondent" (Colonial America)

1771   Charles Burney, *The Present State of Music in France and Italy* (England)

1772   José Cadalso, *Los Eruditos a la Violeta* [*Wise Men Without Learning*] (Spain)

1773   Anna Laetitia Barbauld and John Aiken, *Miscellaneous Pieces in Prose* (England)

1774   Alexander Gerard, *An Essay on Genius* (Scotland)

1775   Thomas Paine, ed. *The Old Bachelor* (Colonial America)

1776   Thomas Paine, *Thoughts on the Present State of American Affairs* (USA); Lemuel Haynes, "Liberty Further Extended: or, Free Thoughts on the Illegality of Slave-Keeping" (USA)

1777   Georg Forster, *A Voyage Round the World in his Britannic Majesty's Sloop, Resolution, Commanded by Capt. James Cook, During the Years 1772, 3, 4, and 5* (Germany)

1778   Vicesimus Knox, *Essays moral and literary* (England)

1779   Henry Mackenzie, *The Mirror* (Scotland); Philip Parsons, *Dialogues of the Dead with the Living* (England)

1780   Natsume Seibi, "San'en no shin" ["Three Monkeys"] (Japan, date appx.)

1781   Jean Jacques Rousseau, *Essai sur l'origine des langues* [*Essay on the Origin of Languages*] (France)

1782   J. Hector St. John de Crèvecoeur, *Letters from an American Farmer* (France); Ignatius Sancho, *Letters of the Late Ignatius Sancho, An African* (England)

1783   James Boswell, *The Hypochondriack* (England, 1777–1783)

1784   Charles Thevenau de Morande, *La Gazette noire par un homme qui n'est pas blanc; ou oeuvres posthumes du Gazetier cuirassé* [*The Black Gazette by a man who is not white*] (France)

1785   Yuan Mei, *Shih-hua* [*Poetry Talks*, written 1785–1788] (China)

1786   Josefa Amar y Borbón, "Discurso en defensa del talento de las mujeres y de su aptitud para el gobierno, y otros cargos en que se emplean los hombres" ["Discourse in Defense of the Talents of Women"] (Spain)

1787   Ottobah Cugoano, *Thoughts and Sentiments on the Evil and Wicked Traffic of the Slavery and Commerce of the Human Species Humbly Submitted to the Inhabitants of Great Britain* (England)

1788   Othello, "An Essay on Negro Slavery" (USA)

1789   José Cadalso, *Cartas Marruecas* [*Moroccan Letters*] (Spain)

1790   Aleksander Radishchev, Путешествие из Петербурга в Москву [*A Journey from St. Petersburg to Moscow*] (Russia); Edmund Burke, *Reflections on the Revolution in France* (Ireland)

1791   Olympe de Gouges, *Déclaration des droits de la femme et du citoyenne* [*Declaration of the Rights of Woman and of the Female Citizen*] (France)

1792   Mary Wollstonecraft, *A Vindication of the Rights of Women* (England)

1793   Motoori Norinaga, *Jeweled Comb Basket* (Japan)

1794   Zhang Dai, *Tao'an mengyi* [*Reminiscences in Dreams of Tao An*](China, composed c. 1650); Xavier de Maistre, *Voyage autour de ma chambre* [*A Journey Around My Room*] (France)

1795   Friedrich von Schiller, *Über die ästhetische Erziehung des Menschen in einer Reihe von Briefen* [*Letters on the Aesthetic Education of Man*] (Germany)

1796   Isaac D'Israeli, "Of Miscellanies" (England)

1797   William Godwin, *The Enquirer: Reflections on Education, Manners, and Literature* (England)

1798   Thomas Malthus, *An Essay on the Principle of Population* (England); Ban Kōkei, *Kinsei kijinden* [*Unusual People of the Modern Age*] (Japan)

1799   Madame de Staël, *De la littérature dans ses rapports avec les institutions sociales* [*The Influence of Literature on Society*] (France)

1800   William Wordsworth, "Preface" to *Lyrical Ballads* (England)

1801   Elizabeth Hamilton, *Letters on the Elementary Principles of Education* (Scotland)

1802   Saul Ascher, *Ideen zur natürlichen Geschichte der politischen Revolutionen* [*Ideas for the Natural History of Political Revolutions*] (Germany)

1803   Alexandre-Laurent Grimod de La Reynière, *Almanach des gourmands*, first pub. [*The Gourmands' Almanac*] (France)

1804   John Wilson Croker, *Familiar Epistles ... on the State of the Irish Stage* (Ireland); Thomas Branagan, *A Preliminary Essay on the Oppression of the Exiled Sons of Africa* (USA)

1805   Nathan Drake, *Essays, biographical, critical, and historical, illustrative of the Tatler, Spectator, and Guardian* (England)

1806   Heinrich von Kleist, *Über die allmähliche Verfertigung der Gedanken beim Reden* [*On the Gradual Production of Thoughts Whilst Speaking*] (Germany)

1807   Louis Claude de Saint-Martin, *Oeuvres Posthumes* [*Posthumous Works*] (France)

1808   Friedrich Schlegel, *Über die Sprache und Weisheit der Indier* [*On the Language and Wisdom of the Indians*] (Germany)

1809   Maria Edgeworth, *Essays on Professional Education* (Ireland)

1810   Johann Wolfgang von Goethe, *Theory of Colours* (Germany)

1811   Shiba Kōkan, *Shunparō's Jottings* (Japan)

1812   Samuel Taylor Coleridge, *The Friend: A Series of Essays* (England)

1813   James Forten, *Letters from a Man of Color* (USA)

1814   Dabney Carr, George Tucker, and William Wirt, *The Old Bachelor* (USA)

1815   Simón Bolívar, *Carta de Jamaica* [*Letter from Jamaica*] (Venezuela)

1816   Petr A. Viaszemskii, На Державине [*On Derzhavin*] (Russia)

1817   Konstantin N. Batiushkov, *Opyty* [*Essays in verse and prose*] (Russia)

1818   Matsudaira Sadanobu, *Kagetsu sōshi* [*Book of Moon and Flowers*] (Japan)

1819	Leigh Hunt, *The Indicator* (England)
1820	Washington Irving, *The Sketch Book of Geoffrey Crayon, Gent.* (USA)
1821	William Hazlitt, *Table-Talk* (England)
1822	Stendhal, *De L'amour* [*On Love*] (France)
1823	Charles Lamb, *Essays of Elia* (England)
1824	Jeremey Bentham, ed. *The Westminster Review* (England)
1825	Jean Anthelme Brillat-Savarin, *Physiologie du Goût, ou Méditations de Gastronomie Transcendante; ouvrage théorique, historique et à l'ordre du jour, dédié aux Gastronomes parisiens* [*The Physiology of Taste*] (France)
1826	Mary Shelley, "On Ghosts" (England)
1827	Thomas De Quincey, "On Murder Considered as One of the Fine Arts" (England)
1828	Elias Boudinot (Galagina Oowatie), ed. *Cherokee Phoenix*, pub. 1828-1834 (Cherokee Nation/USA)
1829	David Walker, *Appeal, in Four Articles; Together with a Preamble, to the Coloured Citizens of the World, but in Particular, and Very Expressly, to Those of the US of America* (USA)
1830	Henry Savery, *The Hermit in Van Diemen's Land* (Australia)
1831	Thomas Carlyle, "Characteristics" (Scotland)
1832	Leopold von Ranke, *Die Grossen Mächte* [*The Great Powers*] (Germany)
1833	Charles Lamb, *The Last Essays of Elia* (England)
1834	Arthur Henry Hallam, "On Sympathy" (England)
1835	Alexis de Tocqueville, *De la démocratie en Amérique* [*Democracy in America*] (France); John J. Audubon, *The Passenger Pigeon* (USA)
1836	Ralph Waldo Emerson, *Nature* (USA)
1837	Esteban Echeverria, *El Dogma Socialista y Otras Páginas Políticas* [*Socialist Dogma and Other Political Pages*] (Argentina)
1838	Flora Tristan, *Peregrinations of a Pariah* (France/Peru)
1839	Charles Darwin, *The Voyage of the Beagle* (England)
1840	Percy Bysshe Shelley, "A Defence of Poetry" (England)
1841	Vissarion Belinskii, "Ideia iskysstva" ["The Idea of Art"] (Russia)
1842	Victor Hugo, *Le Rhin* [*The Rhine*] (France)
1843	Margaret Fuller, "The Great Lawsuit. Men versus Women" (USA); Søren Kierkegaard, *Enten-Eller* [*Either/Or*] (Denmark)

1868   Marcus Clarke, "The Peripatetic Philosopher" (Australia)

1869   John Stuart Mill, *The Subjection of Women* (England)

1870   Fanny Fern, *Delightful Men* (USA)

1871   Florence Nightingale, "The Character of God" (USA)

1872   Oliver Wendell Holmes, *The Poet at the Breakfast-Table* (USA); Rifa'a al-Tahtawi, "The luminous stars in the moonlit nights of al-Aziz" (Egypt)

1873   Walter Pater, *Studies in the History of the Renaissance* (England)

1874   Joseph Howe, *Poems and Essays* (Canada)

1875   Algernon Charles Swinburne, *Essays and Studies* (England)

1876   Friedrich Nietzsche, *Unzeitgemässe Betrachtungen* [*Untimely Meditations*] (Germany)

1877   George Meredith, *An Essay on Comedy* (England)

1878   Ernest Renan, *Mélanges d'histoire et de voyages* [*Miscellany of Histories and Travels*] (France)

1879   Maria W. Stewart, *Meditations from the Pen of Mrs. Maria W. Stewart* (USA)

1880   Edmund Finn, *The Garryowen Sketches* (Australia)

1881   T. H. Huxley, *Science and Culture, and Other Essays* (England)

1882   José Rizal, "El Amor Patrio" ["The Love of Country"] (Philippines)

1883   Alexander Crummell, "A Defense of the Negro Race" (USA); Plotino Rhodakanaty, *Cartilla Socialista* [*Socialist Primer*] (Mexico)

1884   Sully Prudhomme, *L'Expression dans les beaux-arts* [*Expression in the Fine Arts*] (France)

1885   Anténor Firmin, *De l'égalité des races humaines* [*The Equality of the Human Races*] (Haïti); Ken-yūsha, eds. *Garakuta Bunko* (Japan)

1886   José Martí, "The Earthquake at Charleston" (Cuba)

1887   Friedrich Engels, *The Condition of the Working Class in England* (Germany)

1888   Francis N. Zabriskie, "The Essay as a Literary Form and Quality" (USA)

1889   Henri Bergson, *Time and Free Will: An Essay on the Immediate Data of Consciousness* (France)

1890   Oscar Wilde, "The Critic as Artist" (Ireland)

1891   José Martí, "Nuestra América" ["Our America"] (Cuba); Levon Shant, "Mnak barovi irikune" ["Farewell Evening"] (Armenia)

1892	Anna Julia Cooper, *A Voice from the South: By a Black Woman of the South* (USA)
1893	Tudor Jenks, "The Essay" (USA)
1894	Manuel González Prada, "Páginas Libres" ["Free Pages"] (Peru); John Eglinton, *Two Essays on the Remnant* (Ireland)
1895	Victoria Earle Matthews, "The Value of Race Literature" (USA)
1896	Higuchi Ichiyō, *Akiawase* [*Autumn Ensemble*] (Japan)
1897	Leo Tolstoy, *Что такое искусство?* [*What is Art?*] (Russia); William Butler Yeats, "The Celtic Element in Literature" (Ireland)
1898	Emile Zola, "J'accuse!" ["I Accuse!"] (France)
1899	Karl Kraus, ed. *Die Fackel* [*The Torch*, 1899-1936](Germany)
1900	José Enrique Rodó, *Ariel* (Uruguay)
1901	Mark Twain, "To the Person Sitting in Darkness" (USA)
1902	Euclides da Cunha, *Os Sertoes* [*The Backlands*] (Brazil); Zitkála-Šá, "Why I am a Pagan" (Yankton Dakota/USA)
1903	W. E. B. Du Bois, *The Souls of Black Folk* (USA)
1904	Bliss Carman, *The Friendship of Art* (Canada)
1905	Sigmund Freud, *Drei Abhandlungen zur Sexualtheorie* [*Three Essays on the Theory of Sexuality*] (Austria)
1906	Joseph Conrad, *The Mirror of the Sea* (England)
1907	Henry James, *The American Scene* (USA)
1908	G. K. Chesterton, "On Running after One's Hat" (England)
1909	Inazo Nitobe, *Thoughts and Essays* (Japan)
1910	Georg Lukács, *Die Seele und die Formen* [*Soul and Form*] (Hungary)
1911	Benedetto Croce, *Saggi sulla letteratura Italiana del Seicento* [*Essays on Italian Literature of the Seventeenth Century*] (Italy); Rafael Barrett, *El dolor paraguayo* [*The Paraguayan Sorrow*] (Paraguay); John Muir, "My First Summer in the Sierra" (Scotland/USA)
1912	Miguel de Unamuno, *Del sentimiento trágico de la vida* [*The Tragic Sense of Life*] (Spain)
1913	Vasily Vasilievich Rozanov, *Opavshiye listya* [*Fallen Leaves*] (Russia)
1914	Abbas Mahmoud al-Aqqad, الكتب بين ساعات [*Hours Spent Among Books*] (Egypt)
1915	Rubén Darío, *La vida de Rubén Darío escrita por él mismo* [*The Life of Rubén Darío, Written by Himself*] (Nicaragua)

1916   Rabindranath Tagore, *Sadhana: The Realisation of Life* (India)
1917   Alfonso Reyes, *Visión de Anáhuac, 1519 [Vision of Anáhuac, 1519]* (Mexico)
1918   Vilhelm Ekelund, *Metron* (Sweden)
1919   T. S. Eliot, "Tradition and the Individual Talent" (USA)
1920   W. E. B. Du Bois, "On Being Black" (USA)
1921   Adolphe Appia, *L'œuvre d'art vivant [The Work of Living Art]* (Switzerland)
1922   Eric D. Walrond, "On Being Black" (USA)
1923   Kikuchi Kan, *Various Thoughts on the Great Kanto Earthquake* (Japan)
1924   Américo Castro, *Lengua, enseñanza y literatura [Language, Teaching, and Literature]* (Spain)
1925   José Ortega y Gasset, *La deshumanización del Arte [The Dehumanization of Art]* (Spain); José Vasconcelos, *La raza cosmic [The Cosmic Race]* (Mexico); Franz Roh, *Nach-expressionismus: Magischer realismus [Post-Expressionism: Magical Realism]* (Germany)
1926   Langston Hughes, "The Negro Artist and the Racial Mountain" (USA)
1927   José Regio, ed. *Presença - Folha de Arte e Crítica* (Portugal)
1928   José Carlos Mariátegui, *7 ensayos de interpretación para la realidad peruana [Seven Interpretive Essays on Peruvian Reality]* (Peru); Hans Richter, *Inflation* (Germany); Zora Neale Hurston, "How It Feels to Be Colored Me" (USA)
1929   Virginia Woolf, *A Room of One's Own* (England); Dziga Vertov, Человек с кино-аппаратом *[Man with a Movie Camera]* (Russia)
1930   Jean Vigo, *Á propos de Nice* (France); Mario Praz, *La carne, la morte e il diavolo nella letteratura romantica [The Romantic Agony]* (Italy)
1931   Jorge Basadre, *Perú: Problema y posibilidad [Peru: Problem and Possibility]* (Peru); Alain (Émile Chartier), *Entretiens au bord de la mer [Conversations by the Edge of the Sea]* (France)
1932   C. L. R. James, *Letters from London* (Trinidad); Marina Tsvetaieva, *Art in the Light of Conscience* (Russia)
1933   Gilberto Freyre, *Casa Grande e Senzala [The Masters and the Slaves]* (Brazil)
1934   Emma Goldman, *Was My Life Worth Living?* (USA); Marion Milner, *A Life of One's Own* (England); Vũ Trọng Phụng, *The Industry of Marrying Europeans* (Vietnam)

1935   Walter Benjamin, "Das Kunstwerk im Zeitalter seiner tech-nischen Reproduzierbarkeit [The Work of Art in the Age of its Mechanical Reproducibility]" (Germany)

1936   George Orwell, "Shooting an Elephant" (England); Lu Xun, "Death" (China)

1937   M. F. K. Fisher, *Meals for Me* (USA)

1938   Virginia Woolf, *Three Guineas* (England); Antonin Artaud, *Le Théâtre et son Double* [*The Theatre and Its Double*] (France)

1939   P'i Ch'Onduk, "The Essay" (Korea, date appx.)

1940   Simone Weil, "L'Iliade ou le poème de la force" ["The Iliad, or, The Poem of Force"] (France)

1941   James Agee and Walker Evans, *Let Us Now Praise Famous Men* (USA); Richard Wright and Edwin Rosskam, *12 Million Black Voices* (USA)

1942   Albert Camus, *Le Mythe de Sisyphe* [*The Myth of Sisyphus*] (France)

1943   Stefan Zweig, *The World of Yesterday,* English trans. (Austria)

1944   Rachel Carson, "The Bat Knew It First" (USA)

1945   Humphrey Jennings, *A Diary for Timothy* (England)

1946   George Orwell, "Politics and the English Language" (England)

1947   Max Bense, "Über den Essay und seine Prosa" ["On the Essay and Its Prose"] (Germany); Alioune Diop, ed., *Présence Afric-aine* (Senegal/France)

1948   Jean-Paul Sartre, *Qu'est-ce que la littérature?* [*What is Liter-ature?*] (France)

1949   Georges Franju, *Le sang des betes* [*Blood of the Beasts*] (France); Alejo Carpentier, *De lo real maravilloso americano* [*On the Marvelous Real in America*] (Cuba); Aldo Leopold, *A Sand County Almanac* (USA)

1950   Lionel Trilling, *The Liberal Imagination* (USA); Octavio Paz, *El laberinto de la soledad* [*The Labyrinth of Solitude*] (Mex-ico); Aimé Césaire, *Discours sur le colonialisme* [*Discourse on Colonialism*] (Martinique)

1951   Vladimir Nabokov, *Speak, Memory* (Russia); New Intellectu-als of Angola, eds., *Mensagem* (Angola)

1952   Anthony Sampson and Henry "Mr. Drum" Nxumalo, *DRUM Magazine* (South Africa)

1953   Roberto Rossellini, *Viaggio in Italia* (Italy); Vahe Vahian, *Rec-onciliation of the Haralez* (Armenia)

1954   Martin Heidegger, Die Frage nach der Technik ["The Question Concerning Technology"] (Germany)

1955   Roy de Carava and Langston Hughes, *The Sweet Flypaper of Life* (USA); Alain Resnais, *Nuit et brouillard* [*Night and Fog*] (France); James Baldwin, *Notes of a Native Son* (USA)

1956   Hoang Van Chi, *The Fate of the Last Viets* (Vietnam)

1957   José Lezama Lima, *La expresión americana* [*American Expression*] (Cuba)

1958   Theodor W. Adorno, "Der Essay als Form" [The Essay as Form"] (Germany); Gaston Bachelard, *The Poetics of Space* (France); Kawamori Yoshizō, "A Room to One's Self" (Japan)

1959   Nirad C. Chaudhuri, *A Passage to England* (India)

1960   Jorge Luis Borges, *Otras Inquisiciones* [*Other Inquisitions*] (Argentina); Elias Canetti, *Masse und Macht* [*Crowds and Power*] (Germany)

1961   Frantz Fanon, *The Wretched of the Earth* (Martinique)

1962   Natalia Ginzburg, *Le piccole virtù* [*The Little Virtues*] (Italy); Shōno Junzō, "Michi" ["The Road"] (Japan)

1963   Hannah Arendt, *Eichmann in Jerusalem* (Germany/USA); Germán Arciniegas, "Nuestra América es un ensayo" ["Our America is an Essay"] (Colombia); Forough Farrokhzad, خانه سیاه است [*The House is Black*] (Iran)

1964   Ralph Ellison, "The World and the Jug" (USA); James Baldwin and Richard Avedon, *Nothing Personal* (USA); Léopold Sédar Senghor, *Liberté 1* (Senegal)

1965   Glauber Rocha, "Eztétyka da fome" ["The Aesthetics of Hunger"] (Italy/Brazil); Obiajunwa Wali, "The Individual and the Novel in Africa" (Nigeria)

1966   Susan Sontag, "Against Interpretation" (USA)

1967   Malcolm X, "Telephone Conversation with Malcolm X" (USA/France, recorded 1965)

1968   Yukio Mishima, *Taiyō to Tetsu* [*Sun and Steel*] (Japan); Edward Abbey, *Desert Solitaire* (USA)

1969   Fernando Solanas and Octavio Getino, *Hacia un tercer cine* [*Toward a Third Cinema*] (Argentina)

1970   Albert Murray, *The Omni-Americans* (USA)

1971   Roberto Fernández Retamar, "Calibán" (Cuba); John McPhee, *Encounters with the Archdruid* (USA)

1972   John Berger, *Ways of Seeing* (England); Stanley Cavell, *The Senses of Walden* (USA)

1973   Osaragi Jirō, "A Bed for My Books" (Japan, date appx.)

1974   Annie Dillard, *Pilgrim at Tinker Creek* (USA); Alexander Kluge, *In Gefahr und grosster Not bringt der Mittelweg den Tod* [*In Danger and Greatest Need, the Middle Way Brings Death*] (Germany); Jacques Derrida, *Glas* (France)

1975   Eduardo Galeano, *Las venas abiertas de América Latina* [*Open Veins of Latin America*] (Uruguay); Patricio Guzmán. *La batalla de Chile: La insurrección de la burguesía* [*The Battle of Chile*] (Chile)

1976   Wole Soyinka, *Myth, Literature, and the African World* (Nigeria); Wendell Berry, *The Unsettling of America* (USA)

1977   Chinua Achebe, "An Image of Africa" (Nigeria); Roberto Schwarz, *Ao vencedor as batatas* [*To the Victor, the Potatoes*] (Brazil)

1978   Harun Farocki, *Between Two Wars* (Germany)

1979   Joan Didion, "The White Album" (USA)

1980   Roland Barthes, *Camera Lucida* (France); Jamil Dehlavi, *The Blood of Hussain* (Pakistan)

1981   V. S. Naipaul, *Among the Believers* (Trinidad and Tobago)

1982   Richard Rodriguez, *Hunger of Memory* (USA); Rafael Argullol, *El héroe y el único* [*The Hero and the Only*] (Spain)

1983   Chris Marker, *Sans Soleil* (France)

1984   Audre Lorde, *Sister Outsider* (USA); Ángel Rama, *La ciudad letrada* [*The Lettered City*] (Uruguay)

1985   Ayi Kwei Armah, "The Lazy School of Literary Criticism" (Ghana); Susan Howe, *My Emily Dickinson* (USA)

1986   John Akomfrah, *Handsworth Songs* (Ghana/England); Barry Lopez, *Arctic Dreams* (USA); Ngũgĩ wa Thiong'o, *Decolonising the Mind* (Kenya); Malek Alloula, *The Colonial Harem* (Algeria)

1987   Gloria Anzaldúa, *Borderlands/La Frontera: The New Mestiza* (USA); Doris Lessing, *Prisons We Choose to Live Inside* (Zimbabwe/UK)

1988   Jamaica Kincaid, *A Small Place* (Antigua); Italo Calvino, *Six Memos for the Next Millennium* (Italy); W. G. Sebald, *After Nature* (Germany)

1989   Shelby Steele, "Being Black and Feeling Blue: Black Hesitation on the Brink" (USA)

1990   Édouard Glissant, *Poétique de la relation* [*Poetics of Relation*] (Martinique); Sony Lab'ou Tansi "An Open Letter To Africans" c/o The Punic One-Party State, an essay (Belgian Congo)

1991	David Wojnarowicz, *Close to the Knives* (USA); William Least Heat-Moon, *PrairyErth* (USA/Osage)
1992	Philip Lopate, "In Search of the Centaur: The Essay-Film" (USA)
1993	Leslie Marmon Silko, *Sacred Water* (Laguna Pueblo/USA)
1994	Edward Said, *Representations of the Intellectual* (Palestine); Antonio Cornejo Polar, *Escribir en el aire* [*Writing in the Air*] (Peru); Carmen Hermosillo, "Pandora's Vox" (USA)
1995	Anne Carson, "The Glass Essay" (Canada); Marlon Riggs, *Black Is, Black Ain't* (USA)
1996	Sergio Pitol, *El arte de la fuga* [*The Art of Flight*] (Mexico)
1997	Patrick Keiller, *Robinson in Space* (England); Geoff Dyer, *Out of Sheer Rage* (England)
1998	Pankaj Mishra, "Edmund Wilson in Benares" (India); Arundhati Roy, "The End of Imagination" (India)
1999	Nadine Gordimer, *Living in Hope and History: Notes from our Century* (South Africa); Subcomandante Insurgente Marcos, "La Cuarta Guerra Mundial" ["The Fourth World War"] (Mexico)
2000	James Alan McPherson, *A Region Not Home: Reflections on Exile* (USA); Bae Suah, "There is a Man Inside Me" (South Korea)
2001	Apichatpong Weerasethakul, *Mysterious Object at Noon* (Thailand); Roberto Calasso, *Literature and the Gods* (Italy)
2002	June Jordan, *Some of Us Did Not Die* (USA); Nick Denton, ed. *Gawker* (UK/USA)
2003	Shashi Deshpande, *Writing from the Margins and Other Essays* (India)
2004	Sakai Junko, *The Pillow Book REMIX* (Japan)
2005	Rebecca Solnit, *A Field Guide to Getting Lost* (USA); Milan Kundera, *Le Rideau* (Czech Republic)
2006	Sergio González Rodríguez, *De sangre y sol* [*Of Blood and Sun*] (Mexico); F. Gonzalez Crussi, *On Seeing* (Mexico/USA)
2007	Antoni Martí Monterde, *Poética del café* [*The Poetics of the Café*] (Spain); Anna Holmes, ed., *Jezebel* (USA)
2008	Lynda Barry, *What It Is* (USA); Amit Chaudhuri, *Clearing a Space* (India); Paul B. Preciado, *Testo Yonqui* (Spain)
2009	Zadie Smith, *Changing My Mind: Occasional Essays* (England); Choire Sicha and Alex Balk, eds. *The Awl* (USA)
2010	J. M. Coetzee and Arabella Kurtz, "Nevertheless, My Sympathies are with the Karamazovs" (South Africa/England);

	Sayak Valencia, *Capitalismo Gore* (Mexico); John D'Agata, *About a Mountain* (USA)
2011	Damián Tabarovsky, *Literatura de izquierda* (Argentina); Malama Katulwende, "The Clouds" (Zambia); Bill Simmons, ed. *Grantland* (USA)
2012	Jenny Boully, *of the mismatched teacups, of the single-serving spoon: a book of failures* (USA/Thailand)
2013	Hisham Matar, "The Return: A Father's Disappearance, A Journey Home" (USA/Libya)
2014	Ta-Nehisi Coates, "The Case for Reparations" (USA)
2015	Robert Macfarlane, *Landmarks* (England); Maggie Nelson, *The Argonauts* (USA)
2016	Mark Greif, *Against Everything* (USA); Viet Thanh Nguyen, *Nothing Ever Dies* (Vietnam/USA), Amitav Ghosh, *The Great Derangement: Climate Change and the Unthinkable* (India)
2017	Teju Cole, *Blind Spot* (USA); Leanne Betasamoksake Simpson, *This Accident of Being Lost* (Nishnaabeg/Canada); Marina Dimópulos, *Carrusel Benjamin* (Argentina)
2018	Kazim Ali, *Silver Road* (USA); Zoë Wicomb, *Race, Nation, Translation* (South Africa); Silvia Rivera Cusicanqui, *Un Mundo Ch'ixi es posible* [*A Ch'ixi World Is Possible*] (Bolivia); Alessandro Baricco, *The Game* (Italy)
2019	Kathleen Stewart and Lauren Berlant, *The Hundreds* (USA); Verónica Gago, "La potencia feminista o el deseo de cambiarlo todo" ["La Potencia Feminista: Or, The Desire to Change Everything"] (Argentina)
2020	Pau Luque, *Las cosas como son y otras fantasías* [*Things as They Are and Other Fantasies*] (Spain); Kiese Makeba Laymon, "Mississippi: A Poem, in Days" (USA)

Note

1 C. Claire de Obaldia, *The Essayistic Spirit: Literature, Modern Criticism, and the Essay* (Oxford: Oxford UP, 1995), *passim*.

KARA WITTMAN AND EVAN KINDLEY

Introduction

One day in late-sixteenth-century France, Michel Eyquem de Montaigne retired from political life, shut himself in his library, and tried something new. In 1580, he published the first version of the *Essais*, a word that can be translated variously as "attempts," "trials," "experiments" and, of course, "essays." Since then, the world has been reckoning with the form that Montaigne invented (or reinvented, drawing on the long history of dialogues, histories, and self-accountings that preceded him). This book is one such reckoning.

What, after all, is an essay? What can an essay do or think or reveal or know that other literary forms cannot? What makes a piece of writing essayistic? Answers to questions about the essay frequently come in the form of negations, statements of what the essay *isn't*: It's neither poetry nor fiction; it may proceed by experimentation but it isn't a scientific treatise and offers no proof; it deals with concepts and ideas but opposes what Georg Lukács calls the "icy perfection of philosophy"; it may tell the story of a self, but it isn't autobiography or memoir; it may contain facts, but it's certainly not always to be trusted.[1] The essay invites readers down its many and winding paths but isn't so interested in providing a map; it begins a dialogue but doesn't manage the stage. As Thomas Karshan and Kathyrn Murphy admit in the midst of their own efforts to define the form, the "pursuit of common features" might, in the end, be futile: "the essay has made resistance to definition part of its particular work."[2] We might say that resistance and negation themselves are in fact essential to the form: The essay wonders and it doubts, it rejects conclusions, prefers the "not" or the "not yet."

The project of trying to define the essay runs into other complications. For one, essayistic writing is much older than the *Essais* itself. "The word is late," writes Francis Bacon in 1612, "but the thing is ancient."[3] Lately it has come to seem like the essay is as old as writing itself. John D'Agata's three mammoth anthologies, published between 2003 and 2016, have proposed an ambitious and controversial genealogy that traces the essay form as far back as ancient Sumer and encompasses works more commonly labeled philosophy, fiction, and poetry.[4] Montaigne himself draws on a range of Greek and Latin sources: Heraclitus's aphorisms, Seneca's letters, Ovid's verse, Cicero's "eloquence" (which he found constraining),[5] and Plutarch's histories. His magpie gathering of these classical writers helps us see what was essayistic about their work *avant la lettre*. But in our search for the essayistic throughout global literary history, we can also look to texts Montaigne would not have known at all: Azwinaki Tshipala's ribald self-interviews conducted in southern Africa in 315 CE; the wry miscellanies composed by al-Jahiz in eighth-century Basra; Sei Shōnagon's diaristic observations of courtly life in Imperial Japan; Shen Kuo's extensive *Mengxi Bitan*, written around the end of the eleventh century in the Northern Song Dynasty and later translated as *The Dream Pool Essays*; the *Seyâhatnâme* ("books of travels") assembled by Ottoman Turkish explorers; or Bernardino de Sahagún's sprawling, collaborative *Florentine Codex, or The General History of the Things of New Spain*, written in the newly conquered Aztec Empire while Montaigne was still a teenager.

These diverse manifestations point us to the key complexity of the essay: It is at once a literary *genre* and a *mode* of writing, and quite happy to be both without privileging either. Essayism, or essaying – what Montaigne noticed he was doing (trying, experimenting, weighing, exploring) and then decided to name – is a loose and exploratory disposition toward the world, as well as toward representation and writing. Novels can be essayistic, and so can journalistic reportage; we can see aspects of the essay in forms as diverse as prose poems, manifestos, scientific taxonomies, and Internet "listicles" (which might remind us of Sei Shōnagon's lists of "things that quicken the heart"). Claire de Obaldia speaks of "the essayistic spirit": Where "genre remains a question" for the essay, an uneasy reconciliation with the categories and fixed points it essentially rejects, the essayistic spirit is game for almost anything.[6] Writing of this same spirit as it manifests itself in the African American essay tradition, Cheryl Wall – borrowing a phrase from Zora Neale Hurston – calls it "the will to adorn": an aesthetic that values digressiveness, playfulness, embellishment, "and a display of consciousness that language ... is important for its own sake."[7]

Montaigne's coinage, then, more than bringing something wholly new into being, gives us a kind of generic lingua franca, allowing us to consider and talk about writing we now call "essayistic" throughout history and across a wide variety of cultures. Before Montaigne, the word "essay" had never appeared in print to denominate a literary genre. (Some scholars argue that even Montaigne didn't intend it to do so; for him, *Essais* may have been merely a title.) After Montaigne, the word allows us to compare cultural traditions and see both common threads and crucial divergences. This was true even as early as five years after Montaigne's death in 1592: Francis Bacon's 1597 *Essayes* most likely take their name from Montaigne's creations, but they have a distinct ethos and a very different way of approaching both knowledge and authority. They are essays and manifest a recognizably essayistic spirit, but Bacon's essays are not doing exactly what Montaigne's were doing. In other countries, languages, and literary cultures around the world, we can see different traditions of the essay and essayistic writing: some self-consciously following Montaigne, others *sui generis* but sharing the characteristics we generally see in literary works named "essays," and still others adapting Montaignean nomenclature post hoc.

For example, David Pollard, in the introduction to his anthology *The Chinese Essay*, writes: "When English essays were first translated into Chinese on any scale in the 1920s and 30s, there was no agreement on what to call them. The most favored options were *xiaopinwen* (minor works, or short pieces) and *suibi* (occasional jottings) ... Presently the most commonly used term is *sanwen* (prose)." But in classical Chinese literature, *sanwen* refers to anything nonfictional not written in verse, an expansive category that includes "official memorials and rescripts, prefaces, letters, obituaries, prose poems, biographies, excerpts from historical and philosophical works, and more besides."[8] Translating a broad selection of Chinese nonfiction into English, Pollard's anthology brings all of this miscellaneous matter together as "essays." In Japanese, meanwhile, the term that corresponds most closely to "essay" is *zuihitsu*: Steven Carter, in his introduction to *The Columbia Anthology of Japanese Essays*, calls this "a supergenre in which one will often find a mix of subgenres, everything from reportage and travelogue to poetry, literary criticism, biography, confession, journalism – and so on, almost ad infinitum."[9] This genre of writing, according to the scholar Donald Keene, "has no close European counterpart," but Carter tells us "it is generally called 'essay,' or 'miscellany.'"[10] Our own chronology thus traces both essayism and the essay in world literary history after Montaigne, but without fetishizing "the essay" as a term: Some works we include were called essays at their inception, and some weren't; others were translated to English, French, or Spanish as *essays*, *essais*, or *ensayos* (to name just three cognates); some have been described in critical responses or historical descriptions as essays, while still others simply share the wandering, exploratory, self-conscious essayistic spirit.

Does the essay, for that matter, even need to be made of words? In the USA in the 1930s and 40s, photographers such as Margaret Bourke White, W. Eugene Smith, Dorothea Lange, and Arthur Rothstein began publishing photographic essays, sometimes commissioned by the Farm Security

Administration. In 1941, James Agee and Walker Evans collaborated on one of the most famous of these government projects, resulting in the at once delicately lyrical and aggressively political *Let Us Now Praise Famous Men*.[11] The same year, Richard Wright published *12 Million Black Voices*, a trenchant Marxist analysis of African American history juxtaposed with Depression-era photographs by Edwin Rosskam.[12] Later in the century, works such as Susan Sontag's *On Photography*, Roland Barthes's *Camera Lucida*, and John Berger's *Ways of Seeing* explored the critical possibilities of juxtaposing image and text.[13] In 1947 Salvador Dalí illustrated the *Essais*, forging a link between Montaigne's early modern divagations and twentieth-century surrealism, and anticipating later graphic essays such as Philippe Squarzoni's *Climate Changed*, Lynda Barry's *What It Is*, and Eleanor Davis's *Why Art?*[14] Historians of cinema have argued that prototypes of the essay film emerge as early as D. W. Griffith's 1909 *A Corner in Wheat* and Dziga Vertov's 1929 *Man With a Movie Camera*. Hans Richter's 1940 "The Essay Film: A New Type of Documentary Film" suggests that experimental films such as these be called "essays" because they "deal with difficult subjects and themes [in] generally comprehensible form," but also allow the filmmaker to produce "complex thought – thought that, at times, is not grounded in *reality* but can be contradictory, irrational, and fantastic."[15] The addition of the image, still or moving, further complicates the already shifting and unstable form of the essay, raising questions of "how images and words find and lose their conscience," as W. J. T. Mitchell puts it in *Picture Theory*, as well as "their aesthetic and ethical identity."[16]

For twenty-first-century undergraduates, who are one of the intended primary audiences of this book, "the essay" might seem drearily familiar. Most students in the US education system are taught to craft "five-paragraph essays," colorfully known as "hamburger essays," with a top-bun introduction, three body paragraphs (meat, cheese, some veggies), and a bottom-bun conclusion. Scholars have traced these forms both to rhetorical exercises in classical Greece and to the student "themes" assigned in nineteenth-century grammar schools, assignments designed to teach strict style, grammatical correctness, and organized thinking.[17] As Nicole Wallack argues in *Crafting Presence: The American Essay and the Future of Writing Studies*, the problem of defining the essay has played no small part in its being both everywhere and nowhere in schools. The essay, she suggests, "has often been a synecdoche for teachers' and other stakeholders' beliefs about the varied aims of writing in high school and college, and arguably even for the broader cultural functions of education."[18] Students are supposed to learn to write by writing essays, but only essays of a particular kind. The benefit of the five-paragraph essay, especially given the rapidly expanding population of students attending high school and college in the USA in the late 1940s and 1950s, is that it is formulaic and portable: easy to identify, to teach, and to grade. Its boxy outline bears, however, almost no resemblance to Montaigne's tentacular structures, and, in its emphasis on product and assessment, it is in many ways antithetical to his exploratory, wandering spirit.

It's a commonplace for literary critics and theorists (who often, but not always, identify as essayists themselves) to refer to the essay as a neglected or undervalued form, subordinate to the novel and the poem in the literary hierarchy. The essay has also (much like the novel and poetry, come to think of it) periodically been declared to be "dead." If it has been difficult to define the essay, it appears to have been easy to identify its body: Between 1890 and 1940 in the USA, the essay was declared over and over to be "disappearing," "lost," barely surviving, a "Little Old Lady" on the verge of passing away.[19] In a 1902 piece on "The Old-Fashioned Essay" for *Harper's Magazine*, William Dean Howells laments that "the moment came when the essay began to confuse itself with the article, and to assume an obligation of constancy to premises and conclusions, with the effect of so depraving the general taste that the article is now desired more and more, and the essay less and less."[20] Virginia Woolf feels compelled to remind us, in her 1925 "The Modern Essay," that "the essay is alive; there is no reason to despair," perhaps partly in order to walk back her 1905 assertion of its "decay."[21] Ned Stuckey-French has suggested that these hand-wringing obituaries are part of the birth pangs of a more modern version of the essay, born from the decline of a "genteel" essay tradition and the growing desire for a reflective, meditative form in a chaotic and increasingly commercialized literary marketplace.[22]

Yet the essay has never really been out of fashion, and in the twenty-first century it is arguably experiencing something of a renaissance. Graduate and undergraduate courses on the form are proliferating in both literature and creative writing departments. Collections of essays by writers such as Maggie Nelson, Ta-Nehisi Coates, Esmé Weijun Wang, Emilie Pine, Tressie McMillan Cottom, Leanne Betasamosake Simpson, and Durga Chew-Bose are capturing the kind of critical and journalistic attention usually reserved for literary fiction. In 2013 Christy Wampole declared in the *New York Times* that "the essayification of everything" was underway;[23] more recently, the Irish critic Brian Dillon has made the case for "essayism" as a coherent literary aesthetic.[24] Noting the increasingly essayistic character of contemporary fiction, Jonathan Franzen wrote in *The Guardian* in 2016 that "we seem to be living in an essayistic golden age," while also fretting, somewhat counterintuitively, about the essay's imminent "extinction" (along with that of democracy and the human species).[25] Recent works by Ben Lerner, Rachel Cusk, Elif Batuman, Teju Cole, and Karl Ove Knausgaard have troubled the line between novel and essay, just as others by Natanya Ann Pulley, Claudia Rankine, Anne Boyer, and Kazim Ali have blurred those between essay and lyric poem. And then there's the Internet. Twitter and Facebook have revived many of the dialogic and polemical energies that facilitated the rise of the periodical essay in the eighteenth century. Platforms such as YouTube and Vimeo have proven to be fertile soil for video essays, some didactic or instructional, others speculative and meditative; examples of note include John Bresland's *Mangoes*, a patchwork meditation on parenting, consumerism, and masculinity, Elisa Giardina Papa's *Technologies of Care,* an exploration of the precarity of affective labor and the outsourcing of empathy to Internet platforms, Cydnii Wilde Harris's meditations on race and representation in film and television history, and the pointed culture-war commentaries of Natalie Wynn's ContraPoints.

The tradition of trying to define the essay – and it's a very long one – has been dominated for centuries by essayists themselves. Essays on the essay are as old as Montaigne and form a kind of subcanon in their own right. This book participates in that meta-essayistic tradition, but also makes a significant departure from it by bringing the history of the essay into contact with other currents in contemporary literary scholarship. As with any other literary or artistic form, remarks by practitioners can be illuminating, but they can also be arcane or partial, focusing on legitimating a particular practice of essay-writing. We believe the essay is a form that deserves serious theoretical and critical consideration from multiple angles. The mycelial reach of the essay means that all of us who write nonfiction prose for an academic audience, a public audience, or even just for ourselves participate in some way in a tradition of essay writing, but here we've invited our writers to consider the essay in contexts – historical and theoretical – that extend beyond their own individual practice as writers. Our contributors consider essays and the essay form in the contexts of literary theory, political and economic history, postcolonialism, ecocriticism, new media studies, queer theory, and more, and collectively they speak to the range and fecundity of the essay form. We can't, of course, be comprehensive; even the relatively conventional decision to begin with Montaigne, as we do, elides the centuries-long prehistory sketched above. And, while there is some tilt toward the Anglophone tradition in the chapters that follow, we affirm that the essay is a global form. In "440 Years of Essays," the detailed chronology included in this book, we've tried to indicate this expansive geographic and linguistic scope.

The goal of this book is to broaden our ideas of what essays are and have been, how they work, and what work they have done throughout world history (and not just literary history). The chapters in our opening section, "Forms of the Essay," attempt to answer some fundamental questions about the shapes the essay takes: *What is an essay, and what is it good for? How do we know one when we see one?* "Essays are so many and the barriers to entering the category are low, but there are still moments when I find myself saying, *now* this *is an essay*," Jeff Dolven writes in "Remembering the Essay," his reflection on two of the form's sixteenth-century European pioneers, Michel de Montaigne and Francis Bacon. Dolven notes Montaigne and Bacon's mutual concern with memory and situates their work in the context of the humanist educational practices of the early modern period (such as the *ars memoria*), while also broaching the larger question of the essay's "mnemonic affordances," suggesting that we conceive of the essay as a "rebel against memory."

From its inception, the essay has been both an intimately personal genre ("I am myself the matter of my book," as Montaigne famously put it) and a critical one: The *Essais* are built around the texts of others, offering interpretive commentaries on other people's writing on virtually every page. "Originally his book was a collection of the fruit of his reading, with running commentary," Erich Auerbach writes of Montaigne's *Essais* in his magisterial philological study *Mimesis: The Representation of Reality in Western Literature*. "This pattern was soon broken; commentary predominated over text, subject matter or point of departure was not only things read but also things lived – now his own experiences, now what he heard from others or what took place around him."[26] In a pair of early chapters, Merve Emre and Frances Ferguson each explore from different angles this basic bifurcation of the essay form. In "The Personal Essay," Emre argues that the personal has come to dominate over the critical, developing a distinction between the "familiar essay," as practiced by writers such as Charles Lamb and Virginia Woolf, and the more overtly autobiographical "personal essay" as it has evolved since the early twentieth century. Emre sees the personal essay today as a mandatory vehicle of self-revelation and confession perpetuated and incentivized both by a sensationalist Internet media market and by academic institutions, which have required "personal statements" from prospective students since around 1920. "The fiction of private individuality projected by the personal essay allows bourgeois subjects to accrue various cultural, economic, and social rewards," Emre writes, "dispersed by institutions that are, at once, constituted by the fiction of the private individual and responsible for reproducing it."

Ferguson, too, is interested in the interrelation of the individual self and the academic institution. Her chapter, "The Critical Essay," commences with Joseph Addison's "The Pleasures of the Imagination" (first published in his periodical *The Spectator* in 1712; we might note in passing how many critical magazines take the name of a generic individual: the *Spectator*, the *Tatler*, the *Idler*) and traces a short history of Anglo-American literary criticism that runs through the university, encompassing academic critics from I. A. Richards and Cleanth Brooks right up to latter-day practitioners such as D. A. Miller and Eve Kosofsky Sedgwick. "In addressing aesthetic experience and the operation of the senses generally," Ferguson claims, Addison inaugurates a tradition of critical writing about literature founded on a new understanding of sociality: He "assumes that his readers will immediately join him in acts of recognition, that they will see their own experience as matching – and only loosely matching – his." Thus the distance between writer and reader, which the personal essay arguably imposes, is collapsed: The critical essay, à la Addison, "aimed to capture what we might call 'your thoughts as written by someone else' or 'my experience as you already know it.'"

If the essay form is woven from the intricately intermingled strands of self and world, subjective experience and objective reality, what can be said of the relationship between essay and *oikos*, the essay form and our ecological home? In "The Nature Essay," Daegan Miller considers the place of the essay in the broader tradition of nature writing, taking us from the heyday of American transcendentalism to the diverse work being done on climate today in our era of the Anthropocene. "It is not surprising that those who would hew their own original relation to the world have consistently chosen to write essays," Miller declares, and his own essay deftly weaves together powerful examples of the form by Henry David Thoreau, Margaret Fuller, Annie Dillard, Barry Lopez, Camille T. Dungy, and others.

Finally, in "The Essay in Theory," Kara Wittman engages various philosophical attempts to define and delimit the essay, and to use the form to do a kind of philosophy that became increasingly urgent in the shadow of twentieth-century atrocities. Wittman brings together many of the leading lights of Romantic, Marxist, and poststructuralist theory, each of whom saw the essay as essential to their practice. "Essays don't offer data; they offer situated, limited standpoints from which we can perceive something fleeting and meaningful about life itself," Wittman writes, summarizing Georg Lukács's antipositivist conception of the essay in his 1910 *Soul and Form*. For Walter Benjamin, Theodor Adorno, and other German intellectuals associated with the Frankfurt School of Social Research, the essay becomes an indispensable instrument of philosophical critique: of science, of enlightenment, of ideology, of everything that exists. For these thinkers, the essay form offers a way to oppose the totalizing impulses that led to the rise of authoritarianism in the twentieth century. "[T]he essay," according to Wittman, "lets the particulars of existence remain visible and individuated, fugitive from the system builders"; its formal commitment to particularity resists the violence of closed systems.

Our volume's second section, "The Work of the Essay," ranges across centuries and continents in order to illuminate some of the many practical and political uses to which essays have been put. In "Experimental Science and the Essay," Julianne Werlin describes the role of the Baconian essay in facilitating the rise of both experimental science and managed state capitalism in early modern England. Having begun as a humanistic genre for the exploration of self, "essays came to be a medium for the investigation of nature," Werlin writes; and these experimental findings in turn made possible innovations in agriculture, economics, and industry, bringing about nothing less than what Samuel Hartlib called "the reformation of the whole world."

If the essay was instrumental in the rise of modern capitalism, it also proved useful in the articulation of a radical resistance to it, as Anahid Nersessian shows in "Essay, Enlightenment, and Revolution." Nersessian describes the essay's centrality to the European revolutions of the late eighteenth and early nineteenth centuries, tracing an intricate genealogy from the genteel periodical essays of Richard Steele and Joseph Addison to the provocative pamphleteering of Jean-Paul Marat and Karl Marx. While one significant line of essayists agitated for the political transformation of the modern world, another, as David Russell describes in "Ethics and the Essay," was more concerned with providing equipment for living with its everyday anxieties. Focusing on nineteenth-century English "polite essayists" such as William Hazlitt and Charles Lamb, Russell analyzes the essay's contribution to what he calls "an ethics of unknowing" by way of providing a tentative, experimental space in which "established values and habits of response are put into suspension."

Although a preponderance of the theory and history of the essay focuses on its European traditions, the form has been crucial to political and intellectual developments in the Americas and throughout the postcolonial world. As Jesse McCarthy puts it in "The Essay, Abolition, and Racial Blackness": "The violence of colonial settlement, the particular nature of slavery under nascent capitalism, and the rise of new multiracial societies provided a very different context for the essay in the New World than Montaigne's native Dordogne." McCarthy's narrative of the essay's importance to the discourses of abolitionism, civil rights, and racial blackness stretches from Bartolomé de las Casas's *Short Account of the Destruction of the*

Indies (published in 1552, decades before Montaigne's *Essais*) to the twentieth-century interventions of James Baldwin and his contemporary heirs such as Ta-Nehisi Coates and Rachel Kaadzi Ghansah.

Complementing McCarthy's account of the essay's role in the colonial and postcolonial Americas, Ignacio Sánchez Prado's "The Utopian Essay" considers essays that imagine, in form and content, utopia and the "utopian desires of modernity." Although he glances briefly at a long tradition of utopian essay-writing beginning with Thomas More's 1516 *Utopia*, Sánchez Prado is particularly interested in the early twentieth-century "birth of Latin America as a philosophical problem," where the tradition of the Mexican essay established an "intellectual project committed to overcoming Eurocentrism and asserting Latin America as a site of thinking." Focusing on the work of twentieth-century diplomat, critic, and essayist Alfonso Reyes, Sánchez Prado argues for "the utopian essay as part of a political and formal tradition that has its origins in the otherization of the New World as a *tabula rasa* for European ideations," but that was "ultimately claimed in Latin America and other latitudes as an instrument to think liberation."

In "The Essay and Empire," Saikat Majumdar also considers the relationship between the essay form and the logics of control embedded in colonialism. He surveys a range of essayists from across the decolonized world – Nirad C. Chaudhuri, C. L. R. James, Jamaica Kincaid, and Arundhati Roy among them – in order to demonstrate the essay's role in "dismantling ... the notion of mastery" on which colonial domination had been founded. Drawing on Julietta Singh's argument that colonial mastery works in quiet complicity with a range of other forms of mastery (such as mastering an instrument or a language), Majumdar shows us how different postcolonial essayists mobilize the freeing "epistemological failures" inherent in the essay form against this creeping domination. In its "stark refusal of epistemological as well as political mastery," he writes, the essay defies the arrogance and predation of empire.

The section on "The Work of the Essay" concludes with Grace Lavery's "Unqueering the Essay," an examination of the complex relationship between the essay form and normative conceptions of the self, sexuality, identification, and desire. Lavery considers a particular tradition of essays in which "queer literary critics writ[e] about famous queer literary critics," with emphasis on Terry Castle's memoir of the great twentieth-century essayist Susan Sontag. In those essays, writers inhabit the "melancholy" and "eminently queer switch between objective and subjective methods of analysis," while their analysts – the writers-turned-readers – have to confront the "alarmingly monodimensional" nature of their own desires and cathexes: the desire for the writer to "come out" in an essay, a form by its very nature not interested in the full, disclosive *out*. Writing to and in the spirit of another significant contemporary essayist and queer theorist, the late Lauren Berlant, Lavery meditates on the relationship between queer desire, public mourning, and the essay form. Uninterested in making claims for the "essential" nature of the essay, Lavery tests the notion that the form might necessarily (and paradoxically) impose these inadequacies of relation, these evasive and fraught desires between subject and object, writer and reader, wanted and wanting.

Our third and final section, "Technologies of the Essay," considers how the essay has interacted and crossbred with other modes of communication. This section thus points toward the future of the essay form and reflects on its capacity to evolve and adapt to social and technological change. Jason Childs's "The Essay and the Novel" considers the interrelationship of these two infinitely malleable literary forms, arguing that both novel and essay "paradoxically include innovation: Their new instances are torn between the need to observe the formal guide-rails of their antecedents and the urge to do away with these." Thus it should perhaps not be surprising that so many novelists – Virginia Woolf, George Orwell, Milan Kundera, and Zadie Smith, to name only a few – have also been expert essayists, or that the novel itself, in the hands of authors such as Robert Musil, Hermann Broch, and W. G. Sebald, becomes more essay than narrative.

In "Lyric, Essay," Claire Grossman, Juliana Spahr, and Stephanie Young discuss the various hybrids of essay and lyric poetry that have sprung up in the twentieth and twenty-first centuries. Invoking Theodor Adorno, they dub the lyric essay "the subgenre that writers turn to so as to escape the curse of being official," and situate its evolution vis-à-vis the rise of the creative writing program, the memoir boom of the 1990s, the influence of poststructuralist theory, and a global diaspora of writing against the "official" in the USA, the Caribbean, and elsewhere.

The wager of Kevin Adonis Browne's "The Photograph as Essay" is that in order to understand the photographic essay we need to read one. Or rather, we need to look at one. We must, he suggests, spend a different kind of time, and cultivate a different kind of attention. "Time can appear to run differently here," he writes. "The codes will seem foreign. Think of yourself as a visitor or an immigrant and try not to colonize what you have come upon. Try not to control it. Learn the language, its praise songs and its dirges, its long, breathy hymns." There are theoretical texts *about* photographic essays – W. J. T. Mitchell's *Picture Theory* is an excellent example – but Browne's essay, echoing in some ways Roland Barthes's meditative, idiosyncratic *Camera Lucida* or the lyrical "Epilogue" to Teju Cole's *Blind Spot*, suggests that the best way to understand what a photograph *as* essay can do, and be, is to sit with it, to inhabit it.

Nora M. Alter's "The Essay Film" likewise explores the relationship between the written essay and its visual – and also aural – incarnations. "The essay film," she writes, "has developed into a new form of cinema that … progressively transforms the nature of traditional philosophical discourse." That discourse, she shows us, "when filmed, transforms the nature of cinema." Her essay moves from the earliest examples of the essay film in the USA, Europe, and the Soviet Union to twenty-first-century video essays and large-scale video installations in museums and galleries around the world. Alter considers the intersecting aspects of and influences on the essay film: the relationship between the visual and the aural; the influence of the written essay on cinema and cinema on the way essayists explore language; and the way both the essay and the essay film "problematize all binary categories of representation." This ability to problematize categories and modes of representation, she argues, gives the essay film a political dimension and explains the proliferation of essay films "in times of crisis" globally. Because they move beyond traditional forms of objective and linear reportage and representation, essay films can "reveal a problem and bring to attention events that might otherwise be buried for decades."

But the twentieth-century technology that has most radically rejuvenated the essay form, and the one that is most likely to shape its trajectory in the coming decades, is the Internet. In "The Essay Online," Jane Hu locates an essayistic impulse in the bulletin boards and hobbyist forums of the early, precommercial web. The texts generated and disseminated in such spaces were dialogic, in many ways recalling the periodical essays of the eighteenth century: According to Hu, "the online essay evolved from conversations: writing that prompted and compelled other writing." As the Internet became coextensive with mass media over the course of the late twentieth- and early twenty-first century, market forces began to come into play, resulting in "clickbait" personal essays often written by young women and published by websites such as the Huffington Post, Gawker, and Jezebel. While the online personal essay has been a much-maligned genre, Hu insists on its literary and progressive potential; she concludes by considering "personal essays that express interiority not for expression's sake, but in an attempt to mobilize social action," such as the rape survivor Emily Doe's harrowing direct address to her attacker, published by BuzzFeed in June 2016.

We have one final note. We began contacting the authors about contributing to this collection in the fall of 2019; by the end of March 2020 more than 100 countries around the world were on full or partial lockdown trying to curb the spread of the novel coronavirus Covid-19. For some of our contributors, as we write, the lockdown has not yet been lifted. Though we live just 30 miles from each other in Southern California, we coedited this book entirely over Zoom, email, text, and the phone. Aspects of this situation would have been familiar to Michel de Montaigne: Plague ravaged Europe, and his Bordelaisian home, for most of the years he was composing the *Essais*. In "Of Physiognomy," he writes frankly about being "assailed" by the disease "without doors and within," about how much it frightened him. We want to take this space to thank our authors, who wrote through grief and loss and terrible uncertainty, and to honor and mourn the remarkable Cheryl Wall; she is cited frequently in this collection and was working on her own contribution to it when she passed in April 2020. We want to recognize the spirit of collaboration, intellectual kinship, and togetherness across great distances represented by this group of writers. Although he makes much of the solitude in which he composed his *Essais*, Montaigne writes most movingly when he writes of his friends. "Company reassures," he reminds us in the last essay he added to his book, and we have been deeply grateful, in this time of fear and isolation, for these companions.

Notes

1 Georg Lukács, *Soul and Form* eds. John T. Sanders and Katie Terazakis, trans. Anna Bostock (New York: Columbia University Press, 2010), 17.

2 Thomas Karshan and Kathryn Murphy, *On Essays: Montaigne to the Present* (Oxford: Oxford University Press, 2020), 5.

3 Francis Bacon, "To the Most High and Excellent Prince, Henry, Prince of Wales, Duke of Cornwall, and Earl of Chester," as reproduced in Basil Montagu, "Preface," in Francis Bacon, Alexander Spiers, and Basil Montagu, *Bacon's Essays and Wisdom of the Ancients* (Boston, MA: Little, Brown, and Company, 1884), xvi.

4 John D'Agata, *The Lost Origins of the Essay* (Minneapolis, MN: Graywolf Press, 2009); John D'Agata, *The Making of the American Essay* (Minneapolis, MN: Graywolf Press, 2016); John D'Agata, *The Next American Essay* (Minneapolis, MN: Graywolf Press, 2003).

5 Michel de Montaigne, "A consideration upon Cicero," *The Complete Essays of Montaigne*, trans. Donald Frame (Stanford, CA: Stanford University Press, 1958).

6 Claire de Obaldia, *The Essayistic Spirit: Literature, Modern Criticism, and the Essay* (Oxford: Clarendon Press, 1995), 4.

7 Cheryl Wall, *On Freedom and the Will to Adorn: The Art of the African American Essay* (Chapel Hill: University of North Carolina Press, 2018), 6.

8 David Pollard, ed., *The Chinese Essay* (London: C. Hurst and Co, 2000), xi.

9 Steven D. Carter, ed., *The Columbia Anthology of Japanese Essays: Zuihitsu from the Tenth to the Twenty-First Century* (New York: Columbia University Press, 2014), 2.

10 Donald Keene, *Seeds in the Heart: Japanese Literature from the Earliest Times to the Late Sixteenth Century* (New York: Holt, 1993); quoted in Carter, *Columbia Anthology of Japanese Essays*, 1.

11 James Agee and Walker Evans, *Let Us Now Praise Famous Men* (New York: Houghton Mifflin, 2001).

12 Richard Wright and Edwin Rosskam, *12 Million Black Voices* (Battleboro, VT: Echo Point Books and Media, 2019).

13 Susan Sontag, *On Photography* (New York: Picador, 2001); Roland Barthes, *Camera Lucida*, trans. Richard Howard (New York: Hill and Wang, 2010); John Berger, *Ways of Seeing* (London: Penguin Books, 1972).

14 Philippe Squarzoni, *Climate Changed: A Personal Journey Through the Science*, trans. Ivanka Hahnenberger (New York: ABRAMS, 2014); Lynda Barry, *What It Is* (Montreal, Canada: Drawn and Quarterly, 2021); Eleanor Davis, *Why Art?* (Seattle, WA: Fantagraphics, 2018).

15 Nora M. Alter and Tim Corrigan, eds., *Essays on the Essay Film* (New York: Columbia University Press, 2017), 9.

16 W. J. T. Mitchell, *Picture Theory: Essays on Verbal and Visual Representation* (Chicago: University of Chicago Press, 1995), 281.

17 See Anne Berggren, "Do Thesis Statements Short-Circuit Originality in Student's Writing?" in *Originality, Imitation, and Plagiarism: Teaching Writing in the Digital Age* (Ann Arbor: University of Michigan Press, 2008).

18 Nicole B. Wallack, *Crafting Presence: The American Essay and the Future of Writing Studies* (Logan: Utah State University Press, 2017), 10.

19 See Ned Stuckey-French, "Why Does the Essay Keep Dying, and What Do Little Lord Fauntleroy and the 'Lavender-Scented Little Old Lady' Have to Do With It?," *The CEA Critic* 61.2–3 (Winter and Spring/Summer, 1999).

20 William Dean Howells, "The Old-Fashioned Essay," *Harper's Magazine* (October 1902): 802–803.

21 See Virginia Woolf, "The Modern Essay," in *The Common Reader: First Series*, ed. Andrew McNeillie (New York: Harcourt Brace Jovanovich, 1953), 216–217. Also Woolf, "The Decay of Essay-Writing." *The Essays of Virginia Woolf: 1904–1912*, ed. Andrew McNeillie (London: Hogarth, 1986), 24–27.

22 Ned Stuckey-French, *The American Essay in the American Century* (Columbia: University of Missouri Press, 2011).

23 Christy Wampole, "The Essayification of Everything," *New York Times* (May 26, 2013), https://opinionator.blogs.nytimes.com/2013/05/26/the-essayification-of-everything.

24 Brian Dillon, *Essayism: On Form, Feeling and Nonfiction* (London: Fitzcaraldo Editions, 2017).

25 Jonathan Franzen, "Is It Too Late to Save the World?," *The Guardian* (November 4, 2017), www.theguardian.com/books/2017/nov/04/jonathan-franzen-too-late-to-save-world-donald-trump-environment

26 Erich Auerbach, *Mimesis: The Representation of Reality in Western Literature*, trans. Willard R. Trask (Princeton, NJ: Princeton University Press, 2003), 295.

PART I

Forms of the Essay

I

JEFF DOLVEN

Remembering the Essay

What do I remember of Michel de Montaigne's essay "De la Mémoire"? Above all, his vigorous self-deprecation: No one's memory is worse than his. He reads listlessly and without retention. He has forgotten his Greek. He makes reference, as I recall, to Plato's *Meno*, the dialogue in which a slave boy's ability to learn geometry is attributed to a kind of original memory of mathematical law. He doesn't think much of the idea, preferring to treat knowledge as the precipitate of experience. Somewhere along the way, he must retell the story of Simonides, the ancient founder of the *ars memoria*, who stepped out of a dinner party just before the roof caved in and was able to identify the disfigured bodies because he could reconstruct the guests' positions around the table. Simonides' feat is a wonder, but alien to Montaigne's vagrant habits of recall. Or must have been alien, if I know Montaigne. At some point in this increasingly dubious exercise, I pick up my copy of the *Essays* and scan the table of contents to confirm what I half-knew from the start, which is that there is, in fact, no essay on memory there. Though much of what I recalled is be found scattered in his book. There might well have been one, I console myself.

One way of dividing up kinds of writing is to consider how they offer themselves to the memory. How do you remember what you read? You can hang everything about a novel on its story; episodes and atmospheres depend on your recall of what happened next. Somewhere back in the history of the novel is the epic, with its oral formulas to assist the storyteller and its catalogues of famous names. Verse still holds out the hope of memorizing everything, with prompts of meter and rhyme to jog you along. Where recitation fails, it offers abstractions of form, like the structure of a sonnet, to place remembered lines within a whole. In prose, form may be less help, but any writing with an argument has the architecture of its claims and evidence, even the steps of a proof. All of these kinds are constructed according to rules of composition that are also economies of recollection, ways of holding writing together in the mind and bringing it back again at need. Narrative, rhythm, spatial form, and argument all serve the memory. What, then, of the essay? What are its mnemonic affordances – beyond its customary brevity? It is tempting to say that it has none, and moreover that its refusal to make itself convenient to the memory is among its defining properties.

If this is right – that the essay is at its heart a rebel against memory – then forgetful Montaigne proposes himself, once again, as its great instigator. Francis Bacon, the first English essayist, is an antipodal spirit in so many ways, but joins Montaigne in this antagonism, albeit on his own terms. They are both well remembered in the history of the essay after them, and a preoccupation with memory is one of their bequests. Reading them well asks us to think them in the context of the early modern culture of memory against which they wrote, and that is what this opening essay of our volume will do.

*

There used to be a painting at Delphi of a man in Hades braiding a rope, playing it out straight into the mouth of a hungry donkey. Plutarch, the first-century Greek philosopher-historian-priest, tells us in his "On Contentment" that the painting is an image of oblivion. Oblivion "prevents life being a unity of past events woven with present ones," he writes, and such "constant flux makes each person, in theory, different from himself and then different again."[1] What redeems human beings from this tragedy of infinite self-separation is memory, a condition of the continuity of the self, and, for Plutarch's sixteenth-century readers, of the continuity of history. Montaigne was trained up in a veneration of history, especially the classical canon laid down as the foundation of European humanism. He was a nearly native speaker of Latin and, though he had little Greek, he was an avid reader of Plutarch in Jacques Amyot's translations. He credits Plutarch, along with the Roman Seneca, as his two ancient masters: "my book ... is built entirely out of their spoils."[2] Quotations from what have come (under his influence) to be called Plutarch's "essays" are a habit through all stages of his *Essais'* twenty-some years of composition. They must have been among the aphorisms Montaigne inscribed on the bookcases and the rafters of the tower library where he wrote, a circumambient encyclopedia of his life of reading.

And yet he explains, in "Of Vanity," that he loves Plutarch especially for his forgetting. "There are works ... in which he forgets his theme, in which the treatment of his subject is found only incidentally, quite smothered in foreign matter ... Lord, what beauty there is in these lusty sallies and this variation, and more so the more casual and accidental they seem."[3] To make sense of this romance with forgetfulness, it helps to recall how the students of Montaigne's time were expected to remember. The ancient theorists who guided early modern discussions of memory were the usual suspects. Plato's legacy was the idea of memory as a faculty that puts us in mind of forms and laws.[4] Aristotle's empiricism was the greater influence, especially his distinction between remembering and recollection, between the past made present in the course of ordinary life (remembering the way home), and deliberate recall (recollecting the facts of a legal case).[5] Recollection distinguishes humans from animals, for we alone open up the memory to see what is there. To *see*: Memory for Aristotle is fundamentally a matter of images. And see what is *there*: Memory is spatial, and organized topically, which is to say by place, or topos.[6]

Aristotle's influence is important to the *ars memoria* transmitted in the rhetorical tradition, especially the first-century BCE *Rhetorica ad Herennium*, long attributed to Cicero. Its most spectacular form is the technique of the so-called memory palace, which systematizes the principle of Simonides' macabre anecdote. Memory students learn to associate lively images with whatever they want to remember – say, a cup to recall the charge of poisoning in a law case – and then place those images within an imagined building, adding new rooms and corridors and floors as needed, to construct a kind of architectural filing system.[7] By so strongly associating memory and place, the technique masters time. You don't have to reach back into a memory stratified and corrupted by intervening years, because everything is organized synchronically, systematically, just a short stroll away from wherever you start.

In its strong form, the *ars memoria* enjoyed modest uptake in northern Europe.[8] Its spatial arrangement was nonetheless the assumption underneath the almost universal practice, among school-educated readers, of commonplacing, keeping a topically organized notebook for the transcription of useful knowledge. The notebook was a little memory palace; the palace, an unfolded notebook. Readers transcribed jewels of wisdom "on" a given topic, courage, say, or kingship, or melancholy. The impatient could glean the treasures of wide reading on the cheap from printed commonplace books such as Frances Mere's *Palladis Tamia* (1598). Critic Claire de Obaldia, in a formulation to which I will return, has described the essay as literature *in potentia*, drafts or notes toward some more finished form: "the essay is, and it is not literature; or rather the essay *is not yet* literature."[9] The early modern commonplace book is a collection of essays *in potentia*.

The period's most characteristic prose forms, forms fed by these commonplaces, were well adapted to memorization, the persuasive oration and the sermon both affording highly structured, almost architectural homes for

classical *sententiae* and verses of scripture. Montaigne proclaims himself a
serial offender against expectations for a methodical memory, as we will
see. But who remembers better how Plutarch forgets, how his essays wander among their concerns, unencumbered by responsibilities of prospectus
and reprise? For all the quotation, more or less accurate, throughout Montaigne's work, his Plutarch and his Seneca are most reliably present as a
modus scribendi, remembered in their style. (As Seneca would say, writers
must be taken in as nourishment, "otherwise they will pass into the memory, not into the talent," not into the capable self.[10]) The critic Scott Black
treats such essayistic digestions of ancient texts as a convergence of reading
and writing, in "feedback loops" that animate early modern print culture –
ancient text to commonplace book to essay to someone else's commonplace
book and so on. Essays are "more like readerly writing than writerly reading," sponsoring "a way of reading that is neither passive nor productive,
but a process of thinking through."[11] Behind Black's argument is the idea
that everything you read, you read to write with, and that writing, con-
versely, is a way of reading. Or, one might say, remembering not so much
the place names as the way along the way.

*

Montaigne never forgets himself more drastically than in "On Practice." In
the middle of the essay, he recounts an episode from France's civil wars –
"During the third of our disturbances (or was it the second, I do not remember which)"[12] – when he was out riding, a league from his estate, and one
of his men, mounted on a powerful farm horse, ran him down from behind.
His companions take him for dead and carry him the half-league back to the
house; the essay briskly recounts his coming to, vomiting blood, and suffering the attentions of his frightened household. He lingers, however, over the
deliquescence of his swoon. "I found it pleasant to languish and to let myself
go," he recalls; he enjoys "that gentle feeling which is felt by those who let
themselves glide into sleep." The experience confirms what he has long suspected: Death can present a horrible aspect to those who witness it, but that
aspect deceives. Now he can remember it and it was good. "The memory of
this, being deeply planted in my soul, paints for me the face of Death and
her portrait so close to nature that it somewhat reconciles me to her."[13]

   What is this singular episode, this death before death, doing in an essay
on practice, on the daily and the ordinary, "De l'Exercitation"? The opening pages – before he gets to the accident – are a Stoic meditation on the
value of exercising the soul in virtue and hardening the self against life's
travails. "Reasoning and education cannot easily prove powerful enough

to bring us actually to do anything, unless in addition we train and form our Soul by experience."[14] But how to practice for death? Montaigne's accident is an extraordinary gift to a man preoccupied with this question. He observes that he was able even *in extremis* to command his servants and order a horse for his wife. Such acts of domestic competence are automatic, thoughtless, "produced by my senses themselves, doubtless from habit." His inner condition meanwhile is "agreeable and peaceful" and his mind is free.[15] Even his narration afterward lets go happily of details. During which of the several crises of the wars did this happen? Was I a league or half a league away from my house, my library, my affairs? The swoon seems to allow him to forget, and yet to be wonderfully aware, conscious without quite being conscious *of*.

He cuts off these reflections at the point when he finally recalls, days later, the accident itself, a memory that strikes him like a lightning bolt. Still he tries to keep the lesson of the swoon: "This account of so unimportant an event is pointless enough but for the instruction I drew from it for my own purposes: for in truth, to inure yourself to death all you have to do is to draw nigh to it." In the remaining pages he turns to a project of self-study. "I examine nothing, I study nothing, but me; and if I do study anything else, it is so as to apply it at once to myself, or more correctly, within myself."[16] Here is the studious subjectivity for which Montaigne is so famous. That self, under the attentions of the essay, can be laid exactingly, even surgically bare, "the veins, the muscles and the tendons" open to scrutiny; one part of him is revealed "by the act of coughing; another by my turning pale or by my palpitations."[17] But these clues to the quotidian self are also signs of death, and as the essay moves away again from the accident, not to return, Montaigne's new art of self-description becomes an art of forgetting. Plato complained, as Montaigne well knew, that the invention of writing was death to the memory. His essay complies willingly with the loss. It is structured not for recapitulation, not for laying up thought against time, but for letting go as it goes.

Indeed: "I am so outstanding a forgetter," Montaigne writes in "On Presumption," "that, along with all the rest, I forget even my own works and writings." The essay makes a comic survey of his lapses and incuriosities:

> Most of our coins I do not recognize; unless it is all too obvious I do not know the difference between one grain and another, neither in the ground nor in the barn … And since I must reveal the whole of my shame, only a month ago I was caught not knowing that yeast is used to make bread and what was meant by "fermenting" wine.[18]

This performance of embarrassment is sly praise for tacit knowledge, which has served him perfectly well in trade and eating and drinking. It is as though the essays long for their own knowledge to lapse into such wordless practicality. But against such claims the reader must weigh the extraordinary variety of quotations, citations, and anecdotes that leaven the work, their words well remembered even if Montaigne often claims to have forgotten their sources. If a given essay forgets them as it goes – forgets them simply in moving on – it must first remember them, and reproduce them, from what must be a great supply. "Of the Cannibals" begins with three such stories from Plutarch, each recounting an occasion when Greek soldiers first encounter, with surprise, the order and good discipline of the Roman legions. These anecdotes inaugurate a wandering meditation on the natives of the Americas and on who is a barbarian to whom. The connections are metonymic, rather than metaphoric; local associations, from link to link of a chain, report and travel narrative, and Seneca and Virgil, rather than coordinated expressions of a governing conceit.

It is of course still open to the reader to ask, what this essay, "Des Cannibales," is really *about*. What is the metaphor that is the more or less secret meaning of all of its elements – the vertical organization that can explain its lateral travel? One answer might be, cruelty.[19] Near the middle of the essay Montaigne takes up the custom of his title and gives an anthropological account of how the natives dispatch a captive enemy, cook, and eat him, generously "sending chunks of his flesh to absent friends."[20] But he cannot consider their barbarity without reflection on his own culture: There is

> more barbarity in lacerating by rack and torture a body still fully able to feel things, in roasting him little by little and having him bruised and bitten by pigs and dogs (as we have not only read about but seen in recent memory, not among enemies in antiquity but among our fellow-citizens and neighbours— and, what is worse, in the name of duty and religion) than in roasting him and eating him after his death.[21]

No taboo, neither desecrating nor even eating the dead, matters to Montaigne more than living pain. It is a clarion moral judgment, and yet it enjoys little rhetorical punctuation. He passes easily on to the valor of the cannibals' warriors, and then to their polygamy, which he grants may be objectionable to French wives, but then he wonders, what about Leah, Rachel, and Sarah in the Bible, or for that matter, Stratonice of Syria, who (Plutarch tells us) permitted king Deiotarus the attentions of a "very beautiful chambermaid"?

Typical Montaigne. *Do I contradict myself?* he all but asks. Self-contradiction courts the reproach of forgetfulness. Don't you remember, you just said x, and now you are saying not-x? You say you have never been to the Indies; how do you know that their cakes taste "sweet and somewhat insipid"?[22] But contradiction is vital to the essays' moral idiom, their capacity to address complexities of life from which systematic argument could only distract. Memory must make way, must falter, even fail. "Cannibals" ultimately arrives at a scene that would serve, in the hands of another writer, as a narrative climax, the meeting of three natives with Charles IX at Rouen in 1562. At last, the natives speak! Someone in the French party asks a very Montaignian question: What has most amazed the visitors about France? In answer, "they made three points": They are surprised that the boy king Charles, then twelve years old, should command bearded men; that the destitute do not rise up against the rich; and "I am very annoyed with myself for not remembering the third," Montaigne confesses. He does ask one of them about the privileges of rank and learns that a commander will have men to cut a path through the forest for him, wherever he goes. "Not at all bad, that.—Ah! But they wear no breeches ..."[23] And so the essay ends, offhanded, careless, as though it has stopped bothering to remember itself, to read itself.

It is, of course, a memorable ending, but not because it sets the capstone in an arch. It is the abruptness of its abdication that sticks. This is another route to memory, not fitting the system but making an exception. "The learned do arrange their ideas into species and name them in detail," Montaigne writes in "On Experience."

> I, who can see no further than practice informs me, have no such rule, presenting my ideas in no categories and feeling my way—as I am doing here now; I pronounce my sentences in disconnected clauses, as something which cannot be said at once all in one piece.[24]

"On Experience" ends the three-book *Essays* and it inhabits most thoroughly the predicament of Montaigne's self-made idiom. Which is to say, the predicament of an essay *on*, or *of*, or *about* experience. The word "experience" splits in two, then as now, in French as in English, keeping pace with the immediacy of sense-perception while also trailing behind in accumulated skill or familiarity or hard knowledge. Whether that latter kind of experience is memory depends on what you think memory is. Montaigne tends to write of memory as recollection, disciplined recall, precisely so that he can perform its failures, and free himself to handle the past tense of experience differently. If his essays had themselves in mind the same way the memory artist remembers the *Aeneid*, or the facts of a law case, they could hardly continue.

*

In 1594, when he was thirty-three years old, Francis Bacon opened a notebook to begin the project of transcribing from memory all the quotations that he could remember from Erasmus, from Virgil, from the Bible, along with proverbs in Latin, French, Spanish, and Italian. He wrote down over 1,600 before he either emptied his reservoir or grew tired of the exercise.[25] Three years later he published the first edition of his essays. There are ten of them, each consisting of short paragraphs set off by pilcrows, often just a sentence long. Here is a representative pair from "Of Studies":

¶ Read not to contradict, nor to believe, but to weigh and consider.
¶ Some books are to be tasted, others to be swallowed, and some few to be chewed and digested. That is, some books are to be read only in parts; others to be read, but cursorily; and some few to be read wholly and with diligence and attention.[26]

Bacon's essays are works of advice and have some kinship with manuals of conduct or instruction – *A Godlie Forme of Householde Government* (1598) or *A Plaine and Easie Introduction to Practicall Musicke* (1597) – that proliferated in the period. An exemplary *he* and a hortatory *you* are the main characters; the self-scrutinizing, Montaignian *I* is nowhere to be found. The little collection might even be mistaken for another printed commonplace book. But Bacon was wary of how traditional commonplace categories reproduced existing structures of knowledge, "using vulgar and pedantical divisions, not such as pierce to the pith and heart of things."[27] Even in these spare essays *in potentia*, an analytic intelligence shapes their parallelisms, unfolding, in the example above, three distinct reading practices from the figures of tasting, swallowing, and digesting. The book was a notable success, plagiarized even before it was published (it had circulated in manuscript), and reprinted four times.

In the years that separated the first essays from their next edition in 1612 and the last in 1625 – they grew in number and length each time – fortune lifted Bacon up and cast him down again, as he prospered under King James in London's legal and government establishments; made his off-hours contributions to the new science, such works as *The Advancement of Learning* (1605) and the *Novum Organum* (1620); and then in 1621, as Lord Chancellor, at the height of his power, was convicted of accepting bribes and retired to spend the remainder of his life in study. He read Montaigne in French, and likely also in English, in John Florio's brilliant 1603 translation, and his essays, as they lengthened, became increasingly discursive. They retained, however, an ostentatious topical discipline alien to his French contemporary. "To seek to extinguish Anger utterly is but a bravery of the Stoics," he begins the essay "Of Anger." He continues:

We will first speak how the natural inclination and habit to be angry may be attempered and calmed. Secondly, how the particular motions of anger may be repressed, or at least refrained from doing mischief. Thirdly, how to raise anger or appease anger in another.[28]

Bacon is as good as his word: The paragraphs that follow correspond to this initial *partitio*, just as tasting, swallowing, and digesting are opened, in "On Studies," into kinds of reading.[29] Instead of the wayfaring perspective of the Montaignian essay, best seen from wherever you happen to be along its path, Bacon begins with a view from above.

It is tempting to treat such self-conscious architectures as evidence of a preset method, and modern readers of the essays may be encouraged in the assumption by Bacon's place in the history of science. But he could be witheringly skeptical of the methodological programs current in his own moment, and he was at least equally concerned that the structures of formal rhetoric might preempt the recognition and the articulation of new phenomena and new laws. His principal remedy was already center stage in 1597: aphorisms, those pithy sayings drawn from experience. They might start an essay, as in "Of Marriage and Single Life": "He that hath wife and children hath given hostages to fortune; for they are impediments to great enterprises, either of virtue or mischief."[30] They might end one, as in "Of Delays": "For when things are once come to the execution, there is no secrecy comparable to celerity; like the motion of a bullet in the air, which flieth so swift as it outruns the eye."[31] They might erupt in the middle, as in "Of Beauty": "There is no excellent beauty that hath not some strangeness in the proportion."[32] Bacon values their autonomy, their ability to stand alone, and more than that, their resistance to assimilation by their context: "for discourse of illustration is cut off; recitals of example are cut off; discourse of connexion and order is cut off; descriptions of practice are cut off; so there remaineth nothing to fill the aphorisms but some good quantity of observation."[33] The aphorism is cut off, that is, from the prejudices, the fore-judgments, built into the conventional orders of discourse. "This delivering of knowledge in distinct and disjointed aphorisms doth leave the wit of man more free to turn and to toss, and to make use of that which is delivered to more several purposes and application."[34] It is as though the aphorism were a usefully inconvenient phenomenon, a found thing, demanding empirical attention.

Bacon the aphorist is, in his essays and elsewhere, equally a maker of images. If aphorisms break the momentum of an argument, his analogies and metaphors create unexpected eddies of attention. "Of Friendship" analyses two "fruits" of friendship, the "peace in the affections" a friend can bring, and "support of the judgment," before turning in the final paragraph to a third, "which is like the pomegranate, full of many kernels; I mean aid and bearing a part in all actions and occasions."[35] Or again, in "Of Custom and Education":

> In other things the predominancy of custom is everywhere visible; insomuch as a man would wonder to hear men profess, protest, enrage, give great words, and then do just as they have done before; as if they were dead images, and engines moved only by the wheels of custom.[36]

The figure of the man of custom as automaton is startling and memorable, independent of any scheme organizing the essay's larger argument. Bacon has a tendency to take up an idiosyncratic image and develop it as though it were a technical term, as with the fruits of friendship, which can be opened to show the many proxy services of the friend; or elsewhere, in the *Advancement of Learning*, where he develops his four "idols of the mind" (of the tribe, the cave, the marketplace, and the theater) into a taxonomy of bad thinking. The not-quite-deadness of his metaphors, even as they are put to work in argument, sometimes gives the sense of a peculiarly lonely thinker, handling private coin.

Aphorism and image share this strategic estrangement from their context, this refusal to illustrate or ornament. Anne Righter, in a classic essay, describes "the curious configuration of the space" that can open up without warning between any two Baconian sentences.[37] Her example is the beginning of "Of Truth," but "Of Vicissitude of Things" will serve as well:

> Salomon saith, "There is no new thing upon the earth." So that as Plato had an imagination, that "all knowledge was but remembrance"; so Salomon giveth his sentence, that "all novelty is but oblivion." Whereby you may see, that the river of Lethe runneth as well above ground as below. There is an abstruse astrologer that saith, if it were not for two things that are constant (the one is, that the fixed stars ever stand at like distance one from another, and never come nearer together, nor go further asunder; the other, that the diurnal motion perpetually keepeth time), no individual would last one moment. Certain it is, that the matter is in a perpetual flux, and never at a stay. The great winding-sheets, that bury all things in oblivion, are two: deluges and earthquakes.[38]

The three opening quotations and the consequential *so*'s in-between give the feeling of a syllogism. Perhaps it follows from Salomon's stark sententia that all knowledge is remembered, and that anything that seems new must only have been once known and forgotten. One is filling in gaps to say so, and they might be filled otherwise. The ensuing "whereby" has considerable demonstrative confidence, but the image that follows is hard to map to what it demonstrates. Perhaps we forget in life, above ground, as we forget in death, under it? Then immediately on to the abstruse astronomer – he seems to say that without the fixed distances of the stars, and the rhythm of the day, there would be no index for our own mutability. Then one more confident summary, which gives way abruptly to the distinction between the two winding sheets – "winding sheet" becomes for a moment a new term of art – as though our question all along had been, what are the species of destruction that can wipe away all records, all memory? It would be easy to say that the paragraph is itself an exercise in vicissitude. It might be better to say, in ellipsis. Its trajectory is not a wandering line, like Montaigne's, lubricated with apology; rather, a scattering of points for us to connect, or even a blast of shot. Its concession to the economies of memory is minimal. How could we remember it, except part by part, by rote?

And Bacon hates rote. There is an extraordinary moment in "On Atheism" when he dismisses the position of the atheist: "The scripture saith, 'The fool hath said in his heart, there is not God'; it is not said, 'the fool hath thought in his heart'; so as he rather saith it by rote to himself as that he would have, than that he can throughly believe it."[39] In that "saith" he hears the atheist rehearsing an unfelt claim from memory merely. The contrast is with "thought," which is something else again. Here he is in a famous passage from his Latin *De Augmentis Scientiarum* of 1623, two years before the last edition of the essays. The ancients have paid too much attention to memory, imagination, and reason, and have neglected the "thinking faculty":

> For he who remembers or recollects, thinks; he who imagines, thinks; he who reasons, thinks; and in a word the spirit of man, whether prompted by sense or left to itself, whether in the functions of the intellect, or of the will and affections, dances to the tune of the thoughts.[40]

To say that both remembering and recollection, memory involuntary and voluntary, are aspects of thinking is to recognize that the past can only arise in present uses, that memory is as much *for* as *of*. The memory is not a repository of finished thought. The essayist has a corresponding responsibility not to fit thinking to rote recall, a responsibility to refuse the conventional economies of formula and structure, for they ordain their own conclusion. Of the kinds of time that writing correlates – reading time, diegetic time, writing time – the essay's special power is to activate the last, to make the time of the writer's composition salient to the reader's encounter. One might say, with Bacon, that this time is the time of thinking. Thinking is the enemy of memory, or of rote memory, at least, and though he loves premeditated structure, his structures are disrupted, by aphorism, by image, from within – he will not stop thinking to write.

*

The essay is a reluctant genre. Montaigne and Bacon inaugurate that reluctance. But they are continuous points of reference for what becomes a recognizable, salable kind of book in England: In short order, printers put out William Cornwallis's *Essayes* (1600), Robert Johnson's *Essaies, or Rather Imperfect Offers* (1601), D. T.'s *Essaies Politicke, and Morall* (1608), and so on and on. Most modern literary histories that track the essay through the seventeenth century catch up such eccentrics as Sir Thomas Browne and Robert Burton, perhaps Robert Boyle, along their way to the periodical essays of Addison and Steele. But Cornwallis exemplifies the new form's precocious self-knowledge:

> I hold neither Plutarch's, nor none of these ancient short manner of writings, nor Montaigne's, nor such of this latter time to be rightly termed essays, for though they be short, yet they are strong, and able to endure the sharpest trial; but mine are essays, who am but newly bound prentice to the inquisition of knowledge, and use these papers as a painter's boy a board, that is trying to bring his fancy and his hand acquainted.[41]

The figure of the apprentice mixing paints on his palette is a wonderful bit of essayistic diffidence: His work is stubbornly preparatory, unbegun, as though the essay were just a way of teaching the hand to speak. Cornwallis' essays claim to know better than to rise above their own immediacy; they graciously depart when they are done; they recognize themselves in being weak and amateur, minor literature *avant la lettre*, in the sense that they declare no challenge to the way we live, seek only to fit in and make small accommodations of attitude. A novel will keep you up too late; essays suit a scheduled day. (His "Of Sleep" is written in the hour set aside for a midday nap.)

If I find something subtly discouraging about reading Cornwallis now, perhaps it is that he knows his own genre so well. Such confident formulations of modesty become conventional: In 1671, Thomas Culpeper can aver that the essay

> admits of no positive definition, which might be the reason, that neither their great Essays [Essayist] Montaigne, nor the Lord Bacon our more incomparable writer in the same kind, hath thought it requisite to define the word, because it hath so little to do with the matter it handles.[42]

There is a difference between trying to do something in particular, something of a given kind, and just *trying*. I sometimes want to account anything a poem that has a ragged right-hand margin. But sometimes I want to say, with a sense of rare occasion, and according to emergent criteria, *now* this *is a poem*. Essays are so many and the barriers to entering the category are low, but there are still moments when I find myself saying, *now* this *is an essay*. When I do so it is usually because it neither knows what it is, nor knows that it is not supposed to know.

It helps, in vivifying some of the critical commonplaces – that the essay is an attempt, that it is preliminary, that it is subjective – to recognize at any moment in its history what it pushes off against, where it must win its aimless freedom, the sources of its potential shame when it is asked what kind it is. The early modern essay, answering to that question, is especially not an oration. It fails the inherited methods and structures of persuasive speech, refuses the fantasies of virtuoso persuasion in court and courtroom or the dream of a Roman senate. Likewise it is not a sermon. The cathedral memory-patterning of Donne at the pulpit is very different. Perhaps I remember an essay more the way I remember a conversation? Perhaps one conversation of many with a friend, not being sure when it was exactly that she said that, or where. (Could there be a friend of only one conversation? An essayist who wrote only one essay?) Perhaps I remember best the swerve, the startling aphorism, the brilliant image. Not the structure of the argument, but just where the essay defied my expectation for that structure – defied what I remembered about it before I read it. Which might be to say that early modernity teaches the essay to follow what it learned from Plutarch and Seneca, and what it keeps learning from Montaigne and Bacon: that memory is thinking. And also the insight of Jorge Luis Borges, in his story "Funes, His Memory": *pensar es olvidar*, to think is to forget.[43]

Notes

1 Plutarch, *Essays*, trans. Robin Waterfield (New York: Penguin, 1992), 229.
2 Michel de Montaigne, *The Complete Essays*, trans. M. A. Screech (London: Penguin, 2003), 817.
3 Ibid., 1125.
4 The most important discussion is in his *Meno* (81a–98a); also influential is the discussion in the *Phaedrus* of the erosive effects of writing on memory (274b–275b). Plato, *Complete Works*, ed. John M. Cooper (Indianapolis, IN: Hackett, 1997).
5 Andrew Hiscock offers a useful summary of early modern reception of ancient memory theory in *Reading Memory in Early Modern Literature* (Cambridge: Cambridge University Press, 2011), 6–15.
6 Aristotle, *The Complete Works of Aristotle*, ed. Jonathan Barnes (Oxford: Oxford University Press, 1984), 449b5–453b10.
7 The image is from the *Rhetorica ad Herennium*, trans. Harry Caplan (Cambridge, MA: Harvard University Press, 1954), 215. The classic treatment of the *ars memoriae* is Frances Yates's *The Art of Memory* (London: Routledge and Kegan Paul, 1966).

8 Erasmus, the most important educational theorist of the sixteenth century, cautions, "I do not deny that memory is aided by 'places' and 'images';
 nevertheless ... memory largely consists in having thoroughly understood something." *On the Method of Study*, in *The Collected Works of Erasmus*, vol. 24,
 trans. Brian McGregor (Toronto: University of Toronto Press, 1978), 671.
9 Claire de Obaldia, *The Essayistic Spirit: Literature, Modern Criticism, and the
 Essay* (Oxford: Clarendon Press, 1996), 16.
10 Lucius Annaeus Seneca, *Letters on Ethics*, trans. Margaret Graver and A. A.
 Long (Chicago: University of Chicago Press, 2015), 285. "Talent" translates
 Seneca's *ingenium*.
11 Black, *Essays and Reading*, 55.
12 Montaigne, *Complete Essays*, 418.
13 Ibid., 419.
14 Ibid., 416.
15 Ibid., 422–423.
16 Ibid., 423–424.
17 Ibid., 426.
18 Ibid., 741.
19 David Quint finds hatred of cruelty at the ethical center of the *Essays* as a whole.
 See *Montaigne and the Quality of Mercy* (Princeton, NJ: Princeton University
 Press, 1998), 42–74.
20 Montaigne, *Complete Essays*, 235.
21 Ibid., 235–236.
22 Ibid., 234.
23 Ibid., 241.
24 Ibid., 1222.
25 Francis Bacon, "Promus of Formularies and Elegancies," in *The Oxford Francis Bacon*, vol. 1, ed. Alan Stewart (Oxford: Oxford University Press, 2012),
 553–582.
26 Francis Bacon, *Francis Bacon*, ed. Brian Vickers (Oxford: Oxford University
 Press, 1996), 81. References in parentheses in the text are to this edition.
27 Francis Bacon, *The Works of Francis Bacon*, vol. 4, eds. James Spedding, R. L.
 Ellis, and D. D. Heath (Boston, MA: Houghton and Mifflin, 1857–1874), 435.
28 Bacon, *Francis Bacon*, 449.
29 The most comprehensive discussion of Bacon's style remains Brian Vickers,
 Francis Bacon and Renaissance Prose (Cambridge: Cambridge University Press,
 1968). On *partitio*, see pp. 30–60; on aphorisms, see pp. 60–96.
30 Bacon, *Francis Bacon*, 353.
31 Ibid., 383.
32 Ibid., 425.
33 Bacon, *Works*, 3.405.
34 Ibid., 7.321.
35 Bacon, *Francis Bacon*, 395.
36 Ibid., 419.
37 Anne Righter, "Francis Bacon," in *Essential Articles for the Study of Francis
 Bacon*, ed. Brian Vickers (Hamden, CT: Archon, 1968), 319.
38 Bacon, *Francis Bacon*, 451.
39 Ibid., 371.

40 Bacon, *Works*, 4.324. Rhodri Lewis quotes this passage and comments, "Bacon's emphasis on what we *do* when engaging in thought is fundamental to the way in which he approached the memory." "A Kind of Sagacity: Francis Bacon, the *Ars Memoriae* and the Pursuit of Natural Knowledge," *Intellectual History Review* 19.2 (2009): 170.

41 William Cornwallis, *Essayes* (London: 1632), Bb8v.

42 Thomas Culpeper, *Essayes or Moral Discourses on Several Subjects* (London, 1671), B1r. This passage is reproduced in Black, whose modernized spelling I have adopted, in *Essays and Reading*, 132.

43 Jorge Luis Borges, *Collected Fictions*, trans. Andrew Hurley (London: Penguin, 1999), 137. Though my recollection is incomplete: The full sentence is "To think is to ignore (or forget) differences, to generalize, to abstract."

2

MERVE EMRE

The Personal Essay

"The essay form, however, bears some responsibility for the fact that
bad essays tell stories about people instead of elucidating the matter at
hand."
– Theodor Adorno, "The Essay As Form"

To speak of the personal essay is to speak of a genre that is difficult to define
but easy to denounce. The offending element is rarely the essay as a form – it
passes unscathed – but its content, "the personal," "a permanent temptation for a form whose suspiciousness of false profundity does not protect
it from turning into slick superficiality," writes Theodor Adorno.[1] A list of
antonyms to the personal essay might include more admirable imaginary
genres such as the structural essay, the communal essay, the public essay,
the critical essay, and the impersonal essay. Or, as Adorno insinuates in my
epigraph, the good essay, which prioritizes "elucidating the matter at hand"
instead of telling "stories about people," as "bad essays" do.

What makes essays that tell stories about people bad? For Adorno, as for
Walter Benjamin, whom Adorno names as his favorite essayist, essays about
people betray the true object of essayistic criticism: the private individual.
The private individual is not a particular person with a particular story to
tell, no matter how distinctive, original, or purely bizarre that story may
be. The private individual is not a proper name – not "Virginia Woolf" or
"Elizabeth Hardwick," not "Joan Didion" or "Zadie Smith" or whomever
it is you consider your favorite personal essayist to be. Rather, it is the idea
that animates all these figures, the powerful, unobtrusive concept that gives
the personal essay the appearance of ventriloquizing a singular and spontaneous subjectivity. The private individual is the ideological apparatus that
authorizes the genre's first-person address, the "I" that posits itself as both
the subject and the object of its own understanding.

Most essayists and scholars who write about the personal essay agree
that its "I" is, by necessity and choice, an artful construction. Watch, they
say, as it flickers in and out of focus as "a simulacrum,"[2] "a chameleon,"[3]
"a made-up self,"[4] "a distorting representation" of the individual from
whose consciousness it originates and whose being it registers.[5] Yet, having
marveled at its aesthetic flexibility and freedom, few critics put this claim

through its dialectical paces. What if individual subjectivity were as much a fiction as the "I" with which it so prettily speaks? What if stressing the artifice of the first-person were a strategy for masking the personal essay's problematic, "the internal limitations on what its author can and cannot say?"[6] What if the conceptual limitation of the genre were its interpellation of reader and writer into the ideological process of individualism, its glittering veneer of expressive freedom, of speaking and writing as a self-determining subject? What if no performance of stylish confession or sly concealment could shake this ideology loose? What if it only intensified its enchantments?

To answer these questions about the personal essay, its mode of address, and the private individual that enlivens both requires a biography of sorts, though not a personal one. The biographer could be any of the twentieth-century theorists who have heralded the entrance of individual subjectivity into history, but it is Walter Benjamin who emerges as the thinker most interested in its literary aesthetics. According to Benjamin, the private individual was conceived sometime between 1830 and 1848, during the reign of Louis Phillipe, the first "bourgeois monarch." Under his rule, the European ruling class and the middle-class came together to realize their defining goal: the separation of the public from the private domain, where, as Karl Marx observes, the bourgeoisie could retreat to rejoice in "property," "family," "religion," and "order."[7] Once labor had been cordoned off from life, once the productive activity of work had been separated from the supposedly unproductive experience of dwelling, the private individual was born. He was, quite naturally, blind to his own history as a derivative creature, an artifact of political and economic processes that he possessed little incentive to interrogate. The domestic sphere was his incubator, his sanctuary from commercial and social considerations. There he could retreat, wide-eyed and mewling, to probe what he believed to be his thoughts, lodged in his self, his mind, his body, and his home. "The private individual, who in the office needs to deal with reality, needs the domestic interior to sustain him in his illusions," Benjamin wrote, explaining how the ownership of property mirrored the ownership of subjectivity. He continued: "From these derive the phantasmagorias of the interior – which, for the private man, represents the universe."[8]

For Benjamin, the best representative of the private individual was the collector of decorative objects, "the true resident of the interior" as an architectural and an existential space. For us, it might be the personal essay collection, which props up the same ideology. The purpose of this chapter is to trace how the personal essay's historical and aesthetic function has been to persuade us not just that personhood is beautiful or good, but that it is primordial – that individual subjectivity and its expression exist prior to the social formations that gave rise to it. This is a lie, the lie that subtends bourgeois individualism and all its intrusions into language, art, and education, as Adorno explains. "The lie extends from the elevation of historical concepts in historical languages to primal words, to academic instruction in 'creative writing,' and to primitiveness pursued as a handicraft, to recorders and finger painting, in which pedagogical necessity acts as though it were metaphysical virtue," he proclaims.[9] The personal essay appears as the purest, most unflinching aesthetic expression of the lie, for the simple reason that, for an essay to qualify as personal in the first place, the primacy of the private individual must be presupposed, "implicitly but by the same token with all the more complicity," as Adorno writes. "Such essays confuse themselves with the same feuilleton with which the enemies of the essay form confuse it."[10]

*

By my account, the personal essay is a modern formation. It is a wholly different creature from the essay birthed by Montaigne in 1570 and nurtured through the seventeenth century by Sir Thomas Browne, Thomas Fuller, and Abraham Cowley. Each of these essayists is unwilling to disentangle the individual from the condition of man or nature, a commitment reflected by how their prose slides with graceful abandon through the various third-person singulars. The "I" with and of which the modern personal essay speaks proclaims its distinctiveness from the "we's" that crowd the eighteenth-century periodical essays of Joseph Addison and Richard Steele, as well as the "they's" that throng the nineteenth-century metaphysical disquisitions of Leigh Hunt and William Hazlitt. It bears a distant family resemblance to Charles Lamb's *Essays of Elia*, the "quintessence of the spirit of bourgeois intimacy," according to Mario Praz.[11] If Lamb begets the lineage in the mid-nineteenth century, he nevertheless takes care to thwart its autobiographical referentiality. Writing under the pseudonym "Elia" lets him throw a small but shattering wrench into the personal essay's production of individual personhood – its demand for "a single subject whose identity is defined by the uncontestable readability of his proper name," as Paul de Man writes.[12]

"No one has approached the *Essays of Elia*," writes Virginia Woolf in "The Decay of Essay Writing." Published nearly a quarter-century before Benjamin's *The Arcades Project*, and a half-century before Adorno's "The Essay as Form," Woolf's lament about the aesthetic decline of the personal essay grasps the problem of telling stories about people not head on, but obliquely.[13] She does not open by offering a history of bourgeois individualism, but by decrying its most obvious socio-institutional manifestations: first, "the spread of education," which ritualizes subjectivity by stressing the individual nature of failure and success; second, the proliferation of print culture, the "tracts, pamphlets, advertisements, gratuitous copies of magazines, and the literary production of friends" that arrive "by post, by van, by messenger" "at all hours of the day."[14] The churn of both schools and presses results, ultimately, in the flattening of much written matter, Woolf complains, and in a feeling of oversaturation, of boredom on the part of the reader who bears the onslaught. But her boredom is not the boredom one feels when confronted with an apparently infinite, depersonalized expanse of textuality – the boredom of slogging through tightly packed columns in a nineteenth century periodical, for instance. Rather, it is the boredom of having to attend to "a very large number" of people, all of whom demand public recognition through the projection of a private interiority.

The intimate connection between education, the bourgeois public sphere, and the specter of private individuality compels Woolf to judge the personal essay "a sign of the times."[15] It is the genre whose formal conventions – the "capital I" of "I think," or "I feel" – not only draw the individual into public, but also insist upon the primacy of the individual qua individual. This insistence occurs regardless of the quality of the essayist's prose. The personal essay's significance "lies not so much in the fact that we have attained any brilliant success in essay writing, but in the undoubted facility with which we write essays as though this were beyond all others our natural way of speaking," with the "amiable garrulity of the tea room," Woolf writes.[16] It is "primarily an expression of personal opinion," with the stress falling on the "personal," one's "individual likes and dislikes," rather than the strength or the stylishness of the opinion expressed.[17] While these individual likes and dislikes certainly add up to large "numbers," a word that Woolf repeats with scornful amazement, they do not combine in any sensible way.[18] They cannot be imagined as a mass, a totality, cannot be integrated and set to any collective sociopolitical purpose. Even in aggregate, they demand to be recognized as an "actually existing set of potentially enumerable humans," as Michael Warner has described the projection of personhood in the bourgeois public sphere.[19]

Woolf did not hold the desire for recognition to be unethical or untoward, nor did she believe that collective representation is the only purpose to which the essay ought to be directed. Rather, the essay had to maintain the contradictions between individual desires and social demands, between personal being and impersonal experience, to grant the form its unique ability to capture the texture of life – not a particular life, but the impersonal activity of living. "The Decay of Essay Writing" thus concludes with two visions of potential essays, the first permissible, according to Woolf, the second unacceptable. "To say simply, 'I have a garden, and I will tell you what plants do best in my garden' possibly justifies its egoism," Woolf writes.[20] "But to say 'I have no sons, though I have six daughters, all unmarried, but I will tell you how I should have brought up my sons had I had any,' is not interesting, cannot be useful, and is a specimen of the amazing and unclothed egoism for which first the art of penmanship and then the invention of essay-writing are responsible." In the first example, the essayist's objects are her plants, located in the garden outside the home. Their beauty is visible to all who gaze upon them. The history of their climb and blossom is untouched by the presence of the individual gardener. No one appears to fuss over tendrils and buds, to dramatize what needs no drama: growth and decay, the inexorable and universal journey from life to death. In her second example, the essayist's object is herself, how she has managed the intimate affairs of her household. The offspring she has collected cannot be discarded; no one will have them. Their failure to leave the house spurs a banal therapeutic rumination by the writer – "how I should have brought up my sons" – and a wishful allegory by Woolf about the future of the essay. The tacit hope is that one day, the essay too may be blocked from circulating stories about private, homebound people into the wider world.

"The Decay of Essay Writing" appeared in 1905, roughly when the descriptor "the personal essay" began to spread through the English lexicon. To speak of "the personal essay" before then would have been to speak in ciphers and to traffic in redundancies. Prior to the twentieth century, the essay as a form was assumed to be personal but, as the writing of Montaigne and his contemporaries reveals, only in a deliberately circumlocutory manner. Reading across composition textbooks from 1900 to 1940 reveals that the personal was not conveyed through action; not, to echo Woolf, through "the simple words 'I was born'" and a description of the events that followed. Rather, it was through style, a different form of excess from the excesses Woolf decried. Style was marked by the excesses of language, by an author's pace, punctuation, diction, and grammar; her distinctive deployment of adjectives, adverbs, and prepositions, which, as Jeff Dolven observes, "cannot be counted on to shore up first-person as a verb does."[21] Consider, for instance, Woolf's ecstatic tendency to set off adverbs in pairs ("simply and solemnly,"[22] "finely and gaily"[23]). Consider Hardwick's love of trebling adjectives and sometimes hitching an adverb to the last one, so that her prose appears to increase in precision exponentially in the short span of a sentence. ("She is self-absorbed, haughty, destructive."[24] "They are defenseless, cast adrift, and yet of an obviously fine quality."[25]) Consider Didion's habit of beginning with a missing antecedent to create the impression that writer and reader have arrived at a scene in medias res. ("It is an altogether curious structure …"[26]) Framed by teachers of writing as "conversational,"[27] and "chatty,"[28] characterized by its air of "spontaneity,"[29] the essay suggested the author's "personality"[30] as a specular structure. Its refusal to subject its bearer to direct observation was an integral part of its signature.

The essays from earlier centuries that are retroactively designated as "personal" today were commonly referred to as "familiar" essays in the early twentieth century.[31] Their antonyms were "didactic,"[32] "factual,"[33] "informative,"[34] or "instructive" essays.[35] The familiar essay made no claims about the autobiographical nature of its content. It seldom treated the author as its object of interest. Rather, familiarity concerned the relationship projected between the essay's writer and its reader – a relationship between friends. Always, this friendship was mediated by the presence of an object to which the writer had committed her powers of perception and analysis, and, through it, secured her reader's interest: a novel, or a painting; a historic figure such as Cato; a creature such as a moth. The familiar essay unfolded by creating a scene of triangulation between the essayist, her reader, and the object that shared their attention. "One might put it thus," writes Christopher Morley in the 1921 anthology *Modern Essays*: "that the perfection of the familiar essay is a conscious revelation of self done inadvertently."[36] By contrast, the personal essay distinguished itself from the beginning by its failure to maintain the practice of triangulation, its unwillingness to commit to inadvertency. It indulged the temptation to "fall into monologue,"[37] Morley complained, allowing its language to curdle into disclosures that were "too ostentatiously quaint, too deliberately 'whimsical' (the word, which, by loathsome repetition, has become emetic)."

As many of the composition textbooks from the early twentieth century recognized, direct address could not be avoided entirely: It was inherent in the use of the first-person. Yet its influence on the overall scene of essay writing and reading could be minimized, made to harmonize with competing forms of address that were more depersonalized in the kind of friendship they imagined – indeed, that held impersonality to be a sign of the essay's aesthetic and ethical success. "It has seemed to me lately more possible than I know, to carry a friendship greatly, on one side, without due correspondence on the other," writes Ralph Waldo Emerson in "On Friendship," his essay concerning the poetics of familiarity.[38] The asymmetry in the exchange of words between writer and reader was not to be lamented, Emerson reassures his readers: It was to be celebrated for mediating sociality through the cultivated idiosyncrasy of prose. "The higher the style we demand of friendship, of course the less easy to establish it with flesh and blood," Emerson concluded.[39] This was a difficulty to be welcomed, forcing relationality away from face-to-face situations of address and dispersing it across a vast, indefinite public. To write an essay in a conspicuously marked style was to labor to convert one's personality into prose, "cancel[ling] the thick walls of individual character, relation, age, sex, circumstance," he wrote. Whatever prejudices inhered in flesh and blood friendship – indeed, whatever prejudices limited whom one might consider a friend in nineteenth-century America – could be overcome by the skillful diffusion of a marked physicality into an apparently unmarked language.

Any avowal of "impartial publicness" is, of course, never as impartial as it insists.[40] Public styles are always marked by the specifics of nationality, literacy, class, and race; there exists no such thing as a perfectly inclusive or universal language, and Emerson's no doubt depended on the ethos of a specific time and place and way of being to secure his readers' feeling of friendship. Yet his claim to mediating friendship through style nevertheless reveals how, against the rising tide of individualism, the familiar essay demanded that its readers place the highest premium on the imaginative interactions of nonintimate selves. Its social and collective mode of address positions itself as countering the discursive performance of private personhood. It is the friction between these modes of representation that the contemporary personal essay smooths away with increasing vigor in the twentieth and twenty-first centuries.

*

Why are people attracted to stories about individuals? The answer is as obvious as it is petty and perhaps cynical. The fiction of private individuality projected by the personal essay allows bourgeois subjects to accrue various economic, cultural, and social rewards. These rewards are dispersed by institutions that are both constituted by the fiction of the private individual and responsible for reproducing it. The most obvious institution of this kind is the school and, as Adorno observes, its elevation of "pedagogical necessity into metaphysical virtue."[41] Once the production of personhood becomes bound to and administered by pedagogy, its illusions gain in intensity and reach, as does the personal essay.

A more specific genealogy for the genre – and an explanation of its distinctively American quality today – is the "personal statement" that high school students applying to US colleges and universities were asked to produce starting in around 1920, and which has evolved into a cornerstone of the admissions process.[42] Although it is difficult to pinpoint how many students per year write personal statements, 5.6 million applications were submitted in 2019–2020 through the Common App, a generic college admission application that requires the applicant to write at least one personal essay.[43] Orbiting these millions of essays is a burgeoning industry of tutoring, prepping, and editing services, evinced by the popularity of books such as *How to Write the Perfect Personal Statement*, *The Berkeley Book of College Essays*, *College Essays That Made a Difference*, and *How To Write a Winning Personal Statement*. By this measure, the number of published personal essays is a minuscule proportion of the broader field of personal essay writing, which largely deploys its performance of private individuality to secure access to the cultural capital of the university. The personal narrative is the designated genre to reveal the writer's "inner life," an "opportunity to differentiate yourself from everyone else," writes Alan Gelb in *Conquering the College Admissions Essay in 10 Steps*.[44]

To tell this story about the personal essay is to offer a more local account of its function than the story of modernity writ large, showing the mutation of individual subjectivity into an unequally distributed immaterial resource. The first mention of the personal essay as an admissions requirement, according to Jerome Karabel, came during Harvard's drastic changes to its admissions practices in the 1920s. Since the turn of the century, selection based on exam scores had created what administrators called a "Jewish problem":[45] the admission of more Jewish applicants than the university deemed acceptable. "We can reduce the number of Jews by talking about other qualifications than those of admission examination," wrote Harvard's president Abbott Lawrence Lowell in 1922, advocating for a subjective set of criteria.[46] The other qualifications he listed, "character" and "leadership," were to be assessed through three new genres: "a demographic survey, a personal essay, and a detailed description of extracurricular activities."[47] The assumption was that Jewish applicants would fall short of the school's desired "character standard" – that their "centuries of oppression and degradation" meant that they were characterized not by a commitment to individual and personal self-assertion but by a "martyr air."[48]

To weed out Jewish applicants, universities would mobilize the essay as a genre that they treated as "an heir to the Catholic tradition of confession and the later Protestant tradition of narratives of 'saving faith,'" writes Charles Petersen.[49] No doubt the version of individualism championed by administrators drew on the moral culture of the Protestant bourgeoisie, what Max Weber described as its use of education to cultivate a rational, self-assertive personality. This type was marked by its ability to adhere to a consistent and subjective set of values in a disenchanted world. Forced to conceive the meaning of things, and even man's relationship to reality, as an individual matter, Weber's rational personality type formed intellectual arrangements to anoint himself the master and the arbiter of his own destiny, and eventually of those around him. The premise of elite college admissions was that this relation could be cinched, and indeed enhanced, by reversing its terms: that the ability to demonstrate, through the genre of the essay, one's commitment to an idealized model of private and rational individualism marked the applicant as someone well-suited to higher education. Whereas in previous centuries, higher education would have secured a career in the ministry, now it led to executive roles in industry and government. Beyond its discriminatory function, the personal essay sought to identify the students whom the university could transform into the politico-economic leaders of the future.

If students from the 1920s to the present have had only a dim sense of how the personal essay's character standard perpetuated "the rules of order established by class domination,"[50] then their parents and teachers most certainly understood its significance. When, after World War II, the personal essay requirement started to spread from private to public universities, administrators debated whether students were even writing the essays themselves. "The short autobiography called for by most application forms was frequently larded with exaggeration," reports Benjamin Fine in his 1957 book *How to Be Accepted by the College of Your Choice*.[51] Yet the authenticity of storytelling was beside the point. What was being assessed was not the applicant's actual individuality – no doubt there was literally no one else like him in the world – it was his expressive commitment to the value of individuality as a political good, a necessary cultural and economic resource for his *Bildung*. By this logic, parental oversight and meddling were to be welcomed as signs of thoughtfulness, as were the proliferation of how-to books, tutoring businesses, and even paid or unpaid ghostwriters. These forms of assistance all revealed that students were willing, perhaps even eager, to learn how best to express their allegiance to the rules of order perpetuated by higher education. "With all the attention parents pay to their children's admission to Stanford, I don't [think] there's a chance in the world that the students write this answer themselves, or without parental guidance," wrote Frederic O. Glover, assistant to the president of Stanford in 1958. "If my son did, I think he would have holes in his head. Of course he'd ask – if he has any sense, and I'd have my nose over his shoulder as he wrote whatever he'd write." Learning how to "game the system" was only a sign of the system's success at shaping applicants' behavior.

The overtly discriminatory origins of the admissions essay have been superseded by more covert models of calibrating personhood by ethnicity, as in the recent case of Harvard University admissions officers accused of assigning Asian American applicants lower scores in subjective categories such as "positive personality."[52] Yet the value the admissions essay – and the college application process in general – places on the private individual as a self-reflective and self-governing subject, the rightful heir to the spoils of capitalism, remains as powerful as ever. "One significant institutional survival of the personal essay about character is the American college admission essay," write Kathryn Murphy and Thomas Karshan in *On Essays: Montaigne to the Present.* "Applicants are encouraged to draw a moral out of a personal anecdote, often about struggle, and enriched by some element of their reading or studies: 'failure,' an expert on the admissions essay tells us, 'is essayistic gold.'"[53] Far from signaling weakness, the proud narration of failure speaks of character in precisely the terms set by the educated bourgeoisie of the early twentieth century: character as the capacity to maintain one's self-comportment in a moment of distress, to tell a tale of hardship lit by the glow of self-knowledge. The college admissions essay is the central institutional mechanism in the USA responsible for yoking the phantasmagorias of the interior to a distinctive set of cultural and economic rewards. Private individuality is the "gold" the essay spins into its storyline, then reaps as its reward.

*

What Petersen describes as the "Catholic tradition of confession," with its ponderous moral and spiritual accent, its masochistic desire for public exposure and redemption, had yet to enter the scene of personal essay writing and would not do so until the mid-1960s. Almost all the guides mentioned earlier warn applicants away from striking a tone that is too testimonial or therapeutic, working hard to buffer the admissions essay from the sins and perils of what is commonly called confessional writing.[54] Unlike the admissions essay, whose rules and stakes are firmly pegged to the institution of the school, confessional writing speaks to a gestalt shift in the importance of the individual and the technologies used to conceptualize new notions of personhood. "Its development coincides with new cold war cultures of privacy and surveillance, with therapy/pop psychology culture, with the falling away of modernist and 'New Critical' approaches to art and literature, with the rise of the television talk show and the cult of the celebrity," writes Jo Gill.[55]

While one could trace a history of confessional writing that branches back to the writings of Augustine, of Rousseau, of Freud, it was only during the mid-twentieth century that "the confessional" coalesced as a "reinstatement of two closely related literary conventions," details Robert von Hallberg: that literature originates "in its subject matter" and that writers "mean, at least literally, what they say."[56] Perceived by many critics as a rejoinder to New Critical ideologies of reading, the confessional generation appeared to turn away from the university where, surrounded by many successful writers of admissions essays, modernist models of aesthetic autonomy had been institutionalized. The confessional school, by contrast, squatted at the nexus of therapeutic culture, with its air of psychological self-seriousness; second-wave feminism, from which it drew its reputation as a genre of female complaint; and 1960s counterculture, which positioned literary production as a loose and spontaneous activity, a mimetic depiction of a life already lived in accordance with these same aesthetic criteria. "The fictional realism on which we had been shaped seemed to lead almost logically to that further realism which existed in the world of fact," announced Seymour Krim, a second-generation New York beatnik, in his appropriately titled 1971 collection of personal essays, *Shake It for the World, Smartass*. "It was now impossible to restrain ourselves from wanting to go over the edge into autobiography, the confessional essay."[57]

The rise of confessional writing authorized new groups previously excluded from laying claim to personhood to speak as individuals, amplifying the voice of the "voiceless" in testimonies to dispossession. Yet, as Cheryl Butler argues in *The Art of the Black Essay*, the essays of James Baldwin and Rebecca Walker, and recently Ta-Nehisi Coates, are only awkwardly aligned with the tradition of the personal essay. Even if personal experience is what authorizes the essay form, its function as "a weapon for the downtrodden and the desperate-to-be-heard" presumes that personhood was, from the outset, an unequally distributed resource.[58] Nowhere is this more evident than in Baldwin's "Stranger in the Village," in which Baldwin examines himself from the self-estranged perspective of the white villagers who rub his skin and touch his hair, astounded by his blackness: "There was yet no suggestion that I was human: I was simply a living wonder."[59] The uncanniness that Butler identifies in Baldwin's moment of double consciousness – the same uncanniness that marks "the Latina essay," "the Black essay," "the radical feminist essay," she claims – resides in the moment when the essayist recognizes "who I am." Yet this recognition is also the moment when the problematic of the private individual is dissolved by the knowledge that the ability to write and to speak as an "I" is a restricted social and political phenomenon. "Haunted by sociopolitical dramas around issues of race, sex, class, for example, the essay itself might arrive as a racy document with a radical politics left unveiled," Butler writes.[60] Had the personal essay followed in the footsteps of the racy documents of the 1960s, it may not exist anymore, having yielded entirely to the countercultural currents of the political essay.

A genuinely countercultural practice can only flourish for so long before being co-opted by the dominant culture. In this case, co-optation proceeded not through the university, but through the publishing industry, which, as one association report concluded in 1982, had realized that "giving the actual names of girl-friends involved with [one's] sex ventures ... further increased the curiosity of the general reader, and also promoted sales."[61] Running under this gleeful voyeurism were more depressing and commonplace changes in the conditions of publishing after the recession of the 1980s had forced the industry to grow "leaner and meaner." "Confession is a growth industry," announced Catharine Lumby in the 1998 textbook *A Writer's Guide*.[62] On the production side, confession's growth had been spurred by a proliferation in new media forms attractive to amateur or non-professional writers, particularly the rise of blogs and self-publishing, at the same time that professional editorial roles were being made redundant and advances for non-fiction books were beginning to contract. On the consumption side, it was marked by the erasure of meaningful aesthetic differences between "quality media and the tabloids."[63] These economic factors conspired to make individual experience more saleable than ever, simply because it could be bought on the cheap and sold on the regular, especially when tethered to intimate, therapeutic disclosures about transgressive sexual activity, trauma, and family members in crisis.

While one could read individual essay collections to trace how the market emboldened the aesthetics of confession, parody presents a more fruitful opportunity for understanding the personal essay's evolving commercial function through the 1990s and 2000s. "I am a Personal Essay and I was born with a port wine stain and beaten by my mother," declares the Personal Essay who narrates "A Personal Essay by a Personal Essay," published in *McSweeney's* in 2010.[64] "A brief affair with a second cousin produced my first and only developmentally disabled child." Here, in close and crowded quarters, appear the most notable features of confessional writing, beginning with its audacious claiming of the first-person pronoun at the scene of its birth – a wink at Woolf's line in "The Decay of Essay Writing": "The simple words 'I was born' have somehow a charm beside which all the splendours of romance and fairy-tale turn to moonshine and tinsel." Yet the charm of the Personal Essay wears off immediately. It is sullied not by the port wine stain – there is magic to that punning detail – but by the rapid accretion of traumatic disclosures: the observation of physical deformity, the admission of family violence, the recollection of sexual transgression. In aggregate, they do not add up to a story, but, as we will see, a sales pitch.

The Personal Essay speaks to us from "a clinic led by the Article's Director and Editor for a national women's magazine," which will publish the most promising personal essay out of a crowded field of candidates. In attendance, the Personal Essay counts "The Essay Without Arms," "The Exercise Bulimia Essay," "The Divorce Essay," "The Alopecia Essay," and a pitiful, misfit essay who refuses to speak in the first-person and speaks about "Tuesday."[65] "Not the Tuesday of an amputation, just a regular any old Tuesday," the Personal Essay tells us, bewitched by this essay's descriptive prowess and scandalized by its refusal to play by "the rules."[66] Doesn't the Tuesday essay know what it takes to secure a legible social position in the contemporary literary field? she wonders. Our narrator prevails as the winner of this competition, as we know she will from her triumphantly abject beginning. "Anyway, come November I will be buying every copy of *Marie Claire* I can get my one good hand on!" she crows. "If you haven't looked death straight in the eye or been sued by a sister wife, you won't see yourself in my story."[67]

Whereas the narrator of a personal essay draws our attention to the experience of a single individual, the Personal Essay channels the genre's conceptual production of personhood as a saleable commodity. This production takes place through a competitive practice of disclosure, a game of one-upmanship that promises access to publishing's networks of mentorship, distribution, and circulation. Intriguingly, the conventions of confession, the shocking clichés that the personal essays in the clinic must mobilize to perform their singular and embodied personhood, are so overwhelmingly content-based that they short-circuit any consideration of individual style on the part of either reader or writer. We have no idea how these essays are written; we only know what they are about. We see this in the naming of the personal essays at the clinic – not by the readability of the proper name, but by subgenre, a categorical descriptor that could belong to any number of individuals. (Certainly, more than one essayist has written on divorce.) One could imagine the clinic filling up with an infinitely receding horizon of subgenres that, for all their startling combinations, never get any closer to grounding the essay in the peculiarities of prose. The tension between personality and impersonality, essential to early theorizations of the familiar essay, has gone slack, bloated by traumatic content.

Under what conditions is content king? When the personal essay makes the production of personhood not only publicly legible, but also monetizable. "Secretly, we each hoped to out-devastate the other and nail ourselves a freelance contract," confesses the Personal Essay.[68] Her confession is comic, cruel, and pathetic, revealing the mismatch between out-devastating another person through self-exposure and the rewards it yields. In a publishing industry that has largely done away with staff writers, an industry in which art and literature have dwindled into minor cultural forms and creative laborers must create appealing online personae to crowdfund their livelihoods, nothing could be more coveted than a "freelance contract." If there is something painfully anachronistic about buying every copy of *Marie-Claire*, then there is something equally painful in the recognition that the Personal Essay's performance of personhood only gives her access to exploitative labor conditions. But this is as good as it gets.

The Personal Essay's appraisal of the economic situation reveals why the triangulation of reader, writer, and object secured by the familiar essay is no longer viable. Fewer places will pay for it; fewer people are trained to produce it. The confessional has proven a highly successful strategy for extracting literary production from an increasingly deskilled workforce that needs to do little more than share experiences. As Jia Tolentino, a former editor at *Jezebel* and *The Hairpin*, has pointed out, low-budget websites pay young women a pittance for "ultra-confessional essays" that allow them to "negotiate their vulnerability," knowing that these essays will encourage voyeuristic traffic and, by extension, increase the advertising revenue on which these sites depend.[69] The Personal Essay who narrates the conditions of her own existence is more matter-of-fact about what other essayists have failed to recognize, or, in Tolentino's case, have helped to perpetuate: the precarious conditions under which creative labor is performed.

For Tolentino, the end of the personal essay boom is explained by the election of Donald Trump, and the suspicion that, under his reign, the personal is no longer political. Yet its decline is explained more by the structural shift on the Internet toward a "self-branding social media influence economy," as Sarah Brouillette argues.[70] In the last analysis, it is not a decline so much as it is a convergence of the genre with social media platforms that has rendered online venues devoted to personal essays redundant. Whereas personhood, as a collection of tastes, preferences, and experiences, was once bought and sold through long-form narrative, now it can be sold and bought in the form of views, shares, and followers – personal data managed not by editors and the verticals they run but corporations such as Facebook, Twitter, and Amazon. What we ought to mourn, then, is not the decline of the personal essay; its ethos and its aesthetics persist. Rather, it is the much longer, slower death of the conditions that gave rise to the essay's unintimate friendship, a familiarity mediated not by a spectacular personhood but the skillful cultivation of style.

Notes

1 Theodor W. Adorno, "The Essay as Form," in *Notes to Literature*, vol. 1, ed. Rolf Tiedemann (New York: Columbia University Press, 1991), 5–6.
2 Scott Russell Sanders, "The Singular First-Person," *The Sewanee Review* 96.4 (Fall, 1988), 669.

3 Edward Hoagland, "What I Think, What I Am," *The New York Times* (June 27, 1876), 190.
4 Carl H. Klaus, *The Made-Up Self: Impersonation in the Personal Essay* (Iowa City: University of Iowa Press, 2010).
5 Philip Lopate, "Foreword," *The Essays of Elia* (Iowa City, University of Iowa Press, 2003), xv.
6 Louis Althusser, *Reading Capital*, trans. Ben Brewster (London: New Left Books, 1970).
7 Karl Marx, *The Eighteenth Brumaire of Louis Bonaparte* (New York: Cosimo, 2008), 40.
8 Walter Benjamin, *The Arcades Project*, ed. Rolf Tiedemann (Cambridge, MA: Harvard University Press, 1999), 19.
9 Adorno, "The Essay as Form," 20.
10 Ibid., 6.
11 Mario Praz, *The Hero in Eclipse in Victorian Fiction* (Oxford: Oxford University Press, 1969), 68.
12 Paul de Man, "Autobiography as De-facement," *Modern Language Notes*, 94.5 (December 1979), 920.
13 Virginia Woolf, "The Decay of Essay Writing," in *Virginia Woolf: Selected Essays*, ed. David Bradshaw (Oxford: Oxford University Press, 2008), 3–5.
14 Ibid., 3–5.
15 Ibid.
16 Ibid.
17 Ibid.
18 Ibid.
19 Michael Warner, *Publics and Counterpublics* (Brooklyn: Zone Books, 2002), 51.
20 Woolf, 5.
21 Jeff Dolven, *Senses of Style: Poetry Before Interpretation* (Chicago: University of Chicago Press, 2017), 25.
22 Virginia Woolf, "The Pastons and Chaucer," in *The Common Reader: First Series*, ed. Andrew McNeillie (New York: Harvest Edition, 1984), 4.
23 Ibid, 69.
24 Elizabeth Hardwick, *Seduction and Betrayal* (New York: New York Review of Books, 2011), 9.
25 Ibid, 13.
26 Joan Didion, *The White Album* (New York: Farrar, Straus and Giroux, 1979), 68.
27 See James Morgan Hart, *A Handbook of English Composition* (Philadelphia: Eldredge & Brother, 1895), 101; Angeline Parmenter Carey, *The Reader's Basis* (New York: Echo Press, 1908), 64; George Rippey Stewart, *English Composition: A Laboratory Course* (New York: Henry Holt, 1936), 115.
28 Edwin Van Berghen Knickerbocker, *Present-Day Essays* (New York: Henry Holt, 1923), 331; John Buchan, *A Shorter History of English Literature* (New York: Thomas Nelson and Sons, 1937), 202.
29 Wilbert Lorne MacDonald, *Beginnings of the English Essay* (Toronto: University College Toronto, 1914), 88.
30 Glenn Clark, *Personality in Essay Writing* (New York: R. Long & R. R. Smith, Incorporated, 1932), 23.

31 "The Heritage of the Familiar Essay," in Marie Hamilton Law, *The English Familiar Essay in the Nineteenth Century* (Philadelphia: University of Pennsylvania Press, 1934); Stuart Robertson, *Familiar Essays* (New York: Prentice-Hall, Incorporated, 1930).

32 John Baker Opdycke, *Telling Types in Literature* (New York: Macmillan, 1939), 72, 85–87.

33 Ibid., 85–87.

34 Erich Albert Walter, *Toward Today: A Collection of English and American Essays* (New York: Scott, Foresman, 1938), vi.

35 Ibid., vi.

36 Christopher Morley, *Modern Essays: Second Series* (New York: Harcourt Brace, 1924), ii.

37 Ibid., ii.

38 Ralph Waldo Emerson, "Friendship," *The Essential Writings of Ralph Waldo Emerson*, ed. Brooks Atkinson (New York: Modern Library, 2000). 201–214.

39 Ibid., 201–214.

40 Warner, *Publics and Counterpublics*, 76.

41 Adorno, "The Essay as Form," 8.

42 Jerome Karabel, *The Chosen: The Hidden History of Admission and Exclusion at Harvard, Yale, and Princeton* (Boston, MA: Houghton Mifflin, 2005), 130.

43 "Common App Impact," www.commonapp.org/about/common-app-impact, accessed December 30, 2020.

44 Alan Gelb, *Conquering the College Admissions Essay in 10 Steps, Third Edition* (New York: Ten Speed Press, 2017), 102–103.

45 Karabel, *The Chosen*, 130–133.

46 Ibid.

47 Ibid.

48 Ibid.

49 Charles Petersen, "Meritocracy in America, 1930–2000," PhD Dissertation (Harvard: 2020), 19–20.

50 Louis Althusser, *On Ideology* (New York: Verso, 2020), 6.

51 Benjamin Fine, *How To Be Accepted by the College of Your Choice* (New York: Channel Press, 1960), 32.

52 Anemona Hartocollis, "Harvard Rated Asian-American Applicants Lower on Personality Traits, Suit Says," *New York Times* (June 15, 2018).

53 Kathryn Murphy and Thomas Karshan, "Introduction," in *On Essays: Montaigne to the Present* (Oxford: Oxford University Press, 2020), 16.

54 James Dickey, "Spinning the Crystal Ball," in *Sorties: Journals and New Essays* (Baton Rouge: Louisiana State University Press, 1971), 190.

55 Jo Gill, "Introduction," in *Modern Confessional Writing: New Critical Essays* (New York: Routledge, 2006), 3.

56 Robert von Hallberg, *American Poetry and Culture, 1945–1980* (Cambridge, MA: Harvard University Press, 1985), 93.

57 Seymour Krim, *Shake It for the World, Smartass* (New York: Allison and Busby, 1971), 16.

58 Cheryl Butler, *The Art of the Black Essay: From Meditation to Transcendence* (New York: Routledge, 2003), 6.

59 James Baldwin, "Stranger in the Village," in *Notes of a Native Son* (New York: Penguin Books, 2017).

60 Butler, *The Art of the Black Essay*, 6.

61 *Link* (New York: United Periodicals, 1982), 145.

62 Quoted in Irina Dunn, *The Writer's Guide: A Companion to Writing for Pleasure or Publication* (New York: Allen & Unwin, 1998), 31.

63 Ibid., 31.

64 Christy Vannoy, "A Personal Essay by a Personal Essay," *Best American Essays 2011*, ed. Edwidge Danticat (New York: Harcourt Mifflin Houghton, 2011), 210–212.

65 Ibid.

66 Ibid.

67 Ibid.

68 Ibid.

69 Jia Tolentino, "The Personal-Essay Boom is Over," *New Yorker* (May 18, 2017).

70 Sarah Brouillette, "The Talented Mrs. Calloway," *Los Angeles Review of Books* (December 10, 2020).

3

FRANCES FERGUSON

The Critical Essay

A crucial progenitor of the critical essay as we know it emerged in the eighteenth century, in writing that described natural and artistic objects and in the process inspired readers to think about the nature of their experience. In *The Structural Transformation of the Public Sphere*, Jürgen Habermas provides one compelling account of this process when he describes the essay form taking on a new importance and establishing new kinds of subject matter in the early eighteenth century as periodical publication emerged as a print version of the coffee-house culture of conversation. For Habermas, authorship and audience establish a social and implicitly political fact, the entry of a new class of authors who were dependent on a dispersed readership rather than a clearly identifiable patron. Those authors accredited the readership that accredited them and their writing. Essayists did not write in their capacity as experts. They wrote to uncover in themselves things that they thought their readers would recognize as familiar from their own experience. Essays were not argumentative exercises of a kind that lawyers or clergymen might write to debate points of legal or religious doctrine. Critical essays did not simply serve to assist readers, to help them understand what they read. They also provided models for readers who wished to account for their own reactions to what they read. Critical essays helped readers imagine that they themselves could have written them, and prompted readers to notice their own experiences and think of how they might convey them to others.[1]

The commercial facts of the newly expansive public sphere were part and parcel of the periodical's discovery of the commonality of the senses and the capacity to observe them, and Joseph Addison's "Pleasures of the Imagination" essays, published in numbers 411–421 of his periodical *The Spectator*, were particularly striking indicators of the change. Those essays achieved their significance and their popularity by considering faculties that were universal. They created the possibility for the emergence of a new social group by providing a language to talk about the value of those faculties and the acts of judgment that Addison assumed everyone makes in the course of appreciating beauty in the natural world and in art. Addison's perceptual psychology describes his effort to think about his own experience and how he weighed the various senses that provided him information about the world:

> Our sight seems designed to [compensate for all the defects of the sense of touch], and may be considered as a more delicate and diffusive kind of touch, that spreads itself over an infinite multitude of bodies, comprehends the largest figures, and brings into our reach some of the most remote parts of the universe.[2]

By contrast with the drama, where actions and dispositions were localized in individual characters, Addison in his essays performs basic psychological research on himself and in the process encourages the reader to test their own experience. There is no Iago for a reader or viewer to denounce in imagination, no Lear with whom to sympathize in the hope that one's own future would look wildly different. There are only the senses, and chiefly the faculty of sight, and meditations about how it is that we value sight above other faculties and value certain objects of sight more than others.

Addison's writing was not merely the transcription of easy conversation. It conveyed the Lockean argument about the universal operation of the senses and the consciousness that they directed, and in that expansive account of the senses made writing seem simultaneously experimental and experiential. Indeed, Addison's writing contributed to a shift in the relative meanings of "experience" and "experiment." The word "experiment" came less and less to involve observation of one's own first-personal reactions and more and more to establish a lexicon for evaluating one's reactions to writing by others. Addison's literary model, like Locke's educational one, allowed people to think of themselves as being trained up in what they already knew. It refreshed the familiar and made its significance apparent. The apparently private experiences that literary characters such as Pamela Andrews captured in their letters and diaries looked conspicuously available for appreciation and emulation when writers such as Samuel Richardson gave them public form.

The "Pleasures of the Imagination" papers cut in two directions. On the one hand, they inaugurate a sociality that was both proximate and remote: They aimed to capture what we might call "your thoughts as written by someone else" or "my experience as you already know it." On the other hand, Addison's writings inspire worries about how readily that remote sociality might be shattered. In addressing aesthetic experience and the operation of the senses generally, Addison distinguishes these essays from reviews that said of this or that poem or play, "Try it, I think you'll like it" or "You can skip it." By talking about how visuality recognized itself in pleasure, Addison assumes that his readers will immediately join him in acts of recognition, that they will see their own experience as matching – and only loosely matching – his.

That sense of common experience foregrounded contemporaneity and a sense of historical distance in such apparently incidental things as diction and word order that could interrupt the sense of the essay's availability. Even as a scholar such as Hugh Blair in his *Lectures on Rhetoric and Belles Lettres* acknowledged the force of Addison's essays, he recognized the fragility of their bid to provide descriptions that would seem perspicuous to readers. In lecture upon lecture, Blair works through the various "Pleasures of the Imagination" papers, adjusting the syntax here and remedying there a problem of agreement that had escaped Addison's attention. Addison's point about the pleasurable exercise of the senses was a point that could only be delivered if the prose didn't prompt readers to challenge or correct it. Blair was instructing his students in rhetoric and composition, but he was also training them to think of themselves as readers who knew what writing demanded – metaphors that neither died nor tangled with one another, syntax that was easily tracked and undistracted by Latinate periodic sentences. A writing that saw the point of correctness less as an inheritance of educational elites than as a way of preserving the directness of address to one's audience and interlocutors.[3]

Blair's lectures may have tried to sustain Addison's essays as a model by updating Addison's diction and word order to make them seem more natural to English readers, but Blair's educational project itself saddled the essay as a form with a new responsibility. Blair, who came to be known as the first teacher of composition in English, made essay-writing a school subject. Addison had given the essay a new energy by suggesting that anyone could and should write essays, not because they were assigned to write essays but because they were trying to capture the thinking that their experience inspired in them. Although Blair praised the energy that would communicate itself to readers, he was charged with promulgating mere correctness, appealing to social norms rather than to personal expression that might express individual insights.

As the critical essay became a more pervasive literary form, essayists made literature and the critical essay occasions for thinking about psychology outside the confines of strict morality and prudential thought. Two of the most significant essayists of the nineteenth century, William Hazlitt and Thomas De Quincey, built their essayistic careers around demonstrating the importance of individual insight into literary works and the writers who had produced them. On the one hand, they wrote biographical sketches that emphasized the distinctive personal traits of individual writers. Hazlitt, for instance, recalled walks he had taken with Coleridge years earlier, and used Coleridge's inability to keep to a straight path as emblematic of his entire literary career.[4] De Quincey, for his part, developed an account of a poet such as Wordsworth that stressed the importance of Wordsworth's circle of acquaintances and his residence in the English Lake District. Hazlitt and De Quincey, describing their acquaintance with the poets, made readers feel that they understood the writings by virtue of understanding the writers.

Yet Hazlitt and De Quincey did not merely bring out the aspects of Coleridge's and Wordsworth's personalities that seemed unusual and contributed to readers' sense that the two were writers whose distinctive personalities were part and parcel of the distinctiveness of their writing. Hazlitt and De Quincey also plumbed their own consciousnesses to excavate and describe emotions that other writers might have been reluctant to admit. Hazlitt showed the reach of aesthetic emotions when he discovered "gusto" in external objects, and he wrote at length on the pleasures of hating and other negative emotions.[5] The critical essay, sometimes delivered in the form of lectures, offered him an opportunity to see literature as the external representation of inner states, and he discovered in Shakespeare an endless fund of emotions, only some of which one would be willing to claim publicly. De Quincey particularly focused on how literature might not only prompt us to virtuous attention to others but also might enlist us in sympathetic identification even with a murderer. In "On Murder Considered as One of the Fine Arts" (1827), "A Second Paper on Murder Considered as one of the Fine Arts" (1839), and "Postscript" (1854), he describes a notorious crime story that he had first recounted in "On the Knocking at the Gate in Macbeth" (1823).[6] Treating the newspaper accounts of a famous murder as something like found art, he draws on them to think about the planning that had gone into the crime and the suspense that a description of it generated. Beginning with a known outcome – the murders of the married shopkeepers and a serving girl, the survival of a lone infant – De Quincey discovers narrative interest and suspense when he tries to imagine the feelings of an efficient murderer immediately after the crime. De Quincey never argued that society should condone murder, but he did use the essay to suggest how a reader might become conscious of sympathy for the murderer and might feel an anxious identification with a murderer's sudden consciousness of their own vulnerability immediately after a crime. The philosopher and novelist William Godwin, rather than De Quincey, is often credited with having invented the genre of detective fiction in his novel *Caleb Williams,* but De Quincey's essays helped readers to understand crime stories as occasions for identification with victims and potentially vulnerable victimizers alike. What De Quincey observed and articulated was the psychological connection between criminal and detective that has become a convention in crime fiction.

In the twentieth century, I. A. Richards and the American New Critics charted a path for the literary critical essay that made it seem like a twentieth-century analogue to the eighteenth-century essayism of Addison and Blair. Like Addison pondering the force of the human sense of sight, they inquired about the peculiar form of attention that we give to poetry. Like Blair thinking about the importance of effectiveness in prose composition, they provided accounts of close reading that made it possible for readers to think of themselves as trading literary evidence – evidence of literariness – among themselves. The critical essay became the proving ground for readers' demonstrations of their understanding. Richards spoke of books as "machines to think with" and of poems as small-scale exercises in thinking, and the New Critic W. K. Wimsatt characterized poems as objects on the way to laying out "the objective way in criticism."[7] The critical essay had become thoroughly at home in the school, but in a fashion that insisted that remarks about authorial intention and historical research were "private" and thus "external" while a reader's account of their understanding was as "public" as the English language and as "internal" as a poem itself.[8]

Cleanth Brooks, with Wimsatt at his side, accepted what the two of them called an objective account of poetry. Brooks, like Wimsatt, treated a poem as a complete entity, and laundered the notion of paraphrase by appealing to a notion of explication as criticism. The paramount feature of Brooks's critical mode was to arrive at definitions of poetry by sidling up to and rejecting the appropriateness of various nonpoetic understandings of language. The language of poetry was the antitype to the language of logic. Relying on Shakespeare for a description of the game of lawn bowls and the distortions that a particular bowling pitch takes advantage of, Brooks maintained that poetry exploited its difference from logic: its own indirectness. He went further, and characterized poetic language as the language of paradox:

> Mr. Stuart Chase a few years ago, with touching naivete, urged us to take the distortion out of the bowl—to treat language like notation.
> I have said that even the apparently simple and straightforward poet is forced into paradoxes by the nature of his instrument.[9]

Brooks's condescension may have assisted him in affirming the claims of poetry all too quickly, and in suggesting that an argument about the place of logic in language could be rebutted with a quotation from Shakespeare. But Brooks's scorn held a substantial view. It was central to his method to identify several different fields of language and to claim that we need different approaches to its various manifestations. Logic, focusing its attention on the features of our knowledge that can be said to have certainty, operates as a language within ordinary language. It tries to coordinate names and descriptions so as to drive out ambiguity, so that names won't harbor entirely different understandings. Brooks's objection to Chase's naivete, which echoes the logical positivist critique so prominent in philosophy in the middle of the twentieth century, did not so much discredit logic as argue for putting it in its place and seeing how difficult and undesirable it would be to adopt the extreme linguistic simplification of logic. In separating out various different strands of language, Brooks wanted to acknowledge the importance of linguistic formulas such as "Hi, how are you?" that are so readily forwarded by social custom that the speakers who utter them scarcely exert any thought in speaking them. Poetic language, as Brooks suggested in talking about the skill of the poet, was to be distinguished from such automatic speech. It was a skill, whether waged or unwaged. Thus, even though Brooks and his collaborator Robert Penn Warren could include anonymous popular ballads such as "Frankie and Johnny" in the ranks of literature in their anthology *Understanding Poetry*, Brooks was paving the way for thinking of poets and critics as members of a profession.[10]

Poets were poets by dint of their appreciation for "the nature of [their] instrument." They did not confine themselves to the kind of notational language that logicians might use. Nor did they deploy merism, the preferred instrument of contract lawyers when they heap synonym upon synonym to create a field of terms so large and overlapping that the parties to a contract must be able to find mutual agreement even if the terms they use to express it are not identical to one another. Distinguishing poetry from these other uses of language was crucial to distinguishing it from history-writing or journalism. The educational mission of the New Critics was to enable readers to recognize poetry as poetry even as it adopted novel forms. Poets might need, as Wordsworth said, to create the taste by which they could be relished, but students and teachers exercising their efforts at understanding forwarded the movement of taste, made it possible for them to read and enjoy poetry.

As literature became a regular school subject and the critical essay trained on individual poems became a familiar exercise, critics changed the descriptions of poems. The formal features of particular genres became less important: The stanzaic patterns of odes or sonnets, acrostics, or emphatic rhyme mattered less in poetry. One feature of the critical writing about poetry was its emphasis on the discarding of such conspicuous formal elements in favor of a more general characterization of poetic language. The poet's instrument is, in Brooks's account, the language of paradox. In support of this finding, he analyzes a host of poems from different centuries. John Donne's "A Valediction: Forbidding Mourning" with its attention to the squaring of the round earth's corners presents an easy case. Brooks supplements the term "paradox" with others such as "ambiguity," but the reason for highlighting it remains clearly in view. Paradox represents the antitype to logical notation, or the moment at which logic turns back on itself and ceases to be clarifying.

Paradox, strictly conceived, might occur in only a modest portion of a poet's oeuvre, as Brooks conceded even when he talked about Donne's poetry in terms that represented him as the paradigmatic example of the poet. Brooks features paradox, however, not because he was taking a census of rhetorical figures in poetry but rather because poetry, under the banner of paradox, allows him to make a strong claim for literature, and especially poetry, as a distinctive use of language. Logical notation might attempt to restate the sentences of natural speech and make them oases of agreement about existence. But paradox stands as an emblem of the passage of logical statements into an understanding that fictions and fictionality involved something other than or in addition to truth and falsity.

What logical notation eliminated was the notion of voice, and it was precisely voice that Brooks aimed to feature in urging readers to think of understanding poetry on the model of understanding drama. In keeping with the dramatic model for poetry, the New Critics famously installed speakers into accounts of poems, and teachers trained in the New Critical mode were ready with corrective explanations when their students haplessly suggested that they heard Shakespeare's or Wordsworth's voice in their poetry. The insistence on the distinction between poet and poetic speaker may have saved students from rushing headlong into confident statements about what "they thought" in the distant past. Yet that distinction scarcely accorded with the emphasis on poetry as drama. And the New Critical repudiation of both the intentional fallacy and the affective fallacy in favor of the "objective way in criticism" ran headlong into an account of poetry as drama that made readers imagine themselves as speakers and actors. The understanding of virtually all poetry as lyric poetry on the model of drama derived from the claim that poetry was essentially a version of what we call free indirect style in prose: It was the confident inhabitation of one person's thought and feeling by another. The New Critical conviction that it might make "assays of bias" and identify distortions with exactitude may have minimized the prominence of the historical poet and that of the unschooled reader looking for emotional solace in poetry, but what the New Critics called "the objective way" amounts to a claim of expertise in understanding someone's account of someone else's thought and feeling: the poet's representation of an imaginary speaker's.[11]

Neither the American New Critics nor I. A. Richards framed their critical projects as a return to the tradition of essayism that extended from Addison through Hazlitt and De Quincey. Yet they followed those writers in noticing how a book or a poem was always something of a found object. In the Romantic era, poetry itself conspicuously featured descriptions of experience that was unsought, and poems came to document that experience and the claim to it. That movement of thought was crucial in the shift of the word "experimental" to "experiential." In the early eighteenth century, experimental feelings involved certainties that were felt to be immediate. The critical essay existed to unpack those experimental convictions and to describe how one might cling to or modify the certainties of immediate experimental feeling.

Richards, in his most famous work, *Practical Criticism*, strips the titles of poems, names of poets, dates of composition, and publication information from poems.[12] In the process he highlights the extent to which reading a particular poem might resemble perceiving a found object. Because he does not marshal thematic or chronological justifications for the poems he encouraged students to read, each poem challenges the commentators to think of what one owed to a reading experience that expressly eschewed all the usual ways of insisting that poetic meaning and value were simply internal to the poem. However frequently Richards has been lumped together with the New Critics, it was Richards's commitment to highlighting "myself writing" that made *Practical Criticism* a collection of anti-examples and something of an alternative to the models put forward by Brooks. While the claim for "the objective way in criticism" committed Brooks and Wimsatt to imagining that a text was made and given objective existence by being written and published, Richards attended to what we might think of as self-symptomatic readings, the moments in which a poem failed to get a hearing. He particularly featured negative examples, the comments that aimed at correcting the poems they addressed, in the thought that they might be useful as "faults worn by others" usually are.

Brooks and Wimsatt alike identified Richards as an "emotivist," as if he were placing the emphasis on readerly response above all else rather than on nonresponses that announced their impatience with a writer's religion or sentiment. Yet while Brooks and Wimsatt imagined that the aim of criticism was to recognize a text as a complete object that a reader might hope to become adequate to, Richards thought that the stability of a literary text was crucial not because it created a literary object that was complete in its realization but because it created a still point that allowed readers to write, and write repeatedly about it. What made a poem "a machine to think with" was precisely that a reader read differently from one day to another. Doing criticism involved adopting the alienist's attitude, "alienist" being a synonym for "psychoanalyst," but not because criticism could deploy its suspicion on a text.[13] Instead, criticism held out the possibility for readers to engage in self-suspicion. A poem became an occasion, as psychoanalytic sessions are, for altering the conditions of attention to language. Reading was terminable only in practice – because you decided not to keep going back to a text – not because there was an ideal, stable text that could be separated out from the reading. Appeals to dictionaries, encyclopedia, chronologically arranged anthologies, and other people's views might have their uses. But reading was for Richards a first-personal activity: It afforded opportunities for noticing what one noticed, observing one's ideas dawning and waning, seeking out what was sufficiently compelling to be recorded one day, jettisoned or revised another.

Richards's most important contribution to literary criticism was his claim that literature manifested the privacy of minds. While he observes that there are "certain very broad similarities in structure between minds," Richards speaks of that privacy as something that the literary critical essay, on the model of the psychoanalytic case study, might hope to acknowledge with its attention:

> If psychoanalysis has done nothing else for the world it has at least helped us to realize that minds—including author's minds—are private. All that we can ever prove by factual evidence is *an act*—that the author wrote such and such words. But what he meant by them is another matter.[14]

In Richards's *Practical Criticism*, that account of the privacy of minds is a recurrent theme. He speaks of the "poem itself, or some private poem prompted by the material set before the reader."[15] Even in his first iteration of the significant phrase "a book is a machine to think with," Richards rings changes on it to bring out the possibility of a reader's private associations overriding the words on the page: "A book is a machine to think with, but it need not, therefore, usurp the functions either of the bellows or the locomotive."[16]

Richards and the American New Critics may have had considerably opposed notions about what a close reading might involve, but the enduring legacy of their different critical projects was to make "closeness" itself a central issue in literary criticism. On the one hand, closeness was part and parcel of the claim that one could see something in a centuries-old or decades-old text that had not been seen before. On the other hand, closeness needed to provide a rationale for its novel readings, as if to explain why those readings hadn't always been available to critical essays. Moreover, a critical essay that provided a bravura critical reading needed to engage its audience rather than humiliating them with a consciousness that their essays would have prompted Richards to make witty condescending remarks about their deficiencies. The critical essay had become a venue for having a kind of transcendently effective social knowledge, a knowledge that no longer had to think of itself in terms of the class privileges of taste.

Brooks had insisted that reading and understanding a poem such as Donne's "Valediction" was not daunting; it was merely continuous with hearing or singing the unintimidating lines of ballads, and he claimed that no prior expertise or special knowledge was required.[17] Yet later critics found themselves in a paradoxical relation to their audience. They worried about the distribution of closeness, why some texts spoke to them more loudly than others, why some texts were more voluble to them than to other readers. So it came to seem almost inevitable that the critical essay would come to include substantial doses of personal remembrance. Critics who talked about the distinctive cast of their own experience were not self-absorbed and self-promoting; they were instead claiming the importance of recognizing that responding to a text is itself a form of becoming the person one is. D. A. Miller and Eve Kosofsky Sedgwick, for instance, continually used the personal and anecdotal to indicate how they had come to see what they saw in literary texts.[18]

Miller and Sedgwick offered an apology for literature, taking that word "apology" in its almost archaic sense of "defense." Brooks and Wimsatt had insisted that the objective standing of the literary object was the only thing that authorized critical explication and made it possible for readers to arrive at different explications; Richards had pointed to callow youthfulness and ignorance of the world of others as readerly limitations. Miller and Sedgwick, by contrast, made it clear that the love of particular literary texts was a stronger motive force than the "emotivism" that Wimsatt diagnosed in Richards's thinking. Writing a critical essay called for moments of explanation in which the critic imported aspects of their life not so much to explain the text for once and for all as to explain why it had mattered to them. Critical writing and critical reading in the schools might have called for historically oriented reading lists and discussions of the organizing categories of poetry and fiction. Miller, by contrast, makes it clear that you could never write *Jane Austen, or The Secret of Style*, much less a memoir-cum-analysis of Broadway show tunes, unless you went past the point of announcing your literary taste and asked yourself why these things matter to you.[19] And Sedgwick, particularly in her writing with Adam Frank on the work of Silvan Tomkins, emphasizes the many different kinds of attractions that drew specific people to one another and to texts that spoke to them.[20] For both Miller and Sedgwick, the explanation for variability of tastes and variation in the descriptions we provide of the texts we read is not shorter or longer reading lists, not greater or lesser theoretical sophistication. It comes down to personal experience, whether mentioned in passing or elaborated in a full-length essay.

The critical essay came to document what it feels like for a critic to be here, now, with a text: a text that didn't create an anguished sense of the limits of our understanding but was instead a text that seemed to have come expressly for us. Even if corrected in page proofs and commented on in a lecture, this was criticism that left the quotation marks off the texts it analyzed. In that sense, it was supremely alert to the free indirect style of an author like Austen or Flaubert, the intense inhabitation of other characters' consciousness in Henry James. The critical essay always makes a claim to provide a "new and true" subjective account of literary texts. In the process it inevitably generates its own suspicion: The methodological techniques and formal features perceptible enough to be isolated and taught are methods already opening themselves up to the charge that they have betrayed the closeness they aimed for. They look like a turning away from the text to students and colleagues, with critical conventions that are scarcely perceptible appearing under the sign of disingenuousness.

Introducing elements from one's own personal experience, as Miller and Sedgwick did, suggested why they could produce their gimlet-eyed readings. Personal experience unrelated to a particular text had trained them up, had educated them in seeing what was there in the literary texts that called to them. They were able to rely on their confidence in their own experience to speak a truth about the fictions they engaged. But seeing what was hidden in plain sight in literature also raised an uncomfortable issue about the boundaries between fictionality and factuality. They may not have had the slightest interest in Norman Mailer's fusion of the novel and journalism or the historian Jill Ker Conway's claim that the memoir had replaced the novel as the dominant literary form in the Anglophone twentieth century, but their introduction of personal experience participated in much the same collapse of participant and observer that Mailer and Conway had brought to novelistic reporting and social history.[21]

On the one hand, description of the kind that Addison brought to the eighteenth-century essay – an account of what one sees and hears and reads – has become ever more important in literary fiction over the past decades. On the other hand, the self-conscious deployment of at least the names of actual persons, living or dead, has intensified the sense that descriptions may not be the long-sought glue that allows readers to feel that what they are reading is for them. Whether in the magical mode that George Saunders deploys in having Abraham Lincoln haunt the cemetery in which his young son is buried or in the more everyday mode in which Karl Ove Knausgaard recounts what feels like his every movement and thought, fictions insistently represent consciousness out of sync with itself, documenting experience that a narrator has not yet put to rest.[22]

The incursion of historical names and personal memoir into literary fiction has also funded the rise of critical essays that are as committed to a personal and personalizing position as the New Critics thought Richards was. In criticism that blends memoir with literary analysis or focuses on affective responses to literature, the essay can seem to focus as much on the autobiography of the critic as on the details of the literary texts that occasioned it. Though some object to its focus on the critic's response, as in the text that Wimsatt and Monroe Beardsley had insisted had independent objective existence, affective literary criticism can look like a way of rescuing the literary essay from being a purely academic exercise, a product of schools and school assignments.[23]

Historians of universities and their curricula frequently describe the gradual development of literary studies as a professional field. Hugh Blair's eighteenth-century lectures have been hailed as the first instruction in composition in English, and their emphasis on enabling students to learn to write with what Blair called perspicuousness featured students' writing more than students' reading. In the twentieth century, when departments of literary studies consolidated literary curricula and assembled versions of literary canons, efforts to explain the importance of literary studies often took it upon themselves to explain that literature could be a serious concern.

Yet newly invigorated literary studies in twentieth-century universities avoided defining their seriousness in terms of the philological scholarship practiced by those who knew enough to test and challenge the reliability of the very texts they read, and to dispute the idea that a particular text could really have said what later piracies and corruptions had made it appear to say. In keeping with Addison's interest in the universality of the pleasures of the imagination that he had described in the *Spectator*, twentieth-century figures such as Richards and Brooks aimed to focus the critical essay less on texts and more on reading. They thus set aside questions that textual editors had broached about how thoroughly particular texts could be seen as indices to their authors' thinking and focused instead on the textual materials that reading drew out. When Richards asked students to comment on various poems, his chosen method of presenting the poems in effect treated them like summer days, occasions for readers to take their own reactions seriously and not to think about whether there was a misprint in the text or a tradition of poems on summer days that needed to be detailed. While his sardonic remarks on a number of the protocols may have intimidated many readers of *Practical Criticism*, virtually all of his objections were to students' over-confidence in their assertion of their convictions about religion or sentiment and the militancy with which they espoused them.

Richards famously published few critical essays himself, as if in fear that his accounts of poems would themselves assume excessive importance if they came to be taken as models. *The Teaching Archive: A New History for Literary Study* by Rachel Sagner Buurma and Laura Heffernan helps us to understand both Richards's reticence to write critical analyses of poems and Brooks's conversational tone in the critical essays that make up *The Well-Wrought Urn*. Buurma and Heffernan emphasize the importance of the practices that guided the teaching of Caroline Spurgeon, T. S. Eliot, I. A. Richards, Edith Rickert, Saunders Redding, Cleanth Brooks, Edmund Wilson, Josephine Miles, and Simon Ortiz.[24] They aim to describe literary study in the university as it was taught, rather than through the histories of literary criticism that feature doctrinal pronouncements from the New Criticism, historicism and New Historicism, psychoanalytic, Marxist, deconstructive, and affective criticism. The particularly interesting feature of their account of American and British university teaching is that various teachers discovered their methods and sometimes, like T. S. Eliot, their reading lists by thinking about how to find a common language with students more interested in chemistry than literature. Rather than intoning the doctrine of the Intentional Fallacy as W. K. Wimsatt and Monroe Beardsley formulated it, someone such as Josephine Miles developed a practice of counting words in her effort to reach students interested in science and technology rather than literature.[25] Spurgeon's cataloguing of Shakespeare's metaphors and imagery, Miles's examination of word frequencies across decades, and the conversational tones of Brooks and Richards might not have immediately announced themselves as literary scholarship in eras in which rhapsodic appreciation and philological historicism reigned. Buurma and Heffernan, however, suggest a different picture, one in which teaching is the venue that takes most seriously the task of the critical essay as someone such as Addison formulated it in the eighteenth century: the task of recognizing that a reader can take up a text from where they are, can find their object in coming to see how it and they have learned to speak the same language.

Notes

1 Jürgen Habermas, *The Structural Transformation of the Public Sphere: An Inquiry into a Category of Bourgeois Society*, Trans. Thomas Burger (Cambridge, MA: The MIT Press, 1992). As Habermas put the matter, "The issues discussed [in essays in periodical publications] became 'general' not merely in their significance, but also in their accessibility: everyone had to *be able* to participate," 37.
2 Joseph Addison, *The Spectator*, No. 411, June 21, [1712] (London: J. Tonson, [1713], VI:83–87, 83.
3 Hugh Blair, *Lectures on Rhetoric and Belles Lettres* (London: A. Strahan, 1787), II: 59–142.
4 William Hazlitt, *The Complete Works*, ed. P. P. Howe (London: J. M. Dent {1930–34]), XI.
5 Ibid., IV: 77 ff.
6 Thomas De Quincey, *On Murder*, ed. Robert Morrison (Oxford: Oxford University Press, 2009).
7 I. A. Richards, *Principles of Literary Criticism* (New York: Harcourt, Brace & World, n.d. [first published 1924]), I. W. K. Wimsatt, *The Verbal Icon: Studies in the Meaning of Poetry* (Lexington: University of Kentucky Press, 1967), 18.
8 Wimsatt, *The Verbal Icon*, 14.
9 Cleanth Brooks, *The Well-Wrought Urn: Studies in the Structure of Poetry* (Orlando, FL: Harcourt, 1970), 10.
10 See the discussion that Cleanth Brooks and Robert Penn Warren provide of the ballad "Frankie and Johnny," in *Understanding Poetry* (New York: Holt, Rinehart and Winston, 1960), 23.
11 Brooks, *The Well-Wrought Urn*, 10; Wimsatt, *The Verbal Icon*, 18.
12 I. A. Richards, *Practical Criticism: A Study of Literary Judgment* (New York: Harcourt, Brace & World, n.d.).
13 Richards, *Practical Criticism*, 7.
14 I. A. Richards, *How to Read a Page: A Course in Effective Reading with an Introduction to a Hundred Great Words* (London: Routledge & Kegan Paul, 1967), 14.
15 Richards, *Practical Criticism*, 95.
16 Richards, *Principles of Literary Criticism*, 1.
17 Brooks, *The Well-Wrought Urn*, 3–4.
18 D. A. Miller, *Jane Austen, or The Secret of Style* (Princeton, NJ: Princeton University Press, 2003) and *Place for Us: Essay on the Broadway Musical* (Cambridge, MA: Harvard University Press, 1998). Eve Kosofsky Sedgwick, *Touching Feeling: Affect, Pedagogy, Performativity* (Durham, NC: Duke University Press, 2003, esp. 93–122.
19 Miller, *Jane Austen, or The Secret of Style*.
20 Kosofsky Sedgwick, *Touching Feeling*, esp. 93–122.

21 Norman Mailer, *The Executioner's Song* (Boston: Little Brown, 1979); Jill Ker Conway, *When Memory Speaks* (New York: Knopf, 1998).
22 George Saunders, *Lincoln in the Bardo* (New York: Random House, 2017); Karl Ove Knausgaard, *My Struggle* [in six books], tr. Don Bartlett (New York: Farrar, Straus & Giroux, 2013–2019).
23 W. K. Wimsatt and Monroe Beardsley, "The Affective Fallacy," in *The Verbal Icon*, 21–39.
24 Rachel Sagner Buurma and Laura Heffernan, *The Teaching Archive: A New History for Literary Study* (Chicago: The University of Chicago Press, 2021).
25 Josephine Miles, *Eras &Modes in English Poetry* (Berkeley: University of California Press, 1957).

4

DAEGAN MILLER

The Nature Essay

"I used to have a cat," begins Annie Dillard's *Pilgrim at Tinker Creek* (1974), a contemplative book modeled on one of the cornerstones of American nature writing, Henry David Thoreau's *Walden; or, Life in the Woods* (1854). The cat, it turns out, is "an old fighting tom ... stinking of urine and blood," in part cuddly and domesticated, but also wild and rambling and violent; the narrator (who shouldn't be confused with the author) writes in the first person (which shouldn't be confused with the personal voice) that "some mornings I'd awake in daylight to find my body covered with paw prints in blood; I looked as though I'd been painted with roses."

It's a parabolic start, but in its structure, voice, tone, and form, *Pilgrim at Tinker Creek* is a masterclass in the nature essay. A little anecdote of 247 words, grounded in a simple observation; a series of lithe leaps, from the tom, to his bloody footprints, to a short cultural history of roses, all to land steadily at the passage's metaphysical balance point: "We wake, if ever we wake at all, to mystery, rumors of death, beauty, violence...." It's all there: the belletristic prose; the pose of quiet contemplation; the dialectic of human and nature, life and death, wakefulness and sleep, fact and fancy all played out over the course of a year.[1] The entire book is constructed of closely observed moments, carefully penned, that sublime into philosophical meditation – all of which makes for slow reading. Of course, this is the point. To slow the reader down. To give the prose time to work.

Pilgrim at Tinker Creek is also, Dillard tells us, inspired by her distaste for what had only recently come to be known as "nature writing." Dillard had read Henry Beston's *The Northern Farm* (1949) while on a camping trip in Maine and felt that it was too precious, too untethered from fact – Beston didn't know why fireflies light up at night – and fancy: "There was no trace of mind," she scribbled in her journal of Beston's book, "no imagination."[2]

My thanks to Amy Brady, Sumanth Prabhaker, Nicholas Triolo, and Emmanuel Vaughan-Lee whose conversations on nature writing and the essay have done much to shape my thinking.

64

In this, too, *Pilgrim at Tinker Creek* is exemplary. Indeed, disavowal is one of nature writing's defining characteristics. In the earliest collection I've been able to find that names the genre, Henry Williamson's *An Anthology of Modern Nature Writing* (1948), the author opens with a denunciation of the "bad, inefficient, amateurish, imitative, pretentious writing" that had already given nature writing a reputation for cloying-sweet tales of pleasant walks by genteel men through picturesque landscapes.[3] Williamson's sentiment may be nearly seventy-five years old, but the same spleen infuses the English nature writer Richard Smyth's recent critique, "The State of Nature" (2020): "At present the genre is mired in cliché ... Clichéd ideas, views, values, a hackneyed aesthetic, ways of thinking which have become stultifying familiar."[4]

Of course, one can find dozens of writers in every genre who loathe formulaic prose, but they seem to gather especially in nature writing because the modern genre itself is founded on the presupposition that our formulaic, conventional lives – "lives of quiet desperation," Thoreau would call them, lives estranged from nature – are lives in which we've lost the ability to see the wonder that is around us; and having lost the ability to see, we've also suffered a blunting of our moral and ethical obligations.[5] We've lost the ability to really live. When Ralph Waldo Emerson opened his essay *Nature* (1836), "Why should not we ... enjoy an original relation to the universe? Why should we not have a poetry and a philosophy of insight and not of tradition ... Why should we grope among the dry bones of the past?" the weight of his emphasis presses on those two words, "original" and "relation."[6] If we open our eyes – nature writers from Emerson to Dillard consistently play on the metaphors of blindness and sleepwalking – if we can shake off dull convention and get back to something simpler, listening only to the ministrations of the woods and fields, then we'll be liberated to live the way life ought to be lived. "Build," Emerson concludes, "your own world."[7]

Such building begins with the prose itself, and if Emerson privileges poetry and philosophy, it's because he sees in the poet's gift for creativity and the philosopher's knack for incisive thinking models for the original relation that he so desired. But neither, either alone or together, was enough. What was also needed was the close observation of the natural world that marked the work of influential eighteenth-century naturalists Alexander von Humboldt in Germany, Gilbert White in England, and the father-and-son Americans John and William Bartram.

There is only one Western genre that has historically allowed itself such promiscuity, and it is not surprising that those who would hew their own original relation to the world have consistently chosen to write essays. (The proper theme of the essay, wrote Theodor Adorno, "is the interrelationship of nature and culture.")[8] And yet I often wonder if the lingering shade of

Emerson's joyful, iconoclastic spirit that claimed little use for history, biography, and criticism hasn't unintentionally lowered its own veil over the collective eyes of nature writing, and if facing backwards into the past might not temper the blindness of innovation. For one can make something new of nothing about as easily as a life on earth can flourish without sunshine and soil. When Amitav Ghosh argued that the Anthropocene – that catch-all metonym for the artificial degradation of life on Earth – represented a crisis for the realist novel, he made it clear that the quality of a reading public's imagination, and thus the ability of a people to weather existential crisis, depends on the richness of the historical literary mold from which it grows.[9]

And so there's more at stake in a history of the nature essay than merely establishing pedigree. "What we do and do not value in our art," writes poet, critic, and essayist Camille T. Dungy, "reveals what we do and do not value in our times."[10] Nature writing can be silly and overwrought and clichéd and patrician if that's what one wants to see. But if it's true that nature "is the most complex word in the language," as the Marxist literary critic Raymond Williams famously put it ("Any full history of the uses of nature," Williams continues, "would be a history of a large part of human thought"), then it should also be true that *nature* writing ought to be every bit as capacious and multivalent, and that the nature *essay* should be enlivened by poetry and argument and observation and whimsy and philosophy all together.[11]

"To include nature in our stories," writes Barry Lopez, "is to return to an older form of human awareness in which nature is not scenery, not a warehouse of natural resources, not real estate, not a possession, but a continuation of community."[12] Reclaiming a rich legacy of the nature essay won't give us back a pristine Earth, but it may help us to imagine a relation to the universe that is itself original – a word that, when it first appeared in the 1240s, meant "by nature." It might help us simply to imagine.

*

"I long ago lost a hound, a bay horse, and a turtledove, and am still on their trail," Thoreau writes near the beginning of *Walden*.[13] It's hard to know where to begin a history of the essay and nature writing: There's a good case to be made for the Book of Genesis, or Ovid's *Metamorphoses*, or Sei Shōnagon's *The Pillow Book* from 996, or the creation stories of many of the world's Indigenous peoples – perhaps in the beginning all writing was nature writing. Nevertheless, Thoreau highlights the modern genre is characterized in part by an awareness of loss in the face of Western progress. No one has ever figured out what Thoreau meant to signify with his trinity,

66

not exactly; besides, it may be the wrong tack to take. The point, writes Stanley Cavell, is that the narrator of *Walden* "comes to us from a sense of loss" – a loss of familiarity with the world, a loss of connection with living things.[14] It's also important that Thoreau's loss isn't due to getting caught by the gods in trespass – eating apples or stealing fire – but to an arbitrary social and economic order that revalued the living world according to the demands of profit. "What sort of country is that where the huckleberry fields are private property," asked Thoreau in his great anti-capitalist essay, "Huckleberries":

> As long as the berries are free to all comers they are beautiful ... If it were left to the berries to say who should have them, is it not likely that they would prefer to be gathered by the party of children in the hay-rigging, who have come to have a good time, merely?[15]

Anger at the feeling that life's sharp flavor has been dulled by the taste for wealth runs briskly through the history of the nature essay. It's there in Rachel Carson's *Silent Spring* (1962), a book, in part, about how DDT and a host of other synthesized chemicals became increasingly poisonous as they moved up the food chain, but also a furious indictment of prof-it-driven science and technology. One of the most famous lines of American environmental writing comes at the end of the book: "The 'control of nature' is a phrase conceived in arrogance, born of the Neanderthal age of biology and philosophy, when it was supposed that nature exists for the convenience of man."[16] Anger is there, too, in Terry Tempest Williams's *Refuge: An Unnatural History of Family and Place* (1991), a book "of rage. Of women and landscape. How our bodies and the body of the earth have been mined," that chronicles the slow death of her mother from breast cancer, likely caused by fallout from atomic weapons testing that had drifted over the Williams family's Salt Lake City home, and also the slow flooding of Salt Lake that displaced much of the local bird population.[17] It's there in British writer Paul Kingsnorth's *Confessions of a Recovering Environmentalist and Other Essays* (2017), a renunciation of mainstream environmentalism, of modernity itself, in favor of radically anti-capitalist, subsistence living:

> It is a delicious thought that what might save us, in the end, will not be a new economic arrangement or a new politics or another revolution or a series of wonder technologies, but our own inner wildness, pushed under so hard and for so long that it finally bursts to the surface again, hungry for what it has lost.[18]

Yet nature essays are rarely confined solely to elegy, lamentation, or denunciation, and one of the great literary challenges of the nature essay comes in reckoning with the distance between the unnatural loss that is and what should, or could, or would have been had nature been able to run its course. "I do not propose to write an ode to dejection," Thoreau announced in *Walden*, "but to brag as lustily as chanticleer in the morning, standing on his roost, if only to wake the neighbors up": a line so important that Thoreau included it twice.[19]

It's not toward the past, present, or future perfect of the scientist, toward the factual, to which the essayist lets their mind roam, but also the counterfactual and conditional and paradoxical – the ability to see around the edge of fact, to see otherwise: the alluring blue of distance that recurs throughout Rebecca Solnit's *A Field Guide to Getting Lost* (2005); a cat's pawprint left on one's chest; the perfectly rendered "low, sandpapery sounds" of the raven in Susan Hand Shetterly's "Chac."[20] The lushly painted scene or precisely proven fact is the means to then step beyond the bounds of the purely empirical, to look out the window at a swirling storm of snow and see not simply flakes nor weather patterns nor the crystalline molecular behavior of frozen H_2O, but a "beautiful meteor," as Emerson called one such snowstorm – light to live by.[21]

But facts are important: They underscore the unnaturalness of loss, and loss's darkness is the condition fact requires to bloom into revelation. This dialectic is what sets the Transcendentalist essays of Thoreau and Emerson and Margaret Fuller apart from earlier works of nature writing, such as Susan Fennimore Cooper's *Rural Hours* (1850), a seasonal record of the comings and goings of weather, people, crops, flowers, and animals in her native Cooperstown, New York, or Thomas Jefferson's triumphal *Notes on the State of Virginia* (1787), and its interminable lists of rivers, mines, population counts, as well as its explicit defense of white supremacy as natural law. Both Cooper and Jefferson discover whatever it is they already believe to be true.

The challenge for the nature essayist is to see clearly: "Enchantment exists when things are themselves and not their uses," writes Anne Boyer in *The Undying* (2019), another unnatural history of cancer.[22] This is what so worried Emerson, for he saw the rise of a smug, disenchanting triumphalism that understood humanity as separate from and the master of the living world. Though *Nature* is, in total, an optimistic essay, Emerson's writing grew darker and angrier as the stain of the market economy and slavery spread throughout the 1840s and 1850s. By 1846, the Sage of Concord would write "things are in the saddle,/and ride mankind," and it was this purely instrumental outlook that was responsible for both environmental degradation and social exploitation, for deforestation and slavery, alike.[23]

When Margaret Fuller came to write *Summer on the Lakes* (1844), she began with a long, beautifully written though elliptical consideration of Niagara Falls – "here there is no escape from the weight of perpetual creation … Awake or asleep there is no escape" – which one can read as a standard invocation of the sublime.[24] But the deliberate repetition – "there is no escape" – haunts the book, which can be read as a meditation on inescapability. Fuller's thoughts bring her consistently to the unnaturalness of gender roles – a theme to which she would return in her masterpiece, *Woman in the Nineteenth Century* (1845) – as well as the cost of market-driven Progress: "men, for the sake of getting a living, forget how to live."[25] But it's the gravity of what it means to inhabit a land taken from Indigenous peoples that bends her thinking, and the impression she leaves is that everyone and everything, the Indigenous survivors, white settlers, and the landscape itself seems to have suffered. Yet there is no escape. *Summer on the Lakes* is not a book of answers: "what is done interests me more than what is thought or supposed," Fuller wrote. And yet a thing done still has life and the ability to surprise. "Every fact is impure, but every fact contains in it the juices of life. Every fact is a clod, from which may grow an amaranth or a palm."[26]

"What art," Virginia Woolf asked, "can the essayist use…to sting us wide awake and fix us in a trance which is not sleep but rather an intensification of life?"[27] One answer, for the nature essay, is ekphrasis, and, indeed, one of the defining characteristics of the genre is the sensuously rendered scene. I can easily summon a vision of John Muir, who climbed, during a windstorm, to the high top of a Douglas fir on a Sierra ridge in 1874, while the tree "fairly flapped and swished in the passionate torrent":

> The profound bass of the naked branches and boles booming like waterfalls; the quick, tense vibrations of the pine-needles, now rising to a shrill, whistling hiss, now falling to a silky murmur; the rustling of laurel groves in the dells, and the keen metallic click of leaf on leaf.[28]

Or, late at night, sometimes, when I lie insomniac, I feel the bed shift and find myself buried deep beneath the city of Paris, wriggling through chalky straitjacket limestone passageways barely wider than a set of human shoulders, behind Robert Macfarlane, a modern master of the ekphrastic passage: "I shuffle forwards towards the pinch when suddenly – *what the fuck?* – I can feel the stone around me, the stone that encases me, the stone that is measuring me up like a coffin, *starting to vibrate.*"[29] Macfarlane has replaced the gaudy tones of Muir's thickly troweled language with repetition that presses down on your chest: the stone, the stone, the stone.

Much modern nature writing has taken this ekphrastic route, an often present-tense positioning that seeks to dissolve the distance between reader and participant, past and present, "feeling into" an immediate immersion in nature. As Joseph Wood Crutch wrote in 1969, "it is through contact with living nature that we are reminded of the nonmechanical aspects of all living organisms, including ourselves, and can sense the independence, the unpredictableness, and the mystery of the living as opposed to the mechanical."[30] The unspoken chain of reasoning behind much ekphrastic nature writing is that environmental catastrophe is caused by our alienation from nature, that we can be repatriated through close contact, that literature itself can stand in for the non-human world and can help us to realize a sense of kinship. Feeling-into is what drives Henry Beston's bestseller, *The Outermost House* (1928), a delicately sketched account of a year spent alone in a tiny cottage on a deserted Cape Cod beach. "Our fantastic civilization," he writes late in the book, "has fallen out of touch with many aspects of nature, and with none more completely than the night." A few pages later, he writes that "the beach at night has a voice all its own ... with its little, dry noise of sand forever moving, with its solemn, overspilling, rhythmic seas." The ultimate point is to "touch the earth, love the earth, honour the earth."[31]

Just as often, though, modern nature writing has adopted the precise, distanced language of science. This is, in part, a continuation of a much longer cultural trajectory, begun in the sixteenth century, in which the answer to the question "who gets to speak for nature" has shifted from poets and philosophers and religious thinkers (to say nothing of Indigenous peoples) to ecologists and climate scientists. But it's also possible for the intense heat of a poetic or philosophical mind to metamorphose a data point into something else, as does M. F. K. Fisher in *Consider the Oyster* (1941), which begins with an in-depth account of the mollusk's life before transforming into a meditation on cultural mores, environmental ethics, economics, recipes for oyster soups, and a just-below-the-surface exploration of gender and sexuality:

> He—but why make him a he, except for clarity? Almost any normal oyster never knows from one year to the next whether he is a he or she, and may start at any moment, after the first year, to lay eggs where before he spent his sexual energies in being exceptionally masculine. If he is a she, her energies are equally feminine, so that in a single summer, if all goes well, and the temperature of the water is somewhere around or above seventy degrees, she may spawn several hundred million eggs, fifteen to one hundred million at a time, with commendable pride.[32]

It's the sort of essay that Sven Birkerts might have had in mind when he wrote of a form that privileges "exploratory digressiveness" and "allows for picnics along the way."[33]

This leaping out from a fact was perfected by Barry Lopez; his master-piece, *Arctic Dreams* (1986), consists of an enormous quantity of facts and scientific explanations, such as sun-ray mechanics, the differential tempera-ture of various layers of air, and the precise angle of the sun to the Arctic horizon, all of which Lopez marshals to explain the existence of sun dogs – the bright flashes that can be seen on either side of the sun under the right conditions.[34] "To inquire into the intricacies of a distant landscape," Lopez writes in what may as well be the guiding statement of his life's work, "is to provoke thoughts about one's own interior landscape, and the familiar landscapes of memory. The land urges us to come around to an understand-ing of ourselves."[35]

Done poorly, criticism calcifies into screed, ekphrasis fattens into schmaltzy purple prose, and a too-strict reliance on empiricism erupts into the sort of startling anti-intellectual arrogance that mistakes knowledge for meaning. But in the best nature essays, loss and revelation, criticism, ekph-rasis, and empiricism are simply different modes of sharpening one's senses. There's something alive, and enlivening, in the prose itself, like clods turn-ing into amaranths or palms – plants long associated with vigorous immor-tality. Which is ultimately why Dillard reacted so strongly to Beston's *Northern Farm*, a book that is, as Dillard put it, "tired."[36] *Northern Farm* is a rewrite of Beston's *The Outermost House*, penned twenty-one years later, and it follows the same basic structure. But *Northern Farm* plods predictably: Each of the forty-six chapters begins with a description of Beston's daily life, then transitions to an italicized "farm diary," and con-cludes with a thickly spread sermon on the simple life. The game is easily guessed, and once a reader has caught on to the structure, the remaining chapters blur.

"A good essay," writes Woolf, must hold us, "must have this permanent quality about it; it must draw its curtain around us, but it must be a curtain that shuts us in, not out."[37]

*

And we are in need of being held by a world better, a world with more integrity, than this one. If the earliest eruption of the nature essay, at least in the USA, was a reaction to the emerging culture of the commodity, and the mid-century essay a turn from the urban world towards something wilder or more pastoral, today it is the Anthropocene – the intuition that there is no longer any place of natural purity unaffected by human civilization – that casts its hot shadow over the current crop of nature essays. At the same time, forty years' worth of scholarly deconstruction of the idea of nature has revealed how often "nature" has been polished to cast a white, bourgeois, male, urban, and colonial reflection of the world.

However, in the past decade, a crop of revisionary writers have been reworking the nature essay to include women, people of color, and the poor and working class, works such as Lauret Savoy's *Trace: Memory, History, Race, and the American Landscape*.[38] Though Savoy is a scientist – a geologist – her writing is characterized by humility, erudition, and curiosity. "I don't have answers," she writes, "but I do have desires."[39] *Trace* is the desire line Savoy follows as she tries to read herself back into Aldo Leopold's famous land ethic from *A Sand County Almanac* (1949): "A thing is right when it tends to preserve the integrity, stability, and beauty of the biotic community. It is wrong when it tends otherwise."[40]

Leopold famously begins his chapter "The Land Ethic" with ancient Greek slavery. "When god-like Odysseus returned from the wars in Troy, he hanged all on one rope a dozen slave-girls of his household."[41] Leopold's point was that Odysseus's action wasn't out of the ordinary because his slaves weren't people – they were his personal property. But ethics change, wrote Leopold, and just as no one would arbitrarily hang another person anymore, so we shouldn't treat the earth as ours to do with as we please. Except that, over the course of Leopold's life, there were at least 1,023 lynchings in the US.[42] What else, Savoy asks, did Leopold ignore? "Did Aldo Leopold consider me?"[43] We might follow Savoy's lead and begin rereading some of the classic narratives of slavery – including David Walker's *Appeal* (1829), Sojourner Truth's *Narrative* (1850), and Solomon Northrup's *Twelve Years A Slave* (1853) – as early examples of nature writing alongside the more traditional genealogy that I've laid out here.[44]

We might call this strand of contemporary, explicitly political nature writing "revisionist" for the way in it exposes, and rewrites, the pernicious ideologies underlying some traditional notions of nature. Another strand might be better described as "reparative." This is writing explicitly rooted in a practice of care for what remains. "There is power to be generated from cultivating whatever might sustain me, in whatever way I wish," writes Camille Dungy, in "From Dirt," an essay that takes the planting of heirloom Cherokee pole bean seeds, descended from plants grown alongside the Trail of Tears by the Cherokee as the US Army forcibly herded them from their ancestral lands in the Southeast to Oklahoma in the 1830s, as a chance to meditate on race, feminism, violence, and place. It's an essay about refusing "the segregation of the imagination" that separates nature and people, environmental writing and writing about race and gender, an essay about embracing work done well and done carefully.[45]

Part of what marks reparative nature writing is that those who have traditionally been ignored by the literary world are now writing their own stories. "Hold out your hands," Robin Wall Kimmerer begins, in *Braiding Sweetgrass: Indigenous Wisdom, Scientific Knowledge, and the Teachings of Plants* (2013), "and let me lay upon them a sheaf of freshly picked sweetgrass, loose and flowing like newly washed hair."[46] Kimmerer, a member of the Citizen Potawatomi Nation as well as a plant ecologist, pens essays marked by the scientific specificity with which she knows the natural world, as well as the cultural traditions of the Potawatomi. But ultimately Kimmerer's authority comes from her mastery of metaphor, her power to turn sweetgrass, "the flowing hair of Mother Earth," into lines on a page, which she dexterously braids, in a ceremony that enacts the reciprocity lying at the root of her own environmental ethic.[47]

This is not to say that today's nature essayists no longer write about loss. They do. It's there, starkly, in J. Drew Lanham's wryly funny and heartbreaking "9 Rules for the Black Birdwatcher" ("Be prepared to be confused with the other black birder," it begins before moving on to "Don't bird in a hoodie. Ever.") and Garnette Cadogan's "Walking While Black," an essay on race and movement and environment and cultural difference, as well as in Heather Swan's "Dead Owls and Blue Bottle Flies," which uses the work of artist Claire Morgan – gallery spaces filled with dead birds, dead flowers, and dead insects – as a means for Swan to think about unnatural death, natural decomposition, and the human drive to compose meaning.[48]

If the Anthropocene tells us that there is no longer anywhere to turn that doesn't already bear bloody human footprints, then nature is no longer a way out of our problems – tomorrow will be hotter than today whether or not you grow your own food, belong to the Sierra Club, trade in your vehicle for a bike, or vote for the candidate who says they think climate change is real. Perhaps we're all doomed. Then again, perhaps we've all always been doomed. This problem – how, and why, to live a good life given the inevitability of decay and death – is one that philosophers and religious thinkers the world over have been contemplating in their essays for millennia. But, today, what was once a matter of individual reflection has been scaled up to the global, and it's no longer the end of our individual lives that we need to face: "the rub now is that we have to learn to die not as individuals, but as a civilization," as Roy Scranton recently put it in *Learning to Die in the Anthropocene: Reflections on the End of a Civilization* (2015).[49]

Scranton's work reflects an emergent theme in twenty-first-century nature writing: the effort to make sense of what it means to be alive in the era of global climate change. Among the most important of the many recent essays exploring this theme is Emily Raboteau's "Climate Signs," published in 2019 in *The New York Review of Books*. The piece is a virtuosic blend of climate change, race, and a critical consideration of the artist Justin Guariglia's public art exhibition *Climate Signals*, which entailed placing large traffic signs in public spaces throughout New York City that would display messages such as "Climate Change At Work," and "Climate Denial Kills." The essay is also about motherhood: Raboteau begins with her then-four-year-old son's love of trains. Raboteau herself takes public transit around New York to visit Guariglia's installations, and she makes a friend, another artist, named Mikael Awake, the son of Ethiopian immigrants, also drawn to Guariglia's signs and whom Raboteau meets first via Twitter. The essay soars and dives from abstract considerations of the latest global warming data to the logistics of navigating New York's subway system, the growth of a friendship to worrying over her children's future; it's a surefooted, acrobatic performance that is also unpredictable, and though Raboteau turns to artists and scientists, writers and thinkers in the course of her essay to try to understand the losses that compound every day, it's her young son from whom revelation comes. Raboteau introduces him to Awake, worries that he'll "chew Mik[ael]'s ear off about supervillains from the Marvel Universe and the darker actions of Greek Gods," but then stops herself "and thanked my boy for his morbid curiosity. He is teaching us to pay attention."[50]

*

It's a small thing – to pay attention. It won't bring back the passenger pigeon or save the Great Barrier Reef. Yet, as essayists from Thoreau to Dungy, Fuller to Raboteau reaffirm, the world is worth paying attention to.

It is in the nature of the essay to double back and surprise, and there's one more twist in this short history: Nature essays are never only about trees or mountains or rising seas or birds. Essays about nature, that most complex, capacious word, are always in some measure essays about ourselves, our imperfect, blinkered selves, our ability to be held and to hold. Though much has changed over the two-hundred-year course of the modern nature essay, its central focus has remained the near-loss of our greatest human attribute, our "wild holy imaginations," as Brian Doyle put it, about the way contact with plants and stones and weather and animals and other human beings condenses our concentration, revealing to us that we *live* in a world that is both more terrible and more wonder-filled than the one we have grown accustomed to.[51] The world is wild. And whether by scientific fact or careful description, the slow form of the essay itself, its style, is a way of stinging us awake, a way of making the wildness of the world cohere long enough for us to find a deliberate place in it.

Nature essays, the good ones, remind us that there is always more than our minds can hold, that "the bigness of the world is its redemption," as Rebecca Solnit put it.[52] Nature essays, the good ones, remind us that how we read, how we write, how we interpret, and how we live our lives are interrelated, that each, to be done well, demands attentiveness, care, and thoughtfulness. "Can we," writes bell hooks, in *Belonging: A Culture of Place* (2009), "embrace an ethos of sustainability that is not solely about the appropriate care of the world's resources, but is also about the creation of meaning – the making of lives that we feel are worth living?"[53] Nature essays, the good ones, are invitations to imagine.

To have lived a life worth living: This is the dream of the nature essay. "I think," Annie Dillard wrote at the end of *Pilgrim at Tinker Creek*, "that the dying pray at last not 'please,' but 'thank you.'"[54]

Notes

1 Annie Dillard, *Pilgrim at Tinker Creek* (New York: HarperPerennial, 1974), 3, 4. The calendrical structure is one of the most enduring forms of the nature essay, employed by an enormous range of writers, including Thoreau, Aldo Leopold, Henry Beston, Carl Safina, and many others.

2 Ibid., 278; Dillard's reactions to Beston as quoted in Diana Saverin's "The Thoreau of the Suburbs," *The Atlantic* (February 5, 2015), www.theatlantic.com/culture/archive/2015/02/the-thoreau-of-the-suburbs/385128/, accessed March 22, 2022.

3 Henry Williamson, *An Anthology of Nature Writing* (London: Thomas Nelson and Sons, 1948), ix.

4 Richard Smyth, "The State of Nature," *The Fence*, www.the-fence.com/issues/issue-6/state-of-nature, accessed March 22, 2022.

5 Henry David Thoreau, *Walden; or, Life in the Woods*, in *Thoreau: A Week on the Concord and Merrimack Rivers, Walden; or, Life in the Woods; The Maine Woods, Cape Cod* (New York: The Library of America, 1985), 329.

6 Ralph Waldo Emerson, *Nature*, in *The Essential Writings of Ralph Waldo Emerson*, ed. Brooks Atkinson (New York: Modern Library, 2000), 3.

7 Emerson, *Nature*, 39.

8 Theodor W. Adorno, "The Essay as Form," in *The Adorno Reader*, ed. Brian O'Connor (Oxford: Blackwell Publishers, 2000) 107.

9 Amitav Ghosh, *The Great Derangement: Climate Change and the Unthinkable* (Chicago: The University of Chicago Press, 2016), 9.

10 Camille T. Dungy, "Is All Writing Environmental Writing?" *The Georgia Review* (Fall/Winter, 2018), https://thegeorgiareview.com/posts/is-all-writing-environmental-writing/, accessed March 22, 2022.

11 Raymond Williams, *Keywords: A Vocabulary of Culture and Society* (New York: Oxford University Press, 1976), 219, 221.

12 Barry Lopez, "We Are Shaped by the Sound of Wind, the Slant of Sunlight," *High Country News* (September 14, 1998), www.hcn.org/issues/138/

barry-lopez-we-are-shaped-by-the-sound-of-wind-the-slant-of-sunlight, accessed March 22, 2022.

13 Thoreau, *Walden*, 336.

14 Stanley Cavell, *The Senses of Walden*, expanded ed. (Chicago: The University of Chicago Press, 1992) 51.

15 Thoreau, "Huckleberries," in *Thoreau: Collected Essays and Poems* (New York: The Library of America, 2001), 493, 494.

16 Rachel Carson, *Silent Spring*, in *Silent Spring & Other Writings on the Environment*, ed. Sandra Steingraber (New York: The Library of America, 2018), 258.

17 Terry Tempest Williams, *Refuge: An Unnatural History of Family and Place* (New York: Vintage Books, 1991), 10.

18 Paul Kingsnorth, "A Short History of Loss," in *Confessions of a Recovering Environmentalist and Other Essays* (Minneapolis, MN: Graywolf Press, 2017), 57.

19 The line is the book's epigraph. Thoreau, *Walden*, 321, 389.

20 Susan Hand Shetterly, "Chac," in *Settled in the Wild: Notes from the Edge of Town* (Chapel Hill, NC: Algonquin Books, 2010), 62.

21 Emerson, "An Address," in *The Essential Writings*, 72.

22 Anne Boyer, *The Undying: Pain, Vulnerability, Mortality, Medicine, Art, Time, Dreams, Data, Exhaustion, Cancer, and Care* (New York: Farrar, Straus and Giroux, 2019), 33.

23 Ralph Waldo Emerson, "Ode, Inscribed to W.H. Channing," in *The Essential Writings*, 694.

24 Margaret Fuller, *Summer on the Lakes, in 1843* (Urbana: University of Illinois Press, 1991), 3.

25 Ibid., 147.

26 Ibid., 81.

27 Virginia Woolf, "The Modern Essay," in *Virginia Woolf: Selected Essays*, ed. David Bradshaw (Oxford: Oxford University Press, 2008), 13.

28 John Muir, *The Mountains of California*, in *The Eight Wilderness-Discovery Books* (London: Diadem Books, 1992), 399–400.

29 Robert Macfarlane, *Underland: A Deep Time Journey* (New York: W. W. Norton & Company, 2019), 166.

30 Joseph Wood Crutch, *The Best Nature Writing of Joseph Wood Crutch* (New York: William Morrow & Company, Inc., 1969) 17, 22.

31 Henry Beston, *The Outermost House* (New York: St. Martin's Griffin, 1928), 165, 172, 218.

32 M. F. K. Fisher, *Consider the Oyster*, in *The Art of Eating* (New York: Wiley Publishing, 1990), 125.

33 Sven Birkerts, *The Gutenberg Elegies: The Fate of Reading in an Electronic Age* (New York: Faber and Faber, Inc., 2006), xv.

34 Lopez, *Arctic Dreams* (New York: Vintage Books, 1986), 229–232.

35 Ibid., 247.

36 Dillard, *Pilgrim at Tinker Creek*, 278.

37 Woolf, "The Modern Essay," 22.

38 Dillard wrote of the frustration in trying to publish in what is still often seen as a male genre: "It's impossible to imagine another situation where you can't write a book 'cause you weren't born with a penis. Except maybe *Life with My Penis*." There's been a significant recent effort to abolish the penis requirement.

See, for the most recent example, Kathryn Aalto's *Writing Wild: Women Poets, Ramblers, and Mavericks Who Shape How We See the Natural World* (Portland, OR: Timber Press, 2020). Dillard quoted in Saverin, "The Thoreau of the Suburbs."

39 Lauret Savoy, *Trace: Memory, History, Race, and the American Landscape* (Berkeley, CA: Counterpoint, 2015), 113.

40 Aldo Leopold, *A Sand County Almanac*, in *A Sand County Almanac & Other Writings on Ecology and Conservation*, ed. Curt Meine (New York: Library of America, 2013), 188.

41 Ibid., 171.

42 Charles Seguin and David Rigby, *National Lynching Data*, https://osf.io/tvf53/, and Charles Seguin and David Rigby, "National Crimes: A New National Data Set of Lynchings in the United States, 1883 to 1941," *Socius: Sociological Research for a Dynamic World* (January, 2019), https://doi.org/10.1177/237802311984 1780, both accessed March 22, 2022.

43 Savoy, *Trace*, 34.

44 For two recent collections and monographs that have sought to recover non-white voices, see Alison H. Deming, and Lauret E. Savoy, eds., *The Colors of Nature: Culture, Identity, and the Natural World* (Minneapolis, MN: Milkweed Editions, 2002) and Dianne D. Glave, *Rooted in the Earth: Reclaiming the African American Environmental Heritage* (Chicago: Lawrence Hill Books, 2010), among many others.

45 Dungy, "From Dirt," *Emergence Magazine* 1 (2019): 13, 14.

46 Robin Wall Kimmerer, *Braiding Sweetgrass: Indigenous Wisdom, Scientific Knowledge, and the Teachings of Plants* (Minneapolis: Milkweed Editions, 2013), ix.

47 Kimmerer, "Skywoman Falling," in *Braiding Sweetgrass*, 3–10.

48 J. Drew Lanham, "9 Rules for the Black Birdwatcher," *Orion Magazine* (November/December 2013): 7; Garnette Cadogan, "Walking While Black," *Literary Hub* (July 8, 2016), https://lithub.com/walking-while-black/; Heather Swan, "Dead Owls and Blue Bottle Flies," *The Learned Pig* (October 18, 2020), www.thelearnedpig.org/dead-owls-and-blue-bottle-flies/9570, accessed March 22, 2022.

49 Roy Scranton, *Learning to Die in the Anthropocene: Reflections on the End of a Civilization* (San Francisco, CA: City Lights Books, 2015), 21.

50 Emily Raboteau, "Climate Signs," *The New York Review of Books* (February 1, 2019) www-nybooks-com.ezproxy.library.wisc.edu/daily/2019/02/01/climate-signs/, accessed March 22, 2022.

51 Brian Doyle, "What Does the Earth Ask of Us," in *Children & Other Wild Animals* (Corvallis: Oregon State University Press, 2014), 161.

52 Rebecca Solnit, *The Faraway Nearby* (New York: Viking, 2013), 30.

53 bell hooks, *Belonging: A Culture of Place* (New York: Routledge, 2009), 1.

54 Dillard, *Pilgrim at Tinker Creek*, 275.

5

KARA WITTMAN

The Essay in Theory

"In This, I Am the Most Learned Man Alive"

The essay as an idea, as a possibility, goes back much further than Michel de Montaigne's library in sixteenth-century France. It's something we can recognize in history long before history could have recognized it. We might, following John D'Agata's provocative *The Lost Origins of the Essay*, say the essay extends from ancient Sumer, from pre-Christian Babylonia, from classical Greece to the present, that it emerges and coalesces in different cultures, and in different ways, long before it finds a name.[1] The essay is – in theory – very, very old.

The theory *of* the essay is also very old; it coincides with the genesis of the form itself. The essay may not yet "have found its Aristotle," as Carl H. Klaus has it, but it also may not need one: For as long as there have been essays, there have been theories of, theories about, and theories in those same essays.[2] Self-conscious accounts of the essayistic mode appear here and there throughout literary history. "Friends," implores Ziusidra of Sumer in his "List," "Let me give you these instructions."[3] Sei Shōnagon ends her tenth-century *Pillow Book* with a reflection on its form: "jottings ... my thoughts alone ... for the pleasure of it."[4] Or in sixteenth-century Tenochtitlan, Fray Bernardino de Sahagún collects bits of Nahuatl reflections and advice that he seems particularly to admire: "He placed a very good discourse before the common folk," writes Sahagún, "He said to them, 'and I place before you that which is like a mirror. Or I give thee thy model ... from it thou art to take thyself a model ... in order to live well, in order to speak well.'"[5] In other words, the self-conscious impulse to write about one's experiences, about the particulars of the world in their full particularity, and also to write *about* writing about these experiences and particulars, predates Montaigne by hundreds of years. Essaying an object, a system, or a self has always gone hand in hand with "essaying the very vehicle ... in which this essaying is performed."[6] "The essay," Claire de Obaldia observes, "is always its own object."[7]

What Montaigne will give us is a way to focus these existing efforts and to think about their form deliberately *as* a form. Montaigne moves from narrating his own scattershot attempts to acknowledging what he's created: the essay qua essay. The name of his book seems both inevitable and late for precisely this reason; Montaigne arrives at the title *Essais* after he uses the word dozens of times to describe his method. He inaugurates a genre of literature simply by naming his own practice, transforming "essai" from verb to noun to title. In doing so, he also gives us the first recognized consideration of what this genre might be, and what it might mean and do in relation to early modern conceptions of the individual, the self, and life in the world as a political, social, sexual, and emotional actor. "I have ordered myself to dare say all that I dare to do," he writes – and might well have continued, *and then considered how I dared to say it*.[8]

As such, Montaigne offers not only a label and template for the essay, but also a model for theorizing it. "Whatever variety of herbs there may be," he muses in "Of Names," "the whole thing is included under the name of salad." His enthusiastic tolerance, vital for his own self-styled attempts, allows that we can put whatever we want in our own salads – criticism, melancholy, and joy; thumbs and smells and fashion; race and class, sex and suffering – and call them essays. His cooking-show style ("I'm here going to whip up a hodgepodge…") proposes how we might then theorize them, a recipe for recognizing the herby salad or the warm "fricassee" of the essay as different in kind from the genres into whose company it is born.[9] "Others form man," Montaigne writes; "I tell of him and portray a very particular one. […] I cannot keep my subject still. It goes along befuddled and staggering, with a natural drunkenness. I take it in this condition, just as it is at the moment I give my attention to it. I do not portray being; I portray passing."[10] The sense of perpetual becoming he attributes at once to the self and to the essay portraying the self suggests that writing and theorizing an essay are really the same. How *do* you write a self? he asks, which is always already to ask, how do you write an essay?

Theory *in Potentia*

The autotheoretical nature of the Montaignean essay, its intrinsic "self-essaying" impulse, makes it difficult to pinpoint the decisive moment at which the essay joined poetry, drama, and the novel as a fully formed object of literary and critical theory.[11] We could plot any number of key points between the late sixteenth and the mid-nineteenth century at which different essayists turn informally to theorize the epistemological and social affordances of the form, to ask how essays might expand or pervert knowledge and in turn shape society. In 1661, the natural philosopher Robert Boyle tells his readers he's choosing the essay because it will allow them to experiment along with him. This way, he assures them, everyone can learn and no one need write (or know) "an entire body of Physiology" just to do some science.[12] Joseph Addison complains in 1712 that the "Wildness of those Compositions which go by the names of Essays" will leave readers always and only with "confused, imperfect Notions."[13] Samuel Johnson's similar neoclassical worry about the essay's irregularity, the "fatigue" and "irksomeness" of writing without method, is tempered by his admiration for the "fruit" that might ripen out of fresh, unprincipled thinking.[14] In the antebellum USA, Ralph Waldo Emerson finds this wildness and resistance to method sincere, inclusive, and enlivening; he offers the essay as an analog to his country's democratic ambitions.[15] Around this same time, the polymath Venezuelan essayist Andrés Bello makes a similar case defending the capacious and pluralistic periodical essay form, dedicated to "the independence and freedom" of Latin American nations, in his "Prospectus" for *El Repertorio Americano*.[16]

Committed philosophical interest in the essay as form, however, emerges in the late nineteenth century in Britain and Europe, and to some degree in the USA and Latin America, in direct response to what many of its theorists cast as the expansive, arrogating confidence of Enlightenment philosophy and method. Although the essay from its beginnings is a vowedly epistemological – consider Montaigne's celebrated question *que sais-je?* (what do I know?) – growing eighteenth-century interest in philosophies *of* philosophy helped shape the reception and theorization of the essay as a philosophical form. These theories of the essay focus on the form's potential ability to overcome what stands in the way of our really knowing the world: the distance between subject and object; self and surroundings; concept and thing. As the thinkers I consider here understand it, the essay can shuttle between empirical testing, rational system building, and the intuitive, expressive knowledge offered by art and aesthetic judgment without ever being exhausted by any of those forms of knowing. These theorists identify the essay's appeal as its "reject[ion] of monologic scientific totalizations" in favor of aesthetic and dialogic textures and complications.[17]

The Montaignean essay offers a form of aesthetic knowledge that attracted philosophers and critical theorists looking for "a particular kind of inquiry that is neither poetry nor philosophy but a mix of logics, dislogics, intuition, revulsion, wonder."[18] Other coeval essay traditions, in particular the English essay tradition inaugurated by Francis Bacon, subordinate these "essayistic" aspects of the essay to its compact and declarative form. Bacon, perhaps unfairly, falls away in much twentieth-century essay theory partly because of his preeminent career as a natural philosopher, partly thanks to the taxonomic rigidity of his *Novum Organum*, and not least of all because his authoritative style does less to inspire theorists looking to push back against various forms of authority. Although Bacon might be an essayist, his thoroughgoing "scientific mentality" does not, as Theodor Adorno puts it, challenge "the ideal of *clara et distincta perceptio* and indubitable certainty."[19] Adorno goes further: Bacon's resistance to spontaneity implicates him in the "cult of the important," which is regressive, "unfree."[20] Montaigne, on the contrary, is clear and certain about nothing. Or, to put a finer point on it, Bacon, as Orlo Williams says, "writes in his robes of office"; Montaigne, exploratory, spontaneous, and cheerfully haphazard, writes in his bathrobe.[21]

Forms of Doubt

Nineteenth-century British and Continental philosophical interest in the essay form is perhaps best characterized by Friedrich Schlegel's observation that "it is equally fatal for the mind to have a system and to have none. It will simply have to combine the two."[22] Schlegel's witticism captures the paradoxical desire for a way of knowing and representing that is neither paralyzed by orthodoxy nor made irrelevant or illegible by its own lawlessness. The essay offered a form that challenged essential truths and rigid systems, but nevertheless did not abandon the *possibility* of truth or a belief in the common coordinates of existence.

For much of the nineteenth century, the genre of the philosophical fragment served as an essayistic rejection of foundationalism, a disinvestment in totalized or totalizing knowledge, without necessarily ever invoking "the essay" as such. Interest in the fragment collection as a form that could convey both a sense of incompletion and a desire for the whole goes back to Schlegel and his German Romantic colleagues.[23] These writers understood their fragments not as parts of larger extant or forgotten wholes, but rather fragments *ab ovo*. Together, the fragments add up not to a systematic whole, but rather to what Schlegel paradoxically called a "chaotic universality."[24] These fragments are linked to the wider genre of works characterized by incompletion, which, for the critical theorists that follow Schlegel and his peers, is realized in the essay.

Robert Lane Kauffmann credits Walter Pater's 1893 *Plato and Platonism* with inaugurating twentieth-century philosophical essay theory. Pater's brief discussion of the essay names it as the "strictly appropriate form of our modern philosophical literature."[25] Although clearly influenced by the philosophical fragment, Pater views the essay as the literary form most adequate to the way "the human mind relates itself to truth" in the modern world.[26] As Stefano Evangelista suggests, he writes in neither aphorisms nor the fragments characteristic of the German Romantics, but still "understands the essay as a poetic form in the sense theorized by Schlegel": a form of "poetic philosophy."[27] The essay, Pater writes, is "the literary form necessary to a mind for which truth itself is but a possibility, realizable not as general conclusion, but rather as the elusive effect of a particular personal experience."[28] Threaded through Pater's work is the urgent question of how we might perceive an object "as it really is" when our perceptions are always already "ringed round for each one of us by that thick wall of personality through which no voice has ever pierced."[29]

Put simply, Pater recognized that we need philosophy to help us observe and gather up the richness of the world outside us, but he believed we should reject any philosophy that would demand we sacrifice the complexity and variegation of what we see and feel. As such, he is interested in the essay as "lending itself structurally to a many-sided but hesitant consciousness of truth." The essay seemed to him an antidote both to the intuitive flights of poetry and the "dry bones" of dogmatism; it was a generative synthesis "situated midway between these opposites," the inward-looking imagination and the "facile orthodoxy" of a treatise.[30] Pater's discussion of the essay as the "dialectical synthesis of these forms," the creative and critical, sets up three key terms – doubt, dialogue, and dialectic – that will recur with evolving epistemological significance in later Frankfurt School, poststructuralist, and postcolonial studies of the form.[31] Pater's argument for the essay as an art form, and the essayist as an aesthetic critic, also offers an opening gambit in debates about whether the essay belongs to art or science, and what the role of this "aesthetic criticism" is vis-à-vis its objects. Similar debates are emerging elsewhere at this time; Matthew Arnold, T. H. Huxley, and Oscar Wilde take up the gauntlet in Britain, for example, and Victoria Earle Matthews initiates this debate among black intellectuals in the USA at the turn of the century. Matthews's "The Value of Race Literature" (1895) argues that a critical, dialogic relationship to aesthetic objects is imperative to dismantling the harmful conceptual apparatus these objects build up around, in this instance, African American subjectivity.[32] We can trace the legacies of these debates, staged both in the essay form and sometimes about that very form, in different contexts and with various social and political urgency, through the following century.

In *Plato and Platonism*, Pater was interested in the capacity of the essay not only to articulate doubt, but also to suspend its readers, and its writers, in the moment of doubt. He viewed Plato's dialogues as the Ur-form of the modern essay because they embody a particularly social form of doubt, an effort to seek truth "from others ... from [Socrates] himself ... and by the help of his supposed scholars."[33] In an essay, that doubt is registered in its internal dialogism, the essence of which is the method of the dialectic, the constant staging of answers that lead only to more questions. That rhetorical dialectic allows us to orient ourselves toward truth, to seek it not via the dubious reliability of our individual senses or the vanishing certainty of logic, but "by means of question and answer, primarily with oneself."[34] Kauffmann suggests that here Pater extends Montaigne's "unmethodical method, grounded in the somatic self"; he locates a precocious, if implicit, critique of instrumental reason in the *Essais* themselves.[35] The basis of that critique, for Pater, is his sense that the most accurate, perhaps the most ethical, relationship we can have with the possibility of truth is one in which we commit ourselves to doubt.

Strange Bridges

Pater's interest in the philosophical significance of the essay's resistance to system, his identification of the Platonic dialogue as the apotheosis of an essay, and his sense of the essay as an art form, form part of the background for Georg Lukács's 1910 collection of essays *Soul and Form*. Lukács was influenced by Pater's experimental essays and their mix of claim, criticism, and doubt. Participating in a European, and particularly German, tradition of systematic aesthetics, Lukács is the first of these critics to spend serious time theorizing the essay form. Although he would eventually repudiate his Romantic interest in the essential nature of aesthetic categories, his work on the essay is foundational for subsequent theories advanced by members of the Frankfurt School.

Lukács opens *Soul and Form* with "On the Nature and Form of the Essay: A Letter to Leo Popper." The letter is a sustained effort to answer the series of questions with which it opens: Can the essays in *Soul and Form* constitute a recognizable and unified literary form justifiably organized into a single book? Is the essay an independent literary form? If the essay has a critical relationship to its object (following Pater and Wilde, Lukács understood the essay as immanently critical), is it art or is it science? What is the relationship between reality and the aesthetic representation of that reality, between soul and form?[36] These are not easy questions, nor does the "letter" in which they appear offer definitive answers. Rather, this letter-as-essay performs its own resistance to finality as it moves. Hans Gumbrecht writes that for those who succeed Lukács in trying to account for the "aesthetic knowledge" of form, his essay "appears as the gold standard for identifying philosophical and critical conventions of the genre." He also cites both Adorno and the letter's named recipient Leo Popper on the impenetrability of Lukács's prose (Popper: "That these essays are of a lyrical character will become clear to their readers by the sheer fact that they cannot understand them"), which both see not as a drawback but as an excellent defense of his argument.[37]

It helps to understand *Soul and Form* in the context of Lukács's early preoccupations with "the dissonance between subject and object, particular and general, art and philosophy" and the possibility that literary form might overcome or mediate this dissonance.[38] Put differently, Lukács is concerned that the perfect "meaningful and rounded" totality of the world is unavailable to modern individuals; that soul, significance, and "life" (as opposed to mere quotidian "*living*"), have receded from us, leaving us disenchanted, alienated. In the more comprehensive aesthetics of his *Theory of the Novel* (1914), Lukács suggests that what we've lost are the "starry maps" of the epic world. In that world, he tells us, meaning was surely written in the consonance between all things: The map of the stars was at once the map of the world, the stars themselves were our own souls, and those souls were drawn in constellations, replete with meaning. In the epic world, "reading as interpretation, as work, as the discovery or production of significance would be unnecessary [...] form and content, content and expression, story and discourse, part and whole are immediately and self-evidently one and the same."[39] As it stands, however, at the fractured beginning of the twentieth century and on the eve of World War I, there exists no such consonance – and so we must read.

In "On the Nature and Form of the Essay," Lukács looks to the essay as the form that can mediate between an evanescent meaning, the "innermost essence" of our time, and the objective stuff of living to which we are consigned. His opening question "what *is* an essay?" turns with some urgency into *why do we read essays? How do they give us access to reality, to meaning?* Given the disenchanted, abyssal reality in which we find ourselves, what does an essay do to mediate between *life* and living, "between value and fact, life and form, freedom and necessity?"[40]

Lukács's answers are paratactic; we never get the sense that we could find his "essay" in the dictionary or point to its quintessence in some book. He performs in his own prose the same questions-without-answers, the undulating rhythms of criticism and inquiry that he sees as essential to the essay. He does, however, say what the essay is not: It is not the "icy, final perfection" of philosophy; it doesn't contain the seeds of its own obsolescence like "information" or like a "hypothesis in natural science"; it does not lose its value the moment a "new and better one becomes available."[41] Essays don't offer data; they offer situated, limited standpoints from which we can perceive something fleeting and meaningful about life itself. Although it can tell us something about the world, the essay is not really science; it does not offer us "facts and the relationships between facts." And although not a novel, painting, or poem, the essay shares with art a concern with "souls and destinies," with life, and with value. Not science and not exactly art, but touching both, the essay is criticism, an art that "has a form which separates it, with a rigor of law, from all other art forms."[42]

Because it is criticism, the essay remains separate from these incandescent other art forms; it does not lose contact with particularity, with the sensed experience of mere living. The forms of literature and art at whose side the essay stands, without being one of them, are radiant with their own significance. Lyric, for example, clearly illuminates an aspect of reality, of life – the emotive force of the "I" – and then, sublimating this brightly-burning aspect into symbol, severs contact with "life itself." The essay is not this bright light. The essay sees the particularities of life that are "whispers," simple, quiet experiences, questions asked "so softly that beside them the most toneless of events would be crude noise."[43] The essay leans in close to these intimate aspects of life so that they become for a moment significant, replete – and then fade again. "Let me put it briefly," Lukács writes, "were one to compare the forms of literature with sunlight refracted in a prism, the writings of the essayists would be the ultra-violet rays."[44]

As spectral light between what we can see and what we cannot, the essay is connective tissue, a "strange bridge between the world of images and the world of concepts," as the Venezuelan theorist Mariano Picón-Salas, echoing Lukács, puts it a few years later. The essay is an ephemeral bridge between things and ideas, "warning the reader of the dark turns of the labyrinth and hoping to help him seek an opening through which to pass."[45] Lukács speaks of a "gesture," the clear but fleeting circle an essayist draws around a small and humble aspect of life that "melts and condenses" this bit of life into form and allows it for a moment to resonate with significance, with the "reflection of a glow from beyond" that shines through it.[46] The gesture "is the leap by which [the soul] leaves the always relative facts of reality to reach the eternal certainty of forms," the small, fleeting leap an essayist makes.[47] "Form is always in a bind with life," Judith Butler writes of Lukács's melancholy theory, "with soul, and with experience; life gives rise to form, but form is understood to distill life; life wrecks the distillation, only to open us to the ideal that form itself seeks to approach, but cannot. Form is never static."[48] Lukács's essay is therefore essentially ironic, a "penultimate" form: the gesture "ironically emphasiz[es]" its own inadequacy, its inability to represent all life, all soul; the essay offers only "the eternal smallness of the most profound work of the intellect in the face of life."[49]

85

Negatively Dialectical Essays

The essay is not penultimate for Theodor Adorno; there is no longing in his sense of its incompleteness. His pointed rejoinder to Lukács is that the essay is not "a down payment on future syntheses."[50] The transient and fragmentary nature of the essay is the point, and the totality Lukács persists in seeking is fraught with peril. The opening paragraphs of Adorno's 1958 "The Essay as Form" dismiss intellectual waffling about the essay's status and epistemological significance, identifying this "discomfort" as resistance to "intellectual freedom" and overinvestment in "the universal and enduring."[51] The essay for Adorno is "the critical form *par excellence*,"[52] an antidote to suffocating positivism and the malignant dogmatisms of the first half of the twentieth century.

Before turning our full attention to Adorno, however, I want to account briefly for two other German thinkers writing in the intervening years: Max Bense and Walter Benjamin. Although not a member, Bense shared the Frankfurt School's concern with the problem of apprehending reality and what damage we do if we try to measure and describe our reality in only scientific terms, if we cede the rich particularity of life to totalizing systems. He came at this concern, however, not, or not only, as a critical theorist or aesthetic philosopher, but as a physicist and mathematician. "I am convinced the essay is an expression of an experimental method," he writes. "One needs to address it in the same manner as one addresses experimental physics," which is to say, as a form of scrutinizing, engaging, testing.[53] Unlike the mathematical necessities of theoretical physics, he continues, which describe the world axiomatically and deductively, experimental physics flies close to the ground, asks questions, sweats the small stuff. The essay is good for this kind of thinking, this interest in the "kaleidoscopic" "untiring variation" of reality;[54] the essay is a literary "ars combinatoria" in which "configuration is an epistemological category that cannot be achieved through axiomatic deduction."[55] In Bense's theory, as in Lukács's letter, Montaigne's "drunken, staggering self," the subject he "cannot hold still," is not so much a self as a conditional standpoint from which to describe reality.

Although Bense's essay theory appears in Adorno's own, they were not colleagues. Walter Benjamin, on the other hand, had an outsized influence on Adorno's thinking. The two were interlocutors and friends who watched Lukács blend his early interest in aesthetics with his more active commitments to the Communist Party and read his early theories of the essay and the novel. That work shows up in their own thinking about the essay: Lukács's ultraviolet light returns as Benjamin's "profane illuminations," secular light radiating from new "constellations" of the political and material world.[56] Reflecting this profane light demands forms of writing that are not doctrinal, systems of signification that are not totalizing. Benjamin was a prolific essayist, but his meditations on essayistic writing in philosophy appear in *Origin of the German Mourning-Play*, the work he submitted for his *Habilitation*, or thesis, in 1928.

Benjamin "saw his task as that of 'redeeming' concrete phenomena from the refuse of history as they were abandoned by systems in their march to generalization."[57] He viewed the essay as an "alternative philosophical form," committed to the recursive pursuit of "different levels of meaning in its examination of one single object, in which the primary 'method' is digression."[58] Preserving the "distinct and the disparate" even as it represents meanings that exceed those particulars, the essay "return[s] in a roundabout way to its original object" with a "continual pausing for breath ... most proper to the process of contemplation."[59] Benjamin compares this form of writing to the "mosaic," a composition of fragments in which every tiny particular matters, and "the value of fragments of thought is all the greater the less direct their relationship is to the underlying idea."[60] Held together by an idea that gives it shape, in other words – "as constellations are to stars" – the essay nonetheless lets the particulars of existence remain visible and individuated, fugitive from the system builders. And it must be said that for Benjamin, a Jewish intellectual on the eve of World War II, the search for a form of representation that could push against the totalizing machineries of fascist Europe was no mere academic exercise.

The same is true for Adorno, who wrote "The Essay as Form" in the years following his exile to the USA, where he'd fled with other Jewish intellectuals from Nazi Germany. Adorno's belief in "formulating the negative" *requires* the essay's fragmentariness, its failure to achieve the "great aesthetic" for which Lukács, and the Lukácsian essayist, longed.[61] "At the very heart of Critical Theory," writes the Frankfurt School's early chronicler Martin Jay, "was an aversion to closed philosophical systems," and its members gravitated accordingly to aphorisms and essays.[62] Adorno and Max Horkheimer's *Dialectic of Enlightenment* argues that the dominating urges of modern science and instrumentalized reason lead necessarily to a world in which the particulars of nature and human life are made identical with our concepts of them, and the remainders – those that cannot be made identical – are scrubbed.

To avoid this enlightenment dialectic of fear and domination, subordination and exile, Adorno suggests in *Negative Dialectics* that we need to leave open the "consistent sense of nonidentity" in the dialectic.[63] Although, to return to Pater's language, we have no positive access to the nonidentical because we are "ringed round" by our own conceptual subjectivity, we must nonetheless leave room for the nonidentical, a negative space in our thinking and representation for contradiction and diversity. Adorno finds in the essay a form for his negative dialectics, an essentially ironic, self-relativizing, and critical form comfortable with the aporetic nature of reality. "The essay opposes the mean-spirited method whose sole concern is not to leave anything out," he writes; its "epistemological impulse" is to "shrin[k] from any overarching concept" that would offer the dangerous illusion of completion or totality. The essay's totality, paradoxically, "is that of something not total."[64]

Like Bense, Adorno privileges the "methodically unmethodica[l]" essayist who "composes as he experiments, who turns his object around, questions it, feels it, tests it, reflects on it," implicitly rebuking "official culture's" ideological abstractions by engaging and affirming the particular.[65] The essay alone, he writes,

> has successfully raised doubts about the privilege of method. The essay allows for the consciousness of nonidentity, without expressing it directly; it is radical in its non-radicalism, in refraining from any reduction to a principle, in its accentuation of the partial against the total, in its fragmentary character.[66]

Partial, fragmentary, refraining and doubting, *non*identical: Here is Adorno's clearest sense of the essay as a form of negation, an "emancipation" from the "thesis of the identity of thought and its object," a thoroughgoing "heresy" against the orthodoxies that lead to totalitarian thinking.[67] Because the essay's transitions "repudiate conclusive deductions in favor of cross-connections," because it coordinates rather than subordinates, the essay *as form* rejects the logics on which totalizing systems are built. But more than "The Essay as Form"'s final sentence ("the essay's innermost formal law is heresy"), I would suggest Adorno's epigraph, taken from Goethe's *Pandora*, puts the full stop on his conversation with Lukács and Benjamin. Whereas the latter two see the essay as modifying the bright light of knowledge and reason – ultraviolet, profane – Adorno's epigraph turns away from the light back to the world: "Destined to see what is illuminated," writes Goethe, "not the light."[68]

Complications

The political and epistemological urgency of the essay form for the Frankfurt School arguably fades with Jürgen Habermas and the second generation of critical theorists in the 1970s. Theoretical interest in the essay's opposition to certainty, system, and totalizing modes of thought, however, persists in Europe, Latin America, and the USA. The publication of Adorno's "The Essay as Form" in 1958 roughly coincides with the advent of poststructuralism in France and the USA. Jacques Derrida delivers his essayistic lecture "Structure, Sign, and Play in the Discourse of the Human Sciences" at Johns Hopkins University in 1966; a decade later Geoffrey Hartman will note the influence of Lukács's 1910 essay theory on Derrida's work.[69] Roland Barthes feels compelled to "admit" in his Inaugural Lecture for the Chair of Literary Semiology at the Collège de France (1977), that he has "produced *only* essays." Five days later, in his first lecture for the Collège, he tells his auditors that he plans to proceed anti-methodically, that he has "a Nietzschean opposition in mind" between "*method*" and "*culture*." Method, which he admits "to have been taken in by" as a younger philosopher, decodes, explains, describes exhaustively; it "fetishizes the goal as a place and, as a result, by ruling out all other places, enters into the service of a generality." Culture, on the other hand, is essayistic, evokes a "dispatching along an eccentric path, stumbling among snatches ... hostile to the idea of power."[70] His fantasy, he tells his listeners, is that we might live together in this "idiorrhythmic way," harmoniously but heterogeneously, according to our own rhythms. For Barthes, essaying cannot be codified as a noun – a science – it is about motion, testing, understanding the rhythms of objects and languages and texts.[71] We are complicated, and the essay is the genre of complication.

Beyond the poststructuralist movement, other theorists of the essay also engage the anti-systematic, "methodically unmethodical" affordances of the essay, some returning to Pater and Lukács, others taking the Frankfurt School's work on the form in far more explicitly political terms than Adorno himself might have countenanced. Ignacio Sánchez Prado traces a particular tradition of Latin American essayism back to Alfonso Reyes, a contemporary of Lukács who was equally influenced by the German Idealism that animated *Soul and Form*.[72] In *The World, the Text, and the Critic*, Edward Said cites Lukács's ultraviolet definition to emphasize the essay's ironic "marginality" to the texts and objects it discusses. "Necessarily incomplete," in Lukács's terms, the critical essay unsettles the stable value system of the text it touches, and in so doing, Said writes, "is responsible to a degree for articulating those voices dominated, displaced, or silenced by the textuality of texts."[73] Cheryl Wall turns to Adorno in her unparalleled study of African-American essayists' literary resistance to domination and silencing: "The essay," she writes, quoting "The Essay as Form," "'which shakes off the illusion of a simple and fundamentally logical world, an illusion well suited to the defense of the status quo,' was an ideal genre with which to combat the illogic of [African American writers'] positionality and the fundamental injustice of that status quo."[74] And finally, as key texts by Frankfurt School theorists were translated and disseminated, essay films proliferating globally in the late twentieth century incorporated these theories of the essay neatly into their visual, audial, and sometimes explicitly political landscapes.[75] For everyone who experienced West Germany in 1968, writes the film essayist Harun Farocki, "Adorno was an important teacher, even a father figure." I tried, he continues, to imitate his style: "I adopted his aporias."[76]

If there is any constant in the theories of the essay considered here, it is that the essay – exploratory, experimental, essentially incomplete – is heretical: *actually* heretical at moments for their originator; ideologically and formally heretical for his inheritors. Theorists of the essay take up its ability to challenge orthodoxies and question received wisdom while at the same time handling carefully the particulars of experience, representing in ultraviolet those things and those people edged out by totalizing systems and forms of representation. "There is always something in excess of the categories we need to describe a world that is never fully describable through them," writes Martin Jay in his 2020 retrospective on the Frankfurt School; there is always something "that transcends the power to homogenize what is heterogeneous."[77] But perhaps it is better to end four centuries earlier, with Montaigne himself, who always knew this: "We exchange one word for another word, often more unknown," he writes. "To satisfy one doubt, they give me three; it is the Hydra's head."[78]

Notes

1 John D'Agata, *The Lost Origins of the Essay* (New York: Graywolf, 2009).
2 Carl H. Klaus, "Toward a Collective Poetics of the Essay," in *Essayists on the Essay: Montaigne to our Time,* ed. Carl H. Klaus and Ned Stuckey-French (Iowa City: University of Iowa Press, 2012), xv.
3 Ziusidra of Sumer, "List," in *The Lost Origins of the* Essay, ed. John D'Agata (New York: Graywolf, 2009), 7.
4 Sei Shōnagon, *The Pillow Book, The Columbia Anthology of Japanese Essays,* ed. and trans. Steven J. Carter (New York: Columbia University Press, 2014), 31.
5 Bernardino de Sahagún, *Florentine Codex*, vol. 7, trans. Charles Dibble and Arthur Anderson (Salt Lake City: University of Utah Press, 1969), 246.
6 Claire de Obaldia, *The Essayistic Spirit: Literature, Modern Criticism, and the Essay* (Oxford: Clarendon Press, 1995), 100.
7 Ibid.
8 Michel de Montaigne, "On Some Verses of Virgil," *The Complete Essays of Montaigne*, trans. Donald Frame (Stanford, CA: Stanford University Press, 1958), 642.
9 Montaigne, "Of Experience," *The Complete Essays*, 826.
10 Montaigne, "Of Repentance," *The Complete Essays*, 610.

11 See "Literature *in potentia*," in de Obaldia, *The Essayistic Spirit*, 1–64.
12 Robert Boyle, "Proemial Essay," *The Works of Robert Boyle*, vol 2, ed. Michael Hunter and Edward B. Davis (London: Pickering and Chatto, 1999), 10–12.
13 Joseph Addison, "The Spectator 476," in *The Spectator*, ed. Alexander Chalmers (Boston, MA: Sargeant et al., 1810), 115.
14 Samuel Johnson, *Rambler*, no. 184, in *Essayists on the Essay*, ed. Klaus and Stuckey-French, 13–14.
15 Ralph Waldo Emerson, "Montaigne, or the Skeptic," in *Essays and Lectures*, ed. Joel Porte (New York: Literary Classics, 1983), 690–707.
16 Andrés Bello, *Selected Writings of Andrés Bello*, trans. Frances M. Lopéz-Morillas (Oxford: Oxford University Press, 1998), 3.
17 De Obaldia, *The Essayistic Spirit*, 100.
18 Joan Retallack, *The Poethical Wager* (Berkeley: University of California Press, 2003), 4.
19 Theodor W. Adorno, "The Essay as Form," *Notes to Literature*, ed. Rolf Tiedemann, trans. Shierry Weber Nicholson (New York: Columbia University Press, 1991), 34, 38.
20 Adorno, *Minima Moralia: Reflections from Damaged Life*, trans. E. F. N. Jephcott (London: Verso, 2005), 125.
21 Orlo Williams, *The Essay* (London: Martin Secker, 1914), 26.
22 Friedrich Schlegel, "Athenium Fragment 53," in *Philosophical Fragments*, trans. Peter Firchow (Minneapolis: University of Minnesota Press, 1991), 24.
23 Erin Plunkett, *A Philosophy of the Essay* (London: Bloomsbury, 2018), 92.
24 Manfred Frank, *The Philosophical Foundations of Early German Romanticism*, Pt. III, trans. E. Millán-Zaibert (Albany: State University of New York Press, 2004), 210.
25 R. Lane Kauffmann, "The Skewed Path: Essaying as Unmethodical Method," in *Essays on the Essay: Redefining the Genre*, ed. Alexander J. Butrym (Athens: University of Georgia Press, 1989), 227; Walter Pater, *Plato and Platonism* (London: Macmillan & Co., 1901), 174.
26 Pater, *Plato and Platonism*, 175.
27 Stefano Evangelista, *On Essays: Montaigne to the Present,* ed. Kathryn Murphy and Thomas Karshan (Oxford: Oxford University Press, 2020), 244.
28 Pater, *Plato and Platonism,* 175.
29 Walter Pater, *The Renaissance: Studies in Art and Poetry* (New York: Dover, 2013), 152.
30 Ibid.
31 Pater, *Plato and Platonism*, 176, 174.
32 Jesse McCarthy, *Who Will Pay Reparations on My Soul? Essays* (New York: Liveright, 2021), 3. For Matthews's speech see Shirley Wilson Logan, *With Pen and Voice* (Carbondale: University of Southern Illinois Press, 1995), 126–147.
33 Pater, *Plato and Platonism,* 177.
34 Ibid., 179.
35 Kauffmann, "Skewed Path," 225.
36 Georg Lukács, *Soul and Form*, ed. John T. Sanders and Katie Terazakis, trans. Anna Bostock (New York: Columbia University Press, 2010), 16–17.

37 Hans Ulrich Gumbrecht, "Essay, Life, Lived Experience: The Early Georg Lukács and the Situation of Literary Criticism Today," *Republics of Letters*, 4:1 (2014): 11–12; 4.
38 De Obaldia, *Essayistic Spirit,* 100.
39 Kent Puckett, *Narrative Theory: A Critical Introduction* (Cambridge: Cambridge University Press, 2016), 135.
40 Ibid., 144.
41 Lukács, *Soul and Form,* 18.
42 Ibid., 17
43 Ibid., 22.
44 Ibid.
45 Mariano Picón-Salas, from "On the Essay," in *Essayists on the Essay*, ed. Klaus and Stuckey French, 75.
46 Lukács, *Soul and Form,* 21.
47 Ibid., 45.
48 Judith Butler, "Introduction" to Lukács, *Soul and Form,* 5.
49 Lukács, *Soul and Form,* 25.
50 Adorno, "The Essay as Form," 42.
51 Ibid., 29.
52 Ibid.
53 Max Bense, "On the Essay and Its Prose," in *Essays on the Essay Film*, ed. Nora M. Alter and Timothy Corrigan (New York: Columbia University Press, 2017), 52.
54 Ibid., 58–59.
55 Ibid., 57.
56 Walter Benjamin, *Selected Writings*, ed. Howard Eiland and Michael W. Jennings (Cambridge, MA: Harvard University Press, 1991–1999).
57 Kauffmann, "Skewed Path," 229.
58 Walter Benjamin, *The Origin of German Tragic Drama*, trans. John Osborne (London: Verso, 1998), 28.
59 Ibid., 29.
60 Ibid., 30.
61 Max Horkheimer, "Foreword," in Martin Jay, *The Dialectical Imagination* (Berkeley: University of California Press, 1973), xxv.
62 Jay, *Dialectical Imagination,* 41.
63 Theodor Adorno, *Negative Dialectics*, trans. E. B. Ashton (London: Bloomsbury Academic, 1983), 5.
64 Adorno, "The Essay as Form," 42.
65 Bense, "On the Essay and Its Prose" in Adorno, "The Essay as Form," 41–42.
66 Adorno, "The Essay as Form," 47, 35.
67 Ibid., 42, 47.
68 Ibid., 29.
69 De Obaldia, *The Essayistic Spirit*, 139.
70 Roland Barthes, *How to Live Together*, trans. Kate Briggs (New York: Columbia University Press, 2013), 3, 6.
71 Neil Badmington, "Brief Scenes: Roland Barthes and the Essay," in *The Essay at the Limits*, ed. Mario Aquilina (London: Bloomsbury, 2021), 81.
72 Ignacio Sánchez Prado, "The Age of Utopia," *Romance Notes* 53.1 (2013): 93–104.

73 Edward Said, *The World, the Text, and the Critic* (Cambridge, MA: Harvard University Press, 1983), 52–53.

74 Cheryl Wall, *On Freedom and the Will to Adorn: The Art of the African American Essay* (Chapel Hill: University of North Carolina Press, 2018), 4.

75 Alter and Corrigan, *Essays on the Essay Film,* 7.

76 Harun Farocki, "The ABCs of the Film Essay," in Alter and Corrigan, *Essays on the Essay Film,* 297.

77 Martin Jay, *Splinters in Your Eye: Frankfurt School Provocations* (London: Verso, 2020), 161.

78 Montaigne, "Of Experience," 819.

PART II

The Work of the Essay

6

JULIANNE WERLIN

Experimental Science and the Essay

The early essay, like the essay of today, described the vagaries of human experience. Its remit was "moral and political," a phrase that frequently appeared in the titles of essay collections.[1] Michel de Montaigne and Francis Bacon, who each played a pivotal role in the rise of the essay, both regarded their compositions in that light, and most well-known essayists followed suit. Yet for a brief period in the seventeenth century, this humanist form developed a very different set of associations, becoming one of the most important genres of an emerging experimental science. In the hands of Robert Boyle and other members of the early Royal Society, essays came to be a medium for the investigation of nature.

Why did the essay come to seem an appropriate form for experimental science in the second half of the seventeenth century? Most attempts to answer this question have understood the link between the genre and the method in terms of epistemology or textual culture, treating the essay as a "literary technology" that enabled new approaches to the construction and dissemination of knowledge.[2] The essay's tentative, meandering character, scholars have argued, made it a useful genre for an experimental knowledge that was, by definition, uncertain and unfinished.[3] It gave early modern scientists a form in which to negotiate anew the complex relationship between particular, contingent observations and their abstract, formal expression.[4] I draw on these important insights in what follows. But my focus is on a different point of conjunction between the essay and experimental philosophy; that is, on their shared social outlook. Experimental philosophy's methods were intertwined with, and justified by, a sweeping social and ethical vision. Its early practitioners argued for an ongoing, potentially endless accumulation of knowledge, which would, in turn, lead inevitably to material progress. It was a philosophy of *plus ultra*, of going ever further. By the end of the seventeenth century, this much-discussed, much-critiqued ideal had gained a new power and prominence. Understanding this ethos, and the nascent capitalist society in which it developed, is one key to comprehending the connection between the essay and experimental science. For the essay, as it developed in early-modern England, had a surprisingly practical bent, placing a particular emphasis on material success.[5] It was the political and moral commitments of the essay – its humanist orientation – at least as much as its epistemological possibilities that made it attractive to English experimentalists.

Although the birth of the essay and the rise of experimental science are both wider stories, spanning a continent and indeed a globe, in what follows I focus on their development in England. There are two reasons for this. First, it was in England, and especially in the milieu of the Hartlib Circle and in the work of Robert Boyle, that the two most fully converged. A second, related consideration lies in the fact that "essay" and "experimental natural philosophy" are both, in a sense, English terms. The assertion may seem surprising: The essay, of course, derives its name from Montaigne, and his skeptical epistemology and literary interests, including his interest in experience and the experimental, shaped the genre profoundly. Yet despite his formative influence, in France, the word "essay" was not used as a generic label at this point; it was, rather, the title of a particular work, too closely associated with its original author to seem like an imitable model.[6] It was only when the English tradition reached the continent that the term "essay" came into wider use. With a genre as notoriously ill-defined as the essay, tracing the use of the term helps to delimit the field of inquiry. The essay was clearly related to the vernacular prose forms that were developing under other names outside the English-speaking world, but it was never quite identical with them: Essays were typically translated into Italian as *discorsi*, but essays were not precisely *discorsi*. Similarly, although new experimental methods were emerging across Europe, "experimental philosophy" became the name of a particular movement in English, without exact parallel in other languages. Understanding the distinctive resonances and associations both terms possessed is essential to understanding what drew them, briefly, together.

Bacon's Essays

The history of the English essay begins in 1597, toward the close of the Elizabethan era. It was in this year that Bacon published the first edition of his *Essays*, introducing a new genre of English prose and launching his own literary career in the process. In composing essays, Bacon followed the example of Montaigne, whose work he likely learned about from his brother Anthony, a personal friend of the French writer. Yet although Bacon borrowed his predecessor's title and drew on elements of his form, the piece of writing he produced was very different. While Montaigne reflected on the customs of his society and the movements of his mind in searching detail, Bacon gave pointed, impersonal advice on such subjects as managing expenses, taking care of one's health, and cultivating effective study habits. A compendium of glittering aphorisms, Bacon's essays were designed for the ready use of busy individuals.[7] They were to be a lifelong preoccupation for Bacon, reissued in revised and expanded editions in 1612, and again in 1625, a year before his death. He also supervised their Latin translation; in addition, they were translated into French, Italian, and, via Latin, German, becoming one of the first English-language pieces of writing to achieve success in continental vernaculars – perhaps the English language's first true international bestseller.

In the same decades in which Bacon polished and republished his essays, he also set forth the Great Instauration, his ambitious plan to advance the study of nature – and perhaps much else as well – by reimagining its objects of investigation, methods, and aims. It was this project that would forge his reputation in the centuries to come: For later generations, Bacon's vast and varied intellectual output was of interest in large part because of his work as a philosopher of science. In time, even his stylish essays came to be read in light of his scientific writings. Although Bacon's essays were not designated as part of the Great Instauration, similarities of style and ambition, the unavoidable evidences of the same mind at work, made the attempt to find links between the two difficult to resist. Some scholars, noting this affinity, suggested that the essays were an attempt to treat moral and political subjects inductively, or at least to gather the preparatory materials that would make induction possible, along the lines of his natural histories.[8] They were, they argued, an effort toward a science of society, in parallel with the science of nature described in the Great Instauration.

Attractive as this view is in some ways, Bacon's own understanding of the divisions of knowledge, and the methods appropriate to each pursuit, does not ultimately support it.[9] If there are points of contact between the essays and Baconian natural philosophy, it is less because the essays draw on the methods of natural philosophy, and more because the form of natural philosophy Bacon imagined was heavily laden with moral, political, and economic content. It was an approach to knowledge that arose from, and revealed its links to, the social world of Elizabethan England. It is in this respect that the area of overlap between the essays and experimental science stands to be most illuminating: in grounding both in a social and economic context, with its own distinctive values and imperatives.[10]

Early-modern England came comparatively late to the novel mathematical and scientific culture of the European continent. When it finally did so, it was as a result of economic changes that made the adoption of new techniques of calculation and invention increasingly useful. From around the middle of the sixteenth century, merchants began to educate their children in the arithmetic required for techniques of accounting. The needs of industries such as shipping generated interest in the science of navigation, one context for the research of both mathematicians such as Thomas Harriot and experimenters such as William Gilbert, the philosopher of the magnet. Knowledge of surveying, which drove mathematical research, became increasingly important with the emergence of a land market; from the early seventeenth century, the skill began to be taught at the Inns of Court, England's law schools.[11] Likewise, mining, medicine, the cloth industry, and warfare all saw important technical advances, spurring developments in the natural sciences, engineering, and mathematics. By the early modern period, technical knowledge was woven into the social and economic fabric of English life. Without the "ingenious and useful Art" of mathematics, the conduct book writer and essayist Henry Peacham opined in the early seventeenth century, "we can hardly eat our bread, lie dry in our beds, buy, sell, or use any commerce whatsoever."[12]

It is in this context that Bacon's Great Instauration must be understood. Observing his own society, Bacon described the advancement of learning as a social process with material benefits. It would require new forms of intellectual labor and new modes of collaboration, but it would amply justify the resources it demanded. Philosophy would begin to produce "fruit and works," profitable results, not merely "prattle."[13] At the beginning of an age of agricultural improvement – a word that originally meant to make land more profitable – this botanical metaphor was highly suggestive.

Although Bacon did not understand his essays as part of his Great Instauration, they share the practical outlook that characterized his natural philosophy. Indeed, they do much to explain its moral and political presuppositions. The essays speak in the language of advancement, advantage, and profit. They "come home," Bacon wrote in the dedication to the final edition published in his lifetime, "to Mens Businesse, and Bosomes."[14] Their typical tone is brusquely practical: "Houses are built to live in, and not to look on; therefore let use be preferred before uniformity," Bacon begins his essay "Of Building." Individuals should "look into their own estate," while governments should promote "the opening and well-balancing of trade; the cherishing of manufactures; the banishing of idleness" and "the improvement and husbanding of the soil."[15] Style, broadly speaking, complemented matter. In his writings on natural philosophy, Bacon recommended a utilitarian prose, insisting not only on clarity but also on an economy of language that took its bearings from the needs of a commercial society: Writers should avoid ornament, approaching content like a merchant who wishes to "take up as little space as possible in the warehouse."[16] Bacon's essays are too witty and too literary to embody the ideal of a pared-down, pragmatic language in any modern sense. Nevertheless, their short, sharp sentences marked a decided turn away from the elegant periods of Ciceronian prose.[17] In combination with their pragmatic ethos, their vigorous style would do much to recommend them to later experimentalists.

The Essay in the Hartlib Circle

In a dedication to his 1615 *Characters Upon Essaies* addressed to Bacon, the poet and wit Nicholas Breton commented unfavorably on his fellow essayists: "when I lookt into the forme, or nature of their writing, I haue beene of the conceit, that they were but Imitators of your breaking the ice to their inuentions."[18] Even in 1615, this was not entirely fair. Yet it was certainly the case that Bacon's example left a heavy imprint on the essay form in England. In the first half-century or so following the publication of his *Essays*, the genre retained many of the associations it had held in his work. It continued to draw on habits of commonplacing, focusing on the typical subjects of the commonplace book: fame and fortune, riches and poverty, youth and age.[19] By and large, it also shared the moral and political orientation of Bacon's volume. Although some, such as the Pilgrim minister John Robinson, experimented with contemplative religious essays, on the whole the form continued to gather advice for the active life, often with political and commercial overtones.[20] One of Bacon's most ardent followers, Daniel Tuvill, made the collection of profitable advice his chief pursuit, writing both essays and a handbook on the art of "negotiation," or business.[21]

The practical focus of the essay inevitably shaped its perspective on the character of learning. William Cornwallis, whose essays were in general modeled more closely on the writing of Montaigne than Bacon, nevertheless shared his countryman's interest in the practical value of natural knowledge. In "Of the Observation and use of things," Cornwallis describes an encounter with a husbandman:

> I haue sold him an houre of my time, and haue ware for it, good sound principles, In truth beccoming a better fortune: This time hath not bene lost, for his experience, his learning of Tradition, and his naturall witte hath enformed mee of many things, I haue picked out of him good Philosophy, and Astronomy, and other obseruations of Time, and of the world: all which though hee imployes about durt, and allotteth to that ende, hinder not me from making a more worthy vse of them.[22]

The passage has the unmistakable note of the new attitudes toward applied mathematics and mechanics emerging at the time; it also hints at their social basis. In Cornwallis's metaphor, time is money and knowledge is a marketable commodity. His interest in "the use of things," his attention to mathematical calculations, including astronomy, and his keen sense that knowledge ought to be derived from practice – including agricultural work – are all characteristic of the environment that also produced Bacon.

As more and more writers turned their hands to the essay, new English approaches to natural philosophy were also emerging. Although linguistic coinages are an imperfect guide to intellectual history, it is nevertheless suggestive that the phrase "experimental philosophy" first came into use at this moment. It appears to have originated in the 1630s in the circle of the German émigré polymath Samuel Hartlib: Its earliest appearance in print was in the introduction to a new edition of Bacon's *Advancement of Learning* published in 1640 by an associate of his.[23] Samuel Hartlib's wide circle of correspondents and interlocutors has long been understood as one of the crucibles of experimentalism in England.[24] It included such figures as the chemist Robert Boyle, the mathematician John Pell, the doctor and economist William Petty, and the young John Locke; John Milton, for a time, moved on its fringes. A set of overlapping networks rather than a unified movement, Hartlib and his acquaintances embraced an astonishing range of interests, including education, diplomacy, religious reform, mathematics, industry, and agriculture. Their correspondence reveals both plans for a universal Protestant empire and an indefatigable interest in the production of pear cider.[25] This breadth of fascination has, understandably, led some recent scholars to question the coherence of the association.[26] But in fact, their range of interests was inseparable from their intellectual ambitions: The members of the Hartlib Circle were proponents of an applied science, who believed that the investigation of nature had the potential to transform virtually every field of human activity.[27] The goal of experimental philosophy, in Hartlib's words, was "the reformation of the whole world."[28] But the world was not going to be reformed through grand theories of the cosmos, no matter how elegant; real change would come, rather, as a result of new techniques of crop rotation or innovative methods of grafting fruit trees – it was to be, quite literally, a revolution from the ground up.

In what is only an apparent paradox, the Hartlibians' belief in an applied, practical knowledge made them particularly attentive to modes of writing. Because they conceived of experimental philosophy as necessarily collaborative, pursued by many individuals working in different fields and locations, they understood the collection and dissemination of writing as an indispensable element of science.[29] They both wrote in and theorized a range of forms – including, by the 1650s, the essay. Hartlib, for example, assembled the letters of his friend Cressy Dimmock into a work he entitled *An essay for advancement of husbandry-learning* (1651), and, later, "an essay to shew how all lands may be improved in a new way to become the ground of the increase of trading and revenue to this common-wealth" (1653).[30] In a letter to Hartlib, Cheney Culpepper described his written account of a new invention for plowing as "an extemporary essay to which vpon a recollection I cowlde adde yet more," a use that reveals the convergence of the essay and experimentation at this moment.[31] Another, anonymous correspondent mentions "the Essay Sir which I propounded to you about Germination, or rather about a more perfect Inquiry vpon the whole subject of vegetation."[32] As these examples suggest, one of the things that made the essay attractive to members of the Hartlib Circle was its loose, open-ended, and collaborative form, which had obvious advantages for the aggregative, piecemeal mode of the discovery they advocated. But it was not just the essay's formal properties that piqued the interest of the experimentalists. Rather, the ethical resonances attached to the form from Montaigne and Bacon onward were crucial recommendations for men who saw experimental knowledge as a means of social improvement.

It was for this reason that the Hartlib Circle's interest in the essay also extended to more conventionally humanist examples of the form. In 1646, the then nineteen-year-old John Hall (Boyle's exact contemporary) published *Horae vacivae, or, Essays.*[33] Although Hall's essays did not discuss experimental philosophy, or indeed nature, his talent for the genre and moral outlook brought him to the attention of Hartlib, and he too became associated with the group. Other affiliates used the essay to promote the ideals of experimental philosophy, rather than engaging in it directly. Cheney Culpeper's brother Thomas, a theorist of economics, published his *Morall discourses and essayes* in 1655. Attuned to the commitments that animated both experimentalism and the essay, his essays alluded to the importance of mathematics, technical discoveries, and the progress of knowledge. "The learned and able Professors of Arts and Sciences," he pronounced, "should endeavour to render them more clear and Mathematical."[34] Elsewhere he asked, "Why should we acquiesce in Authority, which, though most necessary in Law and Gospel, is the bane of Arts, and a *ne plus ultra* to knowledge?"[35] For figures such as Culpeper, or the similarly situated William Sprigg, the essay remained a short, pointed literary exercise, applied to humanistic subjects.[36] It retained, that is, roughly the form Bacon had used – but within certain circles, that form had come to be understood as aligned with the social, intellectual, and moral ambitions of experimental science.

Boyle's Literary Experiments

It was from within the milieu of the Hartlib Circle that the essay emerged as a major literary vehicle of scientific experimentation. In the Restoration, Robert Boyle became one of the most innovative natural philosophers in Europe. Boyle's experiments, together with that of a handful of contemporaries, helped to give experimentation a new place within the study of nature. But Boyle was not just an experimenter: He was also a writer, and it was through his writings that his experiments, findings, and methodology became widely known. As scholarship of the last decades has pointed out, it is not possible fully to separate his scientific ambitions from his literary techniques.[37] Two of his forms of choice were the essay and the natural and experimental history, genres Bacon had pioneered, which Boyle drew on freely and often amalgamated.[38] The unwieldy full title of Boyle's *Experiments and considerations touching colours first occasionally written, among some other essays to a friend, and now suffer'd to come abroad as the beginning of an experimental history of colours* gives something of a sense of the genres he pulled together. It is an "experimental history," or rather the beginning of one, as well as one of several "essays to a friend" – a designation that blurs the essay and letter. With Boyle's works, essayistic practice and experimental science briefly met and merged; were it not for his example, it is unlikely that a companion to the essay would contain a chapter on the essay and experimental science.

Boyle set out his theory of the essay in a piece he entitled the *Proëmial Essay*, which was published in 1661 but composed in the 1650s. Written while Boyle was still a member of Hartlib's correspondence network, the *Proëmial Essay* is presented as a letter as well as an essay, addressed to one "Pyrophilus." In this meandering but suggestive piece, which has come to be seen as a crucial statement of literary methodology, Boyle describes his approach to literary composition and explains his choice of genre. The essay, he claims, is an apt form for his scientific writing precisely because of its unsystematic character. It is fragmentary and partial, not artificially comprehensive. In contrast to the "compleat Systems of Natural Philosophy" written by previous philosophers, the writer of essays was "not oblig'd to take upon him to teach others what himself [*sic*] does not understand."[39] The result was a method of writing whose flexible, disconnected manner and relatively modest length permitted the accumulation of concrete knowledge.[40] Elsewhere in his writing, when Boyle draws attention to the essayistic form of a composition, it is typically to emphasize its unsystematic character, as when he describes *A Free Enquiry into the Vulgarly Received Notion of Nature* (1686) as a "rhapsody of my own loose papers" and a "maimed and confused essay."[41]

In keeping with his approach to the genre, Boyle tended to use the term "essay" casually. He frequently referred to pieces of writing by turns as essays, treatises, or histories within the same work. Often, the essay, for Boyle, appears to be an approach to composition rather than a genre per se. In this respect, Boyle resembles Montaigne more closely than Bacon.[42] Likewise, his style bears little resemblance to the lapidary aphorisms of his English predecessor. "I have knowingly and purposely transgress'd the Laws of Oratory in one particular," Boyle explains, "namely, in making sometimes my Periods or Parentheses over-long" (17). In contrast to Bacon's sharp, pointed manner in the *Essays*, Boyle's prose was well known for its prolixity, an aspect of his writing that Jonathan Swift would parody in *Meditations Upon a Broomstick* (1701).

Yet Boyle did remain, in a crucial sense, allied to the English essayistic tradition, for his conception of the form was deeply inflected by a Baconian and Hartlibian ideal of applied knowledge. The idea that experimental knowledge is characterized by usefulness was threaded through his early writings. "[T]he barren Philosophy, wont to be taught in the Schools, hath hitherto been found of very little use in humane Life," he remarks in *The Usefulness of Natural Philosophy*, "yet if the true Principles of that fertil Science were thorowly known, consider'd and apply'd, 'tis scarce imaginable, how universal and advantagious a change they would make in the World."[43] In this piece, again written in the 1650s, the allusion to agriculture is not merely a metaphor but a symbol of some of the most urgent social aspirations of experimental philosophy. Even in Boyle's later work, composed after he had moved away from the milieu of the Hartlib Circle, he continued to draw on examples derived from the trades and agriculture.[44] English industry, Boyle suggested, was both transforming, and capable of being transformed by, technical knowledge. A commitment to this vision of experimental philosophy motivates Boyle's use of the essay form. He alludes to the connection between the two in a passage in the *Proëmial Essay*. Distinguishing two modes of inquiry, he remarks, "some Men care only to Know Nature, others desire to Command Her."[45] There is an echo, here, of Bacon's well-known aphorism from the *New Organon*: "Human knowledge and power come to the same thing, for ignorance of the cause puts the effect beyond reach. For nature is not conquered save by obeying it..."[46] But where Bacon's dictum seeks to unite the knowledge of causes with the production of effects – to create a philosophy simultaneously speculative and useful – in this early work, Boyle severs them, choosing to focus solely on the pragmatic and productive.

Philosophers who desire to command nature, Boyle suggests, will turn to the essay rather than the system, for they "may very delightfully &

successfully prosecute their ends, by collecting and making Variety of Experiments and Observations."[47] Essayistic form, experimental philosophy, and an emphasis on applied knowledge were all intimately linked in Boyle's early practice. The tendency of essays, including essays on moral and political topics, to adopt a pragmatic ethos – even to promise useful results – no doubt reinforced the idea of the essay as an appropriate genre for applied learning. In this way, the English essay's humanist commitment to the active life, the very thing that had made it remote from a long tradition of philosophical contemplation, proposed it as a suitable vehicle for a mode of learning dedicated to use. Characteristically, Boyle described the sections of *The Usefulness of Natural Philosophy* as essays.

The Restoration and the Royal Society

Boyle's essays were read with interest both within England and outside it: Like Bacon, he achieved the then-rare feat of becoming a widely translated English-language author.[48] In part as a result of his example, men associated with experimental science and its ambitions continued to write essays throughout the seventeenth century. Abraham Cowley, Joseph Glanville, William Petty, and John Locke, among others, all wrote works they called "essays." In these decades, the category of the essay became both fashionable and fluid, with a surprising range of works designated under that heading. Reference to the genre did not necessarily imply the use of a precise form but could instead invoke a set of intellectual or methodological commitments, as it had begun to do in the Hartlib Circle. In calling his philosophical treatise *An Essay Concerning Human Understanding*, for example, Locke was drawing attention to the influence of experimental science in general, and Boyle in particular, on his thought.[49]

On the whole, however, the paths of the essay and experimental science began to diverge in the last decades of the seventeenth century. In 1663, Boyle, together with Petty, Robert Moray, John Evelyn, William Brounker, and a handful of others, helped to found the Royal Society. In 1665, *The Philosophical Transactions of the Royal Society* was founded under the society's imprimatur. The first scientific journal in English, it pointed forward to an emerging periodical culture in which short prose pieces could be published in journals, rather than amassed in books or circulated via letters.[50] The rise of journals would provide a new context for the essay, propelling it to a position of greater cultural prominence than ever before. Journals would also transform scientific communications. In providing a standing venue for the collection of discoveries, observations, and ideas, the

Philosophical Transactions was a step toward the fulfillment of some of the long-standing aspirations of English experimental philosophers. Its editor, Henry Oldenburg was the former tutor of Boyle's nephew and a one-time member of the Hartlib Circle. Oldenburg, like Hartlib, was a German-born polyglot intellectual with a vast European correspondence, which he also drew on for a publishing project designed to promote new forms of knowledge. But the *Philosophical Transactions* also marked a genuine departure, leading scientific communication in a new and hitherto unanticipated direction.

The same could be said of the Royal Society as a whole. Although the Hartlib Circle's adaptation of a Baconian tradition provided an important antecedent for the Royal Society, many of its cherished ideals evaporated in the Restoration. Its associations with radical religious reform, the political bent of many of its members toward republican government, and its plan for a state-supported institution for applied science were no longer either possible or desirable after the collapse of the Protectorate and the return of the Stuarts. The Royal Society, as has been thoroughly documented, held itself aloof from questions of religious or political policy; its ranks included men with varying religious and political commitments.[51] This very diversity of opinion, however, pointed to the success of some of the underlying assumptions that animated the English experimental tradition. Across the religious and political spectrum, the idea that the growth of scientific knowledge should be a cumulative, collaborative, and ongoing process was more widely accepted than ever before. So too was the idea that such knowledge would lead almost inevitably to material gains.

Even at the end of the seventeenth century, there were many who did not share this view of learning. But the era had clearly seen the transformation of its fortunes. Take, for example, the views of the Stuart kings. James I, who ruled England in the first quarter of the seventeenth century, was an extremely learned monarch. But despite Bacon's attempts to cast him as the new Solomon of natural science, James regarded Baconian natural philosophy with amused incomprehension, preferring Latin disputations, theology, and humanistic learning. His grandson, Charles II, was a far less scholarly figure, but he nevertheless grasped intuitively, as his grandfather could not, that technical knowledge might have pressing implications for English society. A quasi-virtuoso, he delighted in new inventions, discussing the mechanics of shipbuilding with Petty and chemistry with Boyle. The implicit social perspective of the experimental natural philosophy was well on its way to acceptance – as our own world amply testifies. If few later scientists turned to the Baconian essay as a genre of scientific writing, perhaps it was, in part, because they did not need to.

Notes

1 John Florio added a subtitle to his translation of Montaigne's *Essays: Morall, Politike and Militarie Discourses*, inspired by Girolamo Naselli's partial Italian translation, *Discorsi Morali, Politici, et Militari*. See William M. Hamlin, *Montaigne's English Journey: Reading the Essays in Shakespeare's Day* (Oxford: Oxford University Press), 2013, 8.

2 Steven Shapin and Simon Schaffer, *Leviathan and the Air-Pump: Hobbes, Boyle, and the Experimental Life* (Princeton, NJ: Princeton University Press, 1985).

3 Scott Black, *Of Essays and Reading in Early Modern Britain* (Basingstoke: Palgrave Macmillan, 2006).

4 Kathryn Murphy, "Of Sticks and Stones: The Essay, Experiment, and Experience," in *On Essays: Montaigne to the Present*, ed. Thomas Karshan and Kathryn Murphy (Oxford: Oxford University Press, 2020), 78–96.

5 Max Horkheimer and Theodor W. Adorno, *Dialectic of Enlightenment*, trans. Edmund Jephcott (Stanford, CA: Stanford University Press, 2002). See, however, Ellen Meiksins Wood, "Capitalism or Enlightenment?" *History of Political Thought* 21.3 (2000): 405–426.

6 A. M. Boase, "The Early History of the *Essai* Title in England and France," in *Studies in French Literature Presented to H. W. Lawton*, ed. J. C. Ireson, I. D. Mcfarlane, and Garnet Rees (Manchester: Manchester University Press, 1968), 67–74.

7 Black, *Of Essays and Reading*, 21; Paul Salzman, "Essays," in *The Oxford Handbook of English Prose, 1500–1640*, ed. Andrew Hadfield (Oxford: Oxford University Press, 2013), 468–483.

8 Ronald Crane, "The Relation of Bacon's Essays to the Program of the Advancement of Learning," in *Essential Articles for the Study of Francis Bacon*, ed. Brian Vickers (Hamden, CT: Archon Books, 1968), 272–292; Stanley Fish, *Self-Consuming Artifacts: The Experience of Seventeenth-Century Literature* (Berkeley and Los Angeles: University of California Press, 1972); Matthew Sharpe, "Home to Men's Business and Bosoms: Philosophy and Rhetoric in Francis Bacon's *Essayes*," *British Journal for the History of Philosophy* 27.3 (2019): 492–512.

9 Lisa Jardine, *Francis Bacon: Discovery and the Art of Discourse* (Cambridge: Cambridge University Press, 1974), 227–248; Markuu Peltonen, "Politics and Science: Francis Bacon and the True Greatness of States," *The Historical Journal* 35.2 (1992): 279–305.

10 There is, of course, a long tradition of seeking the social correlates of scientific discovery. See Christopher Hill, *Intellectual Origins of the English Revolution* (Oxford: Clarendon Press, 1965). Prominent critiques or revisions of Hill include Mordechai Feingold, "Gresham College and London Practitioners: The Nature of the English Mathematical Community," in *Sir Thomas Gresham and Gresham College: Studies in the Intellectual History of London in the Sixteenth and Seventeenth Centuries*, ed. Francis Ames-Lewis (Aldershot: Ashgate, 1999), 174–188; Michael Hunter, *Robert Boyle: Scrupulosity and Science* (Woodbridge: Boydell, 2000); Deborah Harkness, *The Jewel House: Elizabethan London and the Scientific Revolution* (New Haven, CT: Yale University Press, 2007).

11 Katherine Hill, "Mathematics as a Tool for Social Change: Educational Reform in Seventeenth-Century England," *The Seventeenth Century* 12.1 (1997): 23–36.

12 Henry Peacham, *The Compleat Gentleman* (London, 1622), 72.

13 Francis Bacon, *The Oxford Francis Bacon*, vol. 11, ed. Graham Rees and Maria Wakely (Oxford: Oxford University Press, 2004), 12–13.

14 *Works*, vol. 15, 5.

15 Ibid., 47.

16 Bacon, *The Oxford Francis Bacon*, vol. 11, ed. Graham Rees and Maria Wakely (Oxford: Oxford University Press, 2004), 456–457.

17 John Hoskins, *Directions for Speech and Style*, ed. Hoyt H. Hudson (Princeton, NJ: Princeton University Press, 1935).

18 Nicholas Breton, *Characters Upon Essaies* (London: John Gwillim, 1615).

19 By the middle years of the century, if not before, essay writing was being taught in the classroom. Ted Pebworth, "Not Being, but Passing: Defining the Early English Essay," *Studies in the Literary Imagination*, 10.2 (1977): 17–27.

20 John Robinson, *Nevv essayes or obseruations diuine and morall* (London: Miles Flesher, 1628).

21 D. T. [Daniel Tuvill], *The doue and the serpent* (London: Laurence L'Isle, 1614); John Leon Lievsay, "Tuvill's Advancement of Bacon's Learning," *Huntington Library Quarterly* 9.1 (1945): 11–31.

22 William Cornwallis, *Essays* (London: Edmund Mattes, 1600), J2r.

23 Mordechai Feingold, "Gresham College," 4.

24 Charles Webster, *Samuel Hartlib and the Advancement of Learning* (Cambridge: Cambridge University Press, 1970).

25 On the production of pear cider (perry), see Hartlib Papers, 42/1/34A-35B, 66/22A-B. For observations on the improvement of trade and commerce, British Library Add MS 72437.

26 Vera Keller, "Deprogramming Baconianism: The Meaning of Desiderata in the Eighteenth Century," *Notes and Records: The Royal Society Journal of the History of Science* 72.2 (2018): 119–137.

27 Eric Ash, "Reclaiming a New World: Fen Drainage, Improvement, and Projectors in Seventeenth-Century England," *Early Science and Medicine* 21.5 (2016): 445–469; Antonio Clericuzio, "Plant and Soil Chemistry in Seventeenth-Century England: Worsley, Boyle and Coxe," *Early Science and Medicine* 23.5–6 (2018): 550–583.

28 Hartlib to Boyle, November 15, 1659, qtd. in Walter E. Houghton, "The History of Trades: Its Relation to Seventeenth-Century Thought: As Seen in Bacon, Petty, Evelyn, and Boyle," Journal of the History of Ideas (1941): 33–60, 39. The immediate context is Petty and Hartlib's scheme for a history of trades.

29 Mark Greengrass, Michael Leslie, and Timothy Raylor, eds., *Samuel Hartlib and Universal Reformation: Studies in Intellectual Communication* (Cambridge: Cambridge University Press, 1994); Joanna Picciotto, *Labors of Innocence in Early Modern England* (Cambridge, MA: Harvard University Press, 2010), 116–128.

30 Samuel Hartlib, *An essay for Advancement of Husbandry-Learning* (London: Henry Hills, 1651) and *A Discoverie for Division or Setting Out of Land* (London: Richard Wodenothe, 1653).

31 Hartlib Papers 13/280B; Stephen Clucas, "The Correspondence of a XVII-century 'Chymicall Gentleman': Sir Cheney Culpeper and the Chemical Interests of the Hartlib Circle," *Ambix* 40.3 (1993): 147–170.

32 Hartlib Papers, 8/22/1A, undated.
33 John Hall, *Horae vacivae, or, Essays* (London: J. Rothwell, 1646).
34 Thomas Culpeper, *Morall discourses and essayes* (London: Charles, Adams, 1655), 62.
35 Ibid., 63.
36 William Sprigg, *Philosophical Essays with brief adviso's* (London: Robert Blagrave, 1657).
37 Steven Shapin, "Pump and Circumstance: Robert Boyle's Literary Technology," *Social Studies of Science* 14.4 (1984): 481–520, Peter Dear, "Narratives, Anecdotes, and Experiments: Turning Experience into Science in the Seventeenth Century," in *The Literary Structure of Scientific Argument*, ed. Peter Dear (Philadelphia: University of Pennsylvania Press, 1991), 135–163.
38 Cesare Pastorino, "Beyond Recipes: The Baconian Natural and Experimental Histories as an Epistemic Genre," *Centaurus* 62.3 (2020): 447–464.
39 Robert Boyle, *Works*, vol. 2, ed. Edward B. Davis and Michael Hunter (London: Pickering & Chatto, 1999), 15.
40 Rose-Mary Sargent, *The Diffident Naturalist: Robert Boyle and the Philosophy of Experiment* (Chicago: University of Chicago Press, 1995), 183–185.
41 Robert Boyle, *A Free Enquiry into the Vulgarly Received Notion of Nature*, ed. Edward B. Davis and Michael Hunter (Cambridge: Cambridge University Press, 1996), 7.
42 Terence Cave, *How to Read Montaigne* (London: Granta, 2007), 20.
43 Boyle, *Works*, vol. 3, 296.
44 See, for example, Boyle's comments on fruit in "A Short Excursion about Some Changes Made of Tastes by Maturation," *Works*, vol. 8, 374.
45 Ibid., vol. 2, 23.
46 Ibid., vol. 11, 66.
47 Ibid., vol. 2, 23.
48 Peter Burke, "Lost (and Found) in Translation: A Cultural History of Translators and Translating in Early Modern Europe," *European Review* 15.1 (2007): 83–94.
49 Peter Walmsley makes a case for the influence of the essay form, particularly as practiced by Boyle, on Locke's *Essay* in *Locke's* Essay *and the Rhetoric of Science* (Lewisburg, PA: Bucknell University Press, 2003), 73–95.
50 James Paradis, "Montaigne, Boyle, and the Essay of Experience," in *One Culture: Essays in Science and Literature*, ed. George Levine (Madison: University of Wisconsin Press, 1987), 60.
51 Malcolm Oster, "Virtue, Providence, and Political Neutralism: Boyle and Interregnum Politics," in *Robert Boyle Reconsidered*, ed. Michael Hunter (Cambridge: Cambridge University Press, 1994), 19–36.

7

ANAHID NERSESSIAN

Essay, Enlightenment, Revolution

The essay begins the eighteenth century as a bourgeois form and ends it as a radical one. This is an oversimplification, but it gets at some deep truths about style, purpose, audience, and affinity. The great prose writers of the early eighteenth century were (mostly) men who, eager to earn a place in modern commercial society, cultivated the essay as a form that might demonstrate their lack of hostility to it; their readers were likewise keen to have their own upward mobility reflected back at them. However, by the time Napoleon Bonaparte sunk the last nail into the coffin of the French Revolution, the essay – particularly in Britain and France – had become associated not with deference to the status quo but with the unruly, adversarial postures of the urban working class and its allies. The latter-day fortunes of this shift are especially vivid in the writing of Karl Marx, who represents not the end but rather the apex of the Enlightenment essay and its formal as well as political development.[1]

What was the Enlightenment? In the most benign terms, it was a period of political and cultural liberalization in Western Europe lasting roughly from the late seventeenth to the end of the eighteenth century. As the authority and prestige of the natural sciences grew, that of religious institutions waned. Political systems founded on the old feudal arrangement began to atrophy, and a new set of values emerged to match this increasingly secular world order. Such values, at least for historians who view them through a rose-colored lens, emphasized personal autonomy over group identity, free thinking over dogma and fanaticism, and a belief that the state should not interfere in the private lives of its subjects.

What to make of the fact that all this progress coincided with a massive expansion of the Atlantic slave trade and the kidnapping, torture, abuse, and murder of millions of Africans? Or with the dozens of inter-imperial wars that raged as Britain, France, Spain, Russia, and the Ottoman Empire carved up the globe? In pre-Revolutionary France, where the aristocracy flaunted extreme wealth in the face of grinding poverty, the life expectancy for the average person was twenty-eight and a half years. In England, the enclosure movement privatized public land and forced small farms out of business, driving the rural population to work in brand-new textile factories, or else into the mines that fed those factories with coal. In short, if the Enlightenment was so good, why was it so bad?

Theodor Adorno and Max Horkheimer were not the first to critique the Enlightenment, but their account of its contradictions remains the most persuasive. Rather than view its social and ecological harms as incidental to the strides made in religious toleration or civil rights, Adorno and Horkheimer insist that all these phenomena are embedded in the underlying objective of Enlightenment itself: to liberate society through the domination of nature. Once advances in science and technology allowed humans to understand and thus to begin to modify their environment, they lost not only a fear of God but also all respect for his creation. Anything and anyone could be put to use for any purpose: "Human beings become mere material, as the whole of nature has become material for society."[2]

To be clear, it is not that the horrors of slavery simply coexisted with what Immanuel Kant called "man's emergence from his self-incurred immaturity" but that a new emphasis on *development* – both personal and commercial – at all costs ramified across European culture in seemingly incongruous, ultimately compatible ways.[3] The Enlightenment meant both the emergence of modern feminism and the systematic designation of Black women as less than human, the founding of the first animal welfare society and the use of child labor. Groundbreaking scientific experiments were conducted on the bodies of prisoners, and literacy rates skyrocketed as books were printed on rags stripped from soldiers' corpses. The enormous surplus of wealth required to fund Europe's love affair with the arts and sciences, and to sponsor the careers of its most prominent political reformers – Voltaire, Jean-Jacques Rousseau, Jeremy Bentham, William Godwin, Mary Wollstonecraft – was generated by an economy dependent on the labor of the colonized, the enslaved, and the newly proletarianized.

Adorno and Horkheimer's shorthand for the domination of nature is *reason*, the cognitive faculty that allows us to make judgments in a way that is impartial and objective. It is, Kant argued, through reason that we come to decide that Newton's laws of gravity are true, or if works of art are beautiful and laws just. It is also reason that licenses the destruction of a forest to build a factory. Thus in her 2008 poem, *Zong!*, M. NourbeSe Philip links the juridical concept of *ratio decidendi* to the murder of more than 130 Africans in 1781, when they were thrown overboard from a slave ship so that their owners could collect an insurance payment. "[T]he trap|of rea|son" breaks down human beings until they dissolve in "the sculm of proflits," of no greater value than that assigned by a ledger book or auction block.[4]

In the eighteenth century, the status of reason became the primary point of conflict between those who were for Enlightenment and those who were against it. Reason in this sense is not merely an intellectual capacity but a social attitude and a political affiliation. It could signify good sense, open-mindedness, self-composure, and a generally liberal disposition. It could also signify ruthlessness and calculation, a tendency to dismiss what some might call ethics as mere sentiment, and to value progress – and, as Philip says, profit – above all else. As a general rule, we find critics of the Enlightenment on both ends of the political spectrum agitating against the cool-headed detachment of the moderately progressive mainstream, while the mainstream paints the fringe as hysterical, jejune, or mad.

The essay is the ground on which these skirmishes are fought and which is in turn defined by them. To read the eighteenth-century essay is to see the historical advent of politics *as tone*, such that holding a certain opinion about the world requires expressing that opinion in a distinct emotional register. This has significant consequences for the stylistic development of the genre, particularly when the subject matter at hand is revolution. As it becomes the exemplary prose form for both the expression and the contestation of revolutionary principles, the essay breaks its bond with polite discourse and absorbs the rhetorical habits of less conciliatory kinds of writing, notably satire, polemic, and popular journalism.

The rise of the English periodical essay began in 1711, when Richard Steele and Joseph Addison founded their popular daily *The Spectator* and invented an author – the eponymous "Mr. Spectator" – who might embody its social as well as its writerly ideals. Imperturbably amused by the world, Mr. Spectator was an amiable flâneur who, in Michael Warner's words, exuded "a kind of generality" that allowed him to stand in for polite society per se.[5] His essays in *The Spectator* were aimed at readers who thought that being a smart, sophisticated person meant being able to transcend differences of opinion and background in order to exchange ideas without losing one's cool or taking things personally. Mr. Spectator was their avatar, never buffeted by controversy or unsettled by passion. Even as he took on subjects ranging from aesthetic philosophy to the Atlantic slave trade, he operated decisively above the fray, "ostentatiously avoid[ing] political polemic."[6]

Of course, Mr. Spectator can only exude generality because he is a certain kind of individual: male, well-educated, and white. "I have observed," he remarks in the paper's first issue, "that a Reader seldom peruses a Book with Pleasure 'till he knows whether the Writer of it be a black [i.e., dark-skinned] or a fair Man, of a mild or cholerick Disposition, Married or a

Batchelor, with other Particulars of the like nature, that conduce very much to the right Understanding of an Author." He then describes himself as the heir of "a small Hereditary estate" that has been in the family since the time of William the Conqueror. He spends his days, he says, bopping among London's coffee-houses, talking current events, literature, painting, and a little light philosophy with like-minded company. Wherever he goes, he "observe[s] an exact Neutrality between the Whigs and Tories," having "acted in all the parts of [his] Life as a Looker-on" and being determined to remain so.[7]

Mr. Spectator never does tell us about his own complexion, and he doesn't have to. The ease with which he moves through life is as much a racial privilege as his hereditary estate, which instantly identifies him with the ancestral whiteness of the English gentry. From its first issue, then, *The Spectator* sets up a complex relationship between identity and objectivity. Being white, male, and upper middle class is seen, paradoxically, as a position without a position, the only vantage point from which one might achieve a truly disinterested perspective on the world and its goings-on. This has decisive implications for the journal's style, for its manner, like Mr. Spectator's, is tame and its opinions uncontroversial: A healthy economy is good, gossip and slander are bad, and "a noble Sentiment that is depressed with homely language" is more pleasing than "a vulgar one that is blown up with all the Sound and Energy of Expression."[8]

These three topics – political economy, sociality, and style – are key to the development of the essay during this period. After all, this was a culture whose emphasis on impartiality made it far more welcoming to some than others. Jürgen Habermas famously argues that *only* people who owned private property were thought to have the requisite social skills to take part; others could never separate themselves from the material conditions of their existence and so were saturated by their own economic vulnerabilities, which in turn deprived them of all independence of thought. As Wollstonecraft puts it in her 1792 *Vindication of the Rights of Woman*, economic subordination forces individuals to "fawn like the spaniel" only to indulge in the "excesses" of "slaves and mobs" at the first opportunity.[9] This view of the disenfranchised as having lapsed into an animal state is the flipside of what Habermas describes as the basis of the "literary public sphere" in this era, namely the conflation of "the role of property owners [with] the role of human beings pure and simple."[10]

As Wollstonecraft and Habermas suggest, the linking of economic independence to civility upheld "rational-critical debate" not merely as an ideal but as a form of speciation: In an eighteenth-century world of letters, to be able to engage deliberatively with others was nothing less than a proof of one's humanity.[11] By contrast, taking the conversation too much to heart was to show oneself *less than* – to be, in Wollstonecraft's words, like a dog, a slave, or the faceless member of an angry crowd. The racist character of this train of equivalences is by no means accidental. In eighteenth-century England, opposition to the slave trade was led by religious evangelicals, many of whom were also involved in radical political organizing. Such people were consistently accused of having too much enthusiasm, a moral fervor so intense, so unreasonable, it could easily lead to violence.

How did this premium on easy-going, mild-mannered exchange affect a bourgeois writer's prose? For Samuel Johnson, the essay was "a loose sally of the mind" in which rigorous argumentation would be a faux pas.[12] Any "*good Writer*[,] ... *Gentleman*, or *Man of* WORTH," sniffs the Earl of Shaftesbury, knows that gravity has no place in the essay; it is rather "*Raillery* and *Humour*," along with "Excursions of every kind [that] are found agreeable and requisite." "We have reason perhaps," he continues,

> to be fond of the *Diverting* Manner in Writing, and Discourse; especially if the Subject be of a *solemn* kind. There is more need, perhaps, in this case, to interrupt the long-spun Thred of Reasoning, and bring into the Mind, by many different Glances and broken Views, what cannot so easily be introduc'd by *one* steddy Bent, or continu'd Stretch of Sight.[13]

Here, as throughout his essays, Shaftesbury breaks up the long-spun thread of his own prose with multiple subordinate clauses, a technique that prevents any sentence from gathering undignified steam. Persistently digressive or, to use his word, excursive, Shaftesbury's syntax exchanges the bullishness of a "Bent" – a direction, tendency, or bias – for a noncommittal style uniquely unsuitable for advancing anything like a claim. On one hand, this is the writerly equivalent of Mr. Spectator's studied anonymity, the exemplary rhetorical posture of a professional cipher. On the other, Shaftesbury's "WORTH," which is to say his class, is evident in every genteel pivot away from a declarative statement, in thinking so free it escapes even the faintest compulsion to deliver a point.

Shaftesbury's preferred mode is "the way of the chat," a breezy conversational style that quietly coerces the reader to share in the author's sense of low stakes.[14] A similar obliquity governs the writing of Oliver Goldsmith, David Hume, William Cowper, and Eliza Haywood, the "Addison in petticoats" who founded her mid-century monthly, *The Female Spectator*, to see if women might lay claim to such a roundabout manner for themselves.[15] *The Female Spectator* favors tales of romantic love and illicit sex, but it also builds in opportunities for Haywood to raise political questions before shutting them down as "too ticklish for us to meddle with," thus proving to readers that female essayists could be every bit as evasive as their male counterparts.[16]

This avoidance of politics is typical unless it can be smuggled in through satire. There is no better example than Jonathan Swift's "A Modest Proposal," anonymously published in 1729. There Swift advises the Irish to sell their children as food, a measure that has the double benefit of alleviating hunger in the impoverished colony and providing a bit of population control. The genius of "A Modest Proposal" lies in how scrupulously it copies the etiquette of the Enlightenment essay only to turn it to unexpected ends. Like Mr. Spectator, this essay's author tends to outsource his opinions ("I am assured by our merchants," he'll say, or else "by a very knowing American"), and like Shaftesbury he circumnavigates his subject until, suddenly, he doesn't, breaking from his periphrastic script to inform the reader that "a young healthy child well nursed, is, at a year old, a most delicious nourishing and wholesome food," especially nice in "a *fricasee*, or a *ragout*."[17]

With Swift, the eighteenth-century English essay splits into two distinct subgenres. The first retains an Addisonian commitment to impartiality and detachment and steers clear of political controversy; it concerns itself with light topics and thus paves the way for Romantic essayists such as Charles Lamb, who waxes rhapsodic on roast pig, as well as for the misty introspections of Thomas De Quincey. The second taps satire's vein of righteous indignation to introduce new notes of hostility into the essay form, in particular hostility toward the socioeconomic conditions of eighteenth-century Europe and Britain and their colonies. Crucially, this variant does not abandon objectivity even as it explicitly appeals to the reader's emotions. Rather, like Swift – who litters his proposal with statistics, and ends by assuring his audience that he has nothing to gain from the scheme of selling babies to eat since he has "no children, by which [he] can propose to get a single penny" – they adopt what might be called a passionate indifference to both good manners and rhetorical circumlocution.[18]

In France, literature of all kinds was considerably more politicized than across the Channel. Owing to the repressive political regime under which it unfurled, the ethos of the French Enlightenment had been, from the start, overtly oppositional. From the cunning satire of Montesquieu's *Lettres persannes*, which packages a series of essays on religious toleration and the rights of women as an orientalist fantasy, to the ferocious clarity of Rousseau's treatises on citizenship, the collective message of this writing was unequivocal: "Man is born free, and everywhere he is in chains."[19] Then, of course, there's the Marquis de Sade, who snuck a Swiftian manifesto against private property into his pornographic novel *Philosophie dans la boudoir*.

As for periodical culture, it never achieved the same level of cultural significance in France as it did in England, and that worked against the emergence of the wry, antipolemical tone that defined the classic Enlightenment essay. If the conventional essay had a home in France, it was in the *concours académique*, annual writing competitions hosted by scholarly societies across the country. The *concours* were surprisingly egalitarian: Submissions were anonymous, and anyone could enter regardless of race, gender, class status, or profession. The contests thus went a long way toward merging the high Enlightenment and a more demotic literary culture, and some of the most high-profile journalists of the revolutionary era – including Jean-Paul Marat – cut their teeth on the contest circuit.

During the Revolution, things changed – unsurprisingly. To keep up with the demand for political commentary, the newspaper industry exploded, as did the market for *cahiers de doléances* (lists of grievances) and other cheap, easily produced and widely circulated publications. By the 1790s the *concours* was just one venue among many through which the public could express itself, its once high status a casualty of the "near-universal politicization of French culture" during the period.[20]

In the late eighteenth century, the literary underground finally seized the Enlightenment from high culture. The *libelle*, or slanderous political pamphlet, became the new *essai*, mixing principled critiques of the state into what Robert Darnton memorably terms "anti-social smut."[21] *Libelles* adopted a prose that was punchy, contemptuous, and supercharged with a sense of moral outrage that, while usually devoid of any coherent ideology, nonetheless "communicated a revolutionary point of view."[22] With their taste for long, asyndetonic sentences that pile up scandal after scandal, disgrace after disgrace, they explode the Enlightenment fantasy of a well-ordered world where everyone is an equal player. Take, for example, an attack on Madame du Barry in *La Gazette noire*, which describes the King's mistress as "passing directly from the brothel to the throne, topping the most powerful and redoubtable minister, overthrowing the constitution of the monarchy, insulting the royal family ... by her insolent talk, and the entire nation, which is dying of hunger, by her vainglorious extravagance[.]"[23] Guided by the centrifugal force of its own disgust, the sentence moves outward from intimate to public space and from individual victims to the nation itself, whose starvation du Barry's conspicuous consumption hideously mocks.

This is a "gutter Rousseauism" that takes the antiestablishment attitudes of the mainstream Enlightenment and translates them into the furious vernacular of popular journalism.[24] No one was better at this kind of rephrasing than Marat. Even the title of his paper, *L'Ami de people*, assured its audience that Marat was right there in the struggle, a "friend of the people" who could boil political philosophy down to its practical essence. "Credulous Parisians!" he scolds a population who, having "broken its chains," is now too willing to hand over its power to a government bureaucracy run by lawyers. "Le souverain," he reminds them, "c'est vous ... le législateur c'est aussi vous; la loi, c'est encore vous."[25] This is prose written to be spoken, not – as we saw with Shaftesbury – designed as if to mimic the elaborate interiors of a well-appointed town home.

Marat was a consummate Enlightenment figure. He was well educated, urbane, and for a time he moved comfortably in highborn circles and among aristocratic patrons. His radicalization shows the ease with which the social and discursive norms of eighteenth-century intellectual culture could be turned to incendiary purpose. In his writing, dispassion sharpens into an unsentimental, unforgiving discernment. In a short piece on the execution of Louis XIV, he states flatly that "there's no going back, and this is the position in which we find ourselves today, that we'll have to win or die."[26] Marx will use an uncannily similar formulation when he observes that proletarian revolutions, like the one Marat was trying to foment, seem to "recoil again and again from the indefinite prodigiousness of their own aims, until a situation has been created which makes all turning back impossible, and the conditions themselves cry out: 'Hic Rhodus, hic salta! Here is the rose, dance here!'"[27]

With the Revolution, the Enlightenment ceased to be theoretical, its high-minded ideals irrupting into the streets via newspapers, pamphlets, *libelles*, *cahiers de doléances*, and other forms of popular literature. In England, vernacular interpretations of Enlightenment doctrine also gained traction in response to the events in France, but these have been overshadowed by better-known documents such as Edmund Burke's *Reflections on the Revolution in France* and Wollstonecraft's *A Vindication of the Rights of Men*. Both find the eighteenth-century English essay evolving under the pressures of a suddenly volatile public sphere, in which ideals of polite speech and reasoned debate collide with an unprecedented political situation. They collide, too, with changing notions of gender and class, and with what Burke described as a "revolution in sentiments, manners, and moral opinions" to match the one happening in the domain of state governance.[28]

Facing down Burke's passionately negative response to the Revolution (not to mention his tortuous sentences) Wollstonecraft accuses Burke of what Claudia Johnson terms "the effeminacy of a politics based on practices of foppish sentimentality," and presents herself, by way of contrast, as a Mr. Spectator for the republican set.[29] She disagrees, of course, with Burke's opinions, but her *Vindication* chiefly concerns Burke's muddling together of his political investments and libidinal attachments. As an antidote to his flights of reactionary fancy she offers her own efficient, prosecutorial prose, which not only insists upon but is meant to demonstrate the primacy of rational thought over mere "human feelings."[30]

In the *Reflections*, Burke argues that the French crown, as personified by Marie-Antoinette, upheld "the pleasing illusions, which made power gentle and obedience liberal" by activating the erotic sensibilities of its subjects.[31] To find the queen beautiful was to support feudalism itself, and a democracy – which asks for fidelity to a principle, not a person – could never inspire such ardor. Such claims, Wollstonecraft argues, show "a mortal antipathy to reason."[32] They also show "an unmanly servility" that begs to be reformed by circumspection, as well as a more decorous approach to desire:

> But should experience prove that there is a beauty in virtue, a charm in order, which necessarily implies exertion, a depraved sensual taste may give way to a more manly one–and melting feelings to rational satisfactions. Both may be equally natural to man; the test is their moral difference, and that point reason alone can decide.[33]

The argument here is as much with Burke's style as with his sentiments. Where Burke generates paradoxes (gentle power, liberal obedience), Wollstonecraft presents tidy oppositions and then has one side knock out the other, as if in response to the sheer authoritative force of her prose sensuality might succumb to manliness and the pleasures of emotional self-indulgence to the rigors of sober thought. The movement of the text, in other words, is itself disciplinary or corrective, modeling for readers a smooth, linear progress from error to insight.

Wollstonecraft's emphasis on reason and her distaste for emotional as well as rhetorical excess is typical for a public figure of her era. As Saree Makdisi points out, it places her on one side of a growing divide between "hegemonic" and more extreme variants of radicalism. For Wollstonecraft, "the rational, sovereign, Western bourgeois subject" was the subject of all political thought and action, and that bias shows in her desire to use her essay both to chastise Burke and inoculate her readers against his brand of frenzied nonargument.[34] It shows, too, in her *Vindication of the Rights of Woman*, which salutes the virtues of self-restraint while repeatedly characterizing the working class as dirty and licentious.

The Enlightenment began as a reaction against the sectarian conflict that marked the early modern period. In this new, rational, scientifically informed age, people who disagreed didn't have to be enemies, and sociability was measured by one's capacity to appear to care less than one might about the things that matter most. The polarization of literary as well as political culture after the Revolution did not do away with this set of norms and expectations, but it did render them suspect. By 1820, William Hazlitt could declare that politics "is like military warfare[:] There are but two sides, and once you have chosen your party, it will not do to stand in the midway, and say you like neither."[35] For Hazlitt, partisanship informed literary culture as much as it did civic life; to separate the world of letters from politics was simply delusional. It was an attitude that would become more mainstream as the nineteenth century wore on, even as Hazlitt's stubborn embodiment of it made him the target of defamation campaigns that would jeopardize his career.

Prolific and widely read throughout the nineteenth century, Hazlitt is a figure whose influence on the essay can hardly be overestimated. His writing was persuasion, not mere performance. He was, in a crude sense, the synthesis of Addison and Marat, marrying the former's digressive, improvisatory mode to the latter's militant fury, as well as his journalistic fondness for heckling the reader. The scathing "A Letter to William Gifford, Esq." is composed in maximally aggressive second-person address, as Gifford is in turn labeled "a little person," a "paymaster of the band of Gentlemen Pensioners," and, worst of all, a "Government Critic ... the invisible link, that connects literature with the police." Of the *Quarterly Review*, which Gifford edited, Hazlitt snarls that it "does not contain a concentrated essence of taste and knowledge, but is a receptable for the scum and sediment of all prejudice, bigotry, ill-will, rancour, and ignorance afloat in the kingdom."[36]

What has hitherto gone unacknowledged is the extent to which Hazlitt absorbs the rhetorical gestures of popular, plebeian writing along with its ideological commitments. His letter to Gifford is not far from a Parisian *libelle*, but he is considerably more exorcised by the petit bourgeois than the aristocrat – by "the Bond Street lounger" who, "coming out of a confectioner's shop, where he has had a couple of basins of turtle-soup, an ice, some jellies, and a quantity of pastry," sidesteps the beggar at the door.[37] To be sure, this reflects a change in the composition of Britain's class structure in the early decades of the nineteenth century, but it also betokens a shift in the literary public sphere. The middle class – the vast majority of the reading public – was now the object of censure, particularly from writers who had themselves been born into or achieved a certain level of comfort. If, in its eighteenth-century heyday, the essay had been central to figuring out who could belong to and benefit from commercial society, by the end of the Romantic era it had become a place to describe, criticize, and oppose *from within* the limitations of both capitalism and its cultures.

With this modification or rather expansion of the essay's purpose, there was little room left for the genteel detachment of *The Spectator*. Radicals, reactionaries, and everyone in between embraced a style that subordinated argument to emotional power by stimulating the reader's most basic affective responses: desire, fear, pity, passion, rage, and disgust. It is in these terms that we might understand the early writings of Marx, as well as some of the more lurid passages in *Capital*. Many of those early writings are often characterized as suffering from Marx's early infatuation with German Romanticism, and consequently as relying overmuch on high-flown, poorly grounded notions of what it means to be human and to live with others. This is fair enough. However, Marx, who was also a newspaper man, learns just as much from the irascible phraseology of the gutter Rousseauvians, any one of whom might have said that "No eunuch flatters his despot more basely or uses more infamous means to revive his flagging capacity for pleasure, in order to win a surreptitious favour for himself, than does the eunuch of industry, the manufacturer, in order to sneak himself a silver penny or two or coax the gold from the pocket of his dearly beloved neighbour." Meanwhile Hazlitt, with his hatred for the Bond Street lounger buying out the candy shop, certainly would have agreed that "the refinement of needs" that accompanies the rise of consumer culture forces us to revert "once more to living in a cave, but the cave is now polluted by the mephitic and pestilential breath of civilization."[38]

The point here is not that Marx hates rich people. It is that he exemplifies the marriage of Enlightenment thought and vernacular eloquence that characterized the literary public sphere during the time of the French Revolution. Although we've become accustomed to thinking of the nineteenth century as a time when the great Victorian sages – Thomas Carlyle, John Ruskin, Matthew Arnold – took over the proverbial airwaves with their nostalgic social conservatism and elegantly idiosyncratic phraseologies, the legacy of this volatile period in history has to be acknowledged as a significant influence on English and European culture. More specifically, the rich tradition of popular journalism that repackaged Enlightenment principles for the militant, unpropertied reader exerted a substantial if chronically underacknowledged pressure on the essay, which remained the most user-friendly vehicle through which to distribute critiques of the status quo to a large audience. The coming communist revolution, as Marx had it, might take its poetry from the future, but it took its prose from the past.

It would be a stretch to call *Capital* – all three doorstopping volumes of it – an essay, but it certainly has passages that might be described as essayistic. Even when the text remains tethered to the particulars of political economy, it is no stranger to what appear to be improvised digressions.

These work, to borrow Fredric Jameson's words, to "mark a space of subjectivity and even of sentiment, of a potentially humanistic effusion" whose effect is at once intimate and pedagogical.[39] There is the notable episode when Marx, seemingly carried away by the dark humor of his own conjecture, explains the phenomenological peculiarity of commodities by imagining a table that "not only stands with its feet on the ground, but, in relation to all other commodities ... stands on its head, and evolves out of its wooden brain grotesque ideas, far more wonderful than if it were to begin dancing of its own free will."[40] There are all sorts of vividly speculative formulations that involve likening capital to a vampire or a werewolf, or that compare laborers to spiders and bees.

Most telling, however, is Marx's much-vaunted affinity for satire, and in particular for the carefully modulated aggression he absorbs from Swift, whom he studied closely. In his images of the worker's "human brains, muscles, nerves, hands etc" disappearing into the commodity, interspersed with calculations of the price of labor and goods, we find an industrialized update of Swift's own ghastly number-crunching: "A child will make two dishes at an entertainment for friends," "Infant's flesh will be in season throughout the year, but more plentiful in March," "I believe no gentleman would repine to give ten shillings for the carcass of a good fat child," and, most Marx-like, "Those who are more thrifty ... may flay the carcass; the skin of which, artificially dressed, will make admirable gloves for ladies, and summer boots for fine gentlemen."[41] While Jameson believes *Capital* maintains a tone of "disciplined neutrality," he perhaps misses the fact that such efforts belong to "Marx's memorable practice of satire and caricature."[42] Like Swift, Marx internalizes only to lampoon the remote posture with which the modern essay had been in its early days associated. Just as his critique of political economy does not so much debunk Enlightenment ideas about civilizational development as explode their limitations, so does it find in the glorification of objectivity and disinterest the potential for imagining, at last, how to create a world in which autonomy and collectivity are no longer opposed – in which, in other words, there are no spectators or friends of the people, no government critics or poor man's advocates, but simply human beings.

The radicalization of the Enlightenment does not end with Marx, nor does the radicalization of the Enlightenment essay. Nonetheless, a text like *Capital* stands as the high-water mark of a certain moment in the history of critical prose, when detachment did not necessarily read as dispassion and sincerity was not incompatible with satirical bite. It is born of a careful fusion of placating and highly confrontational idioms, and it articulates a revolution in political thought as an unsettling, sometimes scandalous clash of styles. Although there would be plenty of attempts over the course of the nineteenth century to bring the older model of essay-writing back to prominence – that would avoid controversy, polemic, even argument at all costs – these would now seem deliberately regressive. The critique of Enlightenment now had a literary form as vigorous as its defense, and far more convincing.

Notes

1 This chapter will focus on the emergence, development, and adaptation of the Enlightenment essay in Britain and France, since it is in these two geographically intimate, politically hostile nations that the proletarianization of the essay in response to the French Revolution is most apparent. Marx's relationship to the German literary tradition and particularly to German Romanticism has been well documented, and I don't rehearse it here. The emphasis, rather, is on what Marx learned from both the high and low literary cultures of France and Britain, his countries of residence (excepting a three-year stint in Brussels) from the age of twenty-five until his death in 1883.

2 Max Horkheimer and Theodor Adorno, *Dialectic of Enlightenment*, ed. Gunzelin Schmid Noerr, trans. Edmund Jephcott (Stanford, CA: Stanford University Press, 2002), 68.

3 Immanuel Kant, "An Answer to the Question: 'What is Enlightenment?'," trans. H. B. Nisbet, in Kant, *Political Writings*, ed. H. S. Reiss (Cambridge: Cambridge University Press, 1991), 54–60; 54.

4 M. NourbeSe Philip, as told to the author by Setaey Adamu Boateng, *Zong!* (Middletown, CT: Wesleyan University Press, 2008), 169.

5 Michael Warner, *Publics and Counterpublics* (New York: Zone Books, 2005), 99.

6 Ibid., 98.

7 [Joseph Addison,] *The Spectator*, no. 1 (March 1, 1711), in *The Spectator*, ed. Donald F. Bond, 5 vols. (Oxford: Clarendon Press, 1965), 1.1.

8 [Addison,] *The Spectator*, no. 39 (April 14, 1711), in *The Spectator* 1.165.

9 Mary Wollstonecraft, *A Vindication of the Rights of Woman*, in *A Vindication of the Rights of Woman and a Vindication of the Rights of Men*, ed. Janet Todd (Oxford: Oxford University Press, 2009), 155.

10 Jürgen Habermas, *The Structural Transformation of the Public Sphere: An Inquiry into a Category of Bourgeois Society* (Cambridge, MA: The MIT Press, 1991), 56.

11 Ibid., 55.

12 Samuel Johnson, entry for "Essay," in *A Dictionary of the English Language: An Anthology*, ed. David Crystal (London and New York: Penguin, 2007).

13 [Anthony Ashley Cooper, 3rd Earl of Shaftesbury,] "Miscellany IV," in *Characteristicks of Men, Manners, Opinions, Times*, 3 vols. (London: [John Darby,] 1711), vol. 3, 226.

14 [Shaftesbury,] "Miscellany II," in *Characteristicks*, vol. 3, 96.

15 J. B. Priestley, "Introduction," in *The Female Spectator: Being Selections from Mrs. Eliza Heywood's Periodical (1744–1746)*, ed. Mary Priestley (London: John Lane, 1929), vii.

16 Eliza Haywood, Book XVIII of *The Female Spectator*, in *The Female Spectator*, ed. Kathryn King and Alexander Pettit, 4 vols. (London: Pickering & Chatto, 2001), vol. 3, 178.

17 Jonathan Swift, "A Modest Proposal for preventing the Children of poor People from being a Burthen to their Parents or the Country, and for making them Beneficial to the Public," in Swift, *Major Works*, ed. Angus Ross and David Wooley (Oxford: Oxford University Press, 2008), 492–499; 493–494.

18 Swift, "A Modest Proposal," 499.

19 Jean-Jacques Rousseau, "The Social Contract," in *The Social Contract and other later political writings*, ed. and trans. Victor Gourevitch (Cambridge: Cambridge University Press, 1997), 41.

20 Jeremy L. Caradonna, *The Enlightenment in Practice: Academic Prize Contests and Intellectual Culture in France, 1670–1794* (Ithaca, NY: Cornell University Press, 2012), 205.

21 Robert Darnton, "The High Enlightenment and the Low-Life of Literature in Pre-Revolutionary France," *Past & Present* 51 (1971): 81–115; 105.

22 Ibid., 110.

23 [Charles Thevenau de Morande,] *La Gazette noire par un homme qui n'est pas blanc; ou oeuvres posthumes du Gazetier cuirassé* (1784), quoted in Darnton, "The High Enlightenment," 110.

24 Darnton, "The High Enlightenment," 110.

25 "The sovereign is you; the legislator is also you; the law, that's you too." Jean-Paul Marat, *L'Ami du people* 334 (January 8, 1791), 2, available through The ARTFL Project at https://artflsrvo3.uchicago.edu/philologic4/journauxdemarat/navigate/310/2/, accessed December 1, 2020. My translation.

26 Marat, *Journal de la République Francaise*, 105 (January 23, 1793), 3, at https://artflsrvo3.uchicago.edu/philologic4/journauxdemarat/navigate/770/2/, accessed December 1, 2020. My translation.

27 Karl Marx, *The Eighteenth Brumaire of Louis Bonaparte* (New York: International Publishers, 1994), 106–107.

28 Edmund Burke, *Reflections on the Revolution in France*, ed. J. G. A. Pocock (Indianapolis, IN: Hackett Publishing Co., Inc., 1987), 174.

29 Claudia L. Johnson, *Equivocal Beings: Politics, Gender, and Sentimentality in the 1790s – Wollstonecraft, Radcliffe, Burney, Austen* (Chicago: University of Chicago Press, 2009), 29.

30 Wollstonecraft, *A Vindication of the Rights of Men*, in *A Vindication of the Rights of Woman and a Vindication of the Rights of Man*, 39.

31 Burke, 66.

32 Wollstonecraft, *A Vindication of the Rights of Men*, 5.

33 Ibid., 23; 47.

34 Saree Makdisi, *William Blake and the Impossible History of the 1790s* (Chicago: University of Chicago Press, 2003), 296.

35 Hazlitt, "Of the Spirit of Partisanship," in *The Complete Works of William Hazlitt*, ed. P. P. Howe, 21 vols. (London: J. M. Dent & Sons, 1930–1934), 17:37.

36 Hazlitt, "A Letter to William Gifford, Esq.," in *Works*, vol. 9, 22–23.

37 Hazlitt, "Malthus and the Liberties of the Poor," in *Works*, vol. 7, 109.

38 Karl Marx, *Economic and Philosophical Manuscripts*, trans. Gregor Benton, in *Early Writings*, ed. Rodney Livingstone (London: Penguin, 1992), 359.

39 Fredric Jameson, *Representing Capital: A Reading of Volume One* (London: Verso, 2011), 113.

40 Marx, *Capital*, vol. 1, trans. Ben Fowkes (New York: Penguin, 1990), 163.

41 Ibid., 164; Swift, 494–495.

42 Jameson, *Representing Capital*, 114.

8

JESSE McCARTHY

The Essay, Abolition, and Racial Blackness

"I can honestly say, as God is my witness," the Dominican friar Bartolomé de las Casas testified in his *Short Account of the Destruction of the Indies* (1552),

> that I have solid grounds for believing that the depredations, the harm, the destruction, the depopulation, the atrocities and massacres, the horrible cruelty and barbarism, the violence, the injustice, the plunder and the wholesale murder that all these territories have witnessed and their people suffered (and still suffer) are on such a scale that what I have here been able to relate is no more than a thousandth part of the reality of what has been taking place and continues to take place.[1]

When Las Casas penned this damning account of the genocidal activities of the European conquistadors, the word "abolition" was only just entering the English language.[2] It did not take on our more familiar relation to the context of slavery until the late eighteenth century, when movements spurred by conscientious Quakers in the American colonies and social reformers in England began to employ it as a watchword in a major campaign to shut down the transatlantic system that since the mid-fifteenth century had been deporting African peoples into chattel slavery.[3]

The violence of colonial settlement, the particular nature of slavery under nascent capitalism, and the rise of new multiracial societies provided a very different backdrop for the essay in the New World than Montaigne's native Dordogne. The difference was not in the fact of violence itself. In his celebrated reflection "On Cannibalism," Montaigne had rightly (and wryly) observed that nothing the purportedly savage Indigenous peoples of the Americas did could possibly be any worse than the gruesome tactics deployed by supposedly pious Catholics and Protestants in their wars against each other. What made the Americas different was the scale of the use of force and the entrenchment of an elaborate intellectual *justification* of the dehumanization of subjected peoples. The conquistadors brought with them a *Requerimiento*, a blend of legal, historical, and theological arguments that they publicly pronounced to the Indigenous settlements before they obliterated them. This textual authority mattered to the mission; entire expeditions might be delayed until it could be obtained.[4]

Las Casas wrote with an almost apocalyptic sense of urgency, believing that the fate of the world, or at least the "New" one, lay in his hands. He emphasized the importance of personal experience to his public intervention, even as he marshaled the force of legal rhetoric, social observation, and theological counterargument against the unfolding disaster around him. The Dominican friar hoped and prayed for change; he made himself a tireless advocate for the oppressed; he threw himself into the work of political reform, including, alas, the well-intentioned but misguided idea of incentivizing sugar planters to release their Indigenous workers and replace them with enslaved blacks who could be brought from Spain. In so doing, Las Casas contributed to the emerging logic of the triangular Atlantic trade, the importation of human cargoes from the Guinea coast and exporting of sugar, and other colonial crops, back to Europe. To his credit, Las Casas recognized his mistake and complained that his solution was being abused. It made no difference: The Arawak, like countless other peoples, were effectively liquidated and replaced by enslaved Africans who were made to toil in abominable conditions.

Here, then, is a very different inaugural matrix for a more anguished conception of the essay: a tradition of writing marked by a monumental sense of burden, straining against moral catastrophe, bearing witness and asserting a will to life and self-determination independent of these calamities. Not a series of attempts (*essais*) to *know* oneself as a subject, but a cyclical incantation and assertion of the right *to be* one in the first place. From the retreat of his humanist tower, Montaigne had asked: "*Que sais-je?*" *What do I really know?* From the plantation complexes of the colonies would arise different questions with a more theological bent. How could what had been wrought be undone? Could relations between peoples ever be repaired in the aftermath of such wars of enslavement and extermination? How could one self-fashion and speak freely if one's humanity was suspected of conceptual impossibility and fundamental unworthiness?[5] Given these histories, who would possess the requisite knowledge to address such questions, and on what terms?

And then who would *read* such essays, even if they could be written? The traditionally cultivated and learned readership for the essay was severely limited in the imperial expanses of colonial societies where educated opinion could usually be satisfied with a diet of pamphleteering, newspapers, and public oratory. An essay, especially one interested in making moral and intellectual claims that ran counter to dominant thinking, would enter a marketplace of ideas dominated by the urgencies of commodity trading and the mercantilist projection of power.⁶ The "slavery" most abhorred in the Massachusetts Bay Colony was not the yoke imposed on Negroes but a white merchant's hyperbole about the unfairness of British taxes.

Writers who dare to pull out the seam connecting the facts of social domination and the truth of personal experience, who genuinely attempt to say something new, or at least in a new way, are always rare. Often, they are simply ignored. It is unsurprising, then, that the most perceptive and subtle reception of Las Casas should come in the form of a remarkable yet little-known essay by the Jamaican writer and philosopher Sylvia Wynter. Published in *Jamaica Journal* in 1984, "New Seville and the Conversion Experience of Bartolomé de Las Casas" is at once a scrupulous forensic reconstruction of his reasoning and a powerful meditation on the limits that any ethnocentric – or even anthropocentric – thinking imposes upon our beliefs about who, and what, can ever justify the exercise of dominion.⁷ It is an example of the type of thinking that only an essay can do: deploying scholarly learnedness, illuminating contemporary concern, sweeping up entire historiographies, surveying, like the owl of Minerva, the massive implications generated "at a terrible human cost, of the African presence as a constitutive unit of the post-Columbian civilization of the Caribbean and the Americas."⁸ Wynter's essay exacts a certain poetic justice as well: the reluctant colonizer's plea for humanity rebuked by an Afro-Caribbean descendant of the enslaved, who proposes to reform Humanism precisely by rescinding the perspective of European Man as the agent of global history.

This violent inception foreordained that the writing of essays in the Americas would be stalked by the specter of race and the consequences of racist thinking. Indeed, the centrality of race as a governing American preoccupation was imposed by the intellectual and political architects of the emergent colonial polities. While many of them embraced the European Enlightenment's attack upon feudal aristocratic privilege and obedience to religious authority, they also accepted the enslavement of "Negroes" as a casual fact of political economy; they were still engaged in open conflict with many Indigenous peoples; their own incipient conception of a "white" identity (useless in the European context) had to be consolidated in opposition to these populations.⁹ The instability, and often incoherence, of their conception of race did not deter them. These contradictions were not lost on contemporary observers. "How is it that we hear the loudest yelps for liberty among the drivers of negroes?" Samuel Johnson caustically observed in *Taxation No Tyranny* (1775). His was just one of many rising voices in England and Scotland in the mid- to late eighteenth century that viewed the slave trade as morally repellent and incompatible with professed Christian values.[10]

On the North American side of the Atlantic, such classics of elite opinion as Thomas Jefferson's notoriously negrophobic *Notes on the State of Virginia* (1785) and Benjamin Franklin's "Observations Concerning the Increase of Mankind" (1751) were candid about the demographic prerogatives that their founding settlement arrogated to them. Franklin's opinions were, for example, rigorously ultranativist:

> All Africa is black or tawny. Asia chiefly tawny. America (exclusive of the new Comers) wholly so [...] why increase the Sons of Africa, by Planting them in America, where we have so fair an Opportunity, by excluding all Blacks and Tawneys, of increasing the lovely White and Red?[11]

This racialist discourse (not exclusively, but especially and often ardently antiblack) formed the discursive background against which the abolitionist essay, and especially its African American component, would have to contend with as it made its insurgent forays into public discourse at the end of the eighteenth century.

The more formidable and immediate obstacle, however, was simply the interdiction of literacy for the enslaved. The earliest antiliteracy codes formalizing the penalties for teaching slaves to read and write were passed in South Carolina in 1740 as a response to the threat posed by the Stono Rebellion of 1739. The illegality of literacy (in some states even for free blacks) shaped a tradition among them of adopting "fugitive tactics" in order to obtain and share learning, "stealing away" under cover of night or using subterfuge and secret locations to study.[12] "On Sundays," one freedwoman, Charity Bowery, recounted, "I have seen the negroes up in the country going away under large oaks, and in secret places, sitting in the woods with spelling books."[13] Under such circumstances, the appearance of a black counterdiscourse was, in and of itself, a remarkable act of resistance. Yet we find it springing forth at the birth of the republic.

In 1776, a young man by the name of Lemuel Haynes, born to a white mother and a father said to be "of unmingled African extraction," wrote an essay that was never published but was circulated privately in the rural New England community where he built his career as a charismatic Calvinist minister.[14] It bore the evocative title "Liberty Further Extended: Or Free Thoughts on the illegality of Slave-keeping," and opened with pointed irony by quoting Jefferson's freshly minted formula: "We hold these truths to be self-Evident..." Haynes had worked as an indentured servant, not a slave, until 1774. His first act of freedom was to enlist with the minutemen and fight for independence. Though brief, his essay identified the crux that so much abolitionist writing would reiterate: that doctrines of natural right and republican virtue logically entailed racial equality. "Liberty is a Jewel which was handed Down to man from the cabinet of heaven," Haynes wrote, "it is Coaeval with his Existance [*sic*]."[15]

In response to the Constitutional Convention of 1787, a black writer using the pseudonym "Othello" published "An Essay on Slavery" (1788), emphatically making the same point: Slavery was wildly "inconsistent with the declared principles of the American revolution."[16] In his "Address to the Negroes of New York," and in his recently recovered poem "An Essay on Slavery," the poet Jupiter Hammon called upon his fellow enslaved Africans to trust in a providential Christian telos that would, if they remained pious, inevitably culminate in their liberation.[17] Such arguments for inclusion and in support of the purportedly republican spirit of the nascent USA animate the extraordinary report by Absalom Jones and Richard Allen, "A Narrative of the Proceedings of the Black People During the Late and Awful Calamity in Philadelphia in the Year 1793." Both were clergymen: Allen founded the African Methodist Episcopal Church; Jones, the first black Episcopal congregation. Responding to a yellow fever pandemic, they organized rescue, care, and corpse removal by the local black community while white Philadelphians decamped to safety. Their actions were intended to demonstrate the integrity and "neighborly" contribution of black citizenship. Instead, they were accused spuriously by Matthew Carey, a recent white immigrant, of corruption, hence requiring the defense of their actions in the public sphere.[18] They exemplify the tendency of early essays by black Americans to advocate a cautious hope for inclusion, even in the face of flagrant and malicious white hypocrisy.

The most strident and unapologetic abolitionist essay by a person of African descent to appear in the late eighteenth century was Ottabah Cugoano's *Thoughts and Sentiments on the Evil and Wicked Traffic of the Slavery and Commerce of the Human Species* (1787). Cugoano was a living embodiment of what Paul Gilroy describes as "the Black Atlantic." Born on the Gold Coast, he was transported to Grenada where he knew "the slave-gang," was resold, and worked in "different places in the West-Indies with Alexander Campbell, Esq." before being brought to London in 1772.[19] Cugoano's jeremiad took aim squarely and threateningly at the institution of slavery, with a strong emphasis on divine punishment and retribution that seems not to have gone over well. His essay was assiduously ignored, and Olaudah Equiano, in his celebrated *Narrative* (1789), shifted away from argument to storytelling with an empathetic and forgiving tone, an approach that proved far more effective in converting public opinion and helped establish the slave narrative as the preferred vehicle for abolitionist intervention. In a little commented upon irony, however, Cugoano proposed "that a fleet of some ships of war should be immediately sent to the coast of Africa ... to intercept all merchant ships that were bringing them [slaves] away."[20] This was actually carried out by the Royal Navy's West Africa Squadron after Britain's Parliament abolished the trade in 1807 – a rare instance of an abolitionist demand soon fulfilled. We cannot know if Cugoano lived to see his vision enacted; all trace of his existence is lost after 1791.

Back in the USA, the debate began to turn on the question of "emigration," that is, of the removal or return of blacks to the African continent and the establishment of a colony there. The foundation of the American Colonization Society in 1817 by wealthy whites concerned about the growing numbers of black freedmen (and the growing intensity of abolitionism) set in motion the founding of the colony of Liberia.[21] These projects catalyzed the formation of the first black public sphere, emblematized by the appearance of the first black newspaper, *Freedom's Journal,* established in New York City by John Russwurm and Samuel Cornish in 1827. The intensity of the emigration debate fractured the venture. Only two years in, Russwurm embraced the cause of emigration and crossed the Atlantic to become the first governor of Maryland-in-Africa, a satrapy later merged into Liberia.[22] Cornish defended remaining and started a new paper after his partner's departure called *The Rights of All.*

One of Cornish's agents in Boston was the great abolitionist David Walker, who penned one of the most important African American essays of the nineteenth century, *An Appeal to the Colored Citizens of the World, but in Particular, and Very Expressly, to Those of the United States of America* (1829). Walker wrote with the radical fire of Cugoano, but his support for the remain side in the emigration debates also forced him to shape his arguments not only *against* slavery and white supremacy, but also *for* global democracy and a black national heritage and homeland in the USA.[23] The text was immediately understood to be dangerous; banned in the South, it was smuggled down the East Coast and circulated underground. As one of its foremost scholars puts it, the *Appeal's* "impact – psychological and social – on contemporary African Americans can be compared only to the impact that Thomas Paine's *Common Sense* had on the white patriots of revolutionary America."[24] The *Appeal* is multifaceted and omnivorous, as if Walker knew it would be the only thing he would write and wanted to get everything down for the record. Widely read in the history of slavery, he curses Las Casas ("this wretch"), who features prominently in his pantheon of white iniquity. His most resounding and important idea, however, is that the suffering of the enslaved upon US soil has given them a rightful stake in the nation's meaning and future destiny:

> Will any of us leave our homes and go to Africa? I hope not. [...] Let no man of us budge one step, and let slave-holders come to beat us from our country. America is more our country than it is the whites – we have enriched it with our *blood and tears*. [emphasis in original][25]

In New York that same year, 1829, Robert Alexander Young published *The Ethiopian Manifesto, Issued in Defence of the Black Man's Rights, in the Scale of Universal Freedom*, an essay with a more mystical and millenarian posture but keeping in common with Walker the conviction that black collective self-consciousness is both inevitable and necessary: "Here we are met in ourselves, we constitute but one, aided, as we trust, by the effulgent light of wisdom to a discernment of the path which shall lead us to the collecting together of a people."[26]

As the debate over slavery in the USA heated up, the political oration or address before a public assembly became an increasingly important vehicle to complement the proliferation of abolitionist newspapers. Figures such as Henry Highland Garnet, Mary Ann Shadd Cary, and Frederick Douglass would alternate between these forms, with speeches often being reprinted and diffused in print. This was the case with Garnet's infamous "Address to the Slaves" (1843), the *by all means necessary* militancy of which was opposed for being too radical and inflammatory by Douglass. Garnet was consciously picking up the torch from Walker. He made the lineage textually explicit by having the *Appeal* reprinted together with his own speech in 1848.[27] But Garnet was also taken with emigration schemes and his position declined relative to that of Douglass, whose voice only grew in fame and importance, emblematic of the "democratic eloquence" of the age.[28] Invited to speak at an event commemorating the Declaration of Independence in 1852, Douglass delivered his iconic speech "What to the Slave is the Fourth of July?" at the Corinthian Hall in Rochester, New York. That justly famous jeremiad should be compared to his "Lessons of the Hour" (1894), given just a year before his death, which poignantly captures the keen sense of rage and grave civic concern that imbues so many African American essays tormented by their ambivalent patriotism:

> I cannot shut my eyes to the ugly facts before me. Strange things have happened of late and are still happening. Some of these tend to dim the luster of the American name, and chill the hopes once entertained for the cause of American liberty. He is a wiser man than I am, who can tell how low the moral sentiment of this republic may yet fall. When the moral sense of a nation begins to decline and the wheel of progress to roll backward, there is no telling how low the one will fall or where the other may stop.

How would emancipation come? The abolitionist minister J. W. C. Pennington, in his "The Self-Redeeming Power of the Colored Races of the World" (1859), invokes providential patience: "The race has been preserved mainly by the desperate hope for a better time coming ... their day has been slowly dawning, till, even now, while we speak, the sunbeams appear."[29] Martin Delany's "The Political Destiny of the Colored Race on the American Continent" (1854) combines realpolitik, sangfroid, and racial pride in a vision for autonomous black nationhood. Some of the most withering commentary employed humor: "What for the best good of all shall we do with the White people?" asked William J. Wilson, writing under the name "Ethiop" in the February 1860 issue of the *Anglo-African Magazine*.[30] Edward Wilmot Blyden wrote essays and articles exploring Pan-African themes, and involved himself in the project of emigration and colonization in Liberia.[31] "We Are All Bound Up Together," Frances Ellen Watkins Harper's 1866 address to the National Women's Rights Convention, reminds leaders such as Elizabeth Cady Stanton and Susan B. Anthony that their discourse too easily neglected the difference that race made to the experience of womanhood:

> You white women speak here of rights. I speak of wrongs. I, as a colored woman, have had in this country an education which has made me feel as if I were in the situation of Ishmael, my hand against every man, and every man's hand against me.[32]

Some of the most distinctive essays about race and liberation were penned by Alexander Crummell, an Episcopal priest who spent twenty years as a missionary in Liberia before returning to Washington, DC. His austere and dramatic sermons impressed the young W. E. B. Du Bois, who would become his highly self-conscious (and self-appointed) heir.[33] Committed to an intensely moralizing vision of history, Crummell believed that slavery had corrupted America and that (with proper tutelage) Africa could lead a future generation to a higher state of civilization. In "The Destined Superiority of the Negro" (1877), he warned that the moral decay made evident by slavery would inevitably lead to the collapse of the social order:

> Like the tree "whose root is rottenness," it stands awaiting the inevitable fall. That fall is its property. No fierce thunder-bolt is needed, no complicated apparatus of ethereal artillery. Let the angry breath of an Archangel but feebly strike it, and, tottering, it sinks into death and oblivion.[34]

One expression of this rot was the use of lynching as a tool of terror to undo the modest gains black Southerners, especially, had made during Reconstruction. Although Ida B. Wells is more properly conceived as a founding pioneer of investigative journalism than an essayist, her *Southern Horrors* (1892) deserves mention as an insurgent appropriation of the essay for abolitionist ends.[35] Anna Julia Cooper, famous for her paean to the power of the black woman in *A Voice From the South* (1892), published an important later essay called "The Ethics of the Negro Question" (1902) denouncing the complacency of Gilded Age America's commercially-minded imperialism:

> A nation's greatness is not dependent upon the things it makes and uses. Things without thoughts are mere vulgarities. America can boast her expanse of territory, her gilded domes, her paving stones of silver dollars; but the question of deepest moment in this nation today is its span of the circle of brotherhood, the moral stature of its men and its women, the elevation at which it receives its "vision" into the firmament of eternal truth.[36]

The following year saw the publication of *The Souls of Black Folk* by Du Bois, one of the most significant essay collections ever published in the Americas. It is known primarily for Du Bois's famous theorization of "double-consciousness" and for his description of the "sorrow songs" (Negro Spirituals) as a gift to the US nation and to world culture. Less quoted are those lines full of "troubled eloquence,"[37] which look back to Walker's claims in the *Appeal*:

> Your country? How came it yours? [...] Around us the history of the land has centred for thrice a hundred years; out of the nation's heart we have called all that was best to throttle and subdue all that was worst. [...] Our song, our toil, our cheer, and warning have been given to this nation in blood-brotherhood. Are not these gifts worth the giving? Is not this work and striving? Would America have been America without her Negro people?

From the turn of the century and leading up to the Depression, "the essay became the medium in which debates over aesthetics were waged."[38] James Weldon Johnson's magisterial preface to *The Book of American Negro Poetry* (1922) has often been viewed as the opening act of the Harlem Renaissance and is notable for its assertion, chiming with the spirit of Du Bois, that "the Negro" is "the creator of the only things artistic that have yet sprung from American soil and been universally acknowledged as distinctive American products."[39]

Alain Locke's "The New Negro" and his eponymous landmark anthology heralded a "spiritual Coming of Age" and inaugurated the myth of Harlem as race capital, the "Mecca" of black modernity that eventually came to be known colloquially as the Harlem Renaissance.[40] Young artists, critics, and aspirants clashed over authenticity, cultural belonging, respectability, and advocacy. The "new" attitude, with its slashing, sly urbanity, is evident in the opening sentence of George Schuyler's "The Negro Art Hokum" (1926): "Negro art 'made in America' is as non-existent as the widely advertised profundity of Cal Coolidge, the 'seven years of progress' of Mayor Hylan, or the reported sophistication of New Yorkers."[41] Langston Hughes fought back with "The Negro Artist and the Racial Mountain," calling out a "Nordicized Negro intelligentsia" and sounding the clarion call of a new generation unencumbered by shame or the standards of others. "We build our temples for tomorrow," he declared, "and we stand on top of the mountain, free within ourselves."[42]

The most sophisticated essays on aesthetics to come out of the Renaissance, however, were Zora Neale Hurston's, especially her exploration of the phenomenological relativity of race ("I feel most colored when I am thrown against a sharp white background") in "How It Feels to Be Colored Me" (1928) and the ethnographically influenced "Characteristics of Negro Expression" (1934). The latter, an abstracted, formalist account of the collective aesthetic practices of peoples of African descent, remains a groundbreaking work of enormous influence. With the reevaluation of her work by black feminist scholars in the 1970s, Hurston's aesthetic vocabulary ("jagged harmonies," "angularity," "the will to adorn") and theorization of black economies of the verbal sign laid the foundation for entire subfields within Black Studies. Indeed, the best monograph on the African American essay yet produced, Cheryl Wall's *On Freedom and the Will to Adorn*, is organized around these very categories.[43]

Richard Wright's influence as an essayist is mostly felt through his remarkable "Blueprint for Negro Literature" (1937), his attempt to reconcile the individual artist's relationship to class in the context of political struggle. In *12 Million Black Voices* (1941), a photo-essay collaboration with Edwin Rosskam, Wright adopts a collective folk voice, infusing it with the bleak yet often lucid social vision so characteristically his own:

> As the courts and the morgues become crowded with our lost children, the hearts of the officials of the city grow cold toward us. As our jobs begin to fail in another depression, our lives and the lives of our children grow so frightful that even some of our educated black leaders are afraid to make known to the nation how we exist.[44]

Ralph Ellison, who learned much from Wright, repaid his debt in his 1945 review of Wright's *Black Boy* with its famous definition of the blues as "an impulse to keep the painful details and episodes of a brutal experience alive in one's consciousness, to finger its jagged grain, and to transcend it, not by the consolation of philosophy but by squeezing from it a near-tragic, near-comic lyricism."[45] Ellison's single greatest essay, however, is "The Little Man at Chehaw Station: The American Artist and His Audience" (1977). Its subject is the bewildering problem of "cultural appropriation," which Ellison calls "the enigma of aesthetic communication in American democracy." "We shy from confronting our cultural wholeness," Ellison argues, "because it offers no easily recognizable points of rest, no facile certainties as to who, what, or where (culturally or historically) we are. [...] Deep down, the American condition is a state of unease."[46]

The Civil Rights Movement and the anticolonial struggle shaped the writings that appeared the two decades that followed the end of World War II. Some landmark essays from this period, such as Martin Luther King Jr.'s "Letter from a Birmingham Jail" (1963) and Malcolm X's "The Ballot or the Bullet" (1964), are indissociable from the immediacy of the struggle they address. Others, such as Frantz Fanon's essays in *Black Skin, White Masks* (1952) and *The Wretched of the Earth* (1967), and Aimé and Suzanne Césaire's writings in the Martinican journal *Tropiques*, and above all, *Discourse on Colonialism* (1950), transcend their context and continue to be read as defining documents of our postcolonial historical condition. The relationship of race to revolutionary Marxism, always a tense affair, found ambivalent expressions. Stuart Hall's contributions to the magazines of the English New Left argued for modalities of synthesis and, most notably in "The Great Moving Right Show" (1979), diagnosed the perils of populist backlash. The Afro-Cuban intellectual Walterio Carbonell's *Cómo Surgió la Cultura Nacional* (1961), which argued that Cuba's culture was inherently African, was scuttled and sidelined by Castro's communist regime. So were black Cuban filmmakers such as Nicolás Guillén Landrián and Sara Gómez (one of the first black women to direct her own films), pioneers of the film-essay, a genre that the American Cheryl Dunye's shorts revitalized with a queer lens in the 1990s. Amiri Baraka's "Cuba Libre" (1960) – more searching and less programmatic than some of his other essays on social themes – is an enthralling account of a revolutionist's evolving political education; ultimately though, his cultural writings, especially those on black music such as "Swing: From Noun to Verb" (1963), appear likely to remain his most influential.

One would need a separate chapter entirely in order to account for the importance of James Baldwin to the art of the essay, and especially to the role of the essay as an instrument of public reflection on the relationship of race to liberation, justice, and conscience. There is a tendency to regard the earlier half of Baldwin's career as an essayist as the greater one. This reputation rests on *Notes of a Native Son* (1955), its extraordinary title essay, the classic rebuke to Richard Wright and Harriet Beecher Stowe in

"Everybody's Protest Novel," and the brilliant meditations on diaspora and identity written from Paris. In conjunction with *The Fire Next Time* (1963), they are arguably the most significant essays by a black American writer since *The Souls of Black Folk*. Yet much of the power of Baldwin's writing actually rests in his later work, in *Nobody Knows My Name* (1972) and those late essays that peer into the Reagan era – and into our own – such as "Notes on the House of Bondage" (1980), "Freaks and the Ideal of American Manhood" (1985), and the deeply troubled glimmers of self-destruction haunting *The Evidence of Things Not Seen* (1985). One hears the desperate twilight of this late style, for example, in "A Letter to Prisoners" (1982), Baldwin's response to the grim rise of mass incarceration: "Brethren, please remember, especially in this speechless time and place, that in the beginning was the Word. We are in ourselves much older than any witness to Carthage or Pompeii and, having been through auction, flood, and fire, to say nothing of the spectacular excavation of our names, are not destined for the rubble."[47]

The 1970s and 1980s witnessed powerful reactions, especially by black feminists, to the masculinist militancy of the preceding decades. They include the seminal Combahee River Collective Statement (1977), Angela Davis's *Women, Race and Class* (1981), June Jordan's multifaceted essays, especially her "Report from the Bahamas, 1982," Alice Walker's *In Search of Our Mother's Gardens* (1983), Hortense Spillers's "Mama's Baby, Papa's Maybe" (1987), and the prolific writings of bell hooks. Of these, no essayistic voice has resounded as powerfully as Audre Lorde's elaboration of black feminist philosophy in *Sister Outsider* (1984). In "Uses of the Erotic: The Erotic as Power," for example, one can hear the irruption of a counterdiscourse that has remained vital to the last four decades of social change: "In order to perpetuate itself, every oppression must corrupt or distort those various sources of power within the culture of the oppressed that can provide energy for change. For women, this has meant a suppression of the erotic as a considered source of power and information within our lives."[48]

Throughout this period, a vein of Ellisonian cultural criticism flowed through Albert Murray's *The Omni-Americans* (1970) into the exquisite essays of Gerald Early's *Tuxedo Junction* (1989), James Alan McPherson's underappreciated classics such as "Junior and John Doe" from *A Region Not Home* (2000), Toni Morrison's great literary essays from *Playing in the Dark* (1992), and Greg Tate's jaunty deconstructions in *Flyboy in the Buttermilk* (1992).

Sharp political debates over the devastating effects of mass incarceration and the so-called "crack era" animated political broadsides from the left, such as Cornel West's "Black Nihilism in America" from *Race Matters*

(1993), and those of Glenn Loury and Shelby Steele from the right. The essay practiced as a critical art form thrived like never before in the hands of Stanley Crouch, Hilton Als, Margo Jefferson, Darryl Pinckney, Zadie Smith, Imani Perry, and many others, as traditional outlets opened more space in their pages to black voices. In 2014, Ta-Nehisi Coates's "The Case for Reparations" reminded readers of the power of a well-wrought essay to influence public conversation. Coates made no secret of his debt to Baldwin, whose spirit of righteous indignation he did much to popularize and revive. For a new generation, the essay continues to shape and be shaped by black freedom struggles past and present as it flourishes and fails forward. "What Baldwin knew is that he left no heirs," Rachel Kaadzi Ghansah observes in her essay, "The Weight" (2016), "he left spares, and that is why we carry him with us."[49]

Notes

1 Bartolomé de Las Casas, *A Short Account of the Destruction of the Indies*, trans. Nigel Griffin (New York: Penguin, 1992), 125–126.
2 The OED offers 1529 as an earliest citation, see "abolition, n." *OED Online*, Oxford University Press, www.oed.com/view/Entry/457, accessed May 30, 2021.
3 On Quaker abolitionism see Brycchan Carey, *From Peace to Freedom: Quaker Rhetoric and the Birth of American Antislavery, 1657–1761* (New Haven, CT: Yale University Press, 2012). Compare with John Woolman, *Some Considerations on Keeping Negroes* (Philadelphia, PA: Franklin & Hall, 1754; vol. 2, 1762)
4 Anthony Pagden, "Introduction," in de Las Casas, *A Short Account*, (New York: Penguin, 1992), xxv.
5 See Lindon Barret, *Racial Blackness and the Discontinuity of Western Modernity* (Urbana: University of Illinois Press, 2016), 43.
6 Voices of opposition or at least qualified protest against the enslavement of Africans arose early, and Las Casas was hardly alone. Alonso Sandoval (1576–1672) objected on the grounds of suitability to Christian conversion in *De instauranda Aethiopium salute* (1626); Francisco José de Jaca (1645–1690) made a more forceful case in *Relación sobre la libertad de los negros* (1682). These seventeenth century texts, part of the long history of failed abolitionist discourse initiated by Las Casas, remained largely ignored. See Susana Nuccetelli, Ofelia Schutte, and Otávio Bueno, eds., *A Companion to Latin American Philosophy* (Chichester: Wiley-Blackwell, 2010), 40–42.
7 Wynter's essay appeared in two parts: "New Seville and the Conversion Experience of Bartolomé de Las Casas: Part One," *Jamaica Journal* 17:2 (1984): 25–32; "Part Two," *Jamaica Journal* 17:3 (1984): 46–55.
8 Wynter, "New Seville … Part One": 25.
9 Compare with Nell Irvin Painter, *The History of White People* (New York: W. W. Norton & Co., 2011); Theodore W. Allen, *The Invention of White People Vol. 2: The Origin of Racial Oppression in Anglo-America* (New York: Verso, 1997).

10 See Hugh Thomas, *The Slave Trade: The Story of the Atlantic Slave Trade, 1440–1870* (New York: Simon & Schuster, 1997), 467–485; Samuel Johnson quoted on 467.

11 Benjamin Franklin, "Observations Concerning the Increase of Mankind and the Peopling of Countries (1751)," in *The Autobiography and Other Writings* (New York: Bantam Dell, 1982), 293–294.

12 See Jarvis R. Givens, *Fugitive Pedagogy: Carter G. Woodson and the Art of Black Teaching* (Cambridge, MA: Harvard University Press, 2021), 27–28.

13 James D. Anderson, *The Education of Blacks in the South: 1860–1935* (Chapel Hill: University of North Carolina Press, 1988), 281.

14 See John Saillant, *Black Puritan, Black Republican: The Life and Thought of Lemuel Haynes, 1753–1833* (New York: Oxford University Press, 2003), 9.

15 Ibid., 5.

16 Quoted in Cheryl Wall, *On Freedom and the Will to Adorn: The Art of the African American Essay* (Chapel Hill: University of North Caroline Press, 2018), 12.

17 See Cedrick May and Julie McCown, "'An Essay on Slavery': An Unpublished Poem by Jupiter Hammon" *Early American Literature* 48.2 (2013): 457–471.

18 On the paradoxes of this "good neighbor" strategy, see Derrick R. Spires, *The Practice of Citizenship: Black Politics and Print Culture in the Early United States* (Philadelphia: University of Pennsylvania Press, 2019), 34–78.

19 Vincent Caretta, "Introduction" Ottabah Cugoano, *Thoughts and Sentiments on the Evil of Slavery* (New York: Penguin, 1999), x.

20 Cugoano, *Thoughts and Sentiments,* 100.

21 See Wilson Jeremiah Moses, *Afrotopia: The Roots of African American Popular History* (New York: Cambridge University Press, 1998), 25–26.

22 Irvine Garland Penn, in his classic volume on the black press, is tellingly tart: "Mr. Russwurm's career as an Afro-American journalist, was soon cut short after the suspension of his paper. He was captured by the Colonization Society and sent to Africa." Penn, *The Afro-American Press and Its Editors* (Springfield, MA: Willey & Co., 1891), 31.

23 See Melvin L. Rogers, "David Walker and the Political Power of the Appeal," *Political Theory* 43.2 (2015): 208–233.

24 Peter P. Hinks, *To Awaken My Afflicted Brethren: David Walker and the Problem of Antebellum Slave Resistance* (University Park: Pennsylvania State University Press, 1997), xiv.

25 David Walker, *Appeal to the Coloured Citizens of the World, but in Particular, and Very Expressly, to Those of the United States of America* (Boston, MA: third edition, 1830), 73.

26 Robert Alexander Young, "Ethiopian Manifesto," in *Pamphlets of Protest: An Anthology of Early African-American Protest Literature, 1790–1860,* ed. Richard Newman, Patrick Rael, and Philip Lapsansky (New York: Routledge, 2001), 84–89.

27 See Sterling Stuckey, *Going Through the Storm: The Influence of African American Art in History* (New York: Oxford University Press, 1994), 83–119.

28 Cheryl Wall borrows the term "democratic eloquence" from historian Kenneth Cmiel to describe the essays of this period. See Wall, *On Freedom and the Will to Adorn,* 8–15.

29 Quoted in Moses, *Afrotopia,* 105.

30 Derrick Spires, *The Practice of Citizenship: Black Politics and Print Culture in the Early United States* (Philadelphia: University of Pennsylvania Press, 2019), 162.
31 Blyden is a somewhat dimmed figure today but his thinking and writings were highly influential upon African leaders of the decolonial movement (and later heads of state) such as Nnamdi Azikiwe and Kwame Nkrumah. See Hollis R. Lynch, *Edward Wilmot Blyden: Pan-Negro Patriot, 1832–1912* (New York: Oxford University Press, 1967), 249.
32 Teresa C. Zackodnick, ed., *We Must Be Up and Doing: A Reader in Early African American Feminisms* (Toronto: Broadview Press, 2010), 300–304.
33 "Instinctively I bowed before this man, as one bows before the prophets of the world." W. E. B. Du Bois, *The Souls of Black Folk* (New York: The Modern Library), 218.
34 Quoted in Moses, *Afrotopia*, 102.
35 See Jacqueline Goldsby, *A Spectacular Secret: Lynching in American Life and Literature* (Chicago: University of Chicago Press 2006), 43–104.
36 Anna Julia Cooper, "The Ethics of the Negro Question" (1902), Moorland-Spingarn Research Center Digital Collections, Anna Julia Cooper Papers, "Manuscripts and Addresses," 19, Howard University, Washington D.C. http://dh.howard.edu/ajc_addresses/19, accessed, March 27, 2022.
37 Cheryl Wall borrows the term from Nathaniel Mackey. See Wall, *On Freedom*, 8; 16–18.
38 Wall takes Victoria Matthews's "The Value of Race Literature" (1895) to be inaugural in *On Freedom*, 5.
39 James Weldon Johnson, *The Book of American Negro Poetry* (New York: Harcourt Brace, 1931), 10; Johnson's second edition (1931) concedes the additional example of "American skyscraper architecture."
40 Alain Locke, *The New Negro* (New York: Touchstone, 1997), 3–16.
41 George S. Schuyler, "The Negro-Art Hokum," *Nation* 122 (June 16, 1926): 662–663.
42 Langston Hughes, "The Negro Artist and the Racial Mountain," *Nation* 122 (June 23, 1926): 692–693.
43 Wall's theorizations are based, in part, on exquisite close readings of Hurston's essays on aesthetics.
44 Richard Wright, *12 Million Black Voices,* (New York: Viking Press, 1941), 136.
45 Ralph Ellison *Shadow and Act* (New York: Vintage 1972), 78–79.
46 Ralph Ellison, *The Collected Essays of Ralph Ellison*, ed. John F. Callahan (New York: Modern Library, 2003), 496; 508.
47 James Baldwin, *The Cross of Redemption: Uncollected Writings*, ed. Randall Kenan (New York: Vintage, 2010), 263.
48 Audre Lorde, *Sister Outsider* (Berkeley, CA: Crossing Press, 1984), 53.
49 Rachel Kaadzi Ghansah, "The Weight," in *The Fire This Time: A New Generation Speaks about Race*, ed. Jesmyn Ward (New York: Scribner, 2016), 32.

9

IGNACIO M. SÁNCHEZ PRADO

The Utopian Essay

Any canonical history of the utopian essay would have to begin with Thomas More's *Utopia* (1516), which coined the term and introduced it into world-historical consciousness.[1] Another version could be envisioned centering the Marxist tradition, even though one would have to acknowledge at the outset that Marx conceived the scientific character of his method as a departure from the utopianism of Charles Fourier and others, and that Marx was at best, as Derek Webb calls him, an "accidental utopian."[2] It would perhaps be more urgent and compelling to posit an approach grounded in present concerns and capture in the idea of the essay the utopian desire that stands in stark opposition to neoliberal totalization. One could imagine channeling into that hypothetical essay the force documents such as the manifestos of the Zapatista Army of National Liberation or the desire for a future embodied in the proliferation of speculative fiction.[3] The variety of potential directions speaks to a writing practice that does not have the numbers or visibility of other subgenres of the essay, but is unquestionably inscribed in the intellectual histories, aesthetic desires, and political endeavors of modernity.

To write this chapter, I made the strategic decision to move away from this kind of expected framing and focus my exploration of the utopian essay on a particular place and time. It corresponds to the process that Santiago Castro-Gómez aptly terms "the birth of Latin America as a philosophical problem," in which post-Revolutionary Mexico appears as one of the key intellectual scenes.[4] *Última Tule* and *Visión de Anáhuac (1519)* by Alfonso Reyes and *La raza cósmica* by José Vasconcelos provide unique historical examples of the living legacies of the utopian essay as a genre in a non-European setting. The Mexican tradition of the utopian essay, either directly written within its strict formal parameters or through the appropriation of its devices and traces, fostered an intellectual project committed to overcoming Eurocentrism and asserting Latin America as a site of thinking. It embraced the centuries of European utopian projections – from More's imaginings, to the naturalist fascinations of Alexander von Humboldt's *Political Essay on the Kingdom of New Spain* to Hegel's idea of America as a continent without history – and turned them around into a genre central to the formulation of anti-colonialist and liberationist thought.[5] Their exemplarity arises not only from the fact that they directly appealed to utopia as a literary form to advance their sociocultural projects regarding Mexico and Latin America in the wake of the Mexican Revolution. They write deliberately as the latest participants in a history of utopianism that exists, as Kim Beauchesne and Alessandra Santos discuss, the imagination of a concrete utopia.[6] The utopian essay of post-revolutionary Mexico materializes both historical *longue durée* and the political impulses of its time into a project invested both in the form of literature and in its role in the polis.[7]

I want to advance the case of the utopian essay as part of a political and formal tradition that has its origins in the otherization of the New World as a *tabula rasa* for European ideations but was ultimately claimed in Latin America and other latitudes as an instrument to think liberation and futurity. An exhaustive approach to this multidimensional history not only exceeds this essay's obligation to concision but would also daunt even the most erudite of critics. Simply listing the major interventions would exceed any reasonable word count. Nevertheless, as I write in English, I am keenly aware that the conversation around the utopian essay on which I build this essay exists mostly in Spanish. My hope is to translate the thrust of the Mexican utopian essay into a reflection for non-Hispanophone readers, while providing in the notes enough references to envision its complexity across the fields of Latin American Studies.

The discovery of the New World constitutes the historical horizon of consciousness of the utopian essay as a genre. A long-running debate has been devoted to the extent to which More was acquainted with writings on the New World, from Christopher Columbus and Amerigo Vespucci onwards. As Alfred Cave notes, "the New World in More's conception of utopia is a symbolic construct, a metaphor for both the absence of civilization and a new beginning."[8] Reading the utopian essay, as practiced in Mexico and Latin America, requires breaking away from the narrow definition that centers More and the trope of a deliberately delineated utopian space. Instead, utopia functions as a device that deploys the potentiality of the New World as a mapping of historicity and futurity, concretely grounded in the emergence and development of "América" – the continent, with an accent, as used by Mexican essayists of the twentieth century – as a land of promise and novelty, and as the foundational site of the intersection between modernity, capital, and coloniality.[9]

The very idea of "Latin America" does not name a self-evident geographical space. Rather, it has been shaped through the legacies of this mode of utopian thinking in relation to the region's identity and place within the capitalist world-system.[10] Beatriz Pastor's erudite study of utopian thinking in Latin America between the fifteenth and the seventeenth centuries provides a useful perspective. Decentering More and focusing on his Conquest-era precursors, Pastor notes that utopian thinking emerges from a "precise historical situation – the discovery of the New World – in which desire imposes itself as the dominant element that organizes and articulates the process of reason." Pastor continues: "desire is limited to organizing in particular ways the categories of thinking that functioned in Europe at the time, giving a specific form to the speculative horizon that configures the cognitive processes of the period."[11] In fact, as Eleni Kefala reminds us in her book on the simultaneous falls of Byzantium and Tenochtitlan, there is a long-standing tradition of interpreting the New World as a place where "Europe's utopian imaginings could be forged anew" because of both the treatment of the Americas as a *tabula rasa* and the understanding, from the late fifteenth century onward, of Europe's Middle Ages as an inferior past.[12] Owing to the role of the utopian motif in the process of naming and envisioning the New World, and in shaping the modern European imagination, utopianism becomes one of the bases of the essay genre *avant la lettre*, as the texts of the first colonizers fueled the imagination not only of More but also of Montaigne himself.[13] A crucial task in twentieth-century Latin American literature was to decenter the procedures of the utopian essay away from their Eurocentric configuration, to deploy the imagination of Latin America as a utopian space or to envision heterotopias (Gabriel García Márquez's Macondo most famously, and one of very many) to capture regional histories and cultures.[14]

Alfonso Reyes harnessed the legacies of this utopian thinking and strategically appropriated the utopian essay as part of a repertoire of writing practices in post-Revolutionary Mexico. Influenced by José Enrique Rodó's doctrine of Arielism and a member of the group of young humanists known as the *Ateneo de la juventud*, Reyes became the leading critic and essayist of his generation in Mexico, and one of the most consequential intellectuals in Latin America in the first half of the twentieth century. Owing to his work as a diplomat in Argentina and Brazil in the 1930s, he became one of the leading advocates for the cultural unity of Latin America and the region's right to equal cultural citizenship vis-à-vis Europe. After his return to Mexico, he became a founding figure of major cultural institutions such as El Colegio de México – a public social sciences and humanities research institution that remains one of Mexico's premier intellectual spaces. Reyes's practice of the essay was grounded not only on Montaigne's legacy but also on a deep knowledge of German Idealism, Bergsonian Vitalism, and the Graeco-Latin classics. Reyes used literature and philology to envision the idea of a Mexican and Latin American polis, based on both the careful reading of the classics as moral guides and the deployment of the trope of utopia as a mechanism to decenter Eurocentric understandings of universal culture.[15]

Reyes's most significant engagements with the traditions of the utopian essay date mostly from his period as a diplomat, where utopianism was strongly intertwined with the development of Latin Americanism as an agenda.[16] When Reyes gathered his writings on the idea of Latin America in 1942, he entitled the book *Última Tule*, in reference to the utopian space in the farthest north of Europe.[17] As Reyes himself comments in the philological piece "Utopías americanas," in the mid-1930s there was an increasing interest in More's utopia and its impact as an idea in the New World. Reyes points to the publication of Silvio Zavala's *La "Utopía" de Tomás Moro en la Nueva España y otros estudios* in 1937, among other works, as part of an effort to reclaim the importance of Vasco de Quiroga in implementing utopian thinking for the advocacy and governance of indigenous communities.[18] In more than a historical study, though, Reyes advances both his utopian essays and his philological approximations to utopian writing as mechanisms to convert history into a formal poetics that affords emancipatory thinking. Andrés Zamora observes that, in *Última Tule*, Reyes deploys a sort of "rediscovery" of the New World, in which "América is in essence a discursive field" and "the sole existence of his essay, the act of enunciation, certifies the innate capacity that this América sign has in acting as a perpetual encouragement by others insistent on its continued imagination."[19] The utopian essay, in these terms, is a formal, aesthetic and epistemological tool to envision the past and present of América as a horizon of futurity.

The main utopian essay in *Última tule* is "El presagio de América" or "The Premonition of América." Gathering fragments written and sometimes even published between the 1920s and the 1930s, "El presagio de América" builds a *longue durée* history of the idea of América before the arrival of the Europeans into the New World. Through a number of short sub-essays, Reyes deploys utopian rhetoric, philological research, and poetic language to describe the way in which utopian writing and the reflection on unknown lands in the history of Western culture prefigure the idea of America. "No doubt," Reyes writes, "the first step towards América is the meditation regarding that inspired and hesitant march through which man came closer to the full figuration of the planet."[20] In these terms, Reyes identifies at the core of the utopian essay's lineage not so much the projection of a space for the pure values of society, but rather a site of "presentiment both scientific and poetic."[21] The essayistic procedure here is not so much the imagining of a utopian space, but rather the appropriation of a mode of thinking in which "action has been placed in the service of intelligence in the deepest and most harmonious sense."[22] Reyes performs a takeover of the enunciation of the utopian essay genre, as part of an intellectual mission that uses the history of utopia as a way to fulfill Latin America's political and cultural mission to lead civilization into the future: "philosophers request from the New World a stimulus for the political perfecting of all the peoples. This is the true tradition of the Continent, on which we have a duty to insist."[23]

It is evident from a contemporary perspective that Reyes's humanism remains infused with a Eurocentric conception that centers European intellectual history as the core of universal culture. Nevertheless, his appropriation of the utopian essay was key to gradually breaking away from this mindset and developing a sustained critique of colonial reason. This critique came to be the central concern of Latin American thought across humanistic disciplines, leading to the ulterior development of liberation and decolonial thinking. The utopian essay's constructivist techniques were flipped back, in a Calibanesque gesture, into the critique of the epistemological mechanisms of Western colonial rationality.

It is important to note that Reyes's interventions in and through the idea of utopia are also inscribed in a Mexican tradition of the essay. In Mexico, as in other Latin American countries, the essay has been historically tasked with the elucidation of the nature and spirit of the national, as conceived at the intersection between liberalism and positivism. This form of thinking carried a variety of utopian impulses, as historian Timo Schafer notes, insofar as it carried a "principle of legal equality [that] nevertheless defied the norms governing social relations not only at the time but in any known prior period of history."[24] At the same time, the strong influence of Auguste Comte and Herbert Spencer intertwined liberalism with ideas coming from positivism and scientism, fostering ideas of liberal freedom and governance imbued with notions of progress and evolution.[25] The most canonical entries in the genre in this period were historical essays that read Mexico's history as both an evolution and as a place to make sense of the national essence or destiny of the country. Justo Sierra's *The Political Evolution of the Mexican People* (1900–1902), concerned with reading Mexico's present from its natural historical evolution, is perhaps the most iconic of these works.[26]

Reyes's early essays, gathered in his 1910 book *Cuestiones estéticas*, carried some of the seeds that would allow him to break away from the positivist model right before the beginning of the revolution.[27] He was attentive to the work of Nietzsche and Bergson, and developed his first views of the three writers that would be the subject of many of his later books: Goethe, Góngora, and Mallarmé. A few years later, in 1917, exiled in Spain, he publishes his first and most influential engagement with utopianism, *Visión de Anáhuac (1519)*,[28] written in the wake of the Mexican Revolution as an attempt to provide a view of Mexico as a natural and historical space that elicits "the far deeper community of the daily emotions" and a "sensibility" that "engenders a common soul."[29] The essay takes over the points of view of various conquest and naturalist writings regarding Mexico, from Bernal Díaz del Castillo to Alexander von Humboldt, and narrates a history of the Valley of Anahuac, the site of both ancient Tenochtitlan and contemporary Mexico City. *Visión de Anáhuac* does not speak openly of utopia but undertakes the same procedure that would underlie Reyes's utopian work in later decades. In any case, the richness of the theory of history and the use of poetic language to engage it is undeniable. In fact, there is among scholars a discussion as to whether Reyes puts forward a Hegelian vision of history tied to consciousness, or a poetics of history understood through Bergson's idea of the *élan vital*.[30] It is likely both Hegelian and Bergsonian. These variegated intellectual sources place Reyes not only at the outset of a post-positivist tradition of the Mexican and Latin American essay, but also as a key figure to turn utopianism into a tool for Latin America's claim to universal cultural citizenship.

The uses of the utopian essay in post-Revolutionary Mexico appear in different yet contemporary ideological and intellectual strains. In fact, Reyes did not author the most widely read utopian essay written in Mexico: José Vasconcelos's *La raza cósmica* (1925).[31] A philosopher and contemporary of Reyes, Vasconcelos played the role of organic intellectual in the early years of the Revolution, most notably as minister of education between 1921 and 1924. In this capacity, he set the stage for the revolution's educational reform, and in the fostering of the arts, gave rise to muralists such as Diego Rivera, among others.[32] Vasconcelos would fall out of favor with the regime, first because of his failed presidential campaign in 1929, and later because of his turn to fascism during World War II. Nevertheless, after his repudiation of the Holocaust, he became rehabilitated and remains a major historical figure in Mexican intellectual history. It is unquestionable that *La raza cósmica* played a major part in the history of Latin Americanist thinking, and in the development of utopian and emancipatory thought.

La raza cósmica, subtitled *Misión de la raza ibero-americana*, builds its utopian ideal by intertwining a variety of arguments and intellectual lines.[33] First, it renews and reactivates the Bolivarian ideal by suggesting the consolidation of Latin American nations into spiritual and political unity. Second, it envisions a racial utopia by theorizing *mestizaje* through the lens of

146

eugenics. *Mestizaje* in Latin America refers to the racial and cultural mixture between European, Indigenous, and, in some countries, African peoples and cultures as the grounding of identity. This idea became popular in various national contexts in the early twentieth century, including Mexico, as a way to negotiate social heterogeneity, while being utilized to advocate for the region in contrast to the segregationist model of the USA. Within this framework, Vasconcelos conceptualizes the cosmic race as a race of the future, possible in Latin America as the place where races have already been subject to *mestizaje*, thus bringing about the mixing of the best features of all human groups and the erasure of their (purportedly) undesirable traits. It is an odd read today because many of its intellectual sources are no longer common knowledge. Vasconcelos's work had a strong Catholic inspiration and his work carried influences from both Plotinus's *The Enneads* and St. Augustine's *The City of God*, as well as Bergsonian Vitalism and a deep interest in India and the emerging conceptualization of the Orient in his time.[34]

For both Vasconcelos and Reyes, eclecticism is a tool of thinking afforded by the essay form in its many varieties. Precipitated by their will to break away from positivistic style, which fostered science over humanistic thought and generated a good amount of scholastic writing, Reyes and Vasconcelos find in nonrationalist philosophers and in the essay genre the tools to develop post-revolutionary literature and thought. This is why Reyes, in 1944, called the essay the "centaur of genres, where there is everything and everything fits, the own capricious son of a culture that cannot longer respond to the circular and closed world of the ancients, but to the open curve, to the ongoing process, to the 'Etcetera' already sung by a contemporary poet concerned with philosophy."[35] Both Vasconcelos and Reyes find in the ability of the essay to capture everything a literary form that overcomes the narrow presentism of positivistic inquiry, and opens the mind to both the world at large and the imagination of the future.

La raza cósmica is a more traditional utopian essay in its imagination of an ideal society, Universópolis, to unfold in the middle of the Amazon. For Vasconcelos, the development of this utopia is by no means guaranteed. It is mirrored and threatened by the triumph of the USA and its politics of white supremacy, which would be embodied in a dystopian space: "If the Amazon becomes English, the world metropolis would not be called Universopolis, but Anglotown, and armies would come out of there to impose upon the other continents the harsh law of domination by the blond-haired Whites and the extinction of their dark rivals." On the contrary, should the cosmic race prevail, "the airplanes and the armies will travel all over the planet educating the people for their entry into wisdom."[36] A key feature of Latin American utopian thinking is the notion that, as a region imbued with futurity and the legacies of all the cultures of humankind, America will be the continent to lead all other regions of the planet into a more just world. Reyes says it in a much less bombastic but equally convinced way in his landmark essay "Notas sobre la inteligencia americana." Reyes echoes Vasconcelos's idea of the cosmic race and asserts that – unlike Europeans, who only know their own cultures – Latin Americans enjoy an "innate internationalism" that would foster a peaceful future. The strength of this argument was patent in 1936, when the "threat of armed conflict" was in the air.[37]

In any case, the utopian conception of Latin America and its strong anti-imperialist and anti-supremacist thrust explain well why Vasconcelos's eugenicist (and, from our contemporary perspective, racist) views did not disqualify him from exercising ample influence in the region's emancipatory thinking. This was perhaps best understood by Latinx and Chicano/a thinkers such as his translator Didier T. Jaén or Gloria Anzaldúa, who contributed to the transformation of Vasconcelos's cosmic race into the political idea of La Raza, and into identities such as "La Nueva Mestiza." Jaén is very clear in stating that the cosmic race "is not simply a racist theory, but a theory of the future development of human consciousness," thus defending the urgency of his idea of the "disappearance of all known races" and the "possibility of redemption by continuing on their basic trend of universalism and unity."[38] Similarly, Anzaldúa vindicated Vasconcelos's work as contrary to white supremacy: "Opposite to the theory of the pure Aryan, and to the policy of racial purity that white America practices, his theory is one of inclusivity."[39] One can think about this by recognizing that Vasconcelos's lasting influence is tied to the potentialities of his work's utopian form, in spite of its historically dated and very problematic conception of race. If Reyes performs the utopian essay as a mechanism to harness the historical legacies of the continent into a project of futurity, *La raza cósmica*, perhaps closer to Thomas More's foundational intervention, materialized rising anti-imperial sentiment into what Juliet Hooker calls an "epistemological inversion" of eugenics.[40]

The utopian essay in Mexico – much like the ones written by More, Francis Bacon, Marx and Engels, or Charles Fourier, and the utopian impulse that informs large histories of socialism, struggle and decolonization – is an ephemeral genre because it manifests itself in social change. One will not find many essays that fit the definition canonically, but the utopian impulse is very present in the history of the essay because it is one of the formal and ideological mechanisms through which the future is imaginable. The seminal work of sociologist Ruth Levitas, for example, moved from a historical exploration of the concept of utopia in the West to the proposal of utopia as a method for the imaginary reconstitution of society and the experimentation of alternative futures.[41] The utopian essay in Mexico and Latin America has become tied not only to an intellectual history, but also to a variety of methods fully imbued by the ideals articulated by José Martí's seminal essay "Our America," which, in the words of José David Saldívar, "marks the beginning of a new epoch of resistance to empire in the Americas."[42] There is a case to be made for "Our America" as a utopian essay, on the strength of its conclusion: "From the Rio Bravo to the Straits of Magellan, the Great Cemi, seated on a condor's back, has scattered the seeds of the new America across the romantic nations of the continent and the suffering islands of the sea."[43] This legacy continues to be at the core of utopian writing in Latin America today. As philosopher Horacio Cerutti Guldberg puts it, the utopian essay allows Latin American thought to be not only a theory of the ruptures of the present but also an "auroral thinking, which denounces the nocturnal, and announces the new day like the morning mockingbird."[44]

The major legacy of the utopian essay in Latin America is the many philosophical and historical works that turned Reyes's and Vasconcelos's form into a method, in the way Levitas proposes for today. In 1958, historian and philosopher Edmundo O'Gorman published his powerful book *The Invention of America*, drawing on Reyes and other thinkers of utopian inclination. O'Gorman challenged the idea of the "discovery of America," a commonplace at the time, and described instead the way Europe invented America in its image. From this, O'Gorman derives the seeds of a very influential philosophy of liberation, by liberating the Western world from both "the archaic insular concept of the physical world" and "the no less archaic insular concept of the historical world as something peculiarly belonging to Europe."[45] O'Gorman has more recently become a seminal influence on the thinking of liberation thinkers such as Enrique Dussel and theorists of decoloniality such as Walter Mignolo.[46] This is just one example of how important, generative, and powerful the utopian essay as a form and device has been. As Mario Magallón Anaya notes, the genre may in fact be more urgent, as it embodies "the demand of commitment in transforming the unjust structures of domination that Our America suffers with increasing force in the present, particularly its great majorities."[47] For as long as the need for the horizon of futurity persists, the utopian essay will remain a fundamental literary form.

Notes

1 Thomas More, *Utopia*, eds. George M. Logan and Robert M. Adams (Cambridge: Cambridge University Press, 2002).
2 Darren Webb, *Marx, Marxism and Utopia* (Burlington, VT: Ashgate, 2000). See, of course, Friedrich Engels, *Socialism: Utopian and Scientific*, trans. Edward Aveling (New York: International Publishers, 1935).

3 There are, of course, essays out there that already consider this force. On the Zapatistas, see Eugene Gogol, *Utopia and the Dialectic in Latin American Liberation* (Leiden: Brill, 2016), 119–151 and 402–413. On speculative fiction, see Fredric Jameson, *Archaeologies of the Future: The Desire Called Utopia and Other Science Fictions* (London: Verso, 2005).

4 Santiago Castro-Gómez, "El nacimiento de América Latina como problema filosófico en México (1930–1968)," in *América Latina: Giro óptico: Nuevas visiones desde los estudios literarios y culturales,* ed. Ignacio M. Sánchez Prado (Puebla: Secretaría de Cultura/Universidad de las Américas Puebla, 2006), 435. I would add that Castro-Gómez has done landmark work suggesting Latin America is not a self-evident regional or geopolitical space but rather a humanistic object of knowledge bound to the history of imperialism and colonialism. See Santiago Castro-Gómez, *Critique of Latin American Reason*, trans. Andrew Ascherl (Columbia, NY: Columbia University Press, 2021).

5 More, *Utopia*; Alexander Von Humboldt, *Political Essay on the Kingdom of New Spain*, 2 vols., eds. Vera M. Kutzinski and Ottmar Ette (Chicago: University of Chicago Press, 2019); Georg Wilhelm Friedrich Hegel, *Lectures on the Philosophy of World History*, trans. H. B. Nisbet (Cambridge: Cambridge University Press, 1970).

6 Kim Beauchesne and Alessandra Santos, eds., *The Utopian Impulse in Latin America* (New York: Palgrave Macmillan, 2011).

7 I do not intend to self-cite extensively, and I will limit references to my prior work to this note. The majority of my work relevant to this chapter, including my writings on Vasconcelos and Reyes, are compiled in two books. The first one, *Intermitencias americanistas: Estudios y ensayos escogidos (2004–2010)* (Mexico: Universidad Nacional Autónoma de México, 2013), is a miscellaneous anthology covering many angles and authors. The second one, *Intermitencias alfonsinas: Estudios y otros textos (2004–2018)* (Mexico: Universidad Autónoma de Nuevo León, 2013), gathers all my work on Alfonso Reyes, who is perhaps the most important essayist in Mexican history, one of the five key essayists in the Spanish language. Of the few essays in these collection available in English, two of them are relevant to this collection. One, on utopian thinking is "The Age of Utopia: Alfonso Reyes, Deep Time and the Critique of Colonial Modernity," *Romance Notes* 53.1 (2013): 93–104. The other one, on Reyes and the essay form, "The Alphonsine Literary Form: Idealism, Modernism and the Essay," in *A Scholiast's Quill: New Critical Essays on Alfonso Reyes*, ed. Roberto Cantú (Newcastle upon Tyne: Cambridge Scholars Publishing, 2019), 52–71. This collection includes other chapters on Reyes and the essay.

8 Alfred A. Cave, "Thomas More and the New World," *Albion* 23.2 (1991): 228.

9 The use of "América" with an accent not only decenters the term away from the appropriation of the continent's name by the USA, but also reflects the basic historical fact of its common usage from the independence forward to speak of the continent, without always carrying the linguistic or regional qualifiers of "Hispanic" or "Latin." For a brief and clear discussion of this, see John Charles Chasteen, *Americanos: Latin America's Struggle for Independence* (Oxford: Oxford University Press, 2008), 1–5.

10 As readers might suspect, this is in itself a long discussion, and some of the key texts are discussed in this essay. But it is worth highlighting Miguel Rojas Mix's

América imaginaria (Santiago de Chile: Erdosain/Pehuen/Consejo Nacional de la Cultura y las Artes, 2015). Originally published in 1992, the book is a beautiful visual encyclopedia of the images and ideas in which Europeans built the New World in its utopian otherness. The concept of Latin America as such is discussed in two books worth revisiting: Arturo Ardao, *Génesis de la idea y el nombre de América Latina* (México: Universidad Nacional Autónoma de México, 2019 [1980]) and Walter Mignolo, *The Idea of Latin America* (Malden, MA: Blackwell, 2005).

11 Beatriz Pastor, *El jardín y el peregrino: El pensamiento utópico en América Latina (1492–1695)* (Mexico: Universidad Nacional Autónoma de México, 1999), 44. All translations from text originally in Spanish and without a published English translation are mine. A short English text by Pastor with these ideas is "Utopia in Latin America. Cartographies and Paradigms," in Beauchene and Santos, *Utopian Impulse in Latin America*, 29–49.

12 Eleni Kefala, *The Conquered: Byzantium and America on the Cusp of Modernity* (Washington, DC: Dumbarton Oaks Research Library and Collection, 2020), 11–14.

13 For a discussion of the impact of the New World on Montaigne, see Deborah N. Losse, "Rewriting Culture: Montaigne Recounts New World Ethnography," *Neophilologus* 83.4 (1999): 517–528.

14 A study connecting these aims is Peter G. Earle, "Utopía, Universópolis, Macondo," *Hispanic Review* 50.2 (1982): 143–157. For a continental focus specifically on the essay, see Martin Stabb, "Utopia and Anti-Utopia: The Theme in Selected Essayistic Writings of Spanish America," *Revista de Estudios Hispánicos* 15.3 (1981): 377–393.

15 An excellent discussion in English of Reyes's political use of philology may be found in Robert T. Conn, *The Politics of Philology: Alfonso Reyes and the Invention of the Latin American Literary Tradition* (Lewisburg, PA: Bucknell University Press, 1998).

16 It is worth noting that the emergence of Latin Americanism in this period has many fronts beyond post-Revolutionary Mexico, and is tied to hemispheric and geopolitical questions, including the emergence of the USA as a regional power, the world wars, and the professionalization of Latin Americanism in academic and intellectual fields. In this regard, see Fernando Degiovanni, *Vernacular Latin Americanisms: War, the Market and the Making of a Discipline* (Pittsburgh, PA: University of Pittsburgh Press, 2018).

17 Alfonso Reyes, *Obras completas XI: Última Tule, Tentativas y orientaciones, No hay tal lugar...* (Mexico: Fondo de Cultura Económica, 1997).

18 Reyes, *Obras completas XI*, 97; Silvio Zavala, *La "Utopía" de Tomás Moro en la Nueva España y otros estudios* (Mexico: Antigua Librería Robredo, 1937). An abridged English version of Zavala's work can be found in Silvio Zavala, "The American Utopia of the Sixteenth Century," *Huntington Library Quarterly* 10.4 (1947): 337–347.

19 Andrés Zamora, "Historia y taumaturgia intelectual: La prodigiosa invención de América en *Última Tule* de Alfonso Reyes," *Revista de Estudios Hispánicos* 50.3 (2016): 704. A different take on this idea of history in its relationship to myth may be found in Pol Popovic, "Alfonso Reyes: Myth and History in Última Tule," *Chiricú* (Fall, 2004), 115–133.

20 Reyes, *Obras completas XI*, 11.
21 Ibid., 29.
22 Ibid.
23 Ibid., 59.
24 Timo Schaefer, *Liberalism as Utopia: The Rise and Fall of Legal Rule in Post-Colonial Mexico, 1820–1900* (Cambridge: Cambridge University Press, 2017), 7. For a more general Latin American perspective of this kind of radical liberalism, see James Sanders, *The Vanguard of the Atlantic World: Creating Modernity, Nation and Democracy in Nineteenth-Century Latin America* (Durham, NC: Duke University Press, 2014).
25 The most important study of this period is Charles A. Hale, *The Transformation of Liberalism in Late Nineteenth-Century Mexico* (Princeton, NJ: Princeton University Press, 1989).
26 Justo Sierra, *The Political Evolution of the Mexican People*, trans. Charles Ramsdell (Austin: University of Texas Press, 1969). It is worth noting that the US edition includes texts by both Alfonso Reyes and Edmundo O'Gorman.
27 Alfonso Reyes. *Cuestiones estéticas* (Paris: Librería Paul Ollendorff, 1910).
28 Alfonso Reyes, *Obras completas II: Visión de Anáhuac, Las vísperas de España, Calendario* (Mexico: Fondo de Cultura Económica, 1995), 9–34. An English translation is available in Alfonso Reyes, *The Position of America and Other Essays*, trans. Harriet de Onís (New York: Knopf, 1950), 3–32. This is Reyes's most widely read essay, and as such there is an ocean of bibliography impossible to cite adequately here.
29 Reyes, *The Position of America*, 29.
30 My work on Reyes has developed the Hegel connection. A study more aligned to the question of history and philology can be found in Conn, *Politics of Philology*, 115–126. Sheldon Penn convincingly argues for a Vitalist reading in polemic with Conn and me. See Penn, "*Visión de Anáhuac (1519)* as Virtual Image. Alfonso Reyes's Bergsonian Aesthetic of Creative Evolution," *Journal of Iberian and Latin American Studies* 21.2 (2015): 127–146.
31 José Vasconcelos, *The Cosmic Race/La raza cósmica*, ed. and trans. Didier T. Jaén (Baltimore, MD: Johns Hopkins University Press, 1997). It is worth mentioning that this edition only translates the essay that bears the title. The Spanish-language edition adds his essays and travel notes to Brazil and Argentina, which help foreground both the continental depth of his thinking and the ulterior influence of the text. See José Vasconcelos, *La raza cósmica* (Mexico: Espasa-Calpe, 1994).
32 The best book in English on Vasconcelos is Luis Marentes, *José Vasconcelos and the Writing of the Mexican Revolution* (New York: Twayne, 2000). For the general cultural revolution in which Vasconcelos played such a major part, see Horacio Legrás, *Culture and Revolution: Violence, Memory, and the Making of Modern Mexico* (Austin: University of Texas Press, 2017).
33 Every single aspect of this essay has been discussed extensively in criticism, so I will not refer to these debates individually. I have myself written on *La raza cósmica* as a utopian essay in *Intermitencias americanistas*. English-language readers can consult the introduction by Jaén and the afterword by Joseba Gabilondo in the translation, which do a very good job in foregrounding the piece. For a quick and well-structured discussion of Vasconcelos and the idea of race in Latin

America, see Marilyn Grace Miller, *The Rise and Fall of the Cosmic Race: The Cult of Mestizaje in Latin America* (Austin: University of Texas Press, 2004). For the impact of eugenics in Vasconcelos and other Latin American thinkers, see Nancy Leys Stepan, *The Hour of Eugenics: Race, Gender and Nation in Latin America* (Ithaca, NY: Cornell University Press, 1991). A recent work on Vasconcelos, the essay, and the hemispheric theorization of race is Juliet Hooker, *Theorizing Race in the Americas: Douglass, Sarmiento, Du Bois, and Vasconcelos* (New York: Oxford University Press, 2017).

34 On the peculiar mixture of Plotinus, Bergson and many other disparate thinkers in Vasconcelos's work, see Claude Fell, *José Vasconcelos: Los años del águila (1920–1925). Educación, cultura e iberoamericanismo en el México posrevolucionario* (Mexico: Universidad Nacional Autónoma de México, 1989). On Vasconcelos's Orientalism, see Laura J. Torres-Rodríguez, "Orientalizing Mexico: *Estudios indostánicos* and the Place of India in José Vasconcelos's *La raza cósmica*," *Revista Hispánica Moderna* 68.1 (2015): 77–91.

35 Alfonso Reyes, *Obras completas IX. Norte y Sur. Los trabajos y los días: História natural das laranjeiras* (Mexico: Fondo de Cultura Económica, 1996), 403.

36 Vasconcelos, *The Cosmic Race*, 25.

37 Reyes, *The Position of America*, 38–39.

38 Didier T. Jaén, "Introduction," in Vasconcelos, *La raza cósmica*, xxix.

39 Gloria Anzaldúa, *Borderlands/ La Frontera. The New Mestiza*, third ed. (San Francisco: Aunt Lute, 2007), 99.

40 Hooker, *Theorizing Race in the Americas*, 163.

41 Ruth Levitas, *The Concept of Utopia* (Syracuse, NY: Syracuse University Press, 1990); *Utopia as Method: The Imaginary Reconstruction of Society* (New York: Palgrave Macmillan, 2013).

42 José Martí, "Our America," in *Selected Writings*, ed. and trans. Esther Allen (New York: Penguin, 2002), 288–296; José David Saldívar, *The Dialectics of Our America: Genealogy, Cultural Critique and Literary History* (Durham, NC: Duke University Press, 1991), 7.

43 Martí, "Our America," 296.

44 Horacio Cerutti Guldberg, *Presagio y tópica del descubrimiento (Ensayos de utopía IV)* (Mexico: Universidad Nacional Autónoma de México/Eón, 2007), 42–43.

45 Edmundo O'Gorman, *The Invention of America: An Inquiry into the Historical Nature of the New World and the Meaning of Its History* (Bloomington: Indiana University Press 1961), 145.

46 See, for instance, Enrique Dussel, *Beyond Philosophy: Ethics, History, Marxism, and Liberation Theology*, ed. Eduardo Mendieta (Lanham, MD: Rowman and Littlefield, 2003), 220; and Mignolo, *The Idea of Latin America*, 3.

47 Mario Magallón Anaya, "Ideas sobre ensayo y utopía en América Latina," in *Historia de las ideas latinoamericanas ¿disciplina fenecida?* by Horacio Cerutti Goldberg and Mario Magallón Anaya (Mexico: Juan Pablos/Universidad de la Ciudad de México, 2003), 130.

10

DAVID RUSSELL

Ethics and the Essay

What Do Essays Know?

If every genre of literature offers us a different way of knowing life, then it is perhaps the essay, of all genres, that is the least sure of itself. Since Montaigne, the literary essay has been founded on uncertainty. As has often been pointed out, "to essay" means to try out or to experiment – to give something a go without being sure of the result – and there is a tradition of essay writing, I will propose in this chapter, which makes ethical use of such uncertainties. The essay is a form "which is in morals and manners," William Hazlitt suggested in 1815, "what the experiment is in natural philosophy"; it is one of the functions of the essay, taken as a genre, to remind us that we need modes of experimentation quite as much in ordinary human relations as we do in science ("natural philosophy"). The essay is suited to experiments in morals and manners, Hazlitt proposes, because it is a flexible, tentative, form, good for feeling one's way: It "does not deal in sweeping clauses of proscription and anathema, but in nice distinctions and liberal constructions."[1] As such, it is a mode that comes in handy for Hazlitt in London in the second decade of the nineteenth century; in the densely anonymous encounters of the modern city, the days in which conduct might be regulated by certain rules, and doctrinal laws now seemed to be long gone – if they ever existed.

Essays are like experiments. Hazlitt's analogy is helpful, up to a point, but it is worth noting its limitations. The literary essay may at first appear to offer, like the so-called scientific method, a practice by which knowledge is gained through the testing of hypotheses, but rather quickly we notice that essays are experiments of a strange kind. They are not in pursuit of empirical fact. More often than not, they have nothing to prove. The essay as genre is such a broad and loose category (Hazlitt's "nice distinctions" here could be endless) that any individual essay – or even a whole *Cambridge Companion* – seeking to generalize about it may seem doomed from the outset. But say we wanted to experiment with such a generalization anyway: One place to start is with this genre's own fondness for a kind of generous skepticism, or playful questioning of preexisting forms of knowledge. The literary essay often attends to the most ordinary forms of human experience; it is a form that tends not to take our relations – to ourselves, to other people, and to the world – for granted. Sometimes, this means that approaches to the essay genre seem marked by a tone of tentative humility. Montaigne himself peppered his essays with confessions of his own inadequacies, of method and memory – "*Que sais-je?*" (What do I know?) was his famous question – while Samuel Johnson's 1755 dictionary definition of the essay is "a loose sally of the mind; an irregular indigested piece," which seems nothing too grand. But Johnson also defines the essay as a "first taste," which may grant it, as we will see, a certain ethical and aesthetic significance. And sometimes the essay's incapacity for systematic claims on knowledge appears a point of pride, full of liberatory promise, especially in intellectual environments full of sweeping certainties. "In the realm of thought," claimed Theodor Adorno, "it is virtually the essay alone that has successfully raised doubts about the absolute privilege of method."[2]

Essays are formally equipped for, or lend themselves better to, some uses rather than others. They are usually short. We think of their end even as we begin them, and many a writer has linked this formal quality to reflections on the momentariness of life itself. It was Montaigne who proposed that "to philosophise is to learn how to die." Almost 200 years later, in the final essay of his series *The Rambler*, Johnson said that "we always make a secret comparison between part and whole," so that "the termination of any period of life reminds us that life itself has likewise its termination."[3] Johnson makes the case for life's reflective pauses, "happily and kindly provided." As much as the form's brevity unfits it for certain functions, it equips essays to perform an investment in those kinds of experience that are "proposing frankly to give nothing," as Walter Pater would put it over 200 years later still, "but the highest quality to your moments as they pass, and simply for those moments' sake."[4] Pater is talking about the appreciation of visual art here, but he is also making a point about essayistic ways of looking and relating. Pater made the essay newly artful when he proposed the value of "nothing." He means to suggest that the giving of nothing instrumental, such as rules for life or memorizable data, might have its own uses, and be an important kind of experience, even if only for a moment. He continues a long tradition of essay writing that is aware of the ways – unplannable, incalculable – by which the objects of our attention, through the ways we attend to them, may make more of us.

Pater's student, Oscar Wilde, in an 1891 essay diagnosed the mistake we make when "we teach people how to remember" but "never teach them how to grow."[5] Essays and essayists in very different times and places tend to be united by the fact they are more interested in evocation than in information: Essays often make us realize things – things we can feel are very important – but which we cannot, afterwards, sum up propositionally in the form of information gained, or lessons learned. They teach, not particular "content," but that life is a matter of attention, of feeling one's way, that much of what is valuable does not come in definitive explanation – and doesn't, as it were, get you anywhere. When Ralph Waldo Emerson in his great 1841 essay "Self-Reliance" declares that "I would write upon the lintels of the door post, Whim," he is making the case for a more adventitious direction to life – "I hope it is somewhat better than whim at last, but we cannot spend the day in explanation" – and he leaves unexplained whether he refers to incapacity or disinclination as the source of his vagary.[6] Instead of homing in on a thesis, essays often lead, more indirectly, to exploration of the very grounds or conditions of what we are doing when we are paying attention. You don't have to be a reader of essays to have this kind of experience, of course. In reading poetry, or novels, or in watching films or looking at art, we might find intimations of new ways of seeing or relating, or aspects of experience that we hadn't before known how to name, which we then experience as coming to us, as if from another realm, with the feeling of what Emerson calls, earlier in the same essay, an "alienated majesty."[7] But I am interested, in this chapter, in the more tentative and playful approach to knowledge that the literary essay is often interested in exploring, and in thinking about how this exploration might be the basis for a kind of ethical relation.

Essays do not often unfold a narrative in which facts and values are arranged by the end, in dispositive conclusion. They don't tell someone or something's definitive "story." If they have a front to put up – in the form, say, of the essayist-personae adopted by Jonathan Swift or Charles Lamb, Virginia Woolf, or Hilton Als – they often show you the gaps in it too. Indeed, the very doubts we may have about the essay's moral affordances are the basis of its contribution to ethical life. The most immediate doubt we may have stems from the way much ethical thought has linked morality and narrative. For philosophers such as Aristotle or John Stuart Mill, for example, the good life is a matter of being able to tell one's story aright. (Mill thought biography the most useful genre for ethical education.) After all, rules of good behavior often rely on basic narrative forms: Actions, as your parents may have told you, have consequences. In ordinary language, it is by dint of narratives and the predictions they allow that we may be inducted into habits of good behavior. Novels, as many narrative theorists have pointed out, comport with the ways our moral lives have a "sense of an ending"; they dispense ethical judgment in the ways they conclude, having shown causes leading to their effects. And grander narratives – of nation, or social system, or even of humanity itself – form the basis, as the historian Priya Satia has suggested, of "ethical accountability," of how we explain our actions to ourselves as historical actors – for good or for ill.[8]

Essays are wary of narrative uses. It is not that essays never offer us stories – they very often do – it is just that they often seem averse to giving narrative such a conclusive moral role. Indeed, essays may show us, as Pater suggested, in the course of writing his own essayistic unsettling of a historical narrative, that "our failure is to form habits," which come as the result of having become too settled in our stories.[9] We may form a habit of reading essays, but literary essays do not frequently offer, as textbooks or self-help books do, either the data by which we might justify past decisions and make future projections, or those habits of highly successful people on which we might model our actions. If ethics, as one of the entries for the word in the *Oxford English Dictionary* has it, can be defined as habits of good behavior in the form of "a system or set of moral principles" that both organizes and is revealed by the stories of our lives, then the reading of essays seems to propose frankly to give, if not Pater's "nothing," then very little in assistance towards such definition. When, in our reading of great essays, we allow Virginia Woolf to take us "street haunting," or follow John Berger in looking at animals, or imagine, with Hilton Als, the inner life of Richard Pryor's sister, we are being offered a great deal – but not much in the way of moral imperative, ethical system, or conclusive story.[10]

So when, for instance, Als has Pryor's sister (imaginary, like Shakespeare's) tell us that "being an actress is one of the few jobs on earth that tells the truth about this need that exists in humans – to be told what to do," we are being given a rich provocation instead of a prescription or proscription.[11] When Pater claims that artworks, "like persons, live with us, for a day or for a lifetime," he offers us intimations about the kinds of regard we *could* have for others, for the world, and for ourselves.[12] In experimenting with vivid moments, with roles and personae, modes of approach and ways of handling, the essay reminds us that things don't have to be *this* way. The kinds of relation essays proffer are not so much to be received as right or wrong as they are alternatives to our more habitual ones – or even to our usual sense of the boundaries between us, other people, and the world. ("I, you, me, us, words let alone concepts I struggled with," Als writes in the opening essay to his 2013 collection *White Girls*.)[13] At its best, the essay is a most penetrable form, which performs permeability in language. It is an art of encounter. It is in this art that we may locate its ethical potential.

An Ethics of Unknowing

The essay, then, often makes a virtue of not wanting to know. And this is what can make essays ethically salutary, in their uncoupling, if only for a moment, of ethical life from epistemological or narrative demands. Admittedly, there is something counterintuitive about this. Morality has often been the field where the conflicts and confusions of life have found refuge in certainty. I may be in doubt about all sorts of things, but I know the difference between right and wrong. I know who is good and to be praised, and I know who is bad and to be shunned. There are few accidents in this familiar moral picture, so it provides a secure foundation from which its certainties can radiate to other aspects of life. In fact, this may be the whole point of it. As the philosopher Bernard Williams once suggested, it is in systems of morality that our beleaguered, overwhelmed rationality has itself been able to claim certain foundations though the assumption that morality "must have a claim on one's most fundamental concerns as a rational agent, and in one's recognition of that one is supposed to grasp, not only morality's immunity to luck, but one's own partial immunity to luck through morality."[14] The world may be in chaos, but moral life is not random or accidental; there are rules, you know. It is through those rules that we are protected from the chaos of the world and its broader uncertainties. There is something rueful in Williams's suggestion that "while we are sometimes guided by the notion that it would be the best of worlds in which morality were universally respected and all men were of a disposition to affirm it, we have in fact deep and persistent reasons to be grateful that it is not the world we have."[15] Indeed, following Williams's hint here, we might be tempted to imagine that the more uncertain and unstable the social world becomes, the more ethically certain people feel they need to be: more certain about the categories of right and wrong, and more certain of the identities of the people who fit into them.

In unknowing essays, on the other hand, established values and habits of response are put into suspension. We gain the room to imagine alternatives to precomposed norms. (The artist and essayist David Wojnarowicz called such norms "the preinvented world," which he sought to outwit).[16] Als, in a 2018 interview with the *Paris Review*, describes his own essay writing as "a way of struggling through the intricacies of an anti-empirical sensibility," which is an activity he defines not as the flight from the known world, but as a more unknowing and more imaginative way of encountering how we know it: "not as the construction of an alternate world, but as what your imagination gives you from the real world."[17] The plausible gives way to the possible – even if for just a moment – and the foundation of this process is an attention to one's own imaginative responses to life, which may be wider than one had thought. It is a process analogous to play – where we interact with another person, or an animal, or even an artwork or piece of writing – for its own sake, in careful attention to the impression it gives us.

The fact that essays tend to begin with the personal, the individual impression, and with the place where we happen to be – "Where do we find ourselves?" is how Emerson begins his essay "Experience" – has some-times obscured their more abstract interest in the very terms by which we encounter the world.[18] Essays often begin from the self and its situation, not in the manner of the despairing solipsist or optimistic show-off (like people on social media photographing their dinner), but, perhaps more hopefully, in thinking about the conditions and coordinates of the place from which they begin. In the process, they seek to capture in words the experience of a subject in contact with reality. The characteristic question of the personal or critical essayist of their object of attention is "what does it mean to me?" as Matthew Arnold and Walter Pater both put it in the nineteenth century; or, as the essayist and psychoanalyst Marion Milner wondered of her own attentions in 1936: "might there not perhaps be a private reality, a reality of feeling rather than of knowing, which I could not afford to ignore"? Milner's diary-essays responded with an "experiment" in seeking a "way by which each person could find out for himself what he was like, not by reading what other people thought he ought to be, but directly, as directly as knowing the sky is blue and how an apple tastes, not needing anyone to tell him."[19]

The stakes of such experiments could not be higher. They explore the process by which people, in James Baldwin's words, "renew themselves at the fountain of their own lives." For Baldwin, in a great – seriously play-ful – essay on ethical responsibility, such a capacity was the only basis on which people were able to engage in any authentic way with the world's injustices. It is a matter of trusting one's impressions instead of the known certainties of "historical and public attitudes," because the "person who distrusts himself has no touchstone for reality – for this touchstone can only be oneself."[20] It is precisely this focus on the individual impression that may displace, for a moment, prefigured knowledge: of attitudes, identities, and intentions. As Montaigne famously asked, "when I am playing with my cat, how do I know she is not playing with me?"[21] He suggests that when we are playing with others, we do not need to know what is passing through the mind of the animal we are playing with. All the more so when the ani-mal in question is another person; indeed, the need to know might impede collaborative and playful connections with others. In the sixteenth century, when knowing the core of another person's identity (as race, as religious confession, as social rank) dictated in advance how they were to be treated, Montaigne's playful proposal gains a political function, as the sociologist Richard Sennett has argued.[22] Obviously the question, in different periods of history, has been more or less urgent, more or less violent: Are we ever free of the temptation to treat others according to our presumed knowledge of them, the advance data we have on them, by which we apprehend their identity? The virtue of essays lies in their beginning, often tacitly, with the question of whether there are other things we can do with people, or any objects of our attention, than know them; and whether coming to an answer about, or exposing the truth of, something or someone is the most useful, or the most imaginative, or the most kind thing we can do with them.

All this is not to say that essays are good for us, in any simple terms of consumption or readerly diet, like eating your greens. Some essays present moral or political claims whose urgency we continue to recognize decades later (as we do those made by Baldwin's *The Fire Next Time*). Others seem to propose no obvious moral claims even on their own times (Woolf, for example, on "The Death of the Moth"). In thinking about the ethical function of a given essay, we do not have to agree with its conclusions, or even much like the places it takes us – you don't have to agree with the conservatism, say, in Joan Didion's essays in *Slouching Towards Bethlehem* in order to appreciate their astringent brilliance – but we may find ourselves feeling and thinking differently in the spaces it opens up. It is a simple observation that every piece of writing proposes a way of reading it, of taking it in. Through its language it handles us, so to speak, and shows us a way of handling the world. All art does this. Essays often take it, tacitly, as their subject. It is part of the way our ordinary ways of treating others and ourselves have an art to them (the psychoanalyst Christopher Bollas writes, usefully, of an "aesthetic of handling").[23] The essay, because it often reflects deliberately on how the world and its communications are to be taken, and because it is short – only there for Pater's "moment" – is a very good form for modeling ways of relating and evaluating, ways of handling the world, and the people and other objects we find in it.

It is a characteristic quality of the essay, as a genre, to place the question of knowing temporarily out of bounds, or in parentheses, in order that we may see new purposes or values in a particular encounter. So it is on this basis that we may identify – at least in an essayistic tradition in English, which is the tradition I know best – a set of shared ethical claims. Such claims must be tacit, beginning from the assumption that the most vivid experiences are not to be resolved quickly into knowledge-based and instrumental forms. These are not claims that can be turned to the immediate effect of power, the possession of data, or career advancement. They are claims about the ways and relations by which we come to feel alive – ways and relations that can be difficult to describe, or sum up, in propositional terms. "Forms of closure are perhaps more hospitable to description than forms of openness," Adam Phillips has remarked; this is a descriptive drift we often discern the essayist to be writing against.[24] Phillips, as both a psychoanalyst and an essayist, is a writer who apprehends the shared question that best animates the contact between literature and psychoanalysis: the question of how, or under what conditions, people ever become open to new experiences, and to more vital connections with others. Essays often experiment with language for the kinds of experience, or relations to our thinking, seeing, and reading, that we might not pause to realize if we hadn't been encouraged to do so, but which, when attended to, introduce a new sense of promise. The merit of uncertainty is as foil to the process by which, in Phillips's words, "the omniscience of knowing what we are" sponsors "the omniscience of knowing what we are not." Against which, the "shock of the new, one might say, is the shock of just how knowing we have been about the apparently familiar."[25]

Charles Lamb's Essays in Tact

We have gathered together, under our rubric of essay writing, the broad themes of an unknowing ethics, of handling the world, and of individual practices of attention. It is time we turned in detail to a specific example, which I will draw from my own reading as a scholar of nineteenth-century literature in English. "Now and then it is possible to observe the moral life in process of revising itself," writes Lionel Trilling, and he proposes that such observations come to us in "thinking about literature."[26] The literary essay in early nineteenth-century Britain made full use of the ethical qualities I have described in order to respond creatively to a time when certain knowledge – in the form of the social categories, values, and customs of the "old society" that required people to produce the kinds of signification that matched their station in the social hierarchy – was breaking down under the shock of revolution abroad and urbanization and population growth at home.[27] At a time when more and more people were living ever more closely with people they knew less and less about, guiding social principles were under pressure. The resulting social confusion was at once anxious, as the "truth" of other people could not be grasped as firmly as before, but also full of potential, as many different truths and ways of handling other people, became possible.

Faced with such a situation, one response was to become more knowing: New systems of social classification sprung up, as did innovations in government regulation. This was also the beginning of the ever more minutely regulated etiquette for which the British nineteenth century became famous. There was an anxious demand for good habits. Conduct books boomed again. But this was also the time when some new ideas about a less knowing handling of people and the world were explored in the essay form, which flourished during this era. I have discussed elsewhere the essay's practice of "tact," in the sense of feeling one's way with others, a meaning of the word that first appeared at this time, and I have traced a genealogy of essayistic tact from the romantic essay to the practice of psychoanalytic therapy in twentieth-century Britain. Here I will return to one of the protagonists of that discussion, Charles Lamb, in order to show what an ethic of tact looks like in essayistic practice. The writings in Lamb's *Essays of Elia* make for a particularly good case study because of the way they both perform an ethos of tact in their styles and aesthetic of handling, even as they represent, mimetically, the social situations and street encounters, plays and dreams, to which one might respond more or less tactfully.

Lamb places himself in Montaigne's tradition of declared uncertainty when, in his 1821 essay "Imperfect Sympathies," he ranks himself as part of an "order of imperfect intellects." He describes his preference for a social style constructed from "hints and glimpses, germs and crude essays at a system" to an apprehension of the "full-front" of "Truth."[28] But what looks like an incapacity turns into a resource, Lamb suggests, when contrasted with the kind of relational mode that was on the rise in his time, one that strove for a more utilitarian state of mind in search of "perfect order and completeness" in knowledge.[29] A person so minded "never hints or suggests anything, but unlades his stock of ideas in perfect order and completion ... he never stops to catch a glittering something in your presence, to share it with you, before he quite knows whether it be true touch or not." This way of relating to others, Lamb suggests, misses something through its tidy certainties; it has no care for "middle actions." Between such a knowing person and his interlocutor, there is no "border-land" or space of play: "you cannot hover with him on the confines of truth, or wander in the maze of improbable argument. He always keeps the path. You cannot make excursions with him – for he sets you right." Communication under such conditions shrinks the "border-land" between people to a rigidly demarcated front line: He "stops a metaphor like a suspected person in an enemy's country."[30]

In "Imperfect Sympathies," Lamb's only positive description of a more ethical and essayistic mode of relation is oblique ("a glittering something"), reticent, and tactile (a stopping to "catch," an exploration of a "true touch.") It is an interaction based not on definite information but on the offering of a vague "something." It is temporally imperfect, not being so smoothly finished as to deny its recipient a handhold. One is able to make use of it, to make it one's own. Lamb's essays propose a practice of tact that, through the ways it doesn't want to know, provides a means of preferring the potential of the borderline to the policing of identities. Lamb offers his own most assertive ethical statements in representing the performed practice of this mode. When faced with the tall tales of "Beggars in the Metropolis" (1822), for example, becoming a stickler for truth is the least ethical response. Instead Lamb, writing under his persona of "Elia" advises,

> Shut not thy purse strings against painted distress. Act a charity sometimes.
>
> When a poor creature (outward and visibly such) comes before thee, do not stay to enquire whether the "seven small children," in whose name he implores thy assistance, have a veritable existence. Rake not into the bowels of unwelcome truth merely to save a halfpenny. It is good to believe him. If he be not all that he pretendeth, give and under a personate father of a family, think (if thou pleasest) that thou hast relieved an indigent bachelor ... think them players. You pay your money to see a comedian feign these things.[31]

"It is good to believe him": This is the way Lamb's ethical statements emerge. It is not a matter of sentimentalizing poverty, to turn an act of charity to personal gratification, but to point out that a supposedly practical demand for the facts of the matter can be an equally self-indulgent – even cruel – act. Instead, Elia keeps the "border-land" open; he is doubtful of any rush to occupy unbalanced power relations between knower and known. The kindness of acting a charity is to respond to the virtual in kind, with the essayistic tact of a dramatic imagination: to "think them players" and so be prepared to play oneself.

Lamb offers an essay in ethics because he prefers a renewal of attention (we have seen Als call this "what your imagination gives you from the real world") to the imposition of a single reality. For this single reality would be the reality of the privileged: an absolute moral code, according to which a beggar is considered deserving or not. Truth is "unwelcome" here not in a particular sense (that is, because Elia knows the beggar is a liar and wants to deceive himself on this fact) but in a general one: the notion that he could know the truth of the other is quite inappropriate to the situation. Lamb confronts his reader with the ordinariness of a suspicious critical mode in social interaction, only to propose an alternative relation. Opening a front line into a border-land, Elia evades seemingly inevitable terms of conflictual opposition in favor of more promising possibilities. In his metaphorical mode, Lamb refuses to decide whether the beggar really is in as much trouble as he says. But he also – keeping the metaphorical mode tactfully alive – refuses to treat him, finally, as a stage performer; he and his sufferings are unavoidably in the world, and "concerning these poor people, thou canst not know if they are feigned or not." The tact of Lamb's essay is to keep the precious sense of the virtual, or "as if," in play.

In an earlier essay, "Valentine's Day" (1819), Lamb describes the impersonal pleasures of such a refusal of knowing in the recipient of a gift. This essay links the social intensity of the urban stage – valentines, like city dwellers, "cross and intercross each other at every street and turning" – to social relations of benign unknowing. A friend of Elia sends an anonymous valentine, but Elia's admiration, and the effect of the essay, dwells with the reaction of the recipient rather than the satisfactions of the sender, whose relation to the scene is not described. Lamb is always encouraging us to consider the potential of our impressions and reactions ahead of any knowingness about the outcomes of intended effects. The woman in receipt of an ingenious card is not so "foolish" as to seek to uncover the facts of the matter or become enthralled in a power dynamic of imaginary relations between seer and seen. Rather,

> She danced about, not with light love or foolish expectation, for she had no lover; or, if she had, none she knew who could have created those bright images which delighted her. It was more like some fairy present; a God-send, as our familiarly pious ancestors termed a benefit received where the benefactor was unknown. It would do her no harm. It would do her good for ever after. It is good to love the unknown.[32]

The good to be found here is in the sense of benevolence it evokes and in a connection whose value is found in the fact it has no need to be known. The woman who is the unnamed ordinary hero of this essay eschews knowing (in the form of reading for any plot) in favor of a moment's delight. There is no grand narrative here, no hidden identities to uncover or debts to be repaid. There is only the delight in making the most of the surprises that cross and intercross one's path.

"Little arts of happiness he is ready to teach to others," Pater remarked of Lamb's essays.[33] Other essays of Elia can take on more clearly moral subjects (for instance the fascinating critique of imperialism found in the essay "Distant Correspondents"), but they are all founded in an everyday practice of tact, by which one may suspend suspicion in order to "act a charity" or receive, unknowingly, a valentine. By proposing an essayistic mode of social relation in which people offer their trust to the world through the ways they do not want to know, Lamb makes us wonder how we might have to act and how we might wish to change the world in order to make such trust a more common experience – an experience that is obviously preferable to suspicion, competition, or conflict as dominant social norms. Lamb leaves us with the question, to borrow Baldwin's formulation, of how we might become our own touchstones. The task of responding is up to us, of course, but Lamb's ethical gift is to leave us with a hint, rather than with an imperative or proscription, about the uses of the essay in tact: "It is good to love the unknown."

Notes

1 William Hazlitt, "On the Periodical Essayists," in *Essayists on the Essay: Montaigne to Our Time*, ed. Carl H. Klaus and Ned Stuckey-French (Iowa City: University of Iowa Press, 2012), 16.
2 Theodor Adorno, "The Essay as Form," in *Notes to Literature*, vol. 1 (New York: Columbia University Press, 1991), 9.
3 Samuel Johnson *The Idler* 103 (April 5, 1760).
4 Walter Pater, *The Renaissance: The 1893 Text*, ed. Donald Hill (Berkeley: University of California Press, 1980), 190.
5 Oscar Wilde, "The Soul of Man Under Socialism," in *The Decay of Lying, and Other Essays* (London: Penguin, 2010), 113.
6 Ralph Waldo Emerson, "Self-Reliance," in *Essential Writings of Ralph Waldo Emerson*, ed. Brooks Atkinson (New York: Modern Library, 2000), 135.
7 Ibid., 132.
8 For Satia, the discipline of history itself – that master narrative of the West – has had a pivotal role in managing the conscience and justifying the ethics, of terrible actions on the world stage. Priya Satia, *Time's Monster: History, Conscience and Britain's Empire* (London: Allen Lane, 2020), 12.
9 Pater, *Renaissance*, 189.
10 Virginia Woolf, "Street Haunting," in *Selected Essays*, ed. David Bradshaw (Oxford: Oxford University Press, 2008); John Berger, "Why Look at Animals?" in *Selected Essays*, ed. Geoff Dyer (London: Bloomsbury, 2001); Hilton Als, "You and Whose Army," in *White Girls* (San Francisco: McSweeney's, 2013).
11 Als, "You and Whose Army," 301.
12 Pater, *Renaissance*, 111.
13 Als, "Tristes Tropiques," in *White Girls*, 47.
14 Bernard Williams, *Moral Luck, Philosophical Papers 1973–1980* (Cambridge: Cambridge University Press, 1981), 21.
15 Ibid., 23.
16 David Wojnarowicz, *Close to the Knives* (New York: Vintage, 1991), 87–88.
17 Hilton Als, "The Art of the Essay No. 3," *The Paris Review* 225 (Summer 2018): 138–164; 143.
18 Ralph Waldo Emerson, "Experience," in *Essential Writings*, 307.
19 Joanna Field [Marion Milner], "First Questions," in *A Life of One's Own* (Los Angeles: Tarcher, 1981), 29, 31.
20 James Baldwin, *The Fire Next Time* (New York: Vintage, 1992), 43.
21 Michel de Montaigne, "An Apology for Raymond Sebond," in Montaigne, *Complete Essays* trans. M. A. Screech (London: Penguin, 2003), 505. Sennett's translation (see below) substitutes "playing" for Screech's "passing time."

22 Richard Sennett, "Montaigne's Cat," in *Together: The Rituals, Pleasures and Politics of Cooperation* (New Haven, CT: Yale University Press, 2012). For more detail about Montaigne's essays as a creative response to deadly clashes of doctrinal certainty, see Stephen Toulmin, *Cosmopolis: The Hidden Agenda of Modernity* (Chicago: University of Chicago Press, 1990).

23 See Christopher Bollas, *The Shadow of the Object: Psychoanalysis of the Unthought Known* (New York: Columbia University Press, 1989), 31–37.

24 Adam Phillips, "Narcissism, For and Against," in *One Way and Another: New and Selected Essays* (London: Hamish Hamilton, 2013), 147.

25 Ibid., 151.

26 Lionel Trilling, *Sincerity and Authenticity* (Cambridge, MA: Harvard University Press, 1971), 1.

27 On the transition during this period from the "old society," see Harold Perkin, *The Origins of Modern English Society*, second ed. (London: Routledge, 2002), 17–62.

28 Charles Lamb, *Complete Works and Letters* (New York: Modern Library, 1935), 52.

29 Lamb calls this person the "Scotsman"; he is referring to James Mill, chief codifier of Benthamite utilitarianism and social reformer.

30 Lamb, *Complete Works*, 52.

31 Ibid., 107.

32 Ibid., 63.

33 Walter Pater, "Charles Lamb," in *Appreciations, with an Essay on Style* (London: Macmillan, 1895), 112.

II

SAIKAT MAJUMDAR

Essay and Empire

In "The Novel in Africa," one of the nine fictional sketches that make up J. M. Coetzee's collection *Elizabeth Costello*, fierce arguments about literary form, modernity, and culture shape and disrupt personal relationships.[1] Most of this debate surrounds a lecture given by Emmanuel Egudu, a Nigerian novelist who now makes a living as a speaker on luxury cruise ships. In this particular lecture, Egudu makes certain significant claims about African culture and storytelling. Elizabeth Costello, the Australian novelist who delivers a lecture of her own, finds most of Egudu's arguments pretentious and disingenuous. Costello's and Egudu's lectures occupy centerstage in this text where the arc of a narrative and the claim of an idea appear locked in a mutual bid for dominance. While the lectures and the arguments arising out of them seem to dominate most of the text, it ends with a flash of Costello's memory, one that lays bare aspects of the once-intimate relation between the two leading characters that threaten to belie the intellectual and ideological force of their arguments. Their difference, it suddenly seems, is not merely about ideas: It also runs on a different plane, in the shared past of their sexual encounter, things left behind but not forgotten.

The structure of "The Novel in Africa," as with most of the texts in *Elizabeth Costello*, is deceptive. It is shaped by the play of ideas, which is almost always placed in an inconsistent relation with the behavior of the characters involved. The apparent centrality of the ideational in these texts recalls the European novel of ideas, perhaps best exemplified by the work of Robert Musil. More specifically, it evokes a hybrid mode of intervention that has been described by scholars such as Thomas Harrison and Randi Saloman as "essayism" – a sometimes inchoate fusion of the essay and fiction. Essayism, according to Saloman, is both "a genre and a mode," a rhetorical feature that infiltrates the novel and, in fact, helps to produce the high modern novel itself.[2]

The best-known protagonist of this novelistic essayism is Ulrich in Robert Musil's *The Man without Qualities*, who articulates the defining dilemma of being caught between the contradictory demands of truth and subjectivity: "A man who wants the truth becomes a scholar; a man who wants to give free range to his subjectivity may become a writer; but what should a man do who wants something in between?"[3] Responding to Georg Lukács's claim that the essay belongs to the realm of art, Theodor Adorno points to the inherent modernity of the genre in its fusion of art and science.[4] "In this outlook subscribed to by a wide range of European thinkers from Goethe and Friedrich Schlegel onward," writes Harrison, "experience is a process of flux and becoming, a subsuming of relatively stable forms (configurations of 'being') that 'becoming' breaks down and reconfigures." The impulse behind this hybrid, inchoate genre is human life itself. "Essayism," Harrison argues, is "an even better name for the process, not envisioning its teleology (power, survival, advancement) so much as its self-testing drive."[5]

What I find particularly captivating about the essayism of "The Novel in Africa" is that it posits a contradiction between the ideational and the fictional. A trajectory of argument emerges through the text only to reveal its limitation at the end before other forces of human motivation that fracture its integrity. The contradiction heightens and foregrounds the corrupted quality of the essayistic. As a form simultaneously seduced by the artistic and the scientific, it constitutes a conception of the human subject that is remarkable in its verisimilitude: intimate, vulnerable, and real. The conception of the fallible subject makes up an important model of humanism that has been memorably foregrounded by Edward Said. In his posthumous publication *Humanism and Democratic Criticism*, Said pointed to the "radically incomplete, insufficient, provisional, disputable, and arguable" element of "humanistic knowledge" as noted by Giambattista Vico.[6] The Viconian model of humanism remains for Said a meaningful alternative model of Enlightenment modernity, held in contrast to the objective certainty proposed by the Cartesian vision of apprehending reality that has shaped the Enlightenment more decisively.

The humanism of the European Renaissance was the philosophical context within which Montaigne sought to define and illustrate the modern essay. But his conception of the form, as well as that of the subject that shapes it – "the inner life of the self," as Stephen Greenblatt points out – was remarkably sensitive to the fluidity of the archive.[7] Said, who, in his later work, critiqued postmodern theory's onslaught on the humanist conception of the self, did not draw a particular connection between the form of the essay and the critical ambivalence rooted in his Viconian humanism, but he did make an important note of the genre's amorphous nature in *The World, the Text, and the Critic*. Evoking Lukács, he points to the irony inherent in the genre's interpretative ambition. "Thus the essay's mode is ironic," he writes, "which means first that the form is patently insufficient in its intellectuality with regard to living experience and, second, that the very form of the essay, its being an essay, is an ironic destiny with regard to the great questions of life."[8]

As a tentative, unfinished model of knowledge production – one that is a hybrid of the scientific and the subjective – the essay invokes a dismantling of the notion of mastery. Julietta Singh has recently argued the unmaking of mastery as crucial to the various processes of decolonization. In her book *Unthinking Mastery*, Singh reveals the quiet complicities between colonial domination and other forms of mastery thought to be innocuous or even beneficial – including epistemological and intellectual ones. To master an instrument, an archive, or a language is usually imagined as laudable, and "yet as a pursuit," Singh argues, "mastery invariably and relentlessly reaches toward the indiscriminate control over something – whether human or inhuman, animate or inanimate."[9] Mastery involves an inevitable submission of something. Inasmuch as mastery requires "a rupturing of the object being mastered" – since the object must be rendered weaker than the master – mastery becomes "a splitting of the object that is mastered from itself, a way of estranging the mastered object from its previous state of being."[10] Viewed this way, mastery ends up being a kind of exclusionary humanism, one driven by a decisive master-slave dialectic where the emergence of a victorious human subject is contingent on the violence and domination it can inflict on subordinated modalities.

Failure builds a natural bridge of affinity between the fallible genre of the essay and postcolonial consciousness. The various forms of fallibility historically identified in the genre of the essay – the tentative, the unfinished, and the imperfect – add up to a freedom from mastery that is not only resonant with the Saidian model of flawed humanism, but is also peculiarly conducive to the consciousness of the colonized and continues to resonate with the aspirational narratives of decolonization. One of the most moving instances of the literary articulation of this fallibility is the figure of the postcolonial critic and cultural commentator as an amateur practitioner. The Saidian vision of the ironic critical ambition embodied by the essay is particularly realized in the critical intervention made by the postcolonial essayist from the colonial periphery, in whose work amateur knowledge becomes a perpetually unfinished postcolonial project.

An Epistemology of Flaws

The writer defined by the failure of epistemological mastery populates the expanse of the British Empire. While their limited or flawed epistemology is a function of their liminal position between vernacular displacement and metropolitan aspiration, these writers' personally voiced criticism of cultural and historical phenomena is articulated in sensitively imagined and crafted essays. This tradition connects late-colonial migrants such as V. S. Naipaul and C. L. R. James with early-postcolonial figures such as Nirad C. Chaudhuri, moving to the trenchant anti-imperial voices of Jamaica Kincaid and Arundhati Roy in the late twentieth and early twenty-first centuries. Whether their genre of choice is the memoir or the manifesto, criticism or travelogue, the hybrid, fallible intervention of these writers is caught forever between the sensory embodiment of fiction and the ideational abstraction of the essay. A fractured consciousness that is the inevitable consequence of empire becomes the natural ambience of essayism.

A particularly revealing moment comes in the late twentieth century when a figure from provincial India, Pankaj Mishra, embarks on a project of critical amateurism that is inevitable in a postcolonial periphery as he sets out to interpret culture and literature from a moment in Western culture with which he has no scholarly or affiliative relation. Mishra's memorable 1998 essay "Edmund Wilson in Benares" opens with his failure to write about the American critic Edmund Wilson following the standards of professional Western scholarship.[11] Lacking contextual knowledge of either France or America that might have helped shape a professional commentary on Wilson's writing on Flaubert, Mishra ended up reading the American critic in relation to the people and the atmosphere around him at that time: twentieth-century Uttar Pradesh, with its crime, unemployment, and caste-ridden politics. It is a deeply moving, idiosyncratic reading where the two planes of reality come to cast unexpected light on each other. The essay that emerges from this strange engagement is an intimate and revealing one, where the innate humanism of literature bridges historical realities far apart from each other.

Such failure gives birth to the paradoxical commentator whose lack of mastery over his subject becomes an unexpected source of insight. Elsewhere, I have read this as the peculiar predicament of the colonial or postcolonial thinker who arrives from the provincial periphery with a desire and aspiration for the culture of the metropolis.[12] An ideal protagonist of this desire who straddles the colonial and the decolonized years is the Bengali memoirist and commentator Nirad C. Chaudhuri, whose essays on English culture etch a fascinating trajectory of amateur ethnography as seen from the peculiar vantage point of the formerly colonized. In *A Passage to England*, chronicling the experience of his travels to England and France – his very first trip outside India at the age of fifty-seven – Chaudhuri provides a unique perspective on aspects of English life and culture that makes up a perfect complement to essays on similar subjects by George Orwell and Virginia Woolf.

Unlike Woolf and Orwell, however, Chaudhuri's essays are marked by a clear paradox. This is the gulf between his detailed, bookish knowledge of English culture and his simultaneous lack of real-life experience of it, which often makes for unexpected surprises. It is a strangely productive lack of mastery – which I have sought to elaborate as a form of "provincial cosmopolitanism" – that belongs only to the thinker from the colonial periphery.[13] Its title a clear play on E. M. Forster's novel *A Passage to India*, *A Passage to England* collects essays that outline a (post)colonial subject's relation to the metropolitan heart of the empire so far shaped entirely through books – and suddenly realized for the first time in a trip to England. The nature of this relationship is obvious enough for his family back home to notice. Reading a letter from Chaudhuri describing his experience of England, one of his sons writes in a letter to his friend: "Father has lived too long in the world of books in regard to these places, don't you think so?"[14] Like Mishra a few decades after him, Chaudhuri retains an attachment to Western, particularly European, literature, which he is ready to defend with the force of conviction of one who has, at long last, come to experience the land described in the literature he has read for decades: "English literature is the best guide for foreigners to the English scene because it is more closely the product of its geographical environment, more ecological, than any other literature I have read. I think English literature has gone farthest in fusing Nature and the spirit of man."[15]

Appreciation from Chaudhuri, however, always appears more real when it also reveals the sharp fangs of irony:

> An Englishman of this type resented our devotion to English literature as a sort of illicit attention to his wife, whom he himself was neglecting for his mistress, sport. Therefore he cast the Tenth Commandment in our teeth, tried to cure us of our literary-mindedness, and at the same time sneered at it. The Indians who lent themselves to this treatment and as a result acquired the anti-literary pose, came mostly from the very wealthy and princely classes, who, as Kipling put it, were bear-led by their English tutors.[16]

For Chaudhuri, the most meaningful tie an Indian can have with England is through art and literature: "The only ties felt in the heart that we can have with England are those created by the things of the mind. The Englishmen who did their best to break those ties have lost the Indian Empire, and the Indians who allowed them to do so are the most bored or querulous set of foreigners who visit England."[17]

But the bookish admirer of English literature meets a great surprise at the Shakespeare celebrations in Stratford, on the 391st anniversary of the poet's birthday. Shakespeare, Chaudhuri realizes, continues to be a living and breathing part of English culture, rather than being merely textualized, as he tended to appear from the periphery of empire: "in contemporary England, he seems to have become popular entertainment. England had not degraded the old playwright, actor, and stage manager into a mere author."[18] It was a startling realization, an insight almost after the manner of Raymond Williams, that culture is ordinary, including what appears, from the colonial distance, to be the very pinnacle of literature. Of the enthusiastic audience of the play, he writes: "It seemed to be composed of ordinary middle-class people, who in no way answered my preconceived notion of what a Shakespeare scholar or enthusiast should look like."[19]

Evocative essays by late-colonial and postcolonial aspirants to forms of metropolitan culture reveal ironic reversals at every turn. For the postcolonial subject, lack of mastery shapes a critical performance that is ironical many times over: Celebration and satire reveal impossible mutual entanglements; irony directed at one's epistemological inadequacy gives way to the critique of performative cultures in the metropolis. In Chaudhuri's Trinidadian contemporary C. L. R. James (who started publishing decades before Chaudhuri), we see another model of aspiration for metropolitan modernity. The arc of James's intellectual development clearly marks him out, like Chaudhuri, as an ideological product of the British empire, and yet this development is marked by an odd flirtation with the systematic structure of colonial pedagogy. In pointed contrast to Chaudhuri's barely hidden disdain for the English obsession with sports, James is deeply absorbed in the aesthetics of cricket; indeed, he elevates the sport above literature as a force of culture in nineteenth-century England. There is something of the enlightened amateur, and something powerfully plebeian, in the cultural critic who can thus equate sports with literature. Literary criticism, James unsurprisingly insists, *must* be for a popular audience. This is evident not only in his provocative argument for a popular tradition that continues all the way from classical Greek playwrights to popular twentieth-century filmmakers, but also, and most significantly, through his spirited but eclectic engagement with the literary culture of Bloomsbury.

Two essays from James's *Letters from London*, "The Bloomsbury Atmosphere" and "Bloomsbury Again," together describe about ninety-six frenetic hours spent by James in Bloomsbury in 1932.[20] It is one of the most arresting narrative accounts of the physical environs of the epicenter of literary modernism, its idiosyncratic networks and artistic vibrancy, as well as the seamlessly bohemian lifestyle of its artists. Truly, he spent these four days in a euphoric state of play. It started with a lecture by Edith Sitwell at the Student Movement House, where James crossed swords with Sitwell in the earnest spirit of banter. He followed it with a whole night of conversation with his new London friends and reading the poems of Rabindranath Tagore. Returning home, he barely had a couple of hours of fitful rest between six and eight before another friend showed up at his doorstep, read aloud Sitwell's poetry, and talked about and sang a Handel aria. After he left, James walked around Oxford Street, spent some time in Bumpus's bookshop, came back home to rest for an hour, and then went out again to meet friends with whom he read Chekhov's *Three Sisters*. He came back home that night at the surprisingly early hour of midnight. The following morning, he spent some time in bed reading the newspapers and literary periodicals, and then spent the rest of the morning talking and arguing with friends in cafés and common rooms in the neighborhood, before just about making it in time to the Society of International Studies for a lecture he was scheduled to give there. About the end of the evening, he writes: "You might think that was enough for one day. You simply do not know Bloomsbury."[21] After the lecture, James and his friends went to a café at around midnight, where they spent an hour before going to supper at the home of someone whom he had never met before. After a delightful meal with a fascinating set of people, James went home at around four in the morning. He spent the next morning browsing books at the Times Book Club and went home for lunch, which was a "hopeless failure" as he had no company.[22] At half past two, a couple came to see him, and he spent the rest of the afternoon and evening with them, returning home after one. The stimulants quickly went from tea to beer and whiskey, and by the time they were done with Mussolini, Wagner, Rossini, Verdi, Thackeray, and Shakespeare, they had also made short work of fifty cigarettes between the three of them. In fact, the evening was punctuated merely because they had run out of provisions: "At ten o'clock the beer and the cigarettes were finished and it was time to do something. A typical Bloomsbury problem."[23]

But this high-energy narration leads up to a whimpering anticlimax. At the end of it all, James writes: "Let no one who wishes to write believe that all I have described is life. In one important sense it is not life at all. It is a highly artificial form of living and I would not be surprised if a great deal of what modern work suffers from is not to be traced to that very cause."[24] After quoting a poignant stanza from Wordsworth's "The Solitary Reaper," he continues: "Wordsworth did not learn to write like that by running about in Bloomsbury or any other literary quarter talking about books and art and music. These things come from deeper down."[25]

I don't think it is coincidental that this critique of the idea of "the artistic life," as canonized by Western modernism, comes from a writer from colonial Trinidad who merely steps into this role for a little while as an enthusiastic outsider. One who appears eager to master the life and lifestyle of the metropolitan artist bares ironic cracks in his desire for this mastery; the need to immerse himself in the iconic rhythm of Bloomsbury transforms into an ironic critique of that very rhythm.

All that the immersion into milieus such as Bloomsbury, James goes on to say, can give you is form and technique, which is secondary in importance. Art comes not from the frenetic excitement of the surface, but from the unglamorous calm that lies deeper down, entwined into the marginal moments of the everyday bereft of aesthetic self-consciousness. It is a critique that I believe can also be recognized more obliquely in certain canonized modernists who also migrated from the colonial periphery to the fashionable hubs of metropolitan literary culture, such as James Joyce and Katherine Mansfield. The bustle of Bloomsbury can make us forget that the true source of action is far more deeply rooted in the quotidian world of primal sustenance than in the fashionable milieus of artistic life valorized by metropolitan literary culture. The former world, James reminds us, is "the basis of life and great writing and of great art in any part of the world." Playing the amateur modernist in Bloomsbury for four days, the young writer from Trinidad offers us this anticlimactic caveat.

The Anger of Smallness

The apparent aspiration for the culture of the metropolitan center of empire is fascinating in essayists such as James and Chaudhuri, no less because of the critique of that culture they enact than the immersion into it they embody. No doubt, one enables the other. But the critique of empire embodied in the essay can be far more direct and vitriolic than the apparently aspirational position allowed in these essays. Arguably the most striking instance can be found in the Kenyan writer Ngũgĩ wa Thiong'o's *Decolonising the Mind*. The flagship essay in that collection, "The Language of African Literature," was for a long time seen to be locked in an intense ideological battle with the position assumed by his Nigerian contemporary Chinua Achebe in his essay "The African Writer and the English Language." Taken together, these two essays by these two iconic figures of African literature make up the defining debate about the aesthetic, ethical, and political viability of African writing in English as it raged in the years following the decolonization of sub-Saharan African nations.

Ngũgĩ's essay is a searing reminder of the fact that the soft power of culture and pedagogy is indispensable to the project of colonialism. "The night of the bullet," he writes unforgettably, "was followed by the morning of the chalk and the blackboard." I have taught this essay numerous times as a perfect illustration of the projects of what Louis Althusser calls "repressive and ideological state apparatuses" in colonized societies. These apparatuses work with devastating clarity on the young minds of students, who are particularly sensitive to the hegemonic work of ideology in a postcolonial society. While Ngũgĩ might be held guilty of romanticizing Kenya's precolonial past, his depiction of the shattering of the harmony of the private and public sphere of life by the jarring intrusion of colonial power is devastatingly appropriate.

> And then I went to school, a colonial school, and this harmony was broken. The language of my education was no longer the language of my culture ... English became the language of my formal education. In Kenya, English became more than a language: it was *the* language, and all others had to bow before it in deference.[26]

As colonialism comes to dominate the state, it assumes control over its ideological state apparatuses (crucially, the schools), and begins to unleash psychological violence in the private sphere. With hindsight, ideology reveals itself also as a mode of violence.

Perhaps the greatest insight offered by Ngũgĩ's incisive and polemical essay – one that lyrically fuses the artist, the activist, and the intellectual – is the inexorable relationship between culture and power. This fusion becomes just as evident in the formal structure of his rhetoric as in the themes that are inseparable from that structure: Incisive historical arguments give way to personal reminiscences, which make way for an interpretation of ideologies that takes on the structure of a manifesto; in the end, it is the affective texture of the manifesto that enthralls the reader as they emerge captivated by Ngũgĩ's polemic. English, for Ngũgĩ, is inseparable from the oppressive context of colonialism. It is here that Achebe differs crucially from him; that is, in his belief that English can be productively Africanized to produce a new literature. If for us, in the twenty-first century, Achebe's position seems more convincing, a more pervasive truth about the larger relation between language and power is the great gift of Ngũgĩ's polemic, which serves us well in a postcolonial world that continues to be ridden by the hierarchies of language shaped by the economic and political capital behind them.

The helpless imprisonment in the cage of the colonizer's language tunes the battle cry at the heart of another text of polemical essayism that bears a curious blood-kinship both to James's and Ngũgĩ's work: *A Small Place* by Jamaica Kincaid. For Kincaid, the colonizer's language strangles her within a toxic epistemology whose very values are skewed in the favor of the colonizer:

For isn't it odd that the only language I have in which to speak of this crime is the language of the criminal who committed this crime? And what can that really mean? For the language of the criminal can only contain the goodness of the criminal's deed. The language of the criminal can explain and express the deed only from the criminal's point of view ... the criminal understands the word "wrong" in this way: It is wrong when "he" doesn't get his fair share of profits from the crime just committed; he understands the word "bad" in this way: a fellow criminal betrayed a trust.[27]

A work of terrifying beauty, Kincaid's *A Small Place* is a fated intersection of the political hybridity identified with empire and the epistemological hybridity of the essay as perceived by thinkers from Montaigne to Musil and Adorno to Coetzee and beyond. Anjali Prabhu has pointed to the variegated vocabulary associated with hybridity, terms such as "diaspora, métissage, creolization, transculturation."[28] Hybridity, she reminds us, is represented by Bhabha, Hall, and Lionnet as the resistance and triumph of the subaltern over the hegemonic, but is criticized as an elite concept by Bhabha's critics, such as Benita Parry, who argue that the concept applies far more to "metropolitan elite émigrés and far less to migrant diasporas and even less to those who have 'stayed behind' in the (ex)colony."[29] However it is the third position outlined by Prabhu that resonates most with the tormented legacy that embodies the defiant and promiscuous fusing of form represented by *A Small Place*: "Hybridity, when carefully considered in its material reality, will reveal itself to actually be a history of slavery, colonialism, and rape, inherited in terms of race." As a painful history of "interracial identity," Prabhu reminds us, "it joins up with issues of choosing one's affiliations or having one's affiliations thrust upon one."[30]

It is this lack of choice and freedom that echoes in Kincaid's battle cry from the small place that is Antigua. I would suggest that we would understand the muddling hybridity of rhetoric – that of a letter, an essay, a pamphlet, a memoir, a manifesto, or a chronicle of history – that defines *A Small Place* if we remember this context where hybridity is far from a matter of free choice. The affective hybridity of this polemical text is the inevitable consequence of historical destiny – not only of its oppressions but also of its exclusions, of being relegated forever to "a small place" of slow time, of a nonmodern temporality. Just the way the English language comes to Kincaid as an enslaving force, the hybrid essayism of this text articulates a pain and anger that the author miraculously transforms into an affirmative force by the end of the text.

A powerful achievement of anticolonial essayism, Kincaid's text recalls the deceptive intimacy of Virginia Woolf's *Three Guineas*. Like *Three Guineas*, *A Small Place* speaks in the second person, especially in the striking opening sections, and like Woolf's text, it addresses its adversary. While for Woolf this was the prosperous, upper-class, educated man's son, for Kincaid it is the white tourist, "from North America, or worse, Europe," who comes to Antigua on a leisurely visit. Such a tourist is eager to soak in the island's natural beauty; along with it, he takes a keen anthropological interest in the poverty of its people, and the aesthetic appeal of the island's exclusion from the temporality of modernity: "you might see it as a sort of quaintness on part of these islanders," she writes, "these people descended from slaves – what a strange, unusual perception of time they have ... but perhaps in a world that is twelve miles long and nine miles wide (the size of Antigua) twelve years and twelve minutes and twelve days are all the same."[31]

The ironic beauty of this appeal is mired in the history (and historiography) of British colonialism and its neocolonial afterlife in the debt-traps spun by the International Monetary Fund and the World Bank. The irony comes alive in the "you," where the intimacy of the address simmers with anger, and the blistering anger in turn shapes a corrosive intimacy. Does fighting entail a kind of intimacy? Are we locked in an intimate embrace with those we hate with bitter passion? Kincaid's slim book raises such moving and shocking questions. What historical intimacy binds the colonizer with the colonized? The creditor and the debtor? The slave-owner and the enslaved?

Perhaps the greatest achievement of *A Small Place* is its tone. The pointed sarcasm of the opening section melts into the despair of self-incrimination, which in turn becomes indistinguishable from outrage at the rampage of history. The heartrending beauty of the last section is rooted in the book's innate sense of pain, and it is remarkable how a book of such anger and outrage ends with the celebration of a universal humanism that embraces the oppressor along with the oppressed. Can pain and anger heal? Here Kincaid enters a powerful tradition of Black anger, especially that articulated by women, from Alice Walker to Audre Lorde and beyond, where anger heals even as it burns. It is a deep acceptance of the amoral inevitability of history that makes for the peace of the conclusion:

> The people in Antigua now, the people who really think of themselves as Antiguans, are the descendants of those noble and exalted people, the slaves. Of course, the whole thing is, once you cease to be a master, once you throw off your master's yoke, you are no longer human rubbish, you are just a human being, and all the things that adds up to. So, too, with the slaves. Once they are no longer slaves, once they are free, they are no longer noble and exalted; they are just human beings.[32]

After the opening sections, the "you" vanishes from the book; the accusing finger moves away from the figure of the white tourist to direct its vitriol to larger, more pervasive forces, most crucially, the inevitable violence of modernity that drives the arrogance and avarice of the colonizer and eventually comes to corrupt the colonized – and even the decolonized – in its relentless pursuit of wealth.

The Critique of Capital

Over and above its innate power, A Small Place is a crucial text for postcolonial studies because it brings together the two forms of empire that shaped the twentieth century and held the Global South in a continuum of slavery, chronicling the inevitable passage of post-Renaissance European colonialism to forms of economic neocolonialism. For Antigua, this has meant the transition from British colonialism to the vicious cycle of conditional aid and loans with terms dictated by the International Monetary Fund and the World Bank. Stephanie Black, in her 2001 film Life and Debt, a cinematic interpretation of A Small Place, emphasizes the serpentine noose of neocolonialism, woven by the predatorial capitalism of the West and the unrelenting avarice of its multinational companies that hold the Caribbean islands in a stranglehold.

Over the decades, in an increasingly liberalized and globalized world, the various structures of neocolonial domination have come to gain support from market forces as well as from the ideology of neoliberalism. One of the most trenchant critiques of the different embodiments of twenty-first-century empire – from aggressive capitalism to forms of populist dictatorship – have come from the essays of Arundhati Roy. From waging a war against the building of big dams that displace India's tribal population, to resisting authoritarian rule that stokes hatred for minorities, Roy's essays and lectures have formed an influential part of postmillennial India's critical conscience. This conscience is embodied in a rhetoric that draws fully on Roy's strengths as a novelist. Playing with myth and narrative, in the potently titled essay "The Reincarnation of Rumpelstiltskin," she launches a vitriolic attack on multinational companies who want to restructure the world's water distribution system by putting "a market price on water." It would be a nightmarish excuse for a world. "Evian," she writes, "could own the water. Rand the earth, Enron the air. Old Rumpelstiltskin could be the handsomely paid supreme CEO."[33]

In an essay of delicious and terrifying irony, "The Ladies Have Feelings, So ... Shall We Leave It to the Experts?" Roy brings up the hypocrisy entrenched in the hyphenated term that her polemical essays have sometimes earned her: "writer-activist." A double, foldable term, "writer-activist" embodies a safe and reactionary notion: that to be a writer and an activist are two different things, that no one can be both – and if they are, they deserve an accordingly convertible appellation, "like a sofa-bed."[34] But Roy's essays immediately make it clear that she is at her most incisive and persuasive – and most insightful – when her polemic is directed at language and its various injustices. Unforgettably, in her collection *Listening to Grasshoppers*, she writes:

> Today, words like Progress and Development have become interchangeable with economic "Reforms," Deregulation, and Privatization. Freedom has come to mean choice. It has less to do with the human spirit than with different brands of deodorant. Market no longer means a place where you buy provisions. The "Market" is a de-territorialized space where faceless corporations do business, including buying and selling "futures." Justice has come to mean human rights (and of those, as they say, "a few will do").[35]

Like a diverse range of philosophers and artists before her – from Wittgenstein and Lacan to Orwell – Roy realizes the enormity of this semiotic onslaught. Her relation with language is urgent and intimate enough for her to understand that language is no passive reflection of history. It is rather the linguistic choices we make that shape our consciousness and our sense of reality. The newest, sometimes invisible avatars of imperialism know this well:

> This theft of language, this technique of usurping words and deploying them like weapons, of using them to mask intent and to mean exactly the opposite of what they have traditionally meant, has been one of the most brilliant strategic victories of the tsars of the new dispensation. It has allowed them to marginalize their detractors, deprive them of a language to voice their critique and dismiss them as being "anti-progress," "anti-development," "anti-reform," and of course "anti-national" – negativists of the worst sort. Talk about saving a river or protecting a forest and they say, "Don't you believe in Progress?" To people whose land is being submerged by dam reservoirs, and whose homes are being bulldozed, they say, "Do you have an alternative development model?" To those who believe that a government is duty bound to provide people with basic education, health care, and social security, they say, "You're against the market." And who except a cretin could be against markets?[36]

This is the moment when the hyphen between the "writer" and the "activist" collapses. To be a writer suddenly becomes synonymous with being an activist, and vice versa. The struggle must be launched and sustained on the plane of language. "To reclaim these stolen words," she writes, "requires explanations that are too tedious for a world with a short attention span, and too expensive in an era when Free Speech has become unaffordable for the poor. This language heist may prove to be the keystone of our undoing."

Like Kincaid, who calls out the relentless continuity between colonialism and neocolonialism, Roy has been one of the most powerful essayistic voices of dissent against empire in the twenty-first century. She stages the difficult relation of art with politics, narrative with argument, and she has also received much criticism for these sometimes-difficult juxtapositions. In hindsight, the reasons Roy turned to the essay after the success of her debut novel seem clear enough; while *The God of Small Things*, too, is as trenchant politically as it is poignant, the diversity of marginalized causes with which she has aligned herself over the last couple of decades demands the generic fluidity of the essay, which has moved from the performative urgency of the delivered lecture to the perturbed force of journalistic prose and the anecdotal texture of the personal essay. It is hard to deny that Roy's fiction has suffered from this turn to the essay: To most readers, her second novel, *The Ministry of Utmost Happiness*, was a great disappointment after the power and beauty of *The God of Small Things*, and the jarringly polemical, sometimes pedantic essayisms in the second novel must take their share of the blame. But in the important series of essays she has written between the two novels – and continues to write – she embodies the crux of the relation between the essay and empire. Incensed and sometimes fallible, always warm with life, she inherits a vibrant tradition from Woolf and Kincaid of criticizing the masculinity of political and economic militarism that empire has forced upon the world. She couldn't be more different from the feted Australian novelist of Coetzee's imagination, and yet in the honesty, sincerity, and even the fallibility of her discourse, in the stark refusal of epistemological as well as political mastery, she, like Elizabeth Costello, epitomizes essayism at its most incisive and its most vulnerable, its eternal derision of the arrogance of empire.

Notes

1 J. M. Coetzee, "The Novel in Africa," in *Elizabeth Costello* (New York: Penguin, 2004).
2 Randi Saloman, *Virginia Woolf's Essayism* (Edinburgh: Edinburgh University Press, 2014), 3.
3 Robert Musil, *The Man Without Qualities*, trans. Sophie Wilkins (New York: Vintage, 1996)
4 Theodor W. Adorno, "The Essay as Form," in *Notes to Literature*, ed. Rolf Tiedemann, trans. Shierry Weber Nicholson (New York: Columbia University Press, 1991)
5 Thomas J. Harrison, *Essayism: Conrad, Musil, and Pirandello* (Baltimore, MD: Johns Hopkins University Press, 1992).
6 Edward W. Said, *Humanism and Democratic Criticism* (New York: Columbia University Press, 2004), 12.

7 Stephen Greenblatt, "Shakespeare's Montaigne," in *Shakespeare's Montaigne: The Florio Translation of the Essays* (New York: New York Review Books, 2014), 9.
8 Said, *The World, the Text, and the Critic* (Cambridge, MA: Harvard University Press, 1983), 52.
9 Julietta Singh, *Unthinking Mastery: Dehumanism and Decolonial Entanglements* (Durham, NC: Duke University Press, 2018), 10.
10 Ibid.
11 Pankaj Mishra, "Edmund Wilson in Benares," in *The Picador Book of Modern Indian Literature*, ed. Amit Chaudhuri (London: Picador, 2001), 370.
12 Saikat Majumdar, "The Critic as Amateur," *New Literary History* 48.1 (2017): 1–25.
13 Majumdar, "The Provincial Polymath: The Curious Cosmopolitanism of Nirad C. Chaudhuri," *PMLA* 130.2 (2015): 269–283.
14 Nirad C. Chaudhuri, *A Passage to England* (London: Macmillan, 1959), 14.
15 Ibid., 15.
16 Ibid., 16.
17 Ibid.
18 Ibid., 141.
19 Ibid., 142.
20 Cyril Lionel Robert James, *Letters from London: Seven Essays by C. L. R. James* (Trinidad and Tobago: Prospect Press, 2003), 19.
21 Ibid., 50.
22 Ibid., 48
23 Ibid., 50
24 Ibid., 52.
25 Ibid., 53.
26 Ngũgĩ wa Thiong'o, "The Language of African Literature," *Colonial Discourse and Post-colonial Theory: A Reader*, eds. Laura Chrisman and Patrick Williams (New York: Columbia University Press, 2014), 438.
27 Jamaica Kincaid, *A Small Place* (New York: Farrar, Straus and Giroux, 1988), 32.
28 Anjali Prabhu, *Hybridity: Limits, Transformations, Prospects* (Albany: State University of New York Press, 2007), 1
29 Ibid., 12.
30 Ibid.
31 Kincaid, *A Small Place*, 9.
32 Ibid., 80–81.
33 Arundhati Roy, *The Algebra of Infinite Justice* (New Delhi: Penguin, 2001), 151.
34 Ibid., 196.
35 Arundhati Roy, *Field Notes on Democracy: Listening to Grasshoppers* (Chicago: Haymarket Books, 2009) 12.
36 Ibid.

GRACE LAVERY

Unqueering the Essay

I have a tattoo on my chest that reads "take me out to the beach and I'll tell you my secret name."[1] I won't tell *you* my secret name; in fact, when I was taken out to the beach yesterday (not by *you*, obviously, but the same beach Stephin Merritt was writing about, as it goes) I realized that there might not have been a secret after all. "Everyone knows what the female complaint is: women live for love, and love is the gift that keeps on taking," you wrote.[2] I wonder how the word "female" hit you – and here the "you," until now so intimately addressed to *you*, the reading reader, must be taken to refer to a reader who'll never read this, the late Lauren Berlant – in recent years. You blurbed *Females: A Concern*, a book by a young feminist whose name was anything but secret, but whose complaint was all too real.[3] The title of that book presumably derived from yours, switching the commercial "concern" for the medicalizing "complaint," but its "female" means something quite different, an echo of a powerful ablative absolute:

> Life in this society being, at best, an utter bore and no aspect of society being at all relevant to women, there remains to civic-minded, responsible, thrill-seeking females only to overthrow the government, eliminate the money system, institute complete automation and destroy the male sex.[4]

To begin an essay with this breezy *collatio* is to signal confidence in one's own charisma, and very little in the *SCUM Manifesto* gives us reason to doubt the ferocious intimacy with which its author was almost literally armed. But we also know – you would teach us, let's say – that we would be unwise to assume what this manifesto could demonstrate were it to be used as evidence in *The People v. Valerie Solanas* – whether it proved premeditation for attempted murder, for example, or whether its foreclosed dream of a foreclosed utopia betokened more metaphysical, though perhaps no less murderous, violence. Essays aren't evidence – and "everyone knows" it.

After sitting in a body for over a year, this essay, "Unqueering the Essay," is disgorged onto a laptop on a day in June 2021, the day that I learned of your death. I find myself needing something more, less, or other than what "everyone knows," more than what "there remains [...] only," and yet what I have is the archive, which is what everyone knows. Do *I* know anything else? Emphatically not: I know that on the two occasions when I asked you to do something, and you declined, you were more courteous than demurrals have any right to be; I know that you delivered "Structures of Unfeeling: *Mysterious Skin*" while perched on one leg, like a little yogic stripling.[5] But who am I kidding, I didn't know *you*, except the you that everyone knows. Luckily, that was rather a lot. In the midst of an interview with my friend Charlie Markbreiter, you told him that you were trans, that you had always been trans, that you went by they/them pronouns.[6] To me, and to (I would have guessed) many like me, this was a confirmation of what everyone knew, shifting that past subjunctive ("I would have guessed") into a diffused, deponent present ("everyone knows").

We write *laterally* when we write *essayistically*, etymologically downstream from the Latin *exagium*, meaning both "a weight" and "a weighing," both that which is used to measure the weight of an object and the act of establishing equilibrium on a scale. You were a Scorp, but on the Libra side – a Halloween babe. It often seems as though everyone who loathes me is a Scorp, but of course I merely run afraid of them because I am a double Pisces: flowy, self-indulgent, and vague, albeit that the remainder of my chart, more or less, is in Aries (a cock in a frock). As both weight and weighing, an essay assumes the hydraulically improbable task of being *both* the counterweight against which the value of a given object will be assessed, *and* the act of assessment, both participant and observation. I suppose it is this double-function of the essay that is responsible for an odd feature of the odd genre of "famous queer literary critics writing about famous queer literary critics," a collection that would include (among others) Barbara Johnson's "Bringing Out D. A. Miller," D. A. Miller's "Bringing Out Roland Barthes," Lauren Berlant's "Eve Sedgwick, Once More," and (the primary focus of the present essay) Terry Castle's "Desperately Seeking Susan."[7] The paradoxical feature: an expressed desire to wrest, from the colleague, an avowal that, apparently, the colleague has already performed. The paradoxical nature of this generic expectation is brandished, conspicuously, by its practitioners. Barbara Johnson, beginning her essay on the modalities of outness yielded by Miller's reading of Barthes, begins by acknowledging that the phrase "Bringing Out D. A. Miller" "sounds like the equivalent of "Barging through an Open Door."[8] Not merely redundant, but foolhardy, and liable to trip one up.

We might refer to this double-function – or, really, we might decide not to, and do something else instead – as the *queerness* of the essay. The phrase seems automatically tiresome, doesn't it? In the era of *drones are queer*, for example; or when a resurgent LG-kinda-B movement seems determined to unreclaim the term; when the ontological security of sexuality and the sexual object seems to have become, inexplicably, a going political concern.[9] Fucking *essays* are queer now, great – next, homework. The fatigue tells us a familiar story: that "queer" was to the 2010s what "modernism" was to the 2000s and "deconstruction" was to the 1980s – a ballooning cultural category absorbing and denaturing everything with which it came into contact, migrating far from the recherché scenes of the coalitional LGBT front in opposition to post-HIV/AIDS respectability politics; unpopular European avant-garde literature of the 1920s; and a minor epistemological dimension of Heideggerian phenomenology. This isn't a criticism; on the contrary – *bliss* was it in that bright dawn to be alive, but to be tenured was very heaven. Nonetheless, as the bodies thin, the party dwindles, and now that you have left us, I can't locate the fulcrum on which this sun will be levered over the horizon. Last night, I was at a cabaret show at the Crown and Anchor on Commercial Street, hearing short, hortative anecdotes about the meaning of Pride, and how far "the LGBT community" has come. Soon, I thought, that so-called community will at last summon the self-respect to abandon its feeble attempt to maintain that fourth, unwanted, quarter, and succumb to the antagonisms that bind the first to the second, and the third to the pack. The next morning, I heard that you, Lauren Berlant, the one indisputably trans indisputable genius, had died – and had found myself desperate to protest, all my cynicism in force, that you were just *queering death*, that I am now *queering mourning*, that perhaps you've *transed the eternal binary*, you've *transed gender for the final time, captain*, you've *gone where no nonbinary genius has gone before*. But death isn't subject to the optic switch between observation and participant that conditions the essay – it can't be verbed, much as "Internet" can't be pluralized.

Too much observation, not enough weight. More pedantically: Queer writers have often been drawn to write essayistically, not merely because essayistic writing might be understood and even defined as the writerly showing of a bit of leg, but more because essays differ from other genres of argumentative writing in formalizing the eminently queer switch between objective and subjective methods of analysis. The melancholy consequences of toggling between subject and object are offset, if they are, by the satisfaction of motley. On the other hand, the essayistic glimpse challenges the coalitional dimension of queerness, if it does, by confronting the flirtatiously self-disclosing subject with a reader whose desires, cathexes, aversions, and identities cannot but appear, if they do, alarmingly monodimensional by contrast. Over time, reader becomes writer – in fact, becomes obituarian – and the catalytic chain continues indefinitely. But at the scene of the glimpse, the essay presents the exhibitionist subject herself as scantily clad behind words, while a reader – clumsily arrayed merely in whatever flesh happens to have fallen in place – cannot but hoot for more, different, or contradictory disclosures.

*

At the Paris Dyke March this weekend, a group of women carried a banner that read "les LESBIENNES n'aiment PAS les PENIS," lesbians don't like dicks.[10] No (cis) lesbian reader of the present essay whose advice I sought in composition and editing – does it disappoint *you* to know that you are neither the sole, nor indeed the original, reader of this work? – failed to point out that, whatever this banner's demerits as a political slogan, it's a bust as an empirical claim, as plenty of lesbians (cis) have been enthusiastically heralding penises, their own and others', for a good four decades by now. Nonetheless, its deployment of a putatively unobjectionable descriptive statement as though it were a normative claim has long been one of the characteristic stylistic markers of the anti-trans activists who call themselves "gender critical feminists."[11] The most notorious of these sleights-of-hand is the now ubiquitous slogan "a woman is an adult human female," a line whose iambic-pentametric precision broadcasts its singular aesthetic feature: the self-evidence that contests any "woo" ambiguities that would drag each and every one of these words into the mire the moment that one looks at them for more than a second.[12] The anti-trans literalist's literary mode takes straightforward (albeit inaccurate) self-evidence as the poetic sign for a no-bullshit approach to questions of sexual identity, turning away from the meandering striptease of the essay towards the quickening beat of the catechism, such that each of the slogans, in French as well as English, must be easily adaptable to the tune of "She'll Be Coming Round the Mountain When She Comes."[13] See also, "a female has large, immotile gametes." From prose to verse to formula: The apparent purpose of the descriptive-as-normative move is to sustain the illusion that, although you can't say anything anymore, nonetheless 2 + 2 = 4, and it takes only the necessary impertinence to point out that the emperor is naked; but the dream of such a catechism would not merely be the displacement of one inadequate indexical system by a taxonomy of mathematical self-evidence, but the ontologization (or reontologization) of sexuality as the governing truth of social relations. The strategic gist, though not yet the prosody, of the verse-not-vers crowd was proudly on display on the signage of the group "Get the L Out," an anti-trans lesbian organization that hijacked London Pride in 2018. "Lesbian = female homosexual" especially bears the unmistakable mark of apparent,

unobjectionable self-evidence through the transcription of desires and identities into deductively rationalizable metalanguage. There is more at stake
in these slogans than questions of literary form, but there are *also* questions
of literary form: specifically, the queerness of the essay form, the genre that
denatures the "=" in both "2 + 2 = 4" and "lesbian = female homosexual,"
postulating worlds in which one "two" and another "two" might be irrec-
oncilable into a single "four," or indeed where "lesbian," "female," and
"homosexual" entail complex and perhaps even contradictory predicates.[14]

None of this quite requires calibration; to write an essay claiming that
one cannot write an adequate definition for social types such as "lesbian,"
"woman," and "sexuality" without doing so in the form of an essay might
risk merely affirming the implicit prejudices of the genre. But the claim that
the essay *imposes* such inadequacies of relation might be worth testing by
examining, to my mind, the most vigorously prosecuted essayistic sally of
the century to date, Terry Castle's obituary of the essayist Susan Sontag,
"Desperately Seeking Susan," published in the *London Review of Books*
on March 17 (my birthday: double Pisces), 2005. At the core of the enco-
mium Terry Castle (Libra) writes for her recently deceased friend (Capri-
corn) is the curious relationship that Sontag had to self-disclosure. Curious,
partly because of its lack of curiosity. Sontag's *New York Times* obituary,
it is true, had made no reference to the author's sexuality at all, but Castle notes that Allan Gurganus, in the *Advocate*, had made reference to the
"disparity between her professed fearlessness and her actual self-protective
closetedness," where the visibility of a closet might be thought to imply
the presence of an invisible homosexual.[15] Gurganus and Castle were only
the most prominent of many voices expressing frustration with Sontag's
tight-lippedness regarding sexual identity in the wake of her death. In an
essay in *Out* entitled "Why Sontag Didn't Want to Come Out: Her Words,"
the magazine's editor Brendan Lemon leaves suggestively open the question
of whether or not Sontag was, at the moment of her death, technically out
or not, after "Joan Acocella's profile of her had just come out in *The New
Yorker*, in which Sontag went on record as saying that she had had relationships with both women and men. Sontag didn't name any of them."[16]

Lemon's essay in *Out* transcribes a conversation that the editor had one
night in 2000, after the Acocella profile, in which he goaded Sontag into
coming out with a set of moralizing challenges: "how can you say you're
interested in liberty [...] and be so reticent about asserting your own?" and
"Don't you feel that your ability to awaken people's passions would be
increased if you came out – it would give gay and lesbian readers another
powerful thing to connect to?" All of this took place, in Lemon's recollection, *after* Sontag had, in fact, already come out. To thicken the mystery,

Acocella's brief note in the *New Yorker* contained no reference at all to Sontag's sex life; Lemon, one presumes, had confused it with a more substantial profile in the *Guardian*, in which Sontag had disclosed a great deal about her sexual life, including that she had been in love nine times: "five women, four men."[17] Lemon, of course, declines to see that disclosure as evidence of bisexuality, but in a short note published in the *Los Angeles Times* less than a week after Sontag's death, the gay historian Patrick Moore went much further in excluding that possibility from the record: "In a 1995 *New Yorker* profile, Sontag outed herself as bisexual, familiar code for 'gay.' Yet she remained quasi-closeted, speaking to interviewers in detail about her ex-husband without mentioning her long liaisons with some of America's most fascinating female artists."[18] The phrase "outed herself," as though these carefully organized dances were no more contrived than a wardrobe malfunction, is hardly the most objectionable part of the sentence. Castle raises the possibility of "bisexuality" with less contempt than Moore, but without really taking the word seriously as a descriptor of a person:

> I have to say I could never figure her out on this touchy subject – though we did talk about it. Her usual line (indignant and aggrieved) was that she didn't believe in "labels" and that if anything she was bisexual. She raged about a married couple who were following her from city to city and would subsequently publish a tell-all biography of her in 2000. Horrifyingly enough, she'd learned, the despicable pair were planning to include photographs of her with various celebrated female companions. Obviously, both needed to be consigned to Dante's Inferno, to roast in the flames in perpetuity with the Unbaptised Babies, Usurers and Makers of False Oaths. I struggled to keep a poker face during these rants, but couldn't help thinking that Dante should have devised a whole circle specifically for such malefactors: the Outers of Sontag.[19]

For Castle, "bisexual" is not necessarily "familiar code for 'gay'," as it was for Moore, but it is perhaps evidence of the sophomoric evasiveness whereby a distaste for "labels" could stand for a refusal to grapple with the realities of the real world. One of many comical analogies by which Castle roots Sontag in literary history joins the essayist to Dickens's Mrs. Jellyby, one of the many monstrous matriarchs of *Bleak House*, whose peculiar crime was to care more about the plight of starving orphans in Africa than about her own dilapidated household.[20] At the root of that analogy, one suspects, is Castle's sense that for Sontag sexual identity remained notional, that her fame had allowed her to absent herself from what Gurganus called "what the rest of us daily endure."

To risk a summation, then: It is beyond improbable that what Castle, Moore, Lemon, and Gurganus wanted from Sontag was merely a self-disclosure: The *Guardian* profile had quite clearly yielded one, albeit one that enabled a phobic slippage between bisexuality, ambivalence, and ambiguity, though Sontag can hardly be blamed for that. What these writers wanted was for Sontag to write an *essay* on the subject. Castle acknowledges the fact somewhat explicitly with the double-subject of an especially choice finite clause, "the subject of female homosexuality – and whether she owed the world a statement on it – was an unresolved one for her."[21] Lemon puts the matter directly. After the failure of his moral case for Sontag to write a personal essay describing her sexuality, his final plea is offered in aesthetic terms: "I said all this would make for a fascinating essay, and that it was too bad she had never written it. She said she doubted she would ever take up this topic. Compared to the work, who cares about the biography? Oh, everybody, I replied." Lemon seems to have missed the subtlety of Sontag's response, which did not counterpose *work* to *life*, as Wilde is supposed to have done, but to *biography*, a genre of writing that, we know from Castle, the essayist held in low regard. Indeed, that subtlety indicates a willingness on Sontag's part to allow verbal self-disclosures – chat, discourse – to absorb the subtle tonal and lexical polysemy of the essay form. One derives a similar impression from the notorious 2000 *Guardian* profile by Suzie Mackenzie, in which Sontag adopted the emphatically Anglo argot of her British interviewer, and chatted in a misleadingly cheerful, bright way: "When you get older, 45 plus, men stop fancying you. Or put it another way, the men I fancy don't fancy me. I want a young man."[22] It is as though the very self-disclosure requires the erection of a parodic screen – Sontag as Bridget Jones.[23] Since the life/work futz raised the ghost of a famous Irish homosexual, one might as well recount, then, another sequence of necessary-but-redundant bringings-out: Pater on Winckelmann, Wilde on Pater, Bartlett on Wilde.[24]

*

Among the many juicy tidbits that Castle serves up in "Desperately Seeking Susan" – an essay, I might as well say, that I prefer to anything Sontag herself ever wrote, and which goes some way towards making an otherwise sepulchrally unflapped manifestation of Manhattanite self-regard into someone it might have been fun to know – is that the grand defender of the modernism portion of the Western Civ syllabus adored Patricia Highsmith's *The Price of Salt*. "As far as Sontag was concerned," writes Castle, the "dykey little potboiler – published originally under a pseudonym – was right up there with *Buddenbrooks* and *The Man Without Qualities*."[25] Though Castle's relentless bathos serves her puckish satire of the closeted lesbian, it also establishes a related but distinct contradiction, between modernism and its others, whose relation to the closeted/out distinction remains tantalizingly unspoken. That Sontag placed *The Price of Salt* alongside the voluminous Teutonic masterpieces of Mann and Musil allows a glimpse, we are to think, of the lesbian concealed by "a number of exotic, billowy scarves," yet it also, and more damagingly, aligns Sontag with the vulgar tastes she consistently dismissed. It is this dimension of Castle's obituary, exposing the bourgeois Tucson girl behind the *haute* Manhattanite, that causes "Desperately Seeking Susan" to edge closest to cruelty, but Castle's omnivorous cultural appetites prevent such moments from drifting into contempt. Clearly, when Castle writes that "the famous Sontag 'look' always put me in mind of the stage direction in *Blithe Spirit*: 'Enter Madame Arcati, wearing barbaric jewellery,'" she is at least half remembering Sontag's dismissive categorization of Noel Coward's plays as merely "camping," rather than camp.[26] But whereas Sontag's taxonomy depends upon a classed distinction between the apparently effortless grace of a Ronald Firbank and the belabored gagging of a Coward, Castle's comparisons work, generally, to the benefit of the hacks, rather than the elect. Sontag's "comically huge" feet, "like Bugs Bunny's," knock Sontag off the perch of airy, sophisticated polysexuality, and drag her into a cartoonish and "dykey" space – the misfit gallery from where Castle is lobbing her legumes.

It would be at least an anachronism to frame this maneuver as an instance of the conflict between queer theory and its less rarefied antagonists – Sontag may not have been a lesbian in the sense that her obituarists had wanted, but nor was she a queer theorist in the Berlantian mold. Still, the sense that Castle is a lifer in, and Sontag merely passing through, the historical and cultural setting delineated by the "anthology of lesbian-themed literature I'd been working on for several years," roots itself in Castle's descriptions of the environments in which the two women encountered each other – to be precise, in the complex quasi-institutional setting of lesbian studies, in the era of Judith Butler, Eve Sedgwick, and early Berlant. The assertive unfashionableness of "Desperately Seeking Susan," in other words, coincided with an emerging sense of sexual indeterminacy and anti-identitarianism as the keynotes of scholarly fashionableness. Although that turn, accomplished most grandly in Eve Sedgwick's *The Epistemology of the Closet*, did not in general avow Sontag as an influence, it *did* present itself (as Sedgwick's own career exemplifies, and *Epistemology* narrates) as a move away from the premodernist focus of much lesbian and gay scholarship in the 1980s and towards the promise of modernism as formal pattern for the post-identitarian sexualities that queer theory named.[27] ("Patterning" is Berlant's summary of Sedgwick: She "dedicated her remarkable intellect to asking about patterning, especially in the relation of aesthetics to sexualities.")[28]

The sense of institutional embattlement, of imbrication within this particular cultural conflict, makes itself known in the two crowd scenes that bookend the narrative account of the friendship between Castle and Sontag: one, a triumphant, if embarrassing, moment of lesbian election, and the other, the door being shut in the mob wife's face. The first takes place after a lecture at Stanford's Kresge Auditorium, in which Sontag had read from her "excruciatingly turgid" novel *In America*, after which:

> Sideswiping the smiling president of Stanford and the eager throng of autograph-seekers, she elbowed her way towards me, enveloped me rakishly in her arms, and said very loudly: "Terry, we've got to stop meeting like this." She seemed to think the line hilarious and chortled heartily. I felt at once exalted, dopey, and mortified, like a plump teenage boy getting a hard-on in front of everybody.[29]

Triumphant *if* embarrassing, or triumphant *because* embarrassing? The desire to drag Sontag into the mulch of low cringe comedy, after all, characterizes much of the essay, and here is a moment of plain, stupefied witlessness, whose immediate effect is to endow Castle with an analogical "hard-on," the phallus being, prototypically, the object at which exaltation meets mortification. Yet the giddy little thrill, which feels little enough like an articulation of transsexual desire on Castle's part, also signals the essay's debt to the great nonmodernist plot for which Sontag was, revealingly, a sucker: Highsmith's *The Price of Salt*.[30] Castle may describe the plot with a heavy implication that Sontag identified with the young Therese – "a gifted (yet insecure) young woman who moves to Manhattan in the early 1950s" – but clearly, the "rakish" embrace signals the swagger of Carol herself. (It's too much to suggest, surely, that when Castle has Sontag "chortle," she thereby exhibits her in the role of Carroll: Lewis of that ilk.)[31]

The closing party scene belongs to a different melodrama, and a different institutional setting: Much of Sontag's discourse had worked to set "academics" – pedantic, small-minded, provincial – against the real seat of American intellectualism, the Manhattan art scene. When Castle is finally invited into the latter, she finds herself among the bodies of those whose names have been in circulation as currency: Here is Lou Reed, "O great rock god of my twenties," now merely "silent and surly" – as if to show how far things have fallen, and yet how interbleeding are the social circles of the culturally elect. There is "the freakish-looking lead singer from the cult art-pop duo Fischerspooner," the spondaic phrase "cult art pop duo" coming as close as "Desperately Seeking Susan" ever does to actual clumsiness, rather than its virtuosic imitation.

In the more densely populated setting of a Marina Abramović dinner party, Castle's Dickensian diction neatly moves between an apparently sympathetic free indirect discourse and brutally satirical farce, characters becoming more monstrously cartoonish in the face of the narrator's apparent desire to impress them: "when I asked the man from the Guggenheim, to my right, what his books were about, he regarded me disdainfully and began, 'I am famous for –,' then caught himself. He decided to be more circumspect – he was 'the world's leading expert on Arte Povera' – but then turned his back on me for the next two hours." Castle's eventual retreat from the gay world into that of the "Little People" contains its own wobble: "Turning round one last time, I saw Sontag still slumped in her seat, as if she'd fallen into a trance, or somehow caved in. She'd clearly forgotten all about me." Upon turning, Orpheus (chubby priapic boy?) learns that Euridice has had no intention of following him, whether out of the Lethean *demi-monde* or out of a closet grown to the size of the whole world.

The friction between the various polarities by which "Desperately Seeking Susan" examines its subject affords much of the interpretive interest of the essay: How, exactly, could the half-articulated critique of modernism map onto the half-articulated critique of queerness? Yet rather beautifully, Castle describes a category beyond modernism and its others, beyond lesbianism and its dissolution, or rather a category in which these differences can be experienced, provisionally, as harmonic: music. Fischerspooner and Lou Reed aside, and notwithstanding Sontag's hilariously rendered habit for overstatement ("Yes, Terry, I *do* know all the lesser-known Handel operas. I told Andrew Porter he was right – they *are* the greatest of musical masterpieces"), music is the topic on which Castle's enthusiasm/ambivalence shudders least into mere resentment. After failing Sontag's quizzes on Robert Walser and Thomas Bernhard, Castle gains Sontag's admiration (or at least she is "exempt from idiocy") because she "could hold [her] own with [Sontag] in the music-appreciation department." The nerdy swapping of music strikes Castle as "a peculiar, masculine, trainspotting" kind of pastime, but if it is so, it is one that even in the author's own irreverent style retains contact with German Romanticism, and thus bypasses the aggression at modernist culture that structures much of the affect pointed at Sontag. "I was rapt, like a hysterical spinster on her first visit to Bayreuth. *Schwärmerei* time for T-Ball."[32]

*

Do we just want those we love to be on our teams? I'm aware of how much of this work – not just mine, but Castle's and maybe Sontag's too – seems to collapse into a Carrie Bradshaw strapline, a telegram to *Miss Lonelyhearts*. If Castle's gossipy tribute to her erstwhile unrequited succeeds in making Sontag into more than she might have been, it would be because the emperor inflates with a surprising and sudden pathos at the moment that his nudity has been noted.

> "But he hasn't got anything on," a little child said.
> "Did you ever hear such innocent prattle?" said its father. And one person whispered to another what the child had said. "He hasn't anything on. A child says he hasn't anything on."
> "But he hasn't got anything on!" the whole town cried out at last.
> The Emperor shivered, for he suspected they were right. But he thought, "This procession has got to go on." So he walked more proudly than ever, as his noblemen held high the train that wasn't there at all.[33]

The ending of Hans Christian Andersen's story is, inevitably, far more complicated than its cooption by anti-trans literalists might have suggested. For one thing, the emperor's power, far from being undermined by the child's epistemic interruption, actually grows "more proudly than ever," and the noblemen whom the knavish tailors have cajoled into the ruse continue to carry his train. But it's not just that: It is far from clear, in fact, whether those who repeat the child (oddly genderless) really believe what the child has said. This translation, from the H. C. Anderson Centre and written by Jean Hersholt, introduces some speech from the townspeople, one to the other, that doesn't appear in Andersen's Danish, but neither in Hersholt's formulation ("A child says he hasn't anything on") nor in the original is it clear that the townspeople's perceptions have indeed been freed from ideology. On the contrary, the child's perspective is characterized as both ideologically powerful (it spreads quickly) and political inefficacious (it makes no real difference).

One might expect an essay of this sort to conclude by aligning Castle's dream of an impossibly out Sontag with those of the "les lesbiennes n'aiment pas les penis" crowd. And there is certainly in both cases an articulated desire for a straightforward, no-bullshit, sexuality – the kind that was, a month before Sontag's death, exemplified in a paper published in *Psychological Science*, entitled "A Sex Difference in the Specificity of Sexual Arousal," and collectively authored by a team under the supervision of Meredith L. Chivers and Gerulf Rieger.[34] To investigate the titular difference, Chivers and Rieger isolated three groups – "women, men, and postoperative male-to-female transsexuals" – asked them to describe their sexuality, and then connected their genitals to electrodes while showing them pornography. As rudely physical as an ontologized account of sexuality could be, the electrical circuit convened as porn→electrodes→genitals→sensorium proves, or seems to, a set of hypotheses about the differences between sexual capacity of this tripartite sexual taxonomy. The study claims, interestingly enough, that "transsexuals showed a category-specific pattern [of arousal], demonstrating that category specificity can be detected in the neovagina using a protoplethysmographic measure of female genital sexual arousal," but more provocatively, that of the thirty-three bisexual-identifying men, one-quarter (eight men) experienced arousal when shown straight porn, but not gay porn, and three-quarters (twenty-five men) experienced arousal when shown gay porn, but not straight porn. The study was seized upon as evidence for the long-held prejudice that there are no bisexual men, only gay men in denial and straight men with flexible, not to say questionable, standards. In other words, that sexuality could be fully ontologized, if not as a gene, then at least as a singular capacity, inflexible and ennobling. The gay advice columnist Dan Savage interviewed Rieger, himself a gay man, who wonders of the 25 percent, "they might be straight, but go in for sex with other guys because it's so much easier for a male to have quick sex with another male than with a woman. But their true sexual feelings are still for women." Savage himself used the t word, suggesting that there's a difference between someone's *true* sexual orientation and their sexual capabilities (*emphasis added*).[35] I don't mean to claim that the "true" coming out that Castle would have extracted from Sontag would have had anything in common with the porn→electrode→genitals→sensorium test, whose flaws as a test for sexuality perhaps warrant a footnote but no more, but the study and its reception do illustrate the proposition that the moment of Sontag's death felt like a crisis point for LGBT liberalism in more senses than one.

So, back to Berlant's generous, but devastating, assessment of the place feminist popular culture accords the real ambivalence women so frequently – inevitably – feel when confronted with knowledge of the gap between romantic fantasy and intimate suffering: "in popular culture ambivalence is seen as the failure of a relation, the opposite of happiness, rather than as an inevitable condition of intimate attachment and a pleasure in its own right."[36] So the truth is, I'm no longer convinced that the link between Castle and "les lesbiennes n'aiment pas les penis" is as unbroken as it seems, nor that the queering of identity successfully inoculated those who used it against the fraught desires exhibited in "Desperately Seeking Susan." In the days following the death of Lauren Berlant, a contest emerged on academic Facebook over which pronoun should be used to describe the recently dead. The difficulty of honoring Berlant's request – linked at the bottom of emails they'd sent – for a "they" is made clear in the University of Chicago's published obituary. Berlant's colleague Elaine Hadley (a member, with Berlant, of the Late Liberalisms group and thanked in the acknowledgments to *The Female Complaint*) deploys the repeated proper noun to skirt away from having to use pronouns at all: "Lauren wanted to know what young people were thinking and learn from them, which empowered them. On the other hand, Lauren was incisive and challenged them to work harder and be better [...] Lauren was always organizing reading groups..."[37] It's understandable, kind of: However used to it some of us have become since 2005, to those unused to the syntactical rhythms it produces, the singular "they" can still feel clumsy and a little embarrassing to say out loud – perhaps because it dares to name a utopia in the here and now, an ethical relation whose material presence manifests in the mouths of those who speak, those clothed in the dumb flesh of the respondent. But one couldn't escape the sense that to others in this conversation, those who could claim the intimacy of Berlant, "they" could only refer to someone they had never met – it was a cold and formal textual convention, merely clever. Inevitably, such voices claimed to have felt, and sometimes to have been, "policed" into the deployment of alienated and alienating speech. Berlant, of course, had written a great deal about the conflictual relations between desire and identity that emerge from the collision of public and private spheres (Facebook), generational tension (those who feel that the phrase "cancel culture" means something versus those who are terrorized on account of it), and the charismas of the page and the seminar room. But the queerness of the essay form remains oddly inaccessible: The *out* that you *come* is different from the *out* that you *write*.

Notes

1 The Magnetic Fields, "Living in an Abandoned Firehouse with You," Stephin Merritt, songwriter, track 6 on *Distant Plastic Trees*, PoPuP, 1991.
2 Lauren Berlant, *The Female Complaint* (Durham, NC: Duke University Press, 2008), 1.
3 Lauren Berlant, cover endorsement, *Females: A Concern* by Andrea Long Chu (London: Verso Books, 2019).
4 Valerie Solanas, *SCUM Manifesto* (London: Verso Books, 2004), n.p.
5 Lauren Berlant, "Structures of Unfeeling: Mysterious Skin," *International Journal of Politics, Culture, and Society* 28 (2015): 191–213, https://doi.org/10.1007/s10767-014-9190-y, accessed March 22, 2022
6 Charlie Markbreiter, "Can't Take a Joke: An Interview with Lauren Berlant," *The New Inquiry* (March 22, 2019), https://thenewinquiry.com/cant-take-a-joke/, accessed March 22, 2022
7 Barbara Johnson, "Bringing out D. A. Miller," *Narrative* 10.1 (2002): 3–8; D. A. Miller, *Bringing out Roland Barthes* (Oakland: University of California Press, 1992); Lauren Berlant, "Eve Sedgwick, Once More," *Critical Inquiry* 34.4 (2009): 1089, https://doi.org/10.1086/605402; Terry Castle, "Desperately

Seeking Susan," *London Review of Books* 27.6 (March 17, 2005), www
.lrb.co.uk/the-paper/v27/no6/terry-castle/desperately-seeking-susan, accessed
March 22, 2022

8 Johnson, "Bringing out D. A. Miller," 3.

9 Since the publication in 2015 of the graduate student Cara Daggett's essay
"Drone Disorientations: How 'Unmanned' Weapons Queer the Experience of
Killing in War," the phrase "drones are queer" has become a perhaps-rather-
unfair shorthand among online LGBT communities, signifying the tendency of
academic queer theory to treat the term "queer" as migrating ever further from the
lived experiences and commitments of queer people. Cara Daggett, "Drone Disorientations," *International Feminist Journal of Politics*, 17:3 (2015): 361–379.
The LG-sorta-B movement, which seeks to excise trans people from queer communities altogether, exemplifies the political platform of the British charity "the
LGB Alliance," whose founder Bev Jackson argued in 2020 that "A lesbian is a
biological woman who is attracted to another biological woman. That's obvious. Or at least it was obvious until a few years ago." Any individual attraction,
provided it is "biological," makes a lesbian, apparently. See Camilla Tominey,
"Lesbians facing extinction as transgenderism becomes pervasive, campaigners
warn," *The Telegraph* (December 25, 2020).

10 *Les Lesbiennes N'aiment Pas les Pénis*, https://tetu.com/2021/06/28/pride-paris-
2021-militante-trans-interpellee-altercation-feministes-anti-trans-terf/, accessed
July 13, 2021

11 See Sophie Lewis, "How British Feminism Became Anti-Trans," *New York Times*
(February 7, 2019), www.nytimes.com/2019/02/07/opinion/terf-trans-women-
britain.html, accessed March 22, 2022

12 See, for example, the conversation entitled "How long will the gender woo
movement last?," on *Ovarit*, www.ovarit.com/o/GenderCritical/13360/how-
long-will-the-gender-woo-movement-last, accessed March 22, 2022

13 "She'll Be Coming Round the Mountain" is a traditional American folk song,
which I use here as shorthand for trochaic hexameter. See Carl Sandburg, *The
American Songbag* (New York: Harcourt, Brace, &. Co., 1927), 372.

14 The lesbian feminist Monique Wittig famously distinguished "lesbians" from
"women" along these lines; for example: "it would be incorrect to say that lesbians associate, make love, live with women, for 'woman' has meaning only in heterosexual systems of thought and heterosexual economic systems. Lesbians are
not women." Wittig, "The Straight Mind," *Feminist Issues* 1 (1980): 103–111.

15 Margalit Fox, "Susan Sontag, Social Critic with Verve, Dies at 71," *New York
Times* (December 29, 2004).

16 Brendan Lemon, "Why Sontag Didn't Want to Come Out: Her Words," *Out*,
January 5, 2005.

17 Suzie Mackenzie, "Finding Fact from Fiction," *The Guardian* (May 27, 2000).

18 Patrick Moore, "Susan Sontag and a Case of Curious Silence," *Los Angeles
Times* (January 4, 2005).

19 Castle, "Desperately Seeking Susan."

20 Charles Dickens, *Bleak House* (Ware: Wordsworth Editions, 1993).

21 Castle, "Desperately Seeking Susan."

22 Mackenzie, "Finding Fact from Fiction."

23 Helen Fielding, *Bridget Jones's Diary* (London: Macmillan, 1996).

24 Walter Pater, *Studies in the History of the Renaissance* (London: Macmillan, 1873); Oscar Wilde, *The Picture of Dorian Gray* (Philadelphia: Lippincott's, 1890); Neil Bartlett, *Who Was That Man?: A Present for Mr. Oscar Wilde* (London: Serpent's Tail, 1988).
25 Castle, "Desperately Seeking Susan."
26 Ibid.; Sontag, *Notes on Camp*.
27 Eve Kosofsky Sedgwick, *Epistemology of the Closet* (Oakland: University of California Press, 1990).
28 Berlant, "Eve Sedgwick, Once More."
29 Castle, "Desperately Seeking Susan."
30 Patricia Highsmith, *The Price of Salt* (New York: W.W. Norton, 2004).
31 Lewis Carroll, "Jabberwocky," from *Through the Looking Glass* (London: Macmillan, 1871).
32 Castle, "Desperately Seeking Susan."
33 Hans Christian Andersen, *The Emperor's New Clothes* (Boston, MA: Houghton Mifflin, 1949).
34 Meredith Chivers et al., "A Sex Difference in the Specificity of Sexual Arousal," *Psychological Science* 15.11 (2004): 736–744.
35 Dan Savage, "Savage Love," *The Stranger* 14.44 (July 14, 2005).
36 Berlant, *The Female Complaint*, 2.
37 Sarah Patterson, "Lauren Berlant, Preeminent Literary Scholar and Cultural Theorist, 1957–2021," *University of Chicago News* (June 28, 2021).

PART III

Technologies of the Essay

13

JASON CHILDS

The Essay and the Novel

Novelist and Essayist

According to the dominant mythologies of the novel and the essay, each genre is brought into being by a singular, heroic progenitor: on the one hand, the original novelist, Miguel de Cervantes; on the other, the original essayist, Michel de Montaigne.[1] In these origin stories – narrative symmetries and historical overlap notwithstanding – essayist and novelist are distinct. And it's true that, in the lines of descent from these putative founding fathers, there have certainly been many authors who have identified themselves, or have been identified by critics, as *either* novelists *or* essayists. Yet countless writers have turned their hands to both genres. Indeed, especially since the nineteenth century, when, as Denise Gigante points out, today's common-sense distinction between the two began to become more pronounced,[2] many of our most respected novelists have been equally notable (if less often noted) essayists. Virginia Woolf, Robert Musil, Thomas Mann, Carlos Fuentes, Italo Calvino, George Orwell, Albert Camus, James Baldwin, Milan Kundera, William H. Gass, Umberto Eco, Joyce Carol Oates, J. M. Coetzee, V. S. Naipaul, Joan Didion, Jonathan Franzen, Salman Rushdie, Ursula K. LeGuin, David Foster Wallace, Zadie Smith, William T. Vollmann, Joshua Cohen, Rachel Cusk, Tim Parks, Siri Hustvedt, Karl Ove Knausgaard, Yiyun Li: These are a few of the many who spring readily to mind.

To a degree, this overlap of novelist and essayist has been the result of a seldom-acknowledged pragmatism. To many writers primarily considered novelists, the composition of essays, whether personal, critical, or journalistic, has been an important way of supplementing the income that novels alone, with their longer lead times and uncertain commercial prospects, did not adequately provide. To take a notable example, Virginia Woolf, profoundly influential as both a novelist and an essayist, "did not earn any income from her books until 1919, and even then her books did not start yielding substantial money until the mid-1920s" – that is, until she was already several novels deep into her career. "This meant that writing articles was how Woolf topped up her income," Evelyn Tsz Yan Chan explains, "something she alternately resented for pulling her away from fiction-writing, and was fascinated with because the money she earned gave her a sense of solidity and independence."[3] To take another: George Orwell, though surely best known for his novels *Nineteen Eighty-Four* and *Animal Farm*, was a prolific polemical and critical essayist, reviewing hundreds of books, plays, and films. In his "Confessions of a Book Reviewer," Orwell paints a grimly funny portrait of the writer as jobbing essayist, suggesting it was less for love than money that much of this work was undertaken.

While supporting the composition of novels by moonlighting as a critic and journalist may, for all but a few, seem somewhat less practicable today than it was at points in the nineteenth and twentieth centuries, the essay is today no less essential to the novelist's career. Martin Paul Eve has written eloquently about the form's importance to novelists, not only as a means of marketing their wares and managing their reception (by, for example, inscribing their efforts in certain literary traditions), but also as a site for the cultivation of cultural capital, the establishment of professional networks, and the fulfillment – in the not infrequent cases where the writer holds an academic post – of institutional requirements for a productive publishing agenda.[4] The publication of a novelist's essays in major newspapers – the *New York Times*, say, or *The Guardian* – or in influential periodicals such as the *London Review of Books*, the *Times Literary Supplement*, the *New York Review of Books*, or the *New Yorker* – may tell us something about the author's political predilections, but it also indexes something of his cultural influence and the cachet of his "brand." We might also note instances in which a novelist of illustrious stature is invited to publish essays, whether expounding on grand themes, musing on the quotidian, or both – as in Elena Ferrante's *Incidental Interventions*, which collects weekly columns originally published in *The Guardian*. Such a figure is caricatured in J. M. Coetzee's *Diary of a Bad Year*. "JC," the book's autofictional protagonist and one of its narrators, is invited, alongside five other "*éminences grises* who have clawed our way up to the highest peak," to "pronounce on what is wrong with today's world" in a volume of essays titled *Strong Opinions*.[5] JC expresses a certain degree of apprehension about this transition from novelist to essayist, which seems to represent a neutralization, a culmination of the author's career in impotence rather than importance. Though perhaps traditionally conceived of as the novelist's minor work, the essay can have more than minor significance in his career.

A less cynical view of the essay-writing of novelists might recognize that the practice often kills multiple birds with a single stone. While there may be a variety of material benefits to the practice, the essay often emanates from the novelist's genuine desire to participate more directly or occasionally in public discourse, whether intervening in political or social debate (e.g., Orwell, Vernon Lee, Nadine Gordimer) or, as has perhaps been more common, commenting on matters literary-critical. Often, the novelist will use the essay as a space for sketching out or elaborating on the concerns he either has taken up or intends to take up in his novels, or for exploring ideas about the cultural position and vocation of the novel in general.[6] In some cases – John Barth's "The Literature of Exhaustion," Zadie Smith's "Two Paths for the Novel," or the pieces collected in Alain Robbe-Grillet's *For a New Novel*, for instance – such essays, developing influential critical or theoretical positions, rival in quality or significance the novels they anticipate or accompany into public life. We also owe some of the most widely cited theorizations of the essay itself to essays composed by writers often thought of mainly as novelists: Gass's "Emerson and the Essay," Woolf's "The Modern Essay," Musil's "On the Essay," and Cynthia Ozick's "She: Portrait of the Essay as a Warm Body," to name a few.

Examining such complex acts of critical engagement by novelists might, meanwhile, remind us of instances where authors known primarily as critical essayists have turned their hands to the novel. James Wood, Susan Sontag, and George Steiner, for example, are among the high-profile critics who have published novels, often finding in these projects the same kind of testing ground that the abovementioned novelists have found in the essay. Bryan Cheyette describes Steiner's fiction, for example, as a space in which he can "think against himself"; a space of "humility and openness" that contrasts with "his increasingly closed and orthodox critical work."[7] Lionel Trilling and Walter Pater are notable among earlier essayists who made comparable outings, Trilling with *The Middle of the Journey* and Pater with his innovative *Marius the Epicurean*.

While we may think of novelist and essayist as similar in their focus on the experience of the self in the world, we perhaps tend to think of the essayist as essentially reflective or introspective, whereas the novelist is concerned with dramatic action and events. We might, to invoke the forms' mythic founders once more, picture the essayist Montaigne retiring pensively to his tower while the novelist Cervantes has Quixote venture forth onto unfamiliar ground. "An essay is a fireside thing," Ozick writes, "not a conflagration or a safari."[8] This theory of the difference between forms is as much falsified, of course, by the intense focus of modernist and postmodernist novelists on inner experience as by the essay's close relationship to reportage, especially in the writings of New Journalists such as Hunter S. Thompson, Tom Wolfe, and Joan Didion, which have some precedent in such eighteenth-century periodicals as the *Tatler*. "Essays, unlike novels, emerge from the sensations of the self," Ozick tells us, in another dubious contrast. "Fiction creeps into foreign bodies: The novelist can inhabit not only a sex not his own but also beetles and noses and hunger artists and nomads and beasts. The essay is, as we say, personal."[9] Yet do the essayist's reflections not lead his imagination, as Claire de Obaldia puts it, "to carry him out into the life of other individuals, of places or scenes"?[10]

For Theodor Adorno, it is only the "bad essay" that "chats about people instead of opening up the matter at hand."[11] Yet the distinction between "people" and "ideas" – much like an omniscient and preemptive separation of chat from serious discourse – risks being superficial. Among the earliest modern instantiations of the essay were "character sketches" – such as Thomas Overbury's "A worthy Commander in the Warres," "A mere Pettifogger," and "A fayre and happy Milke-mayd" – written with the aim of distilling a typology of modern persons (a project akin in some ways to Balzac's *The Human Comedy*). The biographical portrait remains an important component of the essay today and is especially common in substantial works of literary journalism and historiography that seek precisely to situate the development of ideas in their subjects' lives. Montaigne himself often chatted about people and, of course, told stories; perhaps not the kind of continuous long-form narratives we associate with the nineteenth-century *Bildungsroman*, but the latter is, after all, only one kind of novel in a long history that includes works that are more episodic (such as *Don Quixote*) or digressive (such as *The Life and Opinions of Tristram Shandy, Gentleman*), as well as works that reflect deep skepticism about the very notion of *Bildung* (such as Gustave Flaubert's *Bouvard and Pécuchet*, Fyodor Dostoevsky's *Crime and Punishment*, and Thomas Mann's *The Magic Mountain*). Such novels, meanwhile, could hardly be said not to deal with ideas, even if their ideas are not amenable to simple paraphrase.

Some theorists contrast the knowledge or expertise – the notions of system or proper form – held by the novelist and essayist in advance of their writing. "A certain scientific or philosophical rigor is ... foreign to the essay," observes William H. Gass. He goes further, however, declaring the essayist not only a non-expert, but "an amateur".[12] "He writes essayistically," Max Bense claims, "who writes while experimenting, who turns his object this way and that, who questions it, feels it, tests it, thoroughly reflects on it, attacks it from different angles, and in his mind's eye collects what he sees, and puts into words what the object allows to be seen under the conditions established in the course of writing."[13] By this definition, many a novelist can be said to write essayistically, following the peregrinations of thought wherever they lead. Indeed, we can readily furnish examples of novels reportedly written with no commitment to a predetermined generic structure, or even in a willful defiance or deferral of structure, from Jack Kerouac's *On The Road* to Knausgaard's *My Struggle*. At the same time, as Jeff Porter warns us, the essay's "apparent informality" is often carefully cultivated, promoting a myth of immediacy belied by what we know of many essayists' inclination to revise: "That the essay seems artless is one of its great ruses."[14]

We might be inclined to think – drawing on a distinction between orders of discourse that goes back to Plato's *Republic* – of the essayist as a writer who speaks in her own voice, where the novelist speaks indirectly through a narrator. "We take the essayist and his narrator or persona ... to be one and the same," avers G. Douglas Atkins; "that is why we say the essay belongs in the category 'nonfiction,' even though the experience there represented is necessarily and inevitably shaped."[15] But what, then, to make of the intense citationality of the essay – not least in Montaigne's *Essais*, but also in more recent works such as David Shields's *Reality Hunger*, a patchwork of lines and passages clipped from other authors? Or of Adam Kirsch's contention that "[t]he essayist is concerned, as a fiction writer is not, with what the reader will think of him or her"?[16] We should hesitate simply to equate the "I" of the essay with that of its author. At the least, the idea that an essayist might care what the reader thinks of him seems cause to suspect unreliable narration. As de Obaldia puts it, the status of the essayist *qua* narrator points to a tension "between the person of the essayist made of flesh and blood and the essayist defined or created out of words alone."[17] Carl Klaus, too, suggests that "the particular personality conveyed in an essay is always in some sense a fiction."[18] To decide whether such problematic self-consciousness distinguishes the essayist from the novelist, meanwhile, we need only consider the long tradition of metafictional or autofictional novels in which author/narrator-protagonists reflect in essayistic asides on their writing *within* the work itself. "I am myself the matter [*la matiere*] of my book," Montaigne famously writes.[19] Authors of innovative memoir-novels, such as Ben Lerner, Sheila Heti, Paul Auster, J. M. Coetzee, W. G. Sebald, Rachel Cusk, Chris Kraus, and Karl Ove Knausgaard evidently share this sense of the book as an ambiguous extension of the self.

Novel and Essay

While it is challenging to clearly distinguish essayist from novelist, defining the difference between novel and essay is even less straightforward. "I recently taught a graduate seminar on the [essay]," writes Christy Wampole in "The Essayification of Everything," "and, at the end of the course, to the question 'What can we say of the essay with absolute certainty?,' all of us, armed with our panoply of canonical essay theories and our own conjectures, had to admit that the answer is: 'Almost nothing.'"[20] Comparable statements on the difficulty of defining the essay appear regularly in the literature. "Some theorists," observes de Obaldia, "have gone so far as to appropriate Montaigne's famous claim to the uniqueness of the species not only to assert that there are as many essays as there are essayists, but even more literally that no one has ever written essays after Montaigne, that his are the only essays that exist in the proper sense of the word."[21]

The novel, likewise, is notoriously resistant to definition. Efforts to nail it down, by its eminent theorists and luminary practitioners alike, have ended in nebulousness. E. M. Forster, for example, famously defined the novel as "a fiction in prose of a certain length."[22] (The recent rise of categories such as creative nonfiction and the nonfiction novel render problematic at least one term of this already spare definition.) Mikhail Bakhtin called the novel "the most fluid of genres," in recognition of the seemingly boundless variety of its instantiations.[23] Guy de Maupassant once remarked that "the critic who dares to write 'this is a novel, this is not' seems to be blessed with a perspicacity that very much resembles incompetence.'"[24] Don DeLillo writes in a letter to Jonathan Franzen that "the novel is whatever novelists are doing at a given moment."[25]

We can at least say with confidence, then, that both the novel and the essay are capacious – perhaps infinitely so. "[W]hereas neither poetry nor philosophy can incorporate the novel," writes Milan Kundera, "the novel can incorporate both poetry and philosophy without losing thereby anything of its identity."[26] De Obaldia views the essay's "resistance to resolving itself into identifiable generic contours" as akin to the power of 'incorporation' that Kundera finds in the novel, identifying it as essentially "a literary hybrid," indeed "a 'baggy monster' which can be stretched in any direction."[27] By the same token, both forms can also be thought of in terms of internal division, of dissonance and disagreement. "The novel's spirit is the spirit of complexity," writes Kundera. "Every novel says to the reader: 'Things are not as simple as you think.' That is the novel's eternal truth."[28] Whereas we perhaps readily accept this idea of the novel as dialogical or polyphonic, we may tend to imagine the essay, by contrast, as univocal – as, for example, a vehicle for advancing a single argument. De Obaldia, however, points out the dialogical quality of the essay, its habit "of approaching the matter from different angles, of choosing arguments for and against in the manner of the heuristic and dialectical method of question and answer": a movement whereby "the topic under investigation becomes the object of a dialogue."[29] Jean Starobinksi, looking at the deep etymological roots of the term "essay" and finding there the Latin *examen*, notes that this ancient word suggestively "designates a swarm of bees, a flock of birds."[30] "The essay," writes Brian Dillon, riffing on this idea, "is diverse and several – it teems."[31]

Part of what makes both genres so hard to define is that their concepts call for innovation: New instances are torn between the need to observe the guiderails of their antecedents and the urge to move past them. Frequently, the novel's innovative extension is characterized as expansion, even a kind of imperialism; Kundera, for instance, refers to the novel's progressive "conquest of being."[32] In the Romantic ideal of the novel as *Gesamtkunstwerk*, we find a yearning for totalization that remains present today in assertions of the novel's (perhaps waning) capacity to comprehend a given cultural moment in its entirety. The individual essay, by contrast, is rarely spoken of in such ambitious terms, even if it is increasingly seen as a form uniquely capable of responding to our fragmented historical moment. One explanation for this perception would be that self-exploration, rather than symbolic patricide or the conquest of existential turf, is usually held up as the motor of innovation in the essay. Wampole writes that Montaigne's invention of the essay, for example, has "little to do with a conscious innovation of form, nor with an iconoclastic destruction of or a steadfast resistance to sixteenth-century forms of written expression"; instead, his *essais* emerge from a sense that "the forms of writing prevalent during his lifetime could not accommodate what he wanted to express through written language."[33]

Some theorists have suggested that we can locate the essence of "essay" and "novel" in our subjective desire for them, rather than in the objective properties of given texts. We speak, for example, about "the spirit of the novel" or "the spirit of the essay." But what do we mean by these hazy invocations? Among numerous possible responses to this question, one that applies to novel and essay alike pertains to their mode of epistemic comportment, their shared constitution as search or research. This spirit is bound up with their modernity. "The novel," writes Georg Lukács, "is the epic of a world that has been abandoned by God."[34] O. B. Hardison tells us that "the essay was born from a moment of profound, even terrifying doubt," and that "its rhetoric has often been adopted by authors who have sensed the power of the forces of dissolution."[35] Montaigne's famous "*Que sais-je?*", the question that propels his *Essais*, can be taken as both an articulation of and a nascent response to such a dissolution. Kundera's claim that the history of the novel, properly understood, is a "sequence of discoveries" – and thus that "[t]he sole *raison d'être* of a novel is to discover what only the novel can discover" – places it within the same horizon of uncertainty.[36]

Of course, against the backdrop of the increasing privilege assigned to the scientific worldview, the novel, like all literature, experiences a kind of cognitive nullification. The essay, to the extent that it is considered literature, is likewise epistemically disenfranchised. But novel and essay both know a desire for knowing, for a knowing in excess of – and, perhaps, in rivalry with – established or official knowledge.

We may nonetheless wish to draw a distinction between these twin spirits. Adam Phillips, reflecting on the relationship between the essay, knowledge, and desire, asks: "[w]hat is the essay a good way of wanting?" One answer to this suggestive question is that, not infrequently, the essay has seemed a good way of wanting the novel. This is the case, first and most straightforwardly, in the tradition of the critical essay – especially where criticism moves from descriptive to normative, as in the manifesto (e.g., Robbe-Grillet's *For a New Novel* or Tom Wolfe's "Stalking the Billion-Footed Beast"). More significantly, the essay has often functioned in a preparatory or "diachronic" relation to the novel – that is, as a draft, rehearsal, or sketch.[37] In such cases, we oppose the informal, spontaneous, incomplete – but also therefore more direct and artless – essay to the novel, the latter being more finely wrought and "worked up." This way of imagining the role of the essay in the genesis of the novel, de Obaldia argues, also implies a qualitative distinction, depicting the former as "a 'simple form' (waiting to be) absorbed into a more complex one,"[38] and thereby conferring upon the essay what has sometimes been called its "second-class citizenship"[39] vis-à-vis the novel. "What the argument of the essay as a precursor recognizably does is to turn the relationship between essay and novel into a *progression*," explains de Obaldia, "and therefore the essay into a supplement or residue which can be discarded once the intended goal has been reached."[40]

On this view, the essay is a novel in a nutshell. Or, to use another metaphor, the novel fleshes out the skeletal essay. The essay is, in a dual sense, finished – both realized and refined – by becoming a novel. This vision of the essay as rough-cut thought or as fragment, on the one hand, and of the novel, on the other, as neat and complete is perhaps at odds with a widely held vision of the novel as formally responsive to the messiness of modern life, just as it conflicts with the sense, espoused by some critics, that the essay is ideally "polished" or "coolly aphoristic," whereas the novel is constitutively imperfect.[41] More strikingly, though, the essay is here dismissed as a literary text in its own right: Its language and form are considered fungible – not only open to paraphrase, but also inchoate.

This diachronic relationship between essay and novel is part of what is at stake in the emergence of the European essay-novels of the twentieth century, particularly insofar as, in signal instances of this hybrid form, the traditional hierarchy of novel over essay is complicated, if not reversed. Far from a mere run-up to the novel, the essay's emergence within the novel – or the novel's devolution, via the insertion of essays, back into something less complete – delivers what some have considered the novel's most advanced instantiations. For Stefano Ercolino, the essay "enters the novel" at a very specific point in the novel's generic history, precisely as a revolutionary way of shoring up its symbolic power at a moment of imminent collapse under the pressure of historical change. Whereas the novel is construed as "the symbolic form of modernity," Ercolino considers the twentieth-century novel-essay "the symbolic form of the *crisis* of modernity."[42] However, while the authors to whom Ercolino attends – chiefly Joris-Karl Huysmans, Marcel Proust, Robert Musil, and Thomas Mann – are certainly concerned with a moment of particular instability within the bourgeois order of meaning, we have seen that the novel and the essay were always already responses to (and expressions of) modernity as crisis.

Indeed, an alternative viewpoint might see such novel-essays returning to an essayism that encompasses the novel from its inception, yet is repressed in the dominant and "anti-essayistic"[43] literary realisms of the nineteenth and twentieth centuries; that is, within the terms of what Kundera calls "the verisimilitude pact."[44] This view is supported by recent revisionist histories of the novel, such as Steven Moore's *The Novel: An Alternative History*, which places experimental and essayistic fictions at its center rather than its periphery.[45] Kundera, whose sense of the novel's history is similar to Moore's, sees the work of Musil and Broch as among the most important events in the novel's development, yet sees the essay, "the specifically novelistic essay,"[46] as developing from within the space of the novel, and so having its truth claims provisionalized by the novel's fictionality. Like Ercolino, Kundera views such essays as embedded in novels, as in Broch's *The Sleepwalkers* or his own *The Unbearable Lightness of Being*. We might contrast this conception of the essay-novel, however, with that embodied in *The Man without Qualities,* which Musil described as "not a novel at all, but an essay of monstrous dimensions."[47] This sprawling – and, significantly, unfinished – work reflects a "generalized essayism," exceeding the novel that it contains.[48]

Critics and theorists have often sharply distinguished the essay-novel from the novel of ideas or *roman à these*, arguing that there is a difference of more than degree, for example, between such works as *The Man Without Qualities,* on the one hand, and Ayn Rand's *Atlas Shrugged* or Sartre's *Nausea* on the other. Usually, the distinction is predicated on the sense that, in the second category, the work merely illustrates or embodies ideas or arguments that existed prior to its composition. Ercolino offers the encompassing term "philosophical mimesis" to suggest a greater family resemblance between these categories, noting that they have in common a refusal to accede to the diremption of particular from universal – and, by extension, of literature from philosophy – in the Western tradition.[49] Yet for Ercolino, works such as Voltaire's *Candide* or Diderot's *Jacques the Fatalist* are still to be separated from those of Broch or Musil, given the "morphological hybridity" of the latter – that is, their formal refusal to enact a reconciliation of the separated orders of discourse, a mixture of and suspension between essay and novel – and a certain "speculative restlessness" in their movement.[50] There remain a great many works, though, that one might hesitate to place in either one of these two buckets, from Thomas Carlyle's *Sartor Resartus* to Robert M. Pirsig's *Zen and the Art of Motorcycle Maintenance*. How, we might ask, does this framework help us to make sense of the highly cerebral works of writers such as William Gaddis, Iris Murdoch, Thomas Bernhard, W. G. Sebald, Nicolas Mosley, Roberto Bolaño, or Michel Houellebecq, or indeed of some philosophers, such as Friedrich Nietzsche or Søren Kierkegaard?

Essayistic and Novelistic

In important recent contributions to the theory and practice of the essay, the genre has often been presented in emphatic opposition to the novel. Indeed, the essay has lately been held up as important *insofar as* it opposes – and, moreover, supersedes – the novel, reversing the traditional hierarchy and order of priority we have noted in this chapter. David Shields's *Reality Hunger*, for example, contains not only reports of the author's own frustrations as a reader of novels – "something has happened to my imagination," he reports, "which can no longer yield to the earnest embrace of novelistic form" – but also sweeping generalizations about its viability: "The novel is dead," as he bluntly puts it at one point.[51] Shields touches on a number of possible explanations for the novel's lost vitality, but perhaps the most important is that, where once the novel functioned ideologically to "impose the image of a stable, coherent, continuous, unequivocal, entirely decipherable universe," today's reality is far too self-evidently fragmented, noisy, and disorienting for such propaganda to be convincing.[52] The novel, seen aright, can be experienced today only as "a form of nostalgia" or a "beautiful illusion."[53] On this view, the very qualities that once relegated the essay to second-class citizenship now become its credentials for primacy: It is precisely insofar as the essay is prenovelistic that it is suited to a post-novelistic world. In not (yet) being "well-made" – in appearing provisional and unintegrated, "seemingly unprocessed, unfiltered, uncensored, and unprofessional," and in taking up a deeply noncommittal attitude to such traditional novelistic trappings as story or plot or character – the essay more accurately reflects a contemporary reality itself perceived as disintegrating.[54] The essay's primacy, however, is a primacy of the secondary: In place of the original literary work that would stand outside and seek to encompass reality, the essay instead intervenes more modestly in a reality with which it is continuous and complicit, self-consciously sampling and remixing cultural elements that are themselves "always already invented."[55] The essay thus affords us more intimate contact with (what we now recognize to be a thoroughly manufactured) reality. The "essayistic," then, becomes a self-conscious aesthetic: a semblance of the absence of semblance.

Not everyone has been convinced by such arguments. For one thing, as our exploration of the topic thus far suggests, the depiction of the novel on which this historical argument about the essay is built is something of a strawman. Reviewing *Reality Hunger*, Zadie Smith writes: "Even in those familiar lists of 'great novels,' classics of the genre, and so on, it's hard to find a single 'well-made' novel among them, if by well-made we mean something like 'evenly shaped, regular, predictable and elegantly designed.'"[56] It is also worth asking whether *Reality Hunger* advances its arguments in the univocal manner that critics such as Smith have asserted: whether it might itself not be more like a novel than a manifesto. "The kinds of novels I like are ones which bear no trace of being novels," Shields (or the book's narrator) writes at one point.[57] And there are many moments in *Reality Hunger* that suggest that the book might be read, and indeed encourages us to read it, not only as "against the novel," but as itself an "antinovel."[58] Pieter Vermeulen argues that "*Reality Hunger*'s death knell [for the novel] cannot avoid sounding a lot like a novel; indeed, the 'novelistic' shape … of Shields's self-designated manifesto belies the clarity of its programmatic intent, and ends up reanimating the form it intends to bury."[59]

We might add that the clearest antecedents to Shields's project are perhaps to be found not in poststructuralist theory, nor indeed in the tradition of the critical essay, but in certain postmodernist novels. In his turn-of-the-millennium study *Cognitive Fictions*, Joseph Tabbi brings attention to a group of writers – Richard Powers, David Markson, and Paul Auster, among others – whom he sees as self-consciously staking out "a new mode of writing about the self": an "essayistic aesthetic" that he describes as "like realism, but not; like postmodern metafiction, but not." The truths of these authors' works, Tabbi contends, "are primarily cognitive rather than representational." They imagine fiction "not as a vehicle for telling stories, but as a medium for holding our stories in thought."[60]

Many of the most engaging and influential works of literature in recent years can be situated in this ambiguous generic space, a space characterized less by the supposedly happy hybridity of postmodern play than by a sense dislocation and difficulty. These texts represent a shift in cultural mood from postmodern celebration to post-truth unease at the way traditional conceptions of authorship and authority are at once persisting and collapsing. In the past decade, there have been works in this vein by Maggie Nelson, Mathias Énard, Geoff Dyer, Ali Smith, Brian Dillon, Maria Tumarkin, Gerald Murnane, Rebecca Solnit, and Simon Critchley, among others: less a mixture of fiction and nonfiction, of creative writing and criticism, than a staging of thoughtful hesitation prior to any commitment to such categories. Needless to say, it is difficult, perhaps impossible, to decide of many such works whether we should consider them novels or as essays. In an interview with James Wood, Knausgaard says that his grand project has emerged from a sense that the "traditional form of the novel" is no longer "eloquent."[61] "The only genres I saw value in, which still conferred meaning," he writes in volume 2 of *My Struggle*, "were diaries and essays, the types of literature that did not deal with narrative, that were not about anything, but just consisted of a voice, the voice of your own personality, a life, a face, a gaze you could meet."[62] Yet throughout *My Struggle*, Knausgaard refers to the work we are reading as a novel. It is as if, to reverse my earlier formulation, the novel had become a good way of wanting an essay. At the opening of *Invisible Yet Enduring Lilacs*, Gerald Murnane provocatively undoes the classification of his previous works: "I should never have tried to write fiction or nonfiction or even anything in-between. I should have left it to discerning editors to publish all my pieces of writing as essays."[63]

Much the same ambiguity can be observed, meanwhile, in works emerging from the domain of criticism. As Peter Boxall writes, the present literary field is marked by the sense that "the distinction between creative and critical writing is becoming more difficult to sustain, and in which critical writing is itself becoming increasingly 'literary,' increasingly belle-lettristic."[64] "Much of what I read in the field of criticism these days is not purely literary criticism or practical criticism in the tradition of I. A. Richards, or theoretical critique," writes Brian Castro, "but essays which are also fictions, perhaps referring to literary works in passing, in order to reference, interrogate and explore culture: its fashions, its trends, its past and future."[65] Ben Lerner argues that "the novel [is] a great vehicle for art criticism, and much of the best art criticism seems to have learned something from fiction." He cites T. J. Clark's *The Sight of Death*, "'an experiment in art writing' [that] has as much in common with novels as it does with most conventional art criticism."[66] Are we dealing, in such cases, with essayistic novels? With novelistic essays? Or with texts uniquely attuned to a context in which such questions have become unavoidably and, indeed, interestingly problematic – a context in which we, as would-be taxonomers, are ourselves implicated?

Some have suggested that the profound uncertainty we face today in dividing and legitimating genres, discourses, and disciplines bears comparison with the uncertainty that attended the moment in which the modern essay and novel first emerged; that there is an equivalence between the institutional, epistemic, technological, and media-ecological upheaval that, in the time of Montaigne and Cervantes, opened the so-called Gutenberg parenthesis and the shifts that, in our own time, may be bringing it to a close. Yet we can also see recent works of essayistic-novelistic writing less as return or repetition than as the continuation of a tradition that has persisted throughout the modern era, albeit mostly at the margins. There is a clear thread, that is to say, connecting the moment of Daniel Defoe, Jonathan Swift, Samuel Richardson, and Laurence Sterne to that of Shields, Knausgaard, Nelson, and Lerner. With that continuity in mind, if we are now, as some theorists suggest, entering a post-literary condition – and if the same forces that have brought this about have helped occasion the resurgence of livelier and more ambiguous modes of writing and reading – then we might also, as Tabbi suggests, "approach digitization not as a prospective 'end' of literary production but its renewal."[67] The end of the era of the book, in other words, or indeed of literature – at least where, following Robert Coover, we construe the latter etymologically, as "things made from letters" – need not spell the end of either the novel or the essay.[68] Instead, these shifts might encourage us to watch with curiosity how novelists and essayists continue to incite and unsettle one another in other media.

Notes

1 These myths, of course, radically simplify the emergence of both essay and novel. However important the influence of particular authors, literary forms are not invented in one fell swoop, but emerge and are consolidated gradually through a complex interplay of thought and practice.
2 See Denise Gigante, "Introduction," *The Great Age of the English Essay* (New Haven, CT: Yale University Press, 2008), xvi–xvii.
3 Evelyn Tsz Yan Chan, *Virginia Woolf and the Professions* (Cambridge: Cambridge University Press, 2014), 74.
4 Martin Paul Eve, *Literature Against Criticism: University English and Contemporary Fiction in Conflict* (Cambridge: Open University Press, 2016), 61. See also Martin Paul Eve, "The Essay in the Career of the Contemporary English Novelist," *The Cambridge History of the British Essay* (Cambridge: Cambridge University Press, forthcoming).
5 J. M. Coetzee, *Diary of a Bad Year* (Melbourne: Text Publishing, 2008), 20–21.

6 Some notable examples would include Don DeLillo's "The Power of History" (published in the *New York Times* in the same year as *Underworld*), Jonathan Franzen's "Mr. Difficult" and "Why Bother?" (both first published around the time of *The Corrections*), David Foster Wallace's "E Unibus Pluram: Television and US Fiction" (published while *Infinite Jest* was being composed), or Tom McCarthy's "The Death of Writing" (published alongside *Satin Island*).

7 Bryan Cheyette, "Between Repulsion and Attraction: George Steiner's Post-Holocaust Fiction," *Jewish Social Studies* 5.3 (Spring/Summer 1999): 69.

8 Cynthia Ozick, "She: Portrait of the Essay as a Warm Body," *Essayists on the Essay: Montaigne to Our Time*, ed. Carl H. Klaus and Ned Stuckey-French (Iowa: Iowa University Press, 2012), 167.

9 Ibid., 168.

10 Claire de Obaldia, *The Essayistic Spirit: Literature, Modern Criticism and the Essay* (Oxford: Oxford University Press, 1996), 11.

11 Theodor W. Adorno, "The Essay as Form," trans. B. Hullot-Kentor and Fredric Will, *New German Critique* 32 (Spring/Summer 1984): 154.

12 William H. Gass, "Emerson and the Essay," *Habitations of the Word* (New York: Simon and Schuster, 1985), 25. See also: G. Douglas Atkins, *Tracing the Essay: Through Experience to Truth* (Athens: University of Georgia Press, 2005), 42.

13 Cited and translated in Adorno, "The Essay as Form," 164. See Max Bense, "Über den Essay und seine Prosa," *Aferkur* 1.3 (1947): 418.

14 Jeff Porter, "Introduction: A History and Poetics of the Essay," *Understanding the Essay*, ed. Jeff Porter and Patricia Foster (Peterborough, ON: Broadview Press, 2012), xxiii.

15 Atkins, *Tracing the Essay*, 148.

16 Adam Kirsch, "The New Essayists, or the Decline of a Form?," *The New Republic* (February 18, 2013), https://newrepublic.com/article/112307/essay-reality-television-david-sedaris-davy-rothbart, accessed March 22, 2022

17 De Obaldia, *The Essayistic Spirit*, 15–16.

18 Carl Klaus, "Essay," *Elements of Literature*, ed. Robert Scholes and Carl Klaus (Oxford: Oxford University Press, 1991), 6.

19 Michel de Montaigne, "To the Reader," *The Complete Essays of Michel de Montaigne*, trans. D. M. Frame (Stanford, CA: Stanford University Press, 1958), 2.

20 Christy Wampole, "The Essayification of Everything," *New York Times* (May 26, 2013), https://opinionator.blogs.nytimes.com/2013/05/26/the-essayification-of-everything, accessed March 22, 2022

21 De Obaldia, *The Essayistic Spirit*, 1. "The title of [Montaigne's] famous book, *Essais*," writes Terence Cave, "was clearly not intended by the author to be a genre title: there was no such genre in his day, only a number of relatively informal modes of writing that might be called 'miscellanies' (*mélanges*) or present themselves under some ad hoc title." Terence Cave, *Thinking with Literature: Towards a Cognitive Criticism* (Oxford: Oxford University Press, 2016), 57–58.

22 E. M. Forster, *Aspects of the Novel* (New York: Rosetta Books, 2002), 17.

23 Mikhail Bakhtin, *The Dialogical Imagination: Four Essays*, ed. M. Holquist, trans. C. Emerson and M. Holquist (Austin: University of Texas Press, 1981), 11.

24 De Obaldia translates this phrase from the 1887 preface to Maupassant's *Pierre et Jean*. See de Obaldia, *The Essayistic Spirit*, 4.

25 Quoted in Jonathan Franzen, *How to Be Alone: Essays* (New York: Farrar, Straus and Giroux, 2007), 95.

26 Milan Kundera, *The Art of the Novel*, trans. L. Asher (London: Faber and Faber, 2005), 64.

27 De Obaldia, *The Essayistic Spirit*, 3–4.

28 Kundera, *The Art of the Novel*, 18.

29 De Obaldia, *The Essayistic Spirit*, 3.

30 This translation comes from Brian Dillon, *Essayism: On Form, Feeling and Nonfiction* (London: Fitzcaraldo Editions, 2017), 17. See Jean Starobinski, "Peut-on définer l'essai?," *Pour un temps* (Paris: Centre Georges-Pompidou, 1985).

31 Ibid.

32 Kundera, *The Art of the Novel*, 14.

33 Christy N. Wampole, "Late Twentieth Century French and Italian Essayistic Fiction," PhD Dissertation (Stanford University, 2011), 9.

34 Georg Lukács, *The Theory of the Novel: A Historico-Philosophical Essay on the Forms of Great Epic Literature*, trans. Anna Bostock (Cambridge, MA: MIT Press, 1974), 88.

35 O. B. Hardison, "In Praise of the Essay," *Poetics and Praxis, Understanding and Imagination: The Collected Essays of O.B. Hardison, Jr* (Athens: University of Georgia Press, 1997), 12.

36 Kundera, *The Art of the Novel*, 6, 5.

37 See de Obaldia, *The Essayistic Spirit*, 16–28. The paradigmatic example is perhaps Marcel Proust's *In Search of Lost Time*. As Vincent Descombes writes: "Literary historians have established the fact ... that the novel began as the unexpected expansion of an essay Proust had undertaken in 1908 or thereabouts ... Scholars who have studied Proust's notebooks describe the way in which this essay was taken over by bits of narrative originally intended as illustrations supporting its theses. Thus the meditation of *Time Regained* was not added to the narrative, as an afterthought, in order to bring out its meaning. What happened was the reverse: The novel was born of a desire to illustrate the propositions of the essay." Vincent Descombes, *Proust: Philosophy of the Novel*, trans. C. C. Macksey (Stanford, CA: Stanford University Press, 1992), 5.

38 De Obaldia, *The Essayistic Spirit*, 16.

39 See Atkins, *Tracing the Essay*, 9–25.

40 De Obaldia, *The Essayistic Spirit*, 17.

41 Zadie Smith, "Revenge of the Real," *The Guardian* (November 21, 2009), 2.

42 Stefano Ercolino, *The Novel-Essay 1884–1947* (New York: Palgrave Macmillan, 2014), 41, xvii.

43 Ibid., 102.

44 Kundera, *The Art of the Novel*, 94.

45 See Steven Moore, "Introduction: The Novel Novel," *The Novel: An Alternative History* (New York: Continuum, 2010), 1–36.

46 Kundera, *The Art of the Novel*, 65.

47 My translation. Musil's original German – "*überhaupt kein Roman, sondern ein Essay von ungeheuren Dimensionen*" – is cited in de Obaldia, *The Essayistic Spirit*, 222, n.112.

48 Ibid., 213.

49 Ercolino, *The Novel-Essay*, 79–103.

50 Ibid., 93.

51 David Shields, *Reality Hunger: A Manifesto* (New York: Vintage, 2011), 199.

52 Ibid., 17.

53 Ibid., 201–202.

54 Ibid., 5.

55 Ibid., 68.

56 Smith, "Revenge of the Real," 2.

57 Shields, *Reality Hunger*, 203.

58 Ibid., 115.

59 Pieter Vermeulen, *Contemporary Literature and the End of the Novel: Creature, Affect, Form* (New York: Palgrave Macmillan, 2015), 22.

60 Joseph Tabbi, *Cognitive Fictions* (Minneapolis: University of Minnesota Press, 2002), xi, 76, 84.

61 Karl Ove Knausgaard and James Wood, "Writing My Struggle: An Exchange," *The Paris Review* 211 (Winter 2014).

62 Knausgaard, *A Man in Love: My Struggle Book 2*, trans. Don Bartlett (New York: Vintage, 2013), 497.

63 Gerald Murnane, "Author's Note," *Invisible Yet Enduing Lilacs* (Sydney: Giramondo, 2005).

64 Peter Boxall, *The Value of the Novel* (Cambridge: Cambridge University Press, 2015), 5.

65 Brian Castro, "Literature and Fashion," *The Sydney Review of Books* (April 23, 2013), https://sydneyreviewofbooks.com/essay/literature-and-fashion, accessed March 22, 2022

66 Ben Lerner, "The Actual World," *Frieze* (June 16, 2013), https://frieze.com/article/actual-world, accessed March 22, 2022

67 Joseph Tabbi, "Is Writing All Over, or Just Dispersed? Digital Essayism in 'Trina, A Design Fiction,'" *The Essay at the Limits: Poetics, Politics and Form*, ed. Mario Aquilina (London: Bloomsbury, 2021), 77.

68 Robert Coover, "The End of Literature," *American Scholar* (September 4, 2018), https://theamericanscholar.org/the-end-of-literature, accessed March 22, 2022

14

CLAIRE GROSSMAN, JULIANA SPAHR, AND STEPHANIE YOUNG

Lyric, Essay

What is the lyric essay?

We know it when we see it. There is the anecdote, the section break. The facts and historical digressions. Like a poem, a lyric essay flashes between ideas or images, leaning on figurative language and musical cadence. Like memoir, the stakes are often personal: *Should I vaccinate my child? What does it mean to feel out of place, to feel shame, or joy? How do I understand my childhood, my body, my mother, the casual racism of my colleagues?* There are pauses. And sentences that act as if they are paragraphs.

The lyric essayist's approach is somewhat scholarly without being too rigorous or argumentative. It is charismatic. Citation is idiosyncratic and irregular; some use footnotes, others list sources in the margin, some rely heavily on quotation.

Perhaps this is why those who describe the lyric essay often turn to metaphor. In blurbs, the lyric essay is said to be pensive and haunted, amulet-like, a dream within a dream. We have seen the lyric essay figured as a lover who doesn't want to leave; a sumptuous, multicourse meal; or, for John D'Agata speaking of "lyric essay" as a genre designation, "an example of lipstick on a pig."[1]

When we performed a simple web search for the "lyric essay," "juxtaposition" appeared in the first sentence of almost every result, as did "hybrid," "new," and "combine."[2]

Almost any definition of "essay" can be used to define "lyric essay" and vice versa. When Montaigne, often understood as the essay's progenitor, describes how he writes in "On Vanity," he speaks of how he gets "lost, but more from licence than carelessness. My ideas do follow on from each other, though sometimes at a distance, and have regard for each other, though somewhat obliquely."[3] Montaigne also claims he, like many a lyric essayist, pulls from the "gait of poetry, all jumps and tumblings."[4] Similarly, when Max Bense describes the essayist as someone who "turns his object around, questions it, feels it, tests it, reflects on it, who attacks it from different sides, and assembles what he sees in his mind's eye and puts into words what the object allows one to see under the conditions created in the course of writing" he could just as easily be describing the lyric essayist.[5] When Cheryl A. Wall in *On Freedom and the Will to Adorn* asks what an essay is – after saying what it is not – she determines that "rather than exhausting a subject, the essayist works around and through a specific aspect of it, proposed usually by a particular and often personal encounter with its implications."[6]

Of course, one could apply these descriptions to genres that are not the essay: The poet and the novelist both turn their objects around, testing and reflecting on them. They too assemble what they see, put objects into words, are not exhaustive.

We played a game as we wrote this. We held up a book and asked: Is this a lyric essay? Claire held up Jean Toomer's *Essentials*. Stephanie held up Simone Forti's *Handbook in Motion*. Juliana held up Gertrude Stein's *Lectures in America*. What about this? Or this? We debated whether or not Samuel Delany's *The Motion of Light in Water*, Kate Millett's *Sita*, and Yvonne Rainer's *Feelings Are Facts* were lyric essays, but decided they were all memoir. Because it includes photographs from medical texts and scholarly discussion of linguistics, we were willing to consider Lisa Linn Kanae's *Sista Tongue* as a lyric essay, even though it too is more or less a memoir. As is Audre Lorde's *The Cancer Journals*. What about Maurice Blanchot's *The Writing of the Disaster*? Philosophy. James Baldwin's *The Fire Next Time*? Essay.

"Lyric essay" is amorphous, maybe more situational than a distinct subgenre. To make things less clear, it also goes by many names: autotheory, autofiction, fictocriticism, hybrid prose, mixed-genre, experimental criticism, fourth genre, braided essay.

When Theodor Adorno noticed the style of Ernst Bloch's 1918 *Spirit of Utopia*, he wrote that the book – a segmented prose meditation – "aroused the expectation of something vast ... I had the feeling," he adds, "that here philosophy had escaped the curse of being official."[7]

A lyric essay is most recognizable by this very impulse: It is the subgenre that writers turn to so as to escape the curse of being official. Arguably it evaded this curse for a long time, circulating as idiosyncratic essay or philosophy prior to being burdened with a name in the 1990s.

Why name "lyric essay" at all? Recent approaches to theorizing the lyric underscore its historical contingency as a genre, describing it as a "project" that twentieth-century literary criticism "took from the nineteenth century and made its own."[8] Originally denoting a short song accompanied by a lyre, "lyric" now might be best understood as the consolidated name for, among other things, overhearing the poet talking to themselves, or the presence of an expressive "I," or short, lineated poetry.[9]

The "lyric" of lyric essay holds this sprawl, naming a sensibility rather than a formal or compositional attribute. And though the lyric essay's "lyric" does not have the imperative of, say, the "lyrical" of *Lyrical Ballads*, its nominal presence alongside "essay" signals a mutualistic arrangement, each genre leaning on the other.

Genres are never quite static categories. Rather, they are a series of conventions that harden into something recognizable. Lauren Berlant calls genre an "affective expectation."[10] Wai Chee Dimock goes for "a self-obsoleting system."[11] Franco Moretti describes genres as "morphological arrangements that *last* in time, but always only for *some* time."[12]

"Lyric essay" is a term that limps along in usage until the 1990s. But then once the 1990s happen, it suddenly seems as if the lyric essay has arrived. David Lazar calls the lyric essay "a market correction to the excesses of slovenly, untheorized autobiographical writing."[13] And while that certainly seems to have some truth, it is also a genre that has been shaped and defined by many of the huge changes to literary production that happen in the 1990s.

*

The turn of the twenty-first century witnessed dramatic changes to US literary production, with rapidly shifting conventions about who writes literature, and what sort of literature is officially literary. These changes were sweeping, complex, and contradictory. At moments it seemed as if literary production was becoming more democratized and inclusive.

Changes in production and distribution allowed writers to publish their work quickly, easily, and outside multinational publishing houses. The culture wars of the late 1980s and early 1990s changed the racial demographics of the works deemed significant or canon-worthy. More and more people attended school to become writers. Colleges and universities, especially private, tuition-driven ones, eagerly expanded their course offerings to meet this demand. The number of Master of Fine Arts (MFA) degrees offered increased dramatically in the 1990s.

At the same time, literature increasingly responded to corporate rather than cultural concerns. Suddenly there was a Borders or Barnes & Noble in every suburban shopping mall. Literature was in some ways becoming more accessible to the middle class. Libraries stopped buying as many books.[14] Multinational publishing houses bought up legacy publishing houses and each other until most of US literature was published by just five big publishers. Both the megabookstore and multinational publishing house answered to the bottom line. They distributed and published less literature.[15] Market-driven literature was given new life when barcodes created a database of national sales numbers, accessible to anyone willing to pay a lot of money. The independent bookstore and its power to point readers to good literature began to disappear.

In short, the production and distribution networks of literature were in some ways more accessible and in other ways more corporate and hierarchical.

All of these forces consolidated sales at the top, giving rise to literary blockbusters, which were often memoirs. In 1996, James Atlas observed this memoir boom, speculated that "the form could turn out to be surprisingly robust."[16] Literature was no longer seen as divorced from the marketplace. Many insisted it was a commodity.

> *Tuesdays with Morrie* (Mitch Albom), *The Liar's Club* (Mary Karr), *Angela's Ashes* (Frank McCourt), *Under the Tuscan Sun* (Frances Mayes), *Girl, Interrupted* (Susanna Kaysen), *This Boy's Life* (Tobias Wolff), *Prozac Nation* (Elizabeth Wurtzel), *The Kiss* (Kathryn Harrison)

The expanding MFA programs, which had traditionally taught poetry and novel-writing, were eager to expand further. They began to offer concentrations in creative nonfiction, which mostly meant memoir. Atlas noted the "literary agents making their annual pilgrimages to the famous writing program at the University of Iowa and signing up memoirists for six-figure deals. (They used to sign up novelists.)"[17]

The MFA became a point of contention. Even those who taught in creative writing programs expressed doubts about them. Some said the degree was useless, or likened the workshops to therapy, or called the programs neoliberal, narcissistic pedagogy. Some argued that it shaped literary production, that it might "increase the abundance of poetry, but ... limit its variety."[18] The "well-crafted" workshop poem was deemed stifling.

The ascendant literary forms of this moment all shared some fealty to a write-what-you-know sensibility, where what the author knows is the author's life experience. There was the workshop poem with its lyric "I"; the first person of the MFA-taught creative nonfiction (with blockbuster memoir aspirations); the "multicultural" autobiography or novel as a distinct and true-to-life observation of minority experience. These approaches were counter to the claims that had been made in the name of "High Theory" or "poststructuralism," counter to the insistence that the author was dead. The poet Harryette Mullen put it this way: "You know, there was a joke that circulated among minority (and some women) graduate students: 'It's that white male subjectivity that needs to be put on hold ... We can just put a moratorium on that, and the rest of us need to step up to the plate, you know (laughter). We *need* our subjectivity.'"[19]

Roland Barthes in "The Death of the Author" describes culture as hollowed-out to the point where "text is a tissue of quotations drawn from the innumerable centers of culture."[20] Lyric essay, we think, takes shape as this form (even as Barthes, a committed essayist, wrote this description long before the subgenre emerged).

*

The lyric essay, like many subgenres, is thus a fighting form. The different groups of writers who all inadvertently produced variations of the lyric essay shared the desire to be other than the workshop poem/story's "I," the memoir's first person, the author as self-observer of marginal identity.

Experimental poets, for example, used a form of the lyric essay in their fight against what Charles Bernstein calls "official verse culture," the dominant poetic mode that had produced both the workshop poem and its close friend the *New Yorker* poem.[21] They wrote things that at the time they often called "poetics" or "poetic statements" or "poet's prose" but would now be called lyric essays. They most often used this form to write about aesthetics, the aesthetics of their influences and their own. And the result was a series of idiosyncratic literary critical works, somewhat more personal and less argument-driven than traditional scholarship. Susan Howe's *My Emily Dickinson*, for instance, describes an antinomian Dickinson, one who "refuses to conform to the Anglo-American literary traditions," one that Howe finds so influential to her own work that she breaks the fourth wall to note that she "wanted to find words to thank Emily Dickinson for the inspiration of poetic daring."[22]

> *Artifice of Absorption* (Charles Bernstein), *The Pink Guitar: Writing as Feminist Practice* (Rachel Blau DuPlessis), *Soft Pages* (Kathleen Fraser), *The Language of Inquiry* (Lyn Hejinian), *My Emily Dickinson* (Susan Howe), *HOW(ever)*, "Notes for an Oppositional Poetics" (Erica Hunt), *Poethics* (Joan Retallack), *Poetics Journal*, "Alarms & Excursions" (Rosmarie Waldrop), *Bad History* (Barrett Watten)

Marjorie Perloff observed that these essays were ballasted by a central principle "that poetry incorporates its own poetics, that it has a theoretical base."[23] These writers embraced poststructuralism. "Alarms and Excursions," for instance, borrowed the style of Wittgenstein's philosophical propositions in *Tractatus Logico-Philosophicus*. Waldrop describes herself as "circl[ing] around this mysterious interaction of private and public that is poetry," proceeding with a numbered set of theses and quotations addressed in intervening commentaries.[24] She intensifies the essay's tendency to circle around.

Perloff characterized what we now call lyric essays as "works that use poetic figuration and structure to present a particular poetics as well. As such," Perloff adds, "*theorypo* or *poetheory* as we might call it, was positioned as the very antithesis of the epiphanic lyric of the Writing Workshop."[25] Put another way, these early examples refused to prioritize personal experience and feelings as the primary concern of poetry. Instead, when they wrote about themselves, they turned their attention outwards. They presented themselves as under the influence of other writers, reversing the conventions of lyric. Scholarship became the domain of poets and poetics.

*

"Poetheory" never caught on. John D'Agata more or less coined the term "lyric essay" in a 1997 issue of *Seneca Review* and then doubled down in a 2014 anthology *We Might As Well Call It The Lyric Essay*. He described a lyric essay as a mode of writing in excess of the conventions of nonfiction, one of "beautiful gangly breadth."[26] Around this time, Ben Marcus called the lyric essay a form of fiction that "seems to invoke a kind of nonfiction not burdened by research or fact, yet responsible (if necessary) to sense and poetry, shrewdly allegiant to no expectations of genre other than the demands of its own subject."[27]

> *On Immunity: An Inoculation* (Eula Biss), *The Body: An Essay* (Jenny Boully), *Autobiography of Red* (Anne Carson), *About a Mountain* (John D'Agata), *Point and Line* (Thalia Field), *Humiliation* (Wayne Kostenbaum), *Break Every Rule* (Carole Maso), *Madness, Rack, and Honey* (Mary Ruefle), *Reality Hunger* (David Shields)

Marcus and D'Agata's definitions of the lyric essay cited idiosyncratic groupings of writers who were already established and often affiliated with MFA programs. Some identified as fiction writers, some as poets, some as writers of nonfiction. This was a markedly different subset of writers than the crowd of experimental poets described in the previous section. And yet what the "workshop poem" was to the experimental poets – conventional, middle brow, unsophisticated – the memoir was to these writers who claimed to be writing lyric essays.

The memoir was, as we mentioned, having a moment in the 1990s. Some might argue that Oprah's Book Club gave rise to this boom with its power to boost book sales or create a bestseller out of a languishing midlist title. The memoirs that Oprah chose were often written by nonprofessional writers who had extraordinary lives, singled out for their authenticity.

This authenticity could be challenged, as when Oprah featured James Frey's *A Million Little Pieces*, originally marketed as a memoir, in her book club. A huge public controversy resulted when the book was quickly revealed to be fictional. Journalists then began to gleefully uncover similar literary frauds every few months. The author Nasdijj, who had published several memoirs about growing up Navajo, was revealed to be a white man named Tim Barrus. Memoirist Margaret B. Jones, a "half-Native" foster child and a member of the Bloods, was in fact Margaret Seltzer, a white woman from Sherman Oaks. At least three fraudulent Holocaust memoirs – one written by the daughter of a Nazi collaborator – were brought to national attention.

For some, this collision of literary and popular culture became one more example of the memoir's debasement. It was now a genre beloved by daytime talk television's mass audience, hungry for any veneer of authenticity.

D'Agata himself wrote a memoir, *About A Mountain*, and a meta-account of writing his memoir, *The Lifespan of a Fact* (with Jim Fingal). The latter is a somewhat parodic account of Fingal doggedly fact-checking the essay that became *About a Mountain*, D'Agata all the while arguing with the memoir industry's stringent, journalistic standards of accuracy. D'Agata bristled at the idea that his personal stories should be strictly fact-checkable. He felt that such a criterion misunderstood artistic autonomy.

*

When we tell the story this way, the lyric essay appears to be an experimental form written mainly by white middle class writers at the turn of the twenty-first century. Its writers were likely to be hesitant about or even oppositional to identity politics, to be philosophically aligned with post-structural critiques of subjectivity. They often believed that excellent literature was rarified and oppositional to marketplace values. And the lyric essay, in the case of the experimental poets, was a genre in which to discuss literature. Or, in the case of the D'Agata types, a genre in which to discuss the self in a postmodern, fact-hostile sort of way.

But these, of course, were not the only writers of lyric essays. A number of theorists working in and around postcolonial studies often used poetic prose to counter simplified accounts of cultural formation. They described and modeled the sorts of aesthetic outlooks that were needed to approach questions of difference, coloniality, diasporic culture, and language, the kinds of writing and storytelling that had arisen out of historical necessity. Their accounts are often marked by the lyric essay's signature section breaks and poetic language; they tack between scholarship and autobiography.

Borderlands/La Frontera (Gloria Anzaldúa), *Dictee* (Theresa Hak Kyung Cha), *The Death of William Gooch: A History's Anthropology* (Greg Dening), *Open Veins of Latin America: Five Centuries of the Pillage of a Continent* (Eduardo Galeano), *Poetic Intention* and *Poetics of Relation* (Édouard Glissant), *Woman Native Other: Writing Postcoloniality and Feminism* (Trinh T. Minh-ha), *Loving In the War Years: lo que nunca pasó por sus labios* (Cherríe Moraga), *Looking for Livingstone* (M. NourbeSe Philip)

Édouard Glissant, for instance, wrote from the mid-twentieth century onward about the necessity of a more complicated view of Caribbean cultural formation, proposing concepts and allegories in service of such an aim. His best-known work, *Poetics of Relation*, reads like a series of short, fragmented philosophical essays; certain sections pause to narrate and reflect on images such as the hold of a slave ship or a burning beach.

Across these works, uncategorizable modes of writing and speech arise from – and respond to – situations of oppression. For Caribbean literatures, Glissant says, "historical marronage intensified over time to exert a creative marronage" in excess of European literary traditions.[28] Approached this way, lyric essay is politically (and not just aesthetically) oppositional. Trinh T. Minh-ha sees "in-between grounds" in knowledge as potentially liberating: "[C]racks and interstices are like gaps of fresh air that keep on being suppressed because they tend to render more visible the failures operating in every system."[29] Much of this work also countered the impulses of memoir. "Writing, for the majority of us who call ourselves writers," Trinh laments, "still consists of 'expressing' the exalted emotions related to the act of creating and either appropriating language to ourselves or ascribing it to a subject who is more or less a reflection of ourselves."[30]

*

The impact of these simultaneous histories is crucial to understanding two important examples of contemporary lyric essay that complicate the relationship between the self, the lyric "I," and representational politics. Claudia Rankine in *Don't Let Me Be Lonely* and Bhanu Kapil in *The Vertical Interrogation of Strangers* both write from a first person that evades self-representation even as they invoke the readerly expectation of it.

We wonder now if, when we first read these books, we fully understood all they were fighting within and against, the structural conditions evoked by their composition. But now they seem exemplary of how lyric essay has the capacity to complicate whatever mode it is working within and against, whether that be lyric address, memoir, or expected narratives of racialized and/or immigrant experience.

Don't Let Me Be Lonely (which is subtitled "An American Lyric") reverses the logic of a fact-checkable memoir about an individual life. Though it appears to describe a period in the poet's life, Rankine in fact assembles a collective life from the facts listed in the notes at the end of the book. These include news stories, statistics, ideas from other writers. Some readers felt betrayed or deceived by this. Rankine says those readers "had trouble with that idea, that the first person could be a structural position unconnected to any particular self."[31]

In a 2007 interview with Major Jackson, Rankine describes how debates about the lyric animated her writing:

> I was very interested in what it would mean to write from the first person when we've had the rhetoric around language poetry about the limits of the first person, and the idea that the lyric is a personal, and perhaps narrow sensibility, and so I thought how can we rescue the first person? How can we take the I back so that the I becomes an extension of the world?[32]

Rankine says that because *Don't Let Me Be Lonely* "contains so many disparate narratives and travels across such a range, I needed an engine that pulled everything together while still allowing things to shift like a gear shift, and that was how the first person was intended to function."[33]

Kapil's *The Vertical Interrogation of Strangers* is written in the voice of a collective first-person taking shape as a series of responses to twelve interview questions. Kapil's collective "I" consists of various Indian women who each answered these same twelve questions; their responses are translated, distilled, and commingled.

Discussing *The Vertical Interrogation of Strangers* ten years after its publication, Kapil's approach to the body and to listening departs entirely from "conventional" understandings of narrative. She writes: "In the collective, the sensations, in repetition, form a kind of boundary or ridge. An accumulate. Is that a word? That then can be broken down into the elements of speech. Choral revenue. Vibration. The place at which colors convert into sound."[34]

*

As the lyric essay developed, the relationship between authorial identity and the first person began to stabilize. The form was increasingly practiced as autobiographical prose engaged with a larger world. Though it maintained a distance from the blockbuster memoir of the 1990s, it was told through the figure of an individual subject generally understood to be the same as the writer. This mode of lyric essay foregrounded the positionality of its narrator, often pointing back at the act of storytelling through a running self-interrogation or metaconversation about narrative itself.

Bright Felon: Autobiography and Cities (Kazim Ali), *Blackfishing the IUD* (Caren Beilin), *The Undying* (Anne Boyer), *Deforestation* (MK Chavez), *Codependence* (Amy Long), *The Argonauts* (Maggie Nelson), *I, Afterlife: Essay in Mourning Time* (Kristin Prevallet), *Grief Sequence* (Prageeta Sharma), *The Collected Schizophrenias: Essays* (Esmé Weijun Wang), *Heroines* (Kate Zambreno)

Still, we can see traces of a more complicated "I" in the tradition of *Don't Let Me Be Lonely* and *The Vertical Interrogation of Strangers*. Sometimes this looks like the chat room chorus that Caren Beilin includes in *Blackfishing the IUD*, the voice of a collective body in pain from illness brought about by insertion of the copper birth control device. This collective voice is interspersed between more traditionally autobiographical accounts of Beilin's own experience. Sometimes this looks like the inclusion of another distinct voice such as Harry Dodge's, who enters *The Argonauts* to comment on his representation by Nelson in her account of their relationship, his gender transition, and her pregnancy. As David Lazar writes in his reflection on the lyric essay, "mothers are where the action is."[35] We can't help but notice how effectively women writers employ the lyric essay to address bodies in transformation, bodies in crisis, bodies failed by a capitalist medical system.

And yet in these examples, the entrance of other voices, whether collective or individual, is kept separate from the book's narrator, who is one and the same as the author. Beilin, for instance, offsets the collective voice in a different, larger font. There is no way a reader of Beilin's work might feel deceived as readers of Rankine's *Don't Let Me Be Lonely* did.

For the most part, today's lyric essays drift back into the memoiristic approach, a closed circuit between author and identity.

*

The lyric essay is now an obvious enough subgenre that it verges on formulaic: The writer recalls some heartache or historic tragedy and cites a critical theorist before pivoting to an image. A Derrida or Foucault quotation provides oblique commentary. This sort of lyric essay almost always takes the self as the subject at its center. This official lyric essay turns the self around, questions it, tests and reflects on it, even as this self-examination is refracted through whatever other subject matter the work is ostensibly about.

But if the lyric essay is less a form and more a means of escaping the curse of being official, then this imagined formula too easily dismisses lyric essay as a space of possibility. The lyric essay moves in and out of institutions, coagulating at certain moments while appearing more diffusely in others. And as the lyric essay does this, it defends itself as a form that is oppositional, that allows its author to find a way around disciplinary conventions. But perhaps it would be more accurate to say that by now, scholars have been shaped by earlier interventions working somewhere between lyric and academic essay, have been galvanized by the interstices, the gaps, the burning beach.

> *The Hundreds* (Lauren Berlant and Kathleen Stewart), *Wayward Lives, Beautiful Experiments: Intimate Histories of Riotous Black Girls, Troublesome Women, and Queer Radicals* (Saidiya Hartman), *Minor Feelings: An Asian American Reckoning* (Cathy Park Hong), *Braiding Sweetgrass: Indigenous Wisdom, Scientific Knowledge and the Teachings of Plants* (Robin Wall Kimmerer), *Threads* (Sandeep Parmar, Nisha Ramayya, Bhanu Kapil), *In the Break: The Aesthetics Of The Black Radical Tradition* (Fred Moten), *The Empire of Love: Toward a Theory of Intimacy, Genealogy, and Carnality* (Elizabeth Povinelli)

The critical lineage here is especially striking in postcolonial and Black diasporic thought; Glissant instead of Barthes. Alexis Pauline Gumbs, for instance, describes herself as "speculative documentarian," writing "from and with the perspective of a researcher, a post-scientist sorting artifacts after the end of the world."[36] Many of these writers explore the complications of race across disciplines and histories and the associational form gives them space for homage and allegiance, or as Hartman puts it, "to tell the stories of those who had left no record of their lives" and "to fill in the blank spaces of the historical record and to represent the lives of those deemed unworthy of remembering."[37] In Hartman's relationship to the missing record, we hear echoes of M. NourbeSe Philip, who writes at the end of *Zong!* about "the telling and un-telling of what cannot, yet must, be told."[38]

> *A Map to the Door of No Return: Notes to Belonging* (Dionne Brand), the trilogy that is *Spill: Scenes of Black Feminist Fugitivity, M Archive: After the End of the World*, and *Dub: Finding Ceremony* (Alexis Pauline Gumbs), *The Black Shoals: Offshore Formations of Black and Native Studies* (Tiffany Lethabo King), *In the Wake: On Blackness and Being* (Cristina Sharpe), *Sentient Flesh: Thinking in Disorder, Poiesis in Black* (R. A. Judy)

Some images necessarily recur and interact between authors, a discussion across works. Glissant's imagining of the hold of a slave ship (in "The Open Boat"), for instance, is revisited by Saidiya Hartman, and later factors into Moten (and Stefano Harney)'s conception of the undercommons. King nods to Glissant when proposing "Black shoals" as an organizing metaphor for how Black thought might intervene in "the normative flows" of Western critical theories about slavery and white settler colonialism.[39] Sharpe uses the metaphor of the wake to conceptualize Blackness as it exists in the path cut by transatlantic slavery, while Gumbs meditates on how marine mammals can offer potential models of human "vulnerability, collaboration, and adaptation."[40]

The sorts of homage and allegiance pursued by these works point towards other understandings of the lyric in a lyric essay: not just the agility to flash between ideas and images, not the figurative language or musical cadence, but the potential for criticism to be powerful, ringing, elegiac.

These works demonstrate that the lyric essay's engagement with scholarship can be as incisive as – more incisive than – other, more official forms of critical writing. Lyric essay as the scholarship of high collective stakes, as rigorous conversation across histories.

Just as we can look back on texts that could be categorized as lyric essays but which circulated as essay, philosophy, or memoir, it may be that the present and future of the lyric essay circulates without being marked as such. Less a subgenre than a signal, this writing escapes the bounds of training, market demands, and disciplinarity. It alerts us to not always obvious arguments within a field, shifts within institutions and markets, and changes to production and circulation.

It fights by doing something else, by turning. The obsession with the oceanic in these recent books makes more sense than the tissue of Barthes. The form is like water, carrying within it the sediment of where it has been, also ebbing and flowing.

Notes

1 John D'Agata and David F. Weiss, *We Might As Well Call It the Lyric Essay* (Geneva, NY: Hobart and William Smith Colleges, 2015), 6.
2 Google, accessed November 13, 2020.
3 Michel de Montaigne, *Complete Essays*, vol. 3 (New York: Penguin Group, 1958), 1124.
4 Ibid., 1125.
5 Max Bense, "On the Essay and Its Prose," quoted in Theodor W. Adorno, *Notes to Literature* (Columbia University Press, 2019), 41.
6 Cheryl A. Wall, *On Freedom and the Will to Adorn: The Art of the African American Essay* (Chapel Hill: University of North Carolina Press, 2018), 1.
7 Adorno, *Notes to Literature*, 467.
8 Virginia Jackson and Yopie Prins, *The Lyric Theory Reader: A Critical Anthology* (Baltimore, MD: Johns Hopkins University Press, 2014), 2.
9 Ibid., 2–3.
10 Lauren Berlant, *Cruel Optimism* (Durham, NC: Duke University Press, 2011), 6.

11 Wai Chee Dimock, "Genre as World System: Epic and Novel on Four Continents," *Narrative* 14.1 (2006): 86.

12 Franco Moretti, *Graphs, Maps, Trees: Abstract Models for Literary History*, illustrated ed. (London New York: Verso, 2007), 14.

13 David Lazar, "Hydra: I'll Be Your Mirror," *The Essay Review* (blog), http://theessayreview.org/hydra-ill-be-your-mirror/, accessed February 12, 2021.

14 Steve Coffman, "How Low Can Our Book Budgets Go?," *American Libraries Magazine* (October 14, 2013), https://americanlibrariesmagazine.org/2013/10/14/how-low-can-our-book-budgets-go/.

15 Dan N. Sinykin, "The Conglomerate Era: Publishing, Authorship, and Literary Form, 1965–2007," *Contemporary Literature* 58.4 (2017): 470.

16 "Confessing for Voyeurs; The Age of The Literary Memoir Is Now (Published 1996)," *New York Times* (May 12, 1996), Magazine, 25.

17 Ibid.

18 John Barr, "American Poetry in the New Century," *Poetry* Magazine (September 2006), p. 434.

19 "A Conversation with Harryette Mullen," interview by Farah Griffin et al., summer 1998, http://writing.upenn.edu/epc/authors/mullen/interview.html.

20 Roland Barthes, "The Death of the Author," in *Image Music Text* (New York: Hill and Wang, 1977), 146.

21 *Content's Dream: Essays, 1975–1984* (Evanston, IL: Northwestern University Press, 2001), 246.

22 Susan Howe, *My Emily Dickinson* (New York: New Directions, 2007), 35.

23 "Avant-Garde Tradition and Individual Talent: The Case of Language Poetry," *Revue Française d'études Américaines* 103 (2005): 129.

24 Charles Bernstein, *The Politics of Poetic Form: Poetry and Public Policy* (New York: Roof Books, 1990), 45.

25 "Avant-Garde Tradition and Individual Talent," 129.

26 D'Agata and Weiss, *We Might As Well Call It the Lyric Essay*, 9.

27 Ben Marcus, "On the Lyric Essay" (2003), http://benmarcus.com/writing/on-the-lyric-essay/.

28 Édouard Glissant, *Poetics of Relation*, trans. Betsy Wing (Ann Arbor: University of Michigan Press, 1997), 71.

29 Trinh T. Minh-ha, *Woman, Native, Other: Writing Postcoloniality and Feminism* (Bloomington: Indiana University Press, 2009), 41.

30 Ibid., 29.

31 "Claudia Rankine, The Art of Poetry No. 102," interview by David L. Ulin, *Paris Review* (2016), www.theparisreview.org/interviews/6905/the-art-of-poetry-no-102-claudia-rankine.

32 Claudia Rankine in conversation with Major Jackson, http://writing.upenn.edu/pennsound/x/Rankine.php, accessed December 15, 2020.

33 Ibid.

34 "Bhanu Kapil by Katherine Sanders," *Bomb* (September 22, 2011), https://bombmagazine.org/articles/bhanu-kapil/.

35 David Lazar, "Hydra: I'll Be Your Mirror," *Essay Review* (2016), http://theessayreview.org/hydra-ill-be-your-mirror/.

36 Alexis Pauline Gumbs, *M Archive: After the End of the World*, illustrated ed. (Durham, NC, and London: Duke University Press, 2018), xi.

37 *Lose Your Mother: A Journey Along the Atlantic Slave Route*, first ed. (New York: Farrar, Straus and Giroux, 2008), 16.

38 M. NourbeSe Philip, *Zong!*, first ed. (Middletown, CT: Wesleyan University Press, 2011), 199.

39 Tiffany Lethabo King, *The Black Shoals: Offshore Formations of Black and Native Studies*, Illustrated edition (Durham, NC, and London: Duke University Press, 2019), 2.

40 Alexis Pauline Gumbs, *Undrowned: Black Feminist Lessons from Marine Mammals* (Chico, CA: AK Press, 2020), 12.

15

KEVIN ADONIS BROWNE

The Photograph as Essay

At Last

Figure 15.1 *Portrait of My Grandfather at Home*, 2016. All photographs by the author

Essaying Is the Art of Wandering

One follows paths, or roads, or rails, or rivers. One goes astray, carves space anew, clearing what might have been covered, lighting what might have been obscured. It is, therefore, a *peripatetic* art, an act of deliberative leisure designed for the human spirit to move independently of the body that contains it – or the institutions that would seek to constrain it. As far as I know, one is *supposed* to wander and drift about – and, if one cannot do these things, one is supposed at least to *want to*.

The wandering occurs as much with the mind as with muscle and bone. It can be envisioned, imagined, dreamed. In whatever form it occurs, it is human to wander. Essaying is natural. This would be the case even if the world were not turned on its head, which it is. Even if my movements were not *literally* constrained, which they are.

This question of wandering matters for people (like me) whose history is borne in transit, but who have lately felt as though we are running out of time, which we are. I am in Trinidad now, writing as the Covid-19 pandemic continues to rage around me. The country has been shut down since March 2020. It's June, now. 2021. The grail of a writer's isolation is now a matter of law, as is the mandate to be masked and distanced. We are locked down and mired in fear. We pretend as if nothing has changed, even though everything has changed; we pretend, to save our lives, imagining ourselves unafraid. There will be an end to this (because things end), but for now we live from spike to spike, as we hope for a greater distance between one and the other. I had thought I was fortunate to belong to a tradition that has prepared me for this time of masking, except it has not prepared me at all. Here, in Trinidad, we are forced to read eyes and brows. Faces here seem censored. Redacted.

Things have taken on different meanings that I must now decipher for myself. Expression has shifted, turning on those whose stillness is a forced stillness – an *enforced* stillness. The irony of "Carnival People" perpetually masked has worn off. We dance mostly in memory, now. Everything, now askew, requires new attention from each of us.

Jolted from the superficiality of symbolic use, the *un*freedom of everyday life has become *literal*. Unaccustomed to this literality, we have tried to do what we always do, what we believe our cultural reflexes demand: *We make light of things*. They have not all worked well, these worn, familiar ways of ours. And yet I wonder what it may mean to make light of things now, however different the time. Stripped of pretense, new urgencies laid bare before me, I want to consider the meanings we make of the things we make with light: photographs and the essaying they enable.

To begin with this end is to be reminded that what has passed never truly passes. Its stillness is a companion to us who regard it, chronicling our intention, articulating lights and shadows, pixels and inks. But that is not the only thing (which can be applied as easily to pandemics as to photographs). More than that, the photograph can reshuffle our assumptions and expectations of what time and space are supposed to be for us – it troubles them as they trouble us. We draw meaning from their symbolic actions to navigate, and perhaps understand, our literal lives.

The photograph is a literal taking of time that invites us to do what photography has always done: *take time*. Take time to see, if that is what you hope to do. To feel, to think. To regard any photograph in such a way as to see its obvious, outdated stillness as a kind of wandering that takes you past the moment of its making, beyond the time we have left, beyond memory or nostalgia. Far from the constrictions of everyday life, this boundless stillness, full of magically mundane things, is a stillness that is so easily missed, its mundane magic so frequently overlooked.

The *essaying* I invite you to do with me takes the photograph and its attendant words as its point of departure, leaving you free to determine what follows and what, if anything, takes form. It is an invitation to go beyond the threadbare triumphs and losses of the will.

Let me show you what I mean.

...

First, consider the following terms:
Photograph Essay
Photographic Essay
Photograph as Essay (my preference, obviously)
Do this at your leisure, distinguishing between what you think are
  their characteristics.

I know, in this postdigital existence of ours, where photography seems (again) to be threatened with irrelevance, these terms will hold a different significance than what they held, say, before the Internet. Take note, anyway, of the interpretive possibilities that begin to unfold merely in your decision to move away from the abbreviation and oversimplification of this form. No more casual references to the "photo essay" for a while.

Now, begin again (as I have). Take a minute. Think of what you have missed, what you may have overlooked in your haste to get to this point. I will ask you to think along with me, but think of other things, too. Let us wander, you and I.

What comes to mind?
Will you make a note?
Will it be handwritten?

Breathe.

Is the air clear where you are?
Is it hazy or putrid, full of smoke or dust
like it sometimes is where I am?

Come back when you feel like it.

Come back.
Or do not come back.
Defy.

Go as far as you wish.

How far have you gone? I can only wish to go.
Curfew from 9pm to 5am; 7pm to 5am on weekends.

Look around.

I will do the same.
I see a wall, a painting on it.
What do you see?
That's my grandfather there,
in the upper firmament of this essay – and throughout.
Did you know?
Did you trust the caption?
...

Perhaps I have asked too much of you. Or too much, too soon. Indulge me, if you can. Indulge yourself, too. Remember that feeling, whatever it is. Try not to make too much of it at this point. Essays are supposed to build, the intensity of their currents are supposed to increase gradually, taking you along and sweeping you away until eventually, buoyed on the drifting sargassum of argumentative thought and reflection, of memory trawled and imagination stirred up like sediment, you forget the betrayal of windless waters and learn, finally, to trust the tide.

Let it happen.

Soon enough, you will have traversed a gulf and come upon the shore of some new understanding. Some new, unknown thing: practices that have not yet announced themselves as traditions, or a set of languages as yet unformed in your mouth. Be careful. These metaphors of discovery can seem benign, but I have found them treacherous: The symbols they invoke can, at times, be jagged. Time can seem unreliable here. The codes will seem foreign. See yourself as a visitor or an immigrant and try not to colonize what you have come upon. Try not to control it. Learn the language, its praise songs and its dirges, its long, breathy hymns. Learn perspective.

To do this with photographs, you will have to look closer, perhaps even at a different angle. Closer, with glazed eyes or with closed eyes, so you can discern the onset of age from the scourge of ruin, so you can comprehend the sublimity in the life of an image as it moves beyond the grasp of passing time. Remember, though: *Do not try too hard.* Overthinking is masochistic. If you must try something, try to feel. These are numbing times.

Feeling is redemptive.
Feeling is the reminder.

A Leisurely Act

I am taking this personally.

Frustrations aside, I still belong, in one way or another, to people who feel things – music will *hit*, food will *lash*, things read will sometimes *soothe*, the photograph will sometimes *touch*. We feel harsher things, too. I belong to people who understand the power of witness, though we sometimes deny it. We recognize what power there is in the collective voice of ordinary people who wish to resist tyranny – in all its contemporary, populist, racist, sexist, and xenophobic forms. Tyranny, however familiar, however accented the accents of its perpetrators.

It is personal, too, because we have been taught to seek and then present knowledge in unfeeling spaces, where we are not welcome, wanted, or represented. Neither seen nor felt, we have learned to speak of ourselves in unfeeling ways, struggled to master the language of numbing. Succeeding at it and failing to find ourselves where we do not belong, we have forged other ways of knowing in the voids created by other, more dominant misrepresentations. Taking the invisibility for proving, the silence as crucible, we know what it means to base our senses of knowing on the ironic acceptance of enduring *un*representation.

Our material lives are real (and remembered), not merely visual but also visible. Sometimes we are *hypervisible*, which, you may know, is a violence to us – to be so visible that we are sometimes not visible at all is not a superpower. Our metaphors are not dreamed up in the wistful musings of explorers or expatriates who find themselves unsure about the implications of heat or sugar or salt on our bodies. We no longer live and die on account of our aspirations to the traps and trappings of Empire or its derivatives. Progressive as these postimperialist times may be, you will understand why I reject the domineering imperatives of "foundational thought," uprooted as I and my people have been.

Figure 15.2 *Portrait of My Grandfather Waiting at the Dinner Table*, 2017

Still, if you find yourself on the outside of my references, try not to worry. Do what I have done. Supplant my work and my words with your own and essay from there. If that measure should fail, consider this: What truly *human* endeavor is impersonal? What is worth doing that would leave our humanity out?

Too much to ask, perhaps? Too soon?

Let us, for the sake of our mutual indulgence, say no. And I will assume that you have begun to consider the *Photograph as Essay* beyond what it appears to offer. I will assume that you have returned again to the photographs, perhaps going over them once, or twice, or more than twice, to guess at or ascertain what logic might be revealed in my sequence. Finding no overt correlation, because I have given none, I hope you will be reminded of your own ability to detect nuances (as commonplace as they may first appear). What's more, if you have done any of these things, you will have engaged in the act of essaying as a form of leisure.

You will have *essayed*.

As for me, I want to dispel the notion that the essay exists as a phenomenon *in stasis*, that its conclusions are always already foregone, its work already concluded. I want to challenge its function as an artifact, or an archive, that can only be examined forensically. I will not concern myself too much with categorizations, except to say that, like the traditional Photographic Essay, the *Photograph as Essay* is an examination of humanity – one's own – taken from a perspective that its composer may have ordinarily overlooked.

Leisure is meant here as a kind of work – a privilege you may not have worked for but have either earned or inherited. Such leisurely acts can engender a sense of identification with the subject. I will not call it *mercy* or *empathy*, though it may look like that in practice. You may feel something. Just remember that what *you* think (of this essay form) will be the only thing that matters in the end. I invite you to feel strategically. So, read by all means, but try to do so *without* the need for explanation. Take the time to see photograph and word, each unencumbered by the other, letting them drift together on their own before you try to think of what they might mean. Then, consider those whose bodies have been inscribed upon, whose faces you once had the privilege of viewing on *their* terms, or your own.

If you have ever attempted an essay such as this, you will already understand that visual texts are not merely subject to being read but are also evidence of layers of subjection – that is, the interminable inscription of meanings on the subject *itself*. If you have ever engaged in these layered subjections, you will have already implicated yourself in their outcomes. Done well, such an essay would illustrate the relationship between veiled meanings and people who have been barred from making their meanings known; between abstractions and their lesser-known points of vernacular origin; between the *Photograph as Essay* as a form to be studied and more organic considerations of the ones for whom such an essay might do some work; between those who make the frame and those who inhabit it. Done well, you may discover that the act of essaying, in my grave present or yours, is how new knowledge will take the shape of the frame *you* have set for it – it is epistemic, but only in the most vernacular sense, like myth or folklore.

I have obviously shown my hand with these binaries.

My objective is not to destroy them or the conventions that produce them, nor is it simply that the notion of an expert (or myself as one) is objectionable, or that taxonomies and structures (still) insist on specialization and the subsequent disciplining of people and their ideas.

No.

It is that I wish to essay, to express my sense of leisure beyond the limits of surveillance and terror, to use photographs and words to imagine myself free of debilitation and injustice, and to have you join me in that imagining. And then, of course, to eventually *accomplish* what we have imagined. This is what these twists are all in aid of, where I hope these turns will eventually lead.

A Type of Form

On Carib Street in San Fernando, near the corner of Upper Hillside Street, there is a former house in the yard belonging to my mother's family, the Pitts and the Wrights. Pitt is my grandmother Muriel's surname before taking the surname of my grandfather, Newallo John Wright. My cousin, Kenrick Pitt, lived there. They called him Ken.

Around the house, almost like a skin but more like bone, another house made of brick and concrete has gone up. Over time, the young has swallowed the old. I am told that zoning laws prevent the complete demolition of this structure because it is too close to the road. I grew up in the house behind that one. 16A Carib Street. That house, too, has gone through some changes, most of its boards replaced with bricks, its wooden beams replaced with steel. I had taken them for granted, as a child would do, these buildings that seemed to wear new buildings like ill-fitting clothes – ironic proof that it was them, the old houses, that no longer fit in this new landscape of things. No place for old places, here.

Ken, my mother tells me, whistled beautifully. "Like a bird." I remember his square jaw, his body chiseled from his imprisoned years, or from playing the Double Second Tenor at Hillside Symphony. I remember those things, but not much else. I can only imagine his whistling now, and I am as apt to

Figure 15.3 *Portrait of My Grandfather Looking South, Toward the Coast*, 2017

replace my imaginings of his melodies with those of a bullfinch or a semp at daybreak – those are birds. I had birds, once.

Why do I remember these things when I should be writing? And why do I refer to sounds I cannot remember when I should be writing about sight (and sites unseen)? Because I am beset – in every aspect of my life – by structures that are built on other structures. They appear to us as new, until some detail emerges from the stubborn ruins of our progress to have us think again in old, forgotten ways. They prod us to look again. Well, not *us*.

It's my own fault that I must contend with these binaries and dilemmas of memory, that I must revisit what I had forgotten until now. I may have brought this on myself – one of the consequences of the form.

Look again. Closer, this time.

Essays about essays can be overcomplicated things, simple only in their redundancy and the drudgery of their retelling. They either do too much or not much at all, depending for their shape and structure on what has come before them, bones built on bones, pretending they are new (sometimes better than new: *original*), defending the thing they have sought to erase. In doing too much, they risk undermining the essence of the form.

I prefer not to take that risk.

I will, instead, risk doing what the essay about an essay may not typically do: locate what exists within the structure, in defiance of the structure that has come up around it. I will not go in search of an old house, its rotted beams, its fallen ceiling. Those are gone. Chasing the implausible logic of my mother's memory, I go in search of the whistle that was like a bird and that I remember from stories, a thing I might have heard. I will not go in search of spirits, but the impossible things that spirits hold. Not the dying man, but the essence of him that a photograph would attempt and fail to capture. Not him, but the light he sees that would eventually make its way through the window to me. Not the spectacle these essays offer, but what it clarifies and, at times, obscures: *Meaning*.

For you, the task is only this: Read the signs as they emerge. Think of your own, whether they are known to you or linger like mysteries. Imagine the spaces their light and sound may have filled. Then try to go there.

(I have the matter of other memories to which I must attend, but I will meet you again shortly.)

A Feeling for Substance

In truth, I should have begun writing before the world changed. If I had, I would have said that I struggle to think of an expressive form more indicative of projected impermanence than the *Photograph as Essay*, adorned as it is in the style of its perishable composer. Before, if I had made such a claim, my conscripted colleagues or friends might have argued the merits of that point. Some might have attacked the claim as if it were blasphemy, while others might have defended it for the same reason. It would have cooled on its way from heated debate to polished prose.

But not now.

We might have argued about what constitutes such an essay, refining versions of a familiar checklist: the photography must take precedence; the writing follows, lest the unattended images be misread or mistaken for an errant series; there is the proportion of photographs to words, what counts as too much or too little of one or the other; then a question of whether that essay would be an end in itself, or a means to some other end. On the undulations of philosophy and wit, items and ideas would have moved from stage to stage, further from their origins like castaways, further away from the ones whose stories they may have been intended to tell. Closer to what we might have argued would be their eventual purpose.

Not now, though.

We might have argued, then, about the *real* work of the essay, each argument serving as an artifact of the indulgence of its creator. From the careful examination of the criteria, some provisional knowledge may have arisen. An essay. But these scenarios feel hollow – like the kind of indulgences I have no time, in this Now, to claim.

And what *Now* is this?

Figure 15.4 *Portrait of My Grandfather Regarding Himself*, 2017

The inescapable kind, of course. The kind in which reflections on knowledge-making feel grave but stagnant, like the realization of one's mortality in the passing of days that go unseized. In this inescapable version – where breathing with no cough is the latest privilege, and the tender, unfevered touch is rare – the charge for making knowledge has seemed to intensify, even as the energy to carry it out has dissipated in the thick, dusty air of every day. The stakes of my defiant stillness and my leisure are different in this inescapable Now.

Higher, in a way. Simpler, too.

"But then," you may say, "aren't these things normal, part of all of our lives and all our everydays? Show me one thing, and you will have shown me all things. What 'new normal' is *actually* new, except to those of us who only now inhabit it? Pandemics have always been here to undo us, to amplify the frailties of our bonds and our bodies. The sea has always raged, outlasting history, never waiting for us to crown its tides or mark its rising levels against the height and depths of a drought. What age has not known overladen boats, or overturned ones, living bodies and dead bodies pouring into the surf or onto the shore? Who has not beheld a horizon, recalled a metaphor of discovery, and mused? The earth has always shaken, claiming neither right nor rebellion when it explodes, blocking the sun, turning the living and unliving alike into frantic ornaments cast about its unkept yard. We swallow its ash, breathe in its dust, revel in its powders. We drink its dirty water.

"How are we any different in this Now from the ages that have come, the ones yet to come? We have always needed air to breathe. We have always been more or less than we have hoped to be, flawed and exquisite, gifted and cruel.

Beautiful. Dangerous."

And, aware of the time, I will say, "Yes. That is all true."

True, that my psychic fugitivity *and* my physical freedom have dissolved like dreams I have dared to dream. These dreams that take me out of hatred's path, away from the barrel of a gun or the point of a knife. They breathe life into me, defying the constricted breath, defying its constrictors. They shield the unriddled body like a secret, holding it close like a myth, like a promise of freedom.

Yes, these things are all true. These mortal times are just as granular as they have always been, just as dangerous. They seem to require no symbolism, breed no metaphor. Like you, I am faced with the same familiar urgency of thinking in seemingly perpetual response to dread – faced, that is, with having to choose not to succumb to its pressures, wandering elsewhere. What is left to be seen in such a time as this? And what part will we play in its making? Knowing that no essay will free us of these times, what will our seeing ultimately yield?

I ask only because in these times, with these higher stakes, it is no small thing to make new meaning of a thing that is already an end in itself, no small thing to forge new knowledge. To see when seeing is luxury. No small thing to resist the flourishing of our anxieties, as they blend into the undignified landscape of our very human troubles. No small thing to dance, as our superficial triumphs fall away like sequins or feathers or any of the accoutrements that are lost in a vast deluge of our tired bodies. No small thing to be still.

No small thing, *Life*, in these dread and disquieting times.

"Try not to panic," I will say. "The subjections *are* infinite, but they are *not* absolute. There is space and light for us, which we must make and keep, where our smallness will not feel so small, and our seeing, feeling hearts will soar."

I will say these things aloud, but mostly to myself.

I have shown my hand again, but I already know that by the time you read this, everything that I have made reference to here will have passed. I hope its essence will remain and, possibly, endure. This can only be a half-hearted hope, one that sees me hoping in mediated ways. For even as they are realized, they will eventually fade. Hope, like other things, will sometimes fade, either ground away to silvered dust, or eaten by bookworms and termites, or overwritten by technology once meant to preserve it. It also manages, in a way, to endure. I have fallen short – more often, lately – but I have also been sustained by what I think the *Photograph as Essay* is designed to invoke: a time that has passed but yet remains, a past that does not pass.

Figure 15.5 *Portrait of My Grandfather Regarding the Southeastern Slope*, 2018

I wonder, though:

What past has passed you by, daring you to remember? What past, not yet passed, has you imagining? You will have to decide for yourself what is worth noting here. And then, you will have to decide what, if anything, you have to say about it. Know that whatever meaning you make, in whatever form, will be foregrounded by the memory of an experience that has been visualized. That visualization will be an antecedent to the expressions intended to articulate or accompany it. And you will be there for all of it – *that* is also true.

I am reminded here that it is possible to run out of time and be unable to escape the very real afflictions of that time – be out of it and in it, at the same time. I try not to despair. Because I am also reminded that it is possible to essay *beyond* the need for escape. In this version, the desire is less relevant, as the aspiring essayist – you or I – would know what it means to traverse the expanse of a photograph's stillness, unbound by the frame.

It is not freedom, only the sense of it.

Though, I wonder, if it is too much to expect that we would eventually want to free ourselves – and use essaying as a means to that end. Who, but we, can say?

Ante Mortem

Photography is functional beyond its received tendency to record moments or highlight events. It allows us to consider how meaning can enable one to reflect on things that are drawn from life – meanings made of light, or which occur in the ostensible afterlife of light. It is an afterlife that is always beginning in an effort to stave off its end. Its embedded meanings remain just beyond – *and* just within – our reach. We therefore are able to arrive at its meanings before we could *know* what they are. How else to get there than to wander? How else to find what has not yet been found, except to imagine its absence and its loss? I may be referring to myself, here. This moment is all too present for me. The yesterday of your reading is the everyday from which I am currently unable to escape. And although we both understand that what you read here is the afterlife of a thought, its past tense has not yet arrived for me.

Understanding this, I treat the *Photograph as Essay* as an instrument with which to craft an elegy to the form – the form, that is, of a thing whose meaning is yet to be, which relies on memory to enact the imaginative potential of its narrative. These imaginings will then be projected into a future where memory is reconstituted, or revised, and represented to the viewer as if the memory itself were an original thing. This is how I see it, at least. It may be something else – may *look* like something else, entirely – when it is your turn to do this. I don't mean to be vague. I want only for us to be free (at least in this space) to make assumptions of what we encounter, to claim whatever we imagine, to make and name as knowledge whatever we choose.

Photography is not *passé*, but hopefully we are no longer concerned with the mythic ability of a photograph to "tell the truth." With the rise of the digital, its platforms and algorithms, and in spite of the obvious cooptation, modification, and arguable perfection of the photographic arts, we have no real need for a license. We are free to think without it, projecting past what we think is its expiration. And yes, it will be that same illusory freedom, but we can practice a bit of autonomy. Until better comes, or until we make it so.

Of course, there will be no way of *knowing* what our acts toward freedom will yield over time. But that is not our concern, right now. Our concern is what may be called the aspirational quality of leisurely work – the inherent conceit of essaying. As one of the most human(e) endeavors we can attempt, this approach to essaying transcends the limitations of originality, or of failure and success. Through it, we are able to reach for new evidence of wonder to endure these times. Let the act of reaching be the elegy you craft. And let that elegy be the lasting mark of life and light that will look and sound to some like a whistling bird that was once a man.

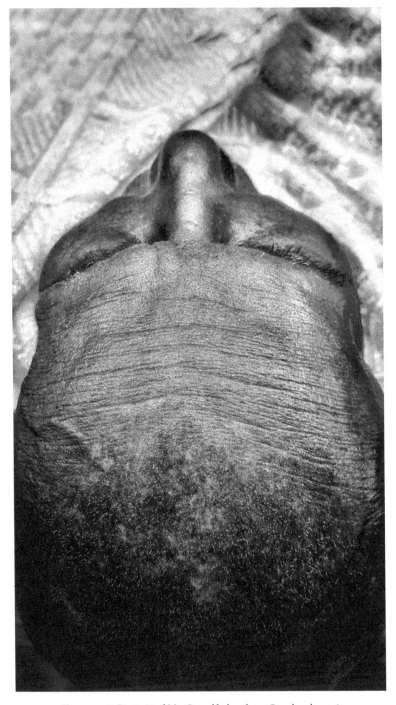

Figure 15.6 *Portrait of My Grandfather from Overhead*, 2018

Post Memoriam

I would have neglected my erstwhile responsibility as a rhetorician if I did not concede a basic point: Every text possesses various degrees of persuasive power. A great deal of that power is derived from the intention of its composer, which is then communicated through the strategic deployment of signs and signifiers. That the composer does or does not make those motives immediately clear makes little difference. A general characteristic of visual texts is that they will never show all there is to see, regardless of how visual they may be or how explicit the language that attends them. With the *Photograph as Essay*, however, we are reminded more of what we have missed – and may, likewise, recall – than simply provided with that which the composer thinks we should see. We sometimes strain to locate the argument, regardless of its apparent universalism. Other times, we are forced simply to guess – often incorrectly. And, even when we are as fully informed as possible, the content itself may nevertheless remain at a level of abstraction that serves only to emphasize the importance of witness in the conjuration of meaning. These, to me, are good things, as they remind us of our agency in the entire process. (These past months have been hard, and I sometimes forget. Things slip by.)

That is to say two things. First, the essayistic photograph, while appearing to offer clarity by way of a definitively visual and authorial perspective,

Figure 15.7 *Portrait of My Grandfather, At Last, Regarded from Distance*, 2018

simultaneously offers a great deal of obscurity by amplifying what the composer can only *attempt* to express about what they *think* they have seen, which they can only *hope* is received and understood by the audience – *you*. Even the clarity is a provisional and troubled clarity, at times altogether troubling (and more reminiscent of obscurity). To come away from such a text with clear answers would mean that you have found a point, a bit of substance in which to base your assumptions and subsequent interpretations. This is a fair outcome. Texts should *do* things – and we, with them. Exactly *what* those things are is matter for some debate. You can decide that.

But this leads to the second thing. To have come away with a point, to which the essay would have *led* (as opposed, say, to that which you would have *found* by means of your own experience and insight), would also suggest that you may have missed the greater, more subtle point of what I think the *Photograph as Essay* can yield: A situation in which the reader engaged in the physical, intellectual act of *essaying* is implicated in the infinitude of interpretive possibility. The acts of reading and reflecting achieve these ends. This is not to suggest that the essay cannot teach particular lessons, or that you should not seek to learn particular lessons from it. Rather, it is to emphasize that the only *definitive* element in the form is the reader – not the photograph, not the essay, but *the one who essays* from it:

You.

An End, Again

Unlike its other derivatives, the *Photograph as Essay* is not simply an appeal to the eye, complemented by a symbolic appeal to the ear or any other part of the body – the heart, for example. It is, instead, an appeal to sense – not the reason or rationality of sense, but an appeal that treats sense *in itself* as its *raison d'être*. Thus, while its components are obvious, the *Photograph as Essay* is not merely what it appears to be, but what we want it to be. As such, it is a visual, textual representation of an interpretive act, a collaborative human desire existing beyond the bounds of persuasion. An aspiration that requires no resolution.

Now, I cannot say if you will be called upon to attempt one of these. But that is not very important. The *Photograph as Essay* and my thoughts on its form are about us, and for us. It is, as I have said, the expressed afterlife of mediated truths, of hardened histories, and of generations of witness accumulated around us. It is ours, but not bound, as we are, by time. Come to it whenever you wish, prompted more by what you have witnessed than by what you have been directed to do. Witness, I tell myself, is a strange privilege. (In the end, it may be the only privilege we can manage in the time we have.) To essay, then, is to see for ourselves what *we* do with what we have witnessed. Having wandered about and found for ourselves that there is no shortage of terrors and joys, we will discover that we have no shortage of causes to which this form can be addressed.

I have opted not to make a study of the conventional form. For, in the absence of that sense of aspiration or autonomy to which I have referred, the enduring relevance of the form would crumble, leaving only the hint of a thing, a frame on which another frame might be built. It would be a monument, of sorts, that would announce the kind of progress that could only take the ruined form of what the essayistic art *might* have been. Like the essay itself, you – reader, viewer, essayist, human – are not bound by any of this. You require no license to practice it.

Either this is what essaying is, or I do not know what I am doing. Either I am clear-headed, or I am exhausted and trying not to come apart at the end. Either I see the course ahead, or I am rudderless and adrift with no beacon for referent, no grounds to anchor the meanings I intend.

Then again, who am I to say?

I have not set out to do what you can do for yourself. As you must have discovered, there are any number of examples that even a cursory search for "photo essay" will yield. Relevant keywords will generate relevant examples. From this probable embarrassment of riches, you are certain to come upon many photographic essayists – Eugene Smith, Gordon Parks, Sebastião Salgado, Gerard Gaskin, Jahi Chikwendiu, DeNeen Brown, Wayne Lawrence, Abigail Hadeed, Nadia Huggins, Maria Nunes – whose work over the last three-quarters of a century would solidify them and the form in the essayistic canon. But, you see, I belong to a people suspicious of canons – of who gets to say where we and our meanings ought to belong, what we ought to be, and how. I hope you are, too, but this may be where I leave you. I have already abdicated my authority as an expert. I have already suggested that you, by virtue of your humanity alone, are fully equipped to make that determination on your own. Perhaps that is enough.

My meanings are much simpler. I worry for my mother who remembers whistling, my aunt who cries when she sees a house on fire. I am still alive but bereft of my objectivity. If asked, now, what have I done, I would say only that I have used photographs to essay. I have used them, too, as an essay to see and read and feel the written word. Or, I have done the opposite. Perhaps I have done neither of those things, or far more.

...

In truth, I have only *essayed*.

That is all.

And only that. And nothing else.

16

NORA M. ALTER

The Essay Film

As we begin the third decade of the twenty-first century, the essay film has achieved a stable position and acceptance as a genre within audiovisual production.[1] The essay film has developed into a new form of cinema that, with its dual audio and visual dimensions, progressively transforms the nature of traditional philosophical discourse, just as that discourse, when filmed, transforms the nature of cinema. Although new genres are constantly emerging within any field of cultural production, the essay film is unusual in that it took so long to gain a foothold within the canon. This is in part because of its uneven development across time and space. Essay films have been around since the implementation of editing techniques and montage to advance narrative in early cinema. Indeed, some critics locate the first essay film with D. W. Griffith's *A Corner in Wheat* (1909), others with Edward S. Curtis's *In the Land of the Headhunters* (1914), and still others with Richter's Inflation (1928). For some scholars, essay films cannot exist before sound cinema, dating its origins with Luis Buñuel's *Land without Bread* (1932). Other historians establish the essay film with its first theorization in writing: Sergei Eisenstein's "Notes for a Film of 'Capital'" (1927), Richter's "The Film Essay: A New Type of Documentary Film" (1940), and Alexandre Astruc's "The Camera Stylo" (1948).

Impressed by James Joyce's *Ulysses,* Eisenstein proposed to film Karl Marx's *Capital* from "thousands of 'tiny details,'"[2] fragments in which "the form of *fait divers* or collections of short *film-essays* is fully appropriate for replacement of 'whole works.'"[3] Eisenstein found the question of how to represent an abstract concept such as capital, which is not a thing but a dynamic, living social relation, to be particularly perplexing. In his project notes, he reflects on a "new form of cinema" that would have to be "discursive" and based on the genre of the essay.[4]

A decade after Eisenstein, Richter wrestled with questions of how to capture abstract thought on film. He proposed a new kind of film that would enable its maker to render "problems, thoughts, even ideas" perceptible and "make

246

the invisible world of imagination, thoughts, and ideas visible."[5] He called this new kind of film an essay film since it "deals with difficult themes in generally comprehensible form."[6] Richter reasoned that unlike documentary film, which presents facts and information, the essay film produces complex ideas not necessarily grounded by reason or in *reality* – ideas that might be contradictory, irrational, and fantastic. For Richter, the essay film no longer binds the filmmaker to the rules and parameters of traditional documentary practice. Instead, it gives free rein to the imagination. Richter chose the term "essay" because the new genre is inherently digressive, playful, contradictory, and political. Echoing Eisenstein's reflections on capital, he cited the stock exchange as an example of a topic that the essay film might confront:

> to show that the function of the stock exchange, is that of a market ... In order to make comprehensible how the stock market functions, one must include other factors: the economy, the needs of the public, market laws, supply and demand, etc. In other words, one cannot rely on simply photographing the object, as is the case in straightforward documentaries, instead one has to try – by whatever means necessary – to reproduce *the idea* of the object.[7]

For both Richter and Eisenstein, the frustration of not being able to represent an abstract economic concept with conventional forms and techniques spurred the conceptualization of the essay film. They both advance the cinematic essay as a new kind of filmmaking that modulates feature, documentary, and art film elements, given each category's perceived limits.

Whereas Eisenstein and Richter were contemporaries and aware of each other's films, though probably not their writings, Astruc emerged out of a different milieu altogether. Writing and making films in France during the postwar era, Astruc penned two critical essays. The first, "The Camera Stylo," promoted the notion of a *camera-stylo* (camera-stylus) that would "become a means of writing, just as flexible and subtle as written language ... [rendering] more or less literal 'inscriptions' on images as 'essays.'"[8] For Astruc, essay films might include textual or graphic inscriptions on the celluloid either materially, or more prevalently, figuratively. The result is a multilayered product: an image track, a soundtrack, and a written track, often accompanied by a voice-over commentary. The textual track or layer is sometimes in direct contradiction with the image track, creating within the total filmic text a jarring collision of opposites and complex levels of meaning that the audience must coproduce. In his second essay, "The Future of Cinema" (1948), Astruc advocated for new technologies that would free cinema from theatrical spectacle. "The cinema that is being born will be closer to the book than the spectacle, its language will be that of the essay, poetic, dramatic, and dialectic all at once," he concluded.[9]

These foundational texts provide the cornerstones upon which subsequent filmmakers and critics conceive of and construct essay films. Early formulations of the essay film find expression in the writings of documentarian John Grierson, playwright Bertolt Brecht, film critic André Bazin, and neorealist filmmaker Roberto Rossellini. It is important to stress that, except for Bazin, most early essay film practitioners and theorists were both writers and makers. This characteristic continues today with essay filmmakers such as Jean-Luc Godard, Harun Farocki, and Hito Steyerl oscillating between writing and moving image-making; they continuously navigate between the two modes of expression. Despite its existence both in practice and formal conceptualization, the essay film has had difficulty finding recognition as a distinct genre. This oversight, in part, is due to the vigilant guardianship of two other dominant practices within nonfiction film: documentary and avant-garde or experimental film.

This failure to acknowledge the essay film as a distinct genre was further perpetrated primarily by Anglo-American film critics and historians.[10] The essay film was, inaccurately, viewed as European and virtually ignored in US scholarly film circles until the 1990s.[11] In contrast, in France, by the 1950s, the term "essai cinematographic" was used frequently, and there was a European confederation of Cinéma d'Art et d'Essai. During the second half of the twentieth century, the essay film, as a minor genre, flourished on the European continent and in the United Kingdom. In Germany, New German Cinema filmmakers such as Rainer Werner Fassbinder, Werner Herzog, and Wim Wenders interspersed their features with short essay films that addressed philosophical questions on various dimensions of image making and the role of the filmmaker. Essay films are often marked by the presence of the director either audially or visually, or both. This leads film critic Frieda Graf to pronounce that "the essay film is the auteur film of the documentary genre." She continues to posit that they were "always a form of film criticism right from the outset."[12]

Stylistically, essay films are marked by a high degree of self-reflexivity, performing an auto-critique of audiovisual media production within the film. For example, Wenders's *Lightning over Water* (1980) compares the medium of video and its relationship to celluloid film to the cancerous cells attacking and destroying the healthy cells in Nicholas Ray's dying body. In Alain Resnais's *All the Memory of the World* (1956), a work centered on Paris's National Library, the director suggests that film supplements the role of printed matter in recording a history of the world. More recently, works by Amos Gitai have been characterized as the self-conscious fabrication of an archive for the future.[13] In some instances, the filmmaker is confronted with the conundrum of representing a history in an image-based medium where visual evidence is either nonexistent or has been deliberately destroyed. Rea Tajiri's *History and Memory: For Akiko and Takashige* (1991) tackles the lack of photographic evidence on the internment of Japanese Americans during World War II. To supplement images where there are none, she turns to Hollywood films: Fictional sources achieve factual status. Rithy Panh in *The Missing Picture* (2013) adopts a different tactic to tell the story of the genocide of Cambodians by the Khmer Rouge; in the absence of visual evidence and recorded archives, he recreates scenes using small clay figurines. Themes of history, memory, recording, and representation are staples of the essay film.

From Europe, the essay film spread globally through a variety of educational and immigrational circuits and routes. For example, in the late 1950s and early 1960s, Latin American filmmakers such as Glauber Rocha, Tomás Gutierrez Alea, Fernando Solanas, and Octavio Getino studied in Rome. Collectively, they developed the concept of Third Cinema, which both in practice and theory acknowledges the essay as an essential alternative to dominant cinematic practices. Third Cinema reached the USA and Britain through the work of US-based Ethiopian filmmaker and scholar Teshome Gabriel, who expanded its parameters to include emergent filmmaking of decolonization coming out of Africa. Belgian-born British scholar Paul Willemen discovered Gabriel's work in the early 1980s and introduced Third Cinema to Black British diasporic communities in the UK, including Sankofa and the Black Audio Film Collective. Meanwhile, Gabriel taught at UCLA from the mid-1970s onwards, where he trained a cohort of Black filmmakers, including Charles Burnett, Julie Dash, Haile Gerima, Barbara McCullough, Billy Woodberry, and others. Later called L.A. rebellion films, the resulting works eschewed traditional genre distinctions and were marked by an essayistic style that combined documentary, experimental, and fictional elements.

A different migratory path of the essay film unfolds within the field of fine arts. Richter trained as an artist, immigrated to the USA, and immediately began producing essay films with fellow European exiles such as Marcel Duchamp, Fernand Léger, and Max Ernst.[14] In the 1960s and 1970s, conceptual artists such as Vito Acconci, Dan Graham, and Robert Smithson experimented with film- and videomaking self-reflexive aesthetic meditations. A decade later, Judith Barry, Dara Birnbaum, Martha Rosler, and Tony Cokes explored video's potentiality for sampling from and appropriation of pre-existing sources to produce insightful critiques on commodity culture and mass entertainment. Not only did they source visual found footage, but they also employed popular music as a crucial structural signifier. In the 1990s, the transition from analog to digital production systems profoundly affected the essay film. It not only facilitated editing and montage, but also dramatically increased accessibility to an archival database of images and sounds. Moreover, in the last decade of the twentieth century, moving images found their place in art exhibition venues. Today, one is more likely to view essay films in museums and galleries than in movie theaters. Furthermore, with the shift from single-channel projections in cinema houses to television sets in open architectural spaces comes a proliferation of screens whereby the essay film takes on a sculptural dimension in its installation mode. Finally, digital streaming platforms have established an alternative distribution and reception model for the essay film.

Many definitions of the essay film include understanding it as a translation of the literary-philosophical written essay. Thus, some critics refer to it as "filmed philosophy," while others such as Laura Mulvey refer to "theory films," and Thomas Elsaesser declares Harun Farocki's films to be a "form of intelligence."[15] Some essay filmmakers engage in an intense reflection on the medium as medium. Already with Dziga Vertov's *Man with a Movie Camera* (1929) we see a preoccupation with how images are made. Later essay films on this topic include Farocki's *As You See* (1986) and *Images of the World and the Inscription of War* (1988), Wenders's *Notebooks on Cities and Clothes* (1989), Orson Welles *F for Fake* (1973), Valie Export's *Invisible Adversaries* (1977), Helke Sander's *Redupers* (1977), and Jean-Luc Godard's *Histoire(s) de Cinema* (1988). In *Parallel* (2014), Farocki produces an in-depth four-channel installation essay on the evolution of video game technology and virtual reality. Finally, in works such as *This is the Future* (2019) and *SocialSim* (2020), Hito Steyerl investigates the potential of Artificial Intelligence to generate texts and images. Essay films question the differences between film and photography, video and electronic imaging, and between film and the man-made environment as forms of visual representation; they trace the interrelated histories of "mechanical reproduction," "vision," and "visuality," "operative images," and finally of digitally generated images, manipulation, and intermediality.

In the broadest sense, the essay film is a hybrid that fuses the three long-established categories of film: fiction, documentary, and art film. But it also goes beyond this amalgamation to cross the boundaries of traditional disciplines. Producers of audiovisual essays include feature filmmakers, documentarists, avant-garde filmmakers, and artists who produce installations for gallery and museum display, and scholars who seek an alternative to writing to communicate their ideas. Indeed, reasons for the proliferation of the essay film in the twenty-first century include the broad accessibility of video cameras and digital editing systems. This technology has enabled individuals with little or no training in filmmaking to become practitioners of the craft. The facility to post recordings on sites such as YouTube and through social media networks has contributed to the proliferation of the genre. Further, the more general shift away from literacy toward visual culture in the late twentieth century has spurred production within this medium.

The form of an essay film is determined by which formulation of the written essay the filmmaker follows. Thus, postwar French filmmakers such as Chris Marker or Resnais were profoundly influenced by Michel de Montaigne, for whom "essay" meant the testing of ideas, himself (slyly qualified as "so frivolous and vain a subject"), and society.[16] The essay was a wide-ranging form of cognitive perambulation that reflected upon fundamental questions of life and human frailty, tensions, and overlaps between "fact" and "fiction," and their consequences for social order and disorder. For Montaigne, the distinguishing features of the essay include humor, irony, satire, paradox; its atmosphere is one of contradiction and the collision of opposites. German essay filmmakers such as Farocki or Hartmut Bitmosky follow German-language theorists such as Theodor W. Adorno, Walter Benjamin, Max Bense, and Georg Lukács. Lukács, in his "On the Nature of the Essay," posited the essay as both a work of art and a critique. He situated the essay between scientific and aesthetic production and defined it as "criticism as a form of art."[17] This duality forms the constitutive base of many essay films that perform film theory through the filmic medium itself. In other instances, rhetorical devices such as "chiasmus," or the oscillatory "crossing" of categories are adapted to the cinematographic medium. Further, Adorno's evocation of the puzzle picture that at once both shows and hides two images serves as a method of reading Farocki's image production. It is important to recall that Adorno was mobilizing this trope to address the occlusion of the worker and labor during a period of late capitalism. In his discussion of the puzzle picture, Adorno asks "where is the proletariat?," a question that Farocki tries to answer with his *Workers Leaving the Factory* (1995). Puzzle pictures are like the painterly and psychological technique of "anamorphosis," whereby a "change of perspective," in the extended or narrow sense, alters meaning.[18]

Some practitioners of the essay film, such as Steyerl, use various techniques of layering images and sounds to create a filmic version of what Benjamin referred to as the "dialectical image." In her essay film, *The Empty Center* (1998), on reunification and the city of Berlin, Steyerl sifts through the layers of history that comprise the Potsdamer Platz, once the center of Weimar Germany. Through elaborate superimpositions and overlays, images from the past are projected onto the present and cast into the future. As Steyerl explains, "The film makes use of slow superimpositions to uncover the architectonic and political changes of the last eight years ... [I]t traces back the history of ostracism and exclusion, especially against immigrants and minorities, which always have served to define the notion of a powerful national center. Its form evokes an archeology of amnesia where every single item refers to absence and erasure." Steyerl thus encodes a dialogic understanding of history, in which the past informs the present and vice versa, in the filmic technology itself. In addition to the theories of Benjamin, Siegfried Kracauer's philosophy of history forms a discursive scaffold in Steyerl's essay film. The archeology of Berlin is not just rendered visually but sonically, and *The Empty Center* opens with the sound of hammering as citizens use simple household tools to dismantle the wall. Steyerl's cinematic essay rings an alarm bell and signals a serious social and political crisis that the dominant media attempt to bulldoze over. *The Empty Center* warns that as old borders are torn down, new ones will be quickly erected with their own exclusions. Steyerl employs the form of the essay film to weave a self-reflexive critique of the documentary genre through the sociopolitical theme of reunification and the power of capital.

The field out of which it emerges determines the shape of the essay film. As evident from its beginnings, practitioners from radically different backgrounds, training, and institutional affiliations make essay films: film, art, anthropology, journalism, and many other disciplines. Godard and Anne-Marie Miéville come out of film and media; Yvonne Rainer out of dance; Martha Rosler and Isaac Julien are trained in the fine arts; Trinh T. Minh-ha and Jean Rouch are anthropologists; Alexander Kluge has a law degree; and Manthia Diawara comes from the humanities. Most essay filmmakers are educated (either formally or as autodidacts) in multiple fields ranging from philosophy to psychoanalysis, sociology, history, and social criticism. They translate their theoretical knowledge into the filmic medium using creatively the latest audiovisual technologies. The essay film thus bridges institutional divides between literary history, intellectual history, artistic practice, and film studies. One question that is often raised is how an essay film is different from a documentary. Here I follow Bense, who uses the example of a Green Woodpecker in his definition of the essay. Bense explains: "An analytic description leads to nothing more than a piece by Brehm (a German zoologist). But if one has an idea while looking at the Green Woodpecker, let's say concerning the concept of rhythm, and reflects this idea in the Green Woodpecker ... the experimental enters into the report which elevates it."[19] Bense thus stresses the intervention of subjectivity, aesthetics, and an ethical position that transforms an encyclopedic entry into an essay.

The essay film is inherently interdisciplinary, and many of its practitioners are part of a global diaspora that crosses borders and national boundaries. They are internationals, cosmopolitans, displaced from their country of origin, living a hyphenated existence between multiple cultures. This transnationalism figures prominently in their work. For example, US-educated, Philippine-based filmmaker Kidlat Tahimik explores the legacy of first Spanish and then US colonialism in his essay film *Perfumed Nightmare* (1989), the protagonist, self-reflexively played by Tahimik, leaves his small island for Europe. Objects of syncretism populate *Perfumed Nightmare* such as the "Jeepney," brightly painted and custom-designed vehicles that have been refashioned from standard-issue US military jeeps. Tahimik draws an analogy to his recourse to the essay film, a combinatory genre that brings together disparate elements to produce a new text. French-educated, Vietnamese-born, US-based anthropologist Trinh T. Minh-ha highlights displacement, dislocation, and myths of authenticity in *Surname Viet: Given Name Nam* (1989). Through a series of ruses, the film calls into question generic tropes and stylistic techniques that produce what Roland Barthes referred to as the "reality effect." Trinh demonstrates that what viewers accept as "truth" or "documentary" (in this case, the everyday life of women in contemporary Vietnam) is constructed out of a conventional set of institutional codes and superficial forms. For Trinh, the documentary genre has conditioned a public to blindly accept what is delivered as truth instead of interrogating its construction as text. Indeed, in her writings, she declares: "There is no such thing as documentary – whether the term designates a category of material, a genre, an approach, or a set of materials."[20]

Existing at the interstices of disciplines and methodologies, the essay film is a transgressive genre that willfully breaks the rules, conventions, and institutional strictures. This tendency manifests generically, formally, stylistically, thematically, and nationally. For example, formally, some essay films, such as Mark Lewis's *Cane Toads: An Unnatural History* (1988), willfully blend fact and fiction, in this case to produce a scathing allegorical critique on the legacy of the importation of foreign laborers to Australia. At the beginning of Ulrike Ottinger's *Johanna D'Arc of Mongolia* (1989), the character of Lady Windermere asks the provocative question: "Was it a confrontation with reality or with the imagination ... must imagination shun the encounter with reality? Or are they enamored of each other? Can they form an alliance?" The film, a voyage across the tundra of Mongolia on the former Trans-Siberian Express train, explores the intertwined relationship between travel, cinema, and ethnography. This problem is transformed into epistolary and travel essay films such as Marker's *Sunday in Peking* (1956), *Letter from Siberia* (1958), and *Sunless* (1982), as well as Chantal Akerman's *News From Home* (1991), Wenders's "filmed diary" *Tokyo-Ga* (1985), and Ottinger's *Chamisso's Shadow* (2016). This type of essay film is a form of "anthropological bricolage": a way of mapping psychological space and time onto geophysical space and time in order to offer an escape from national identity's conceptual and geophysical limitations, only to encounter new limits abroad and at home.

The essay film is often used to treat subjects that directly confront identity and fluid subject positions that refuse binary distinctions and constraints. Because the essay and the essay film are positioned between more stable genres, they problematize all binary categories of representation. These include topics such as gender; as for example, in Sue Friedrich's *Sink or Swim* (1990) or Monica Treut's *The Virgin Machine* (1988). Sexuality is conjoined with issues of race in Marlon Riggs's *Tongues Untied* (1989). And the AIDS crisis is the focus of Derek Jarman's *Blue* (1993), Rosa von Praunheim's *A Virus knows No Morals* (1986), and the omnibus *Silence=Death* (1990), featuring contributions by David Wojnarowicz, Keith Haring, Allen Ginsberg, and others. Although its literary-philosophical antecedent is the product of a singular voice, some essay films respond to a pressing or urgent crisis with a collective endeavor that seeks to diminish the hierarchy of auteurship in favor of community-based activism. Both *Far from Vietnam* (1967), a sharp critique of the US war in Vietnam, and *Germany in Autumn* (1978), response to the escalation in violence by both the Red Army Faction and the West German state, exemplify quickly made essays that respond to an immediate crisis.

Formally, some practitioners seek to expand the frame of film. Thus, Godard and Miéville in *Here and Elsewhere* (1974) challenge traditional single-channel viewing formations and develop a split-screen aesthetic to show multiple sets of moving images. Two systems of montage are at play; a sequential series of images that unfold within each quadrant and a montage that comprises the placement of the different sequences next to each other within the larger cinematic screen. Anticipating the emergence of multichannel installations, Godard and Miéville forge a new form of relationships in which the viewer beholds multiple-image tracks simultaneously. Contemporary multiscreen installations range from simple dual projections on a single surface as in Farocki's *The Silver and the Cross* (2010) to double-sided screens such as Stan Douglas's *Hors-champs* (1992) or Steve McQueen's *Ashes* (2015) that encourage the viewer to circle round the images, or Isaac Julien's nine double-sided screen installation, *10,000 Waves* (2010), which immerses the spectator into a sea of sounds and images. Many contemporary essay filmmakers create both single and multiscreen versions of their work in order to maximize accessibility. Thus, in 2013 John Akomfrah made the single-channel DVD, *The Stuart Hall Project*, and its companion three-channel installation, *The Unfinished Conversation*. Both works draw from the same database of sounds, images, recordings and archival footage; however the single channel is structured chronologically and musically following Miles Davis's compositions, whereas the installation eschews linear organization and includes quotations from literary texts by Virginia Woolf, Charles Dickens, and Mervyn Peake. The single-channel format allows for the concentrated reception of a compositional structure built on accretion. In contrast, the unstructured viewing environment of a gallery installation is more suited to discrete units or fragments of meaning.

As important as the visual track in an essay film is the soundtrack. Essay filmmakers follow the dictum of the Soviet directors Eisenstein, Vsevolod Pudovkin, and Grigori Alexandrov, who argued in 1929 that, unless it was used contrapuntally, sound would "destroy the culture of montage."[21] Sound, for these filmmakers, was never to be used as a suturing device. Pudovkin vehemently proclaimed that "music ... in sound film [must] *never be the accompaniment*. It must retain its own line."[22] Sound manifests in different ways; it can be heard as the voice who may be the director or their stand-in who provides a commentary for the film that may or may not correspond directly to the images show. In Hollis Frampton's *Nostalgia* (1971), there is a temporal lag between the image described on the screen and the one that is shown. Disjunctive strategies manifest in Yvonne Rainer's *Kristina: Talking Pictures* (1976), drawing attention to gender relations and subject formation by constructing a contradictory commentary. In Dan Eisenberg's *Persistence* (1997), photographs described by the director are from a different time than those that appear on the screen. Thus, a description of leave-taking from the late 1940s accompanies an image of a contemporary train platform. Eisenberg purposefully confuses the present and past to underscore how the contemporary moment is indelibly marked by history. Sometimes, contradictions and alternative messages manifest in the use of music. Dan Graham's *Rock My Religion* (1983) and Tony Cokes's *Black Celebration: A Rebellion Against the Commodity* (1988) turn to contemporary music to construct elaborate sonic structures that encase their social critiques. Marcel Ophuls's *November Days* (1991) is a "Musical Comedy," about the fall of the Berlin Wall and its aftermath. At times, a director uses music as a structuring device such as Godard's employment of the fugue in *Germany Year 90 Nine Zero* (1991) to account for Berlin's multiple narratives and histories. And Manthia Diawara turns to the popular form of opera in his *An Opera for the World* (2017) based on a Sahel tradition, which confronts the viewer directly with the tragic consequences of attempts to migrate. In many of his films, Godard creates "sound images," or what Gilles Deleuze refers to as "sonsigns." For Godard, both sound and images must be activated to produce critique; as he has it in *Here and Elsewhere* (1974): "To learn to see in order to hear elsewhere. To learn to hear oneself speaking, in order to see what others are doing." Sound can evoke an elsewhere, a political space often just off the visual frame on the margins. Sound may be recruited to enact the change in perspective, making a different image apparent from the dominant one.

Historically, essays emerge in times of crisis. Accordingly, they may be seen to have a functional dimension. Nevertheless, their appearance may also be symptomatic. As Homi Bhabha put it in a widely quoted phrase, "In every state of emergency there is an emergence," and essay films have often been produced in response to just such a state.[23] Lukács related the growing importance of the essay to the crisis of modernism. Bense, commenting immediately following the horrors of World War II, saw the essay as a crucial instrument for ethical and critical thought in the wake of a breakdown in humanity. As he concluded in "On the Essay and Its Prose," "[d]ue to the critical situation as a whole, due to the crisis which mind and existence thrive, the essay has become a characteristic of our literary era. The essay serves the crisis and its conquest by provoking the mind to experiment, to configure things differently, but it is not simply an accent, a mere expression of the crisis."[24] Adorno posited the essay as perhaps the only genre capable of resisting the massive instrumentalization that characterizes the contemporary moment. As curator Okwui Enwezor observes, "in the modern era artistic and intellectual collectives tend to emerge during moments of crisis. This crisis can be social, cultural, political or economic; however, its effects seem always to generate environments of *disillusion* and *disaffection*, leading to a counter challenge by artists."[25] Essay films become more pointed and effective during periods of cultural, social, and political crisis. Crisis and emergency can be productive in terms of artistic practice. For example, in the past ten years, a proliferation of works directly confront migration, climate crisis, and the Anthropocene.

In the past two decades, essay films and installations investigating migration and the border as a zone of violence have multiplied dramatically. Works such as Ursula Biemann's *Performing the Border* (1999), set on the USA–Mexico border, track the precarity and systemic abuse that marks the everyday lives of those who reside in such zones of indeterminacy. Julien's *10,000 Waves* and Akomfrah's *Vertigo Sea* (2015) launch their aesthetic meditations from recent disasters resulting in the death of migrants. The deaths are presented on the soundtrack as eyewitness recordings. Julien turns to a 2004 news item detailing the death of twenty-three undocumented Chinese workers who, unaware of the dramatic tides, drowned in Morecambe Bay in northwestern Britain. Julien replays a desperate call made to an emergency first responder team informing them of the impending disaster.

We only hear half of the conversation, which ends with the wrenching assessment, "just people, just people." In *Vertigo Sea*, it is a news report that imparts the recent accident of a boat carrying migrants. Waves crash as details of the disaster unfold, including the information that few on board knew how to swim; apparently, the captain abandoned his human cargo and made it safely to shore. The voice of a man murmuring "Oh Jesus save me, oh Jesus save me" overlaps that of the reporter. The traumatized plea echoes metonymically across centuries, as the sea is cast as a watery grave that has swallowed the bodies of many souls and regurgitated some on idyllic beaches. As an age-old medium for transportation, the sea in Akomfrah's film at once connotes hope and despair. Side by side and one after another in *Vertigo Sea*, kaleidoscopic configurations of images and sounds appear. However, it is stories such as that of the news report that impart the horror. The voice-over relates a story of a baby tossed off a slave ship into the sea for the crime of crying too much. The narrator pauses and voices a question over shots of black corpses washing up on a beach: "Why do I speak of one child when we have heard of many hundreds of men cast into the sea?" The sea is both passage and a watery grave that has swallowed the bodies of many souls, regurgitating some on idyllic beaches. The challenge is how to return to the singularity of the importance of an individual so that they are not merely rendered as part of a series of constant figures and statistics. How to make each human death count?

Candice Breitz tackles this same conundrum in *Love Story* (2016). She asks, "What kind of stories are we willing to hear? What kind of stories move us? Why is it that the same audiences that are driven to tears by fictional blockbusters, remain affectless in the face of actual human suffering?" The seven-channel work comprises a space divided into two parts. The first room contains a large screen. Against a green screen background, the actors Julianne Moore and Alec Baldwin alternate reading a monologue composed of fragments of stories of migration. In the second space, there are six small monitors; on each, there is a medium shot of a man or woman from diverse ethnic and racial backgrounds seated and looking directly into the camera, delivering a narrative. These individuals tell the same stories ventriloquized by Moore and Baldwin. Each person explains why they left their country. For Shabeena Francis Saveri it was because of persecution for being transgender; Jose Maria Joao sought to escape his past as a former boy soldier in Angola; Luis Ernesto Nava Molero is a political dissident from Venezuela. The youngest of the six refugees interviewed by Breitz is Sarah Ezzat Mardini, a former junior champion swimmer from Syria. She and her sister fled because of the civil war. They traveled to Turkey via Lebanon and then paid a smuggler for passage across the Aegean from Izmir to Greece. Mardini describes how their overloaded dinghy meant for eight people but holding twenty began to take in water, and how, as one of the few swimmers on board, she went into the sea at night and for three-and-a-half hours swam and pushed the boat, keeping it afloat until it miraculously reached the shore of Lesbos. Mardini eventually made it to Germany via Macedonia, Serbia, Hungary, and Austria.[26] In her work, Breitz challenges the division between the performance or reenactment of the real. Is there a difference in the "truth" conveyed? Moore and Baldwin attract immediate attention; their celebrity status makes the invisible visible, the inaudible audible. They serve as lures, hooking the spectator and drawing her in.

A different approach is operative in Nika Autor's *Newsreel 63 The Train of Shadows* (2017), which also begins from a real piece of evidence. In this instance, it is an anonymous fragment, a shard of reality circulating on the Internet as a brief video posting taken from a smartphone camera held by someone riding on the bottom of a train between the wheels. The fugitive image (literally and materially) conveys the desperate and cramped conditions of hanging on for dear life while somehow trying to record some images for a possible future viewer. The anonymous posting is evidence of a "here I was," "this was my journey." The identity of the "passenger" remains unknown and whether they ever made it to their destination is unclear. Out of a few seconds of footage, Autor generates an essay film that examines cinematic history of the train as a sign for modernity as it courses across screens over decades, carrying goods, passengers, and fantasies from one place to another. Time and space collapse, and the unthinkable and previously unreachable are possible. The destinations are often unknown, and the future is an open journey that may lead to a dead end. In *Newsreel 63*, Autor reminds us that these phantom rides may lead to death, whether by a horrific accident of those who ride the undercarriage and slip or by suffocation for those who ride in the containers. The train becomes a vehicle to transport shadows of those who once were across borders. After its opening sequences composed of found footage (fictional and documentary) from train travel, Autor focuses on the stretch of rails between Belgrade and Ljubljana, a heavily trafficked stretch by refugees moving north to Austria. She documents the communities that arise along the tracks of those forced to wait, to live in limbo, in anticipation of which train will be the one to possibly transport them out their everyday purgatory to either heaven or hell.

In their response to contemporary crises, history, and politics, essay films function as an alternative journalism. For example, the breakup of Yugoslavia led to an immediate response by French essay filmmakers, with Marker's *Prime Time in the Camps* (1993), Ophuls's *A Call to Arms* (1994), and Godard's *Forever Mozart* (1996). Adorno wrote that the essay "detects traces of the eternal in the transient" yet also "tries to render the transient eternal."[27] Essay filmmakers respond to failings, gaps, and omissions in dominant media coverage. The form of the essay film allows for a more immediate response, in part because it does not have to be 100 percent verifiable, and its viewing platforms are more direct and less encumbered by bureaucratic distribution formalities. Because documentary film is linked to truth claims, it reinforces and produces a truth determined by those in power. The result is a hegemony of the same regimes of truth and images that circulate globally, reinforcing dominant power structures. By contrast, the essay allows for competing narratives, which, through specific cinematic techniques such as dissolves, superimpositions, or contrapuntal soundtracks, address the complexity of history and unearth and restore those subjects that exist at the margins and are often invisible and inaudible. Many politically committed essay films begin with documentary facts and archival evidence, which are then set into play to produce scathing exposés on contemporary topics – those that mainstream journalism ignores or cannot address. Artists and filmmakers use archives differently than journalists or historians. In a recent example, journalist and documentary filmmaker Laura Poitras teamed up with the art collective Forensic Architecture and produced a triptych of essay films entitled *Edgelands* (2021) for an art exhibition space. Poitras and codirector Sean Vegezzi investigated and exposed three cases spanning the period of the Covid-19 pandemic in New York City. The first shows the extensive use by police surveillance technology, TARU, to track protestors and ostensibly prevent domestic and civil unrest; the second case, through intercepted sound-recordings, brings attention to a prison barge located in the East River where the deadly conditions during the pandemic threaten the safety of the incarcerated; the third details the continued use of prison labor from Rikers Island to bury unclaimed bodies of the poor. Immediately after *Edgelands* opened at the n.b.k. in Berlin on June 18, 2021, the Associated Press reviewing the exhibition reported the stories and transmitted them across media venues globally. The essay film could respond immediately to a crisis, reveal a problem, and bring attention to events that might otherwise be buried for decades.

In Raoul Peck's *A Profit and Nothing But! Impolite Thoughts on the Class Struggle* (2001), the narrator repeats at regular intervals the refrain: "I come from a country that technically doesn't exist." Peck's essay film about Haiti examines the fate of a people and a nation when it falls off the grid of capital and is determined unprofitable. He addresses what happens when natural environmental catastrophes such as hurricanes and famines combine with war and political corruption to exile a land and its people. His thesis is that capital is a crime that buys silence and renders inaudible and nonexistent those who do not play the game and therefore fail. Peck's poetic eulogy intercuts between beautiful verdant shots of Haiti and images taken from New York, London, Paris – capitals of capital in the first world. "Capital has won, for how long?" the narrator repeatedly asks. Peck calls attention to the role of culture more generally and film, specifically, in the struggle against global inequalities. The commentary laments: "Figures no longer mean anything nor do words. 40,000 children die every day in the world – an intolerable thought – no, figures no longer mean anything." Over shots of urban architecture, the narrator asks, "Why should we continue to create images anyway? As a memento of lost battle to leave something behind for what future? … How can you express the experiences of a lifetime, show a generation's failures; how can you narrate an irreversible history? [On the image track he shows newsreel footage of police brutality against people of color] What words, what images to say, for once, something different?" The final sequence shows children in Port-a Piment who have gathered to watch public screenings of films. Peck includes shots from popular films such as *Apocalypse Now* and US Westerns valorizing genocide, but also alternatives such as Gerima's *Ashes and Embers* (1982), Naoeur Khemir's *Les Baliseurs de Desert* (1984), and Mohamed Chouikh's *La Citadelle* (1988). These film-makers sought to find a new cinematic language for fighting oppression and making visible and audible that which many would prefer to remain unseen and unheard. Peck as narrator in his film asks, "Why make films? Perhaps because we don't know better, because it is more respectable than burning cars." He continues, over shots of Haitians going about their everyday lives:

> What will they remember when it is time to remember, when memory is all that remains: films that make the heart beat faster, said Chris Marker … The collective memory of battles that were not always ours. So much commitment for so little … Yet some images stick in your mind, rare moments of truth, just enough time to glimpse another horizon through a window.

Essay films are composed of fragments of "thousands of tiny details," as Eisenstein put it: slivers and shards of a much larger reality. The essay film functions as a kaleidoscope. Audiovisual constellations coalesce and are momentarily held together by invisible bonds. A twist of the maker's hand changes the image and allows for a new one to emerge out of the pieces. In *An Image Book* (2018), Godard claims it should take an hour to represent a second, a day to represent a minute, a week for an hour, and a year for a day – moving images compress reality to fragments. Perhaps, to paraphrase Brecht, reality today can only exist in the fragment. Some may say that in this era of fake news and competing realities where truth is manufactured regardless of its veracity and received within an echo chamber, the inherently ambiguous nature of the essay film has turned it into a problematic category of production calling for a return to documentary. However, I disagree. Today, more than ever, at this time of obscurity where lies are constructed and celebrated and events are drowned in a sea of unfathomable data, the essay as a form of political critique needs to be sustained.

Notes

1 For the sake of brevity, I will use the term "essay film" regardless of media to refer to audiovisual essays, including film, video, and digital.
2 Sergei Eisenstein, "Notes for a Film of 'Capital,'" *October* 2 (1976): 3–26, here 7.
3 Ibid., 9.
4 Ibid., 4.
5 Hans Richter, "The Film Essay: A New Form of Documentary Film" [1940], in *Essays on the Essay Film*, ed. Nora M Alter and Timothy Corrigan (New York: Columbia University Press, 2017), 89–92, here 91.
6 Ibid.
7 Ibid., 90.
8 Alexandre Astruc, "The Birth of a New Avant-Garde: La Caméra Stylo (1948)" in *Film and Literature: An Introduction and Reader*, ed. Timothy Corrigan (Upper Saddle River, NJ: Prentice Hall, 1999), 158–162.
9 Alexandre Astruc, "The Future of Cinema" [1948], in *Essays on the Essay Film*, ed. Alter and Corrigan, 93–101; 95.
10 This practice continues to this day with Jonathan Kahana's compendium on the documentary in which the essay film does not even appear as a category. See Jonathan Kahana, *The Documentary Film Reader: History, Theory, and Criticism* (Oxford: Oxford University Press, 2016).
11 The first mentions of the essay film in English surface in the 1990s by essayists such as Philip Lopate, critics such as Jonathan Rosenbaum, and film historians including Michael Renov. It is not until the new millennium that book-length studies emerge devoted to the essay film as a genre. See Laura Rascaroli, *The Personal Camera: Subjective Cinema and the Essay Film* (London: Wallflower Press, 2009), Timothy Corrigan, *The Essay Film: From Montaigne, after Marker* (Oxford: Oxford University Press, 2011), and Nora M. Alter, *The Essat Film After Fact and Fiction* (New York: Columbia University Press, 2018).
12 Frieda Grafe, "Found Fictions: Better Documentaries" [1991], in *Frieda Grafe*, ed. Volker Pantenburg, Sissi Tax, and Else de Seynes (Berlin: Harun Farocki Institute, 2020), 15–19; 15.
13 Jean-Michel Frodon, *Amos Gitai et l'enjeu des archives* (Paris: Collège de France, 2021).
14 See Hans Richter, *Dreams that Money Can Buy* (1947).
15 Laura Mulvey, "Riddles as Essay Film" [2015], in *Essays on the Essay Film*, ed. Alter and Corrigan, 314–321. Thomas Elsaesser, "Working at the Margins: Film as a Form of Intelligence," in *Harun Farocki: Working at the Sight-Lines*, ed. Thomas Elsaesser (Amsterdam: Amsterdam University Press, 2004), 95.

16 Michel de Montaigne, "To the Reader," *The Complete Essays of Montaigne*, trans. Donald Frame (Stanford, CA: Stanford University Press, 1958), 2.

17 Georg Lukács, "On the Nature and Form of the Essay" [1910], in *Essays on the Essay Film*, ed. Alter and Corrigan, 21–40; 22.

18 Theodor W. Adorno, *Minima Moralia: Reflections on a Damaged Life*, trans E. F. N. Jephcott (New York: Verso, 2005), 124.

19 Max Bense, "On the Essay and Its Prose," in *Essays on the Essay Film*, ed. Alter and Corrigan, 49–59; 57.

20 Trinh T. Minh-ha, 'The Totalizing Quest of Meaning," in *When the Moon Waxes Red* (New York: Routledge, 1991), 90–107; 90.

21 S. M. Eisenstein, V. I. Pudovkin, and G. V. Alexandrov, "A Statement," in *Film Sound: Theory and Practice*, ed. Elisabeth Weis and John Belton (New York: Columbia University Press, 1985) 83–85; 84.

22 V. I. Pudovkin, "Asynchronism as a Principle of Sound Film," in ibid., 86–91; 89.

23 Bhabha as cited by Reece Auguiste and the Black Audio Film Collective, "Black Independents and Third Cinema: The British Context," in *Questions of Third Cinema*, ed. Jim Pines and Paul Willemen (London: BFI, 1989), 212–217; 214.

24 Bense, "On the Essay and Its Prose," 59.

25 Enwezor, "Coalition Building: Black Audio Film Collective and Transnational Postcolonialism," in *The Ghosts of Songs: The Film Art of the Black Audio Film Collective*, (Liverpool: Liverpool University Press, 2007), 106–123; 122.

26 Subsequently, Mardini was arrested by Greek authorities for aiding refugees to reach Greece.

27 Theodor W. Adorno, "The Essay as Form," in *Notes to Literature*, ed. Rolf Tiedemann and trans. Shierry Weber Nicholson (New York: Columbia University Press, 2019), 36.

17

JANE HU

The Essay Online

In researching the origins of the online essay, I looked – where else – online. In the Google search box, I typed "first online essay" and then "first essay online" followed by "first essay posted on the internet," none of which led me to the first online essay, but instead to a series of websites that sold essays and dissertations online. In a final effort, I typed "first online essay" again and clicked the "I'm Feeling Lucky" button. The result was an article about India's first national online essay contest from 2006.[1]

What struck me about my search was how much it mirrored the experience of reading, or writing, an essay: meandering, digressive, a scattering of miscellaneous information in search of a more general form. Perhaps this shouldn't be surprising. After all, the Internet itself emerges as a miscellany of forms – the "convergence," as Henry Jenkins calls it, of old and new media that "alters the relationship between existing technologies, industries, markets, genres and audiences."[2] Technological convergence on the Internet gathers a range of media: broadcast television, radio, telephones, newspapers, and, we might imagine, the essay. Media scholars of essayistic writing on the Internet generally focus on the rise of blogging and social media in the wake of the dot-com bubble – that is, online essays in the era of Web 2.0.[3] In contrast, this chapter argues that the story of the online essay begins slightly earlier, during the era of the precommercial Internet, when communication occurred largely over message boards, forums, and listservs.

The history of the online essay starts not with the personal blog but with the personal computer. While most of its technical features were already in place by 1972, the microcomputer was not widely available to the public until the late 1970s.[4] Even then, the device was not immediately associated with "the ethos of personalness," as Fred Turner describes it, "to which small computers have since become attached."[5] As Turner's history of postwar cyberculture explains, it was the synergy between the Bay Area countercultural and hobbyist communities during the 1960s and 1970s that transformed the idea of computing from a tool of corporate control into one of collaboration, flexibility, and utopian social change. This ideological shift involved reframing the computer not as a device that merely received information (as with broadcast TV), but one with which users could also engage in two-way communication. In Kevin Driscoll's account, the early homespun "bulletin-board systems" (BBSs) where computer hobbyists exchanged files eventually "linked a more diverse group of people and covered a wider range of interests and communities."[6] In 1985, Stewart Brand and Larry Brilliant founded a BBS known as the WELL (or Whole Earth 'Lectronic Link), helping to gather the countercultural community already constituted by Brand's influential *Whole Earth Catalog* into a digital space. The WELL specifically emphasized dialogue among its users, enabling them "to *become* an interactive collectivity in real time."[7] By the 1980s, most online systems had taken Brand and Brilliant's lead by encouraging conversation on their BBSs, where netizens could meet to discuss topics ranging from hacking to erotica to the Gulf War. The average WELL post ran to about eight lines, but some, especially when a user was impassioned by a thread's topic, could go on for multiple paragraphs, and were sometimes even explicitly framed as essays.[8] Not unlike Seneca's letters to Lucilius, which Bacon once described as "but Essays, – That is dispersed Meditations, though conveyed in the form of Epistles," the online essay evolved from conversations: writing that prompted and compelled other writing.[9] That is to say, the first online essay was never one essay, but necessarily at least two.

One candidate for the first online essay is "Pandora's Vox," written by a user named Carmen Hermosillo, who went by the alias "humdog." Posted on the WELL in 1994, the 2,946-word text immediately set off what was then referred to as a "flame war," a series of long-running and often acrimonious debates that often broke out over public message boards. A research analyst of Cuban descent, Hermosillo had been an active WELL user for years, but at the time of her post she was growing skeptical of the liberatory potential associated with virtual communities. Instead of the expressive freedom promised by techno-utopianists, what Hermosillo experienced online felt more akin to a perverse commodification of the personal. "i have seen many people spill their guts on-line," she writes, rather presciently, "and i did so myself until, at last, i began to see that i had commodified myself."[10] For Hermosillo, this commodification of selfhood unfolded primarily through written words: the constellation of, to use her words, "user-ids," "rhetoric," and "language in cyberspace" that formed the "illusion" of authentic expression on the Internet.[11] "Pandora's Vox" begins by rejecting the premise of free speech online ("rhetoric in cyberspace is liberation-speak," she scoffs at one point), arguing instead that "language in cyberspace is a frozen landscape" of "sign-value" and "surface-sign" untethered from material reality or struggle.[12] To be sure, Hermosillo's language, suffused with the influence of postmodernist thought, dates her essay to the early 1990s, yet its warnings about the reification of words online ring uncannily ahead of its time. "i created my interior thoughts as a means of production for the corporation that owned the board i was posting to," she reflects, "and that commodity was being sold to other commodity/consumer entities as entertainment."[13]

Written almost entirely in lower case letters, "Pandora's Vox" is a BBS post that might pass for a lyric essay, or perhaps what Lukács, quoting Schlegel, would describe as an "intellectual poem."[14] Yet for all its generic flexibility, what marks "Pandora's Vox" as a prototypical online essay is not how it is written but how it was taken up: It, to use a phrase that did not exist at the time, went viral.[15] "Carmen's vox immediately set off a firestorm," recalls Peter Ludlow in a 2009 blog post: As WELL users logged on to protest the insinuation that they "were commodifying their inner lives [...] nearly every discussion thread exploded into flame wars when humdog appeared."[16] While these WELL discussion threads are no longer accessible, Hermosillo's influence is evident in how "Pandora's Vox" continues to circulate elsewhere, reposted on multiple sites and even reprinted in an anthology of essays in 1996.[17]

If anything, "Pandora's Vox" has only grown *more* representative of online culture over time. This is not only because almost everything it warns of about the Internet – from its monetization of individual expression to its modes of surveillance – is now a truism. Hermosillo's essay also anticipates a genre attuned to gender, to the promises and perils of writing as a woman online. Fourteen years after posting "Pandora's Vox," Hermosillo would be found dead in her bedroom in what has since been interpreted, at least by family, friends, and acquaintances on the Internet, as a response to Hermosillo's own romantic troubles with a man she met over Second Life. In retrospect, it's hard not to read "Pandora's Vox" as a cautionary tale about Hermosillo's own fate as a woman who increasingly negotiated her personal life online. Of course, almost all I know about Hermosillo I found on the Internet, from reading her words remediated and reframed by others. "i suspect that my words have been extracted," muses Hermosillo near the end of her 1994 post, "and that when this essay shows up, they will be extracted some more."[18] But the way Hermosillo's essay and her life dovetail suggest, at least, both the difficulties and necessities of disambiguating the two.

In 1999, five years after Hermosillo's post, the WELL was acquired by *Salon*, an early news and opinion website established shortly after the 1994 San Francisco newspaper strike by former *San Francisco Examiner* editor David Talbot. Having grown tired of traditional print media, Talbot sought to explore the "potential of the new medium" in *Salon*, which he pitched as a specifically "literary-oriented Webzine."[19] The site began as a mix of opinionated storytelling and arts commentary, while also hosting a popular BBS-style feature called "Table Talk" where readers could comment on the site's content. With its entrepreneurial spirit and irreverence for official mainstream culture, *Salon* seemed a natural fit for the WELL. Both were, after all, outgrowths of the left-leaning ethos of the Bay Area, and many of *Salon*'s early participants were already active members of the WELL community.

Even as the WELL migrated officially to *Salon*, its countercultural ideal of a virtual community on a public Internet was reaching a wider audience. After the early dial-up BBSs of the 1980s, which remained largely local affairs, the mid-1990s saw the emergence of a more scattered community of writers online who maintained personal "weblogs" – a term coined by Jorn Barger in 1997 to describe the process of "logging the web," later condensed to "blogs."[20] "Logging the web" – recording, and linking to, interesting content you discovered elsewhere on the Internet – quickly became inseparable from logging, and commenting on, the events of your own daily life. Even before Barger's inspired portmanteau, writers had been experimenting with online diaries as early as 1994.[21] Remediating existing literary forms such as the confessional essay, the memoir, and, indeed, the diary entry itself, the personal blog enacted a new form of life writing for an unprecedented online public.

At the start of 1999, there were only a few dozen weblogs known to be in existence, but the introduction of Blogger – a publishing tool developed by Pyra Labs – in August of that year made it easier for anyone to start a blog. Applications such as LiveJournal, Diaryland, and Xanga soon joined the bandwagon. Yet whereas Blogger presented itself neutrally as "an automated weblog publishing tool," subsequent popular platforms such as Live-Journal, as suggested by its name, encouraged writers to adopt a diaristic attitude that was simultaneously community-oriented.[22] In 1999, LiveJournal presented itself as "an up-to-the-minute log of whatever you're doing, when you're doing," a definition that feels not far off from the mandates of today's social media platforms.[23] Similarly, Xanga defined itself as "a community of online diaries and journals" that was also a "weblog community."[24]

By the turn of the twenty-first century, personal blogging had gone mainstream. As Rebecca Mead explains in an oft-cited 2000 *New Yorker* essay about the rise of Blogger, "Having a blog is rather like publishing your own, on-line version of *Reader's Digest*, with daily updates. [...] Then other people who have blogs ... read your blog, and if they like it they blog your blog on their own blog."[25] Mead's essay introduces Blogger and blogging by first introducing us to a specific blogger: Meg Hourihan, cofounder of Blogger, who also published the blog Megnut.com. As Mead's essay lingers over details about Hourihan's personal life (even opening and closing by focusing on her romantic relationship with Evan Williams, another Blogger cofounder who would go on to cofound Twitter), her prose begins to absorb the anecdotal, private quality of her subject's. Reading Megnut, as Mead tells us, reveals "all kinds of things about its author." "I know that she's a little dreamy and idealistic," Mead muses, and "that she fervently believes there is a distinction between 'dot-com people,' who are involved in the Internet for its I. P. O. opportunities, and 'Web people,' who are in love with the imaginative possibilities presented by the medium, and that she counts herself among the latter."[26] In describing Blogger by way of profiling the specific blogger that is Meg, Mead frames the platform's entrepreneurial ethos around the individual personality of its creator. For Meg, the personal blog enables a liberatory self-expression (and indeed self-mythologization), where the most minute and intimate aspects of one's life might become relevant.

While Hourihan's confessional mode of writing was hardly new, online writing increasingly used this intimate, essayistic voice to draw in new readers and writers, expanding the Internet's circuits of engagement and attention. The pre-2000s web belonged mostly to hobbyists and tech workers who had their cultural roots in the noncommercial history of countercultural communities, but online writing in the era of Web 2.0 started to move beyond this milieu. Print newspapers were slow to adapt their content to the web, worrying about the unreliability of online journalism and what Clay Shirky describes as "the mass amateurization of a job previously reserved for media professionals."[27] Meanwhile, personal bloggers flexibly adapted to new styles of media commentary and reporting. Not only were there now personal blogs such as Megnut that read like public-facing diaries, but there was also a surge of political blogs, from Glenn Reynolds's conservative Instapundit to Josh Marshall's left-leaning Talking Points Memo (TPM). While the ideological tilt of these early 2000s sites may have varied, they nonetheless shared a general rhetorical attitude: They were written in a first-person voice that was informal, conversational, and, we might even say, essayistic. ("But anyway, back to my story," Marshall pivots at one point in his first TPM post, six days after the 2000 presidential election – a Montaignian digression that would come to characterize his chatty tone.[28])

As more people started their own blogs to wax private or political, the blurring of the journalistic and essayistic impulse online also influenced the creation of media sites featuring writing that was increasingly quippy, irreverent, and personal. On May 10, 2005, the Huffington Post was launched as an online aggregator of news, blogs, and related media coverage. Billed under cofounder Arianna Huffington's name, the site was more accurately the brainchild of Jonah Peretti, who pitched it as a counterweight to right-wing blogs such as the Drudge Report. In addition to the name recognition of Huffington herself, the Huffington Post attracted attention early on with celebrity bylines, from the historian Arthur M. Schlesinger Jr. to *Seinfeld* producer Larry David. Over time, the site began to include contributions by students, politicos, and activists, in addition to celebrities, though its pursuit of viral content (or "spreadable media," as Jenkins calls it) never waned.[29] Under Peretti's influence, the site's strategy involved coming up with sensational headlines such as "Watch Naked Heidi Klum in Seal's New Video," often paired with provocative photos, while also dialing up the snark (a style of writing characterized by its snide and sarcastic attitude). In short, the Huffington Post "pioneered what would become known as clickbait," as Tim Wu puts it, a sensationalizing approach to media that was influential in shaping how attention gets captured online.[30] Even relatively staid and literary-leaning online establishments such as Salon and Slate grew more gossipy in tone and clickbait-driven in response.

Whereas sites such as the Huffington Post attracted readers by publishing writing by celebrities, others started capitalizing on the allure of writing *about* celebrities. The pseudonymous Perez Hilton rose to fame during the mid-2000s by posting gossip and media items about celebrities in a notoriously venomous tone. Drawing on the star quality of known names, Perez Hilton's ascent to celebrity status himself was further enabled by the plausible deniability of his own name – a détournement of the name of another celebrity (Paris Hilton) already associated with Internet-fueled celebrity scandals into a "wildly popular fictive persona made possible by the anonymity of the web."[31] Not unlike the gossipy personae of such eighteenth-century periodicals as the *Tatler* and *Spectator*, Hilton branded himself as an authorial entity whose name was neither identical with nor entirely distinct from the writer himself (whose real name was Mario Armando Lavandeira Jr.). Recapitulating the history of the periodical essay, Hilton's blogposts shifted the realm of online essays into an increasingly public sphere, where, as William Hazlitt once put it, "the philosopher and wit here commences newsmonger."[32] In this way, Hilton exemplified a genre of Internet writing that would grow increasingly familiar over the course of the twenty-first century, one in which anonymous or unknown "nobodies" could attain, however briefly, the status of Internet celebrity.[33]

As more figures competed for pockets of attention online, the blogger's path to microfame grew yet more snarky and sensationalist. In 2002, the

British ex-pat Nick Denton launched the New York media gossip site Gawker, a name that wouldn't be out of place among the eighteenth-century periodicals that covered coffee house and city talk. "The basic concept," as Denton put it, "was two journalists in a bar telling each other a story that's much more interesting than whatever hits the papers the next day."³⁴ Denton's first move was to hire editor Elizabeth Spiers, whose "tart prose" and mocking authorial commentary on established New York media immediately set the tone for Gawker.³⁵ As Carla Blumenkranz tells it, Spiers made herself the "winning protagonist" of her posts even when writing about the famous icons of New York publishing such as Anna Wintour: Spiers was "the heroine in the sitcom she and her readers could imagine of their upwardly mobile lives."³⁶

While Spiers pioneered the style, it was arguably Jezebel, Gawker's sub-blog of writing by women and for women, that saw the fullest evolution of the blogger as heroine protagonist.

Launched in 2007 by founding editor Anna Holmes, Jezebel was framed as an explicitly feminist counterpoint to traditional women's magazines. Following Gawker, Jezebel pitched itself as the more iconoclastic and undisciplined successor to established print media, with an approach that valued a no-holds-barred directness. As the site's first features editor Moe Tkacik wrote in her 2007 "Jezebel Manifesto: The Five Great Lies of Women's Magazines," Jezebel was "a blog for women that will attempt to take all the essentially meaningless but sweet stuff directed our way and give it a little more meaning, while taking more the serious stuff and making it more fun, or more personal, or at the very least the subject of our highly sophisticated brand of sex joke."³⁷ Tkacik's manifesto modeled an informal tone that would characterize much of Jezebel's writing, a version of the "familiar style" of Hazlitt's essays, which, for Charles Lamb, "resemble occasionally the *talk* of a very clever person, when he begins to be animated in a convivial party."³⁸ This was writing that wanted to have it both ways: to attack mainstream women's magazines from a more radical feminist perspective while still vying for the same audience. Jezebel sought to eschew the oppressive commodification of women's desires by presenting a different brand of womanhood: one that was messy, crude, possibly drunk at a party, and unabashed about dragging what had previously been deemed private into the public sphere.

A brief list of headlines gives a snapshot of the Jezebel sensibility: "If A Guy Gets A Nose Bleed While Performing Oral Sex, Should I Worry?"; "We Have a Rape Gif Problem and Gawker Media Won't Do Anything About It"; "Interview With a Woman Who Recently Had an Abortion at 32 Weeks"; "I am the Anonymous Model"; "If Comedy Has No Lady Problem,

Why Am I Getting So Many Rape Threats?" The essay that best exemplifies this aggressive scrambling of public and private might be the candidly titled "Ten Days In The Life Of A Tampon," written by Tkacik herself about a year after Jezebel's founding. The clickbait headline's semantic ambiguity – it's unclear at first whether the story will be narrated from the perspective of the tampon itself or its user – only heightens the aura of scandalous intrigue surrounding the essay. "WARNING," runs Tkacik's opening disclaimer,

> The following is a really, really gross story. It may even qualify as 'beyond gross.' It also: signifies nothing, gives you wayyyy too much information, and is told by a total idiot. Its sole redeeming trait is that it involves a scenario we've all feared before – the one where you get a tampon stuck up inside you for a treacherously, perilously long period of time – and it has a (marginally) happy ending. Read at your own risk, folks.[39]

The writing here is representative of Tkacik's prose throughout the essay: casual, chatty, even intentionally artless. In providing a preface that summarizes the essay's arc, Tkacik presents a clue for how to read it: not for plot ("it has a (marginally) happy ending") or even aesthetics (the story "may even qualify as 'beyond gross'"), but for the everyday familiarity of its content (the essay's "sole redeeming trait is that it involves a scenario we've all feared before"). For many seasoned bloggers, the form of Tkacik's essay would have been profoundly familiar, unfolding in what reads like a series of diary entries.

"Ten Days in the Life of a Tampon" relishes the abandonment of decorum. To be warned to "read at your own risk" is, of course, only to entice the desire to read further. And what Tkacik delivers in this 1,878-word tour-de-force is the public display of the most private aspects of a woman's life in writing, including excerpts from her private text messages. On her meandering way, Tkacik hits all of the sweet spots of Jezebel content – sex, drugs, the beauty myth – before ending rather anticlimactically on what readers have known to be the problem all along: the forgotten tampon, now ten days old. The essay culminates in the anticipated Gothic reveal ("The tampon emerged, grayish brown and bloated like a corpse in the harbor"), before closing with an intimate domestic dialogue between Tkacik and her friend ("'But hold on,' I panicked. 'I had sex *three times* with that thing. Do you think it absorbed a bunch of sperm? Do you think I should get Plan B? Holy shit, you think I'm *already pregnant?*'"). "Ten Days In The Life Of A Tampon" dramatizes the work of the personal essay in a literal sense: What is being written about for consumption is not the discovery of sentimental interiority, but the narrative dramatization of *revealing* one's insides as a rhetorical performance whose merits lie in the boldness of the telling.

This genre of the personal women's essay, whose aesthetic value lies in precisely such acts of narrative self-exploitation, was arguably mastered at Jezebel. Its mode of flagrant confession would go on to influence sites such as xoJane and columns such as Vox First Person that were almost entirely devoted to personal essays that repackaged women's private experiences (from the banality of period blood to the trauma of late-term abortions) for public consumption. xoJane has since taken down its site, though one can find traces of its most popular stories in aggregators and roundups at sites such as Jezebel, which list, among xoJane's greatest hits, essays such as "My Gynecologist Found a Ball of Cat Hair in my Vagina" and "My Former Friend's Death Was a Blessing."

If "the hallmark of the personal essay is its intimacy," as Philip Lopate writes, wherein "the personal essayist sets up a relationship with the reader, a dialogue – a friendship," the online essay is increasingly pitched toward generating not private intimacy or friendship but public scandal, reactiveness, and virality.[40] In a 2015 Slate essay titled "The First-Person Industrial Complex," the writer Laura Bennett asks, "when did the harrowing personal essay take over the internet?"[41] Bennett's question targets a broad phenomenon, though her motivating example is the Jezebel essay "On Falling In and Out of Love With My Dad," written by Natasha Chenier. The piece was edited by Jia Tolentino, who had offered Chenier the option of publishing it under a pseudonym given its explosive contents, but Chenier felt adamant that "this [was the] story I'd always wanted to tell."[42] The essay, as predicted, went viral. Unlike those penned by staff writers such as Tkacik, personal essays on women's media sites were increasingly capitalizing on intensely intimate acts of self-exposure by freelancers that were less avenues or auditions for more writing gigs than extractive one-offs. These were stories by nobodies, in other words: the online essay version of the gimmick, or one weird trick, that might bring you microfame at best or sometimes at worst.

The commercial Internet generated an economy of attention that rewarded stories that were at once sensationalist and relatable – personal and universal – in a drive for content that would go viral among the broadest range of readers. The personal essay became a quick way to drum up clickbait that would then feed into the advertising industry that financially supported so many of these sites. "It is now commonplace to assume that personal identity work is foundational to the production of social media and even of hardware interfaces," explain Anna Poletti and Julie Rak. What came of the personal writing of the early personal computer was now "the constant directive to 'share' personal information on social media" that asks, rather teleologically, "users to create a specific type of identity, one that can be shared."[43]

By 2017, however, the online "personal essay boom" was being pronounced "over" by none other than Tolentino, who, as an editor at both
Jezebel and The Hairpin, had done so much to sustain it. Tolentino pins
the rise of these essays, written mostly by women who dwelled on "*too
personal*" topics that either "seemed insignificant, or else too important"
for public airing, to the need for easy clickbait at a time when magazine
budgets were being slashed.[44] But the market for confession quickly became
oversaturated, and personal essays began to give way to "think-pieces" in
which autobiographical anecdote was linked to a broader cultural or political "take." These essays, as Bennett wrote in an email to Tolentino, were
more likely to "center on systemic rather than personal trauma" than their
predecessors. Especially in the wake of Trump's election, online cultural
discourse swung toward explicitly politicized reflections, with women's personal essays, in particular, embracing a revival of second-wave feminist discourse exemplified by phenomena such as #MeToo.

Yet while some mourned the death of the personal essay, others noted
the insularity of the obituaries lamenting its decline. "The personal essay
was an economic problem and a social problem dressed up as a cultural
taste problem," writes Tressie McMillan Cottom in *Thick*, her collection of
personal essays in which the personal is the necessary mediator for critical
and political statements by marginalized writers.[45] When it came to black
women, Cottom explained, the personal essay "was the only point of access
for telling creative stories of empirical realities. Latinas said the same. Queer
women and trans women and all manner of women stepped forward to add
dimensions to what the personal essay form is and what it is assumed to
be."[46] For Cottom, this is not to pose the aesthetic style of the mainstream
white woman's personal essay against the political utility of everyone else's
personal protest essay, but to clarify the strategic essentialism of underpriv-
ileged voices who must capitalize on the personal essay's cachet simply to
be heard. What obituaries such as Tolentino's had missed, Cottom insisted,
was how "the personal essay had become the way that black women writers
claim legitimacy in a public discourse that defines itself, in part, by how well
it excludes black women."[47] The personal essay enabled minority voices
who typically had no claim to speaking with authority in public to occupy a
genre of persuasive speech acts that was political, to be sure, but necessarily
woven through the performance of individual personhood. These were personal essays that expressed interiority not for expression's sake, but in an
attempt to mobilize social action.

One version of the political personal essay might look like this: On June
3, 2016, at 4:17 p.m. ET, BuzzFeed (a website specializing in "contagious
media," founded in 2006 by the Huffington Post's Jonah Peretti) published

a 7,137-word essay under the title "Here's The Powerful Letter The Stanford Victim Read To Her Attacker."[48] The letter had been read out loud just
the day before, in court, by the woman who was raped by a Stanford under-
grad named Brock Turner. Written in the legal genre of the victim impact
statement, which works to express the social harms and traumas that might
otherwise go unaccounted for, the essay failed to do its rhetorical work in
court: Turner received six months in jail, a relatively lenient sentence given
by the judge who also took into account flattering character testimonials
by Turner's family and friends. Rape narratives crucially rest on narratives about character, as Frances Ferguson teaches us, in which "credibility
revolves around the credit of the person rather than around the facts of the
narrative" and whose litigation works, much like the classical psychological
novel, through "a confrontation between other people's accounts of one
and one's own account."[49] In response to Turner's light sentence, the victim shared her statement with BuzzFeed news reporter Katie J. M. Baker,
who posted it online the next day. Much to the victim's surprise, the post
went viral: Not only widely disseminated over social media, it was also
republished in venues such as *The Guardian*, the *Washington Post*, the *Los
Angeles Times*, and the *New York Times*. CNN staged a reading of it. At
one point, it even started trending on Twitter.

To what genre does this initially unsigned text belong? Originating within
a legal context, the statement was, of course, never written with the intention
of going public, much less online. Yet even as a victim impact statement, it
tweaks the genre, addressing not the judge but, instead, the defendant, Brock
Turner, himself. In this way, BuzzFeed is correct in calling it a "letter." This
particular victim impact statement is written in epistolary format, read out
loud in court as a kind of open letter whose rhetorical force lies in the awareness that it will be heard by more than the defendant alone. "You don't
know me," the statement begins, "but you've been inside me, and that's why
we're here today."[50] In the courtroom, these lines of intense intimacy – about
literal interiority – are directly addressed to Turner. But online, detached
from the particular bodies of speaker and receiver, their vectors of address
shift, requiring the reader to inhabit the anonymous voice of the author,
but also to imagine being on the receiving end of her "you." Throughout
the text, the author's voice switches between a first-person direct address to
Turner ("Your life is not over, you have decades of years ahead to rewrite
your story") and a third-person narrative addressed to the judge ("Brock had
a strange new story [...] and most importantly in this new story, there was
suddenly consent"), while sometimes acknowledging a more general public
audience ("To conclude, I want to say thank you [...] to the girls across the
nation that wrote cards to my DA to give to me, so many strangers who

cared for me"). The post went viral partly owing to the public awareness already surrounding the highly mediatized case, but also to the flexible intimacy of its first-person voice that invites a porous community of readers.

In many ways, the text presents itself as an intensely intimate personal essay – an essay that, by definition, means to testify to the trauma of what happened specifically to the writer. Yet owing to the necessary anonymity of the victim, both on and offline, it is also a profoundly impersonal essay, in which impersonality is not so much the negation of the person, as Sharon Cameron theorizes it, "but rather a penetration through or falling outside of the human particular."[51] As with the first-person "I" of writing by Ralph Waldo Emerson or Simone Weil (the essayists that Cameron examines), the "I" in Buzzfeed's Victim Impact Statement expresses a precarious identity that plays with the dissolution, denuding, and even degradation of a singular individual personality. Here, the author is a kind of "nobody" and thus also anybody – an impersonal identity that enacts rape's unmaking of personhood through the reparative rewriting of selfhood that is the personal essay's *raison d'être*. This is the personal essay taken to a kind of limit case: a personal essay that, owing to legal stipulations, gets published under a pseudonym that renders it impersonal again. And it is this context, of a generic "nobody" who tells a familiar story of rape in the context of Buzz-Feed's surrounding social media apparatus that enabled its virality, shared by readers who, by their own words (in tweets or the comment section), related personally to the author's experience.

Yet despite all the mediation entailed by its virality, Doe's essay, in its artifactual particularity, returns us to some of the fundamental questions of the essay form, online or off. It enacts many of the features of the classical essay, in being persuasive, argumentative, and digressive. (And the digressiveness is to its point, since this is a narrative that cannot be fully, chronologically recalled: The essay dramatizes its author's recollection of waking up after being raped while unconscious and coming to terms with what has happened to her body.) But it is an online essay whose digressiveness enacts the process of coming to oneself through remediation – to know one's most intimate self through the scrutiny of others. "I had grown up in the margins," the author reflects in her memoir *Know My Name*, which not only reveals her real name (Chanel Miller) but also her ethnicity as a half-Chinese woman. "In the media Asian Americans were assigned side roles, submissive, soft-spoken secondary characters," she reflects, in the wake of going viral. "It did not feel possible that I could be the protagonist."[52] But in the context of her anonymous statement, Miller's ethnicity was dissolved in the generality of a rape story that allowed an Asian American woman to be, hidden in plain sight, a heroine protagonist on the Internet.

Miller's victim impact statement, in being remediated online, converges with much of what already defines the Internet as well as the essay on the Internet: It is a deeply personal text that becomes impersonal and generic again. In its shift to the impersonal personal essay online, Miller's victim statement also becomes available to the public in ways that would have been impossible in court. As the essay went viral many times over, extracted for clicks on multiple news and social media sites, it also spurred mass political action, precipitating enough public outrage to result in the recall of the judge on Miller's case, the first instance of judicial recall in California in over eighty years.

From "Pandora's Vox" to "Ten Days In The Life Of A Tampon" to Chanel Miller's Victim Impact Statement, the online essay has long been associated with the personal essay insofar as the personal essay expresses the unruly, unregulated, and utopic freedoms associated with the first personal computers. While Hermosillo's early BBS post incited an unintentional flame war owing to its warnings about the commodification of the private self online, subsequent essays in the era of Web 2.0 were engineered to go viral precisely by commodifying such selfhood. The women's personal essay is only one example of how the Internet has capitalized on personal writing, given how the genre already flirts with the potentially hazardous relationship between private interiority and public consumption that defines the online essay. Yet, as humdog's and Miller's essays show us, the online essay contains multitudes, in which – even now, with the Internet at its most commercialized – the personal might still be political.

Notes

1 "India Inspired: First Online Essay Contest," *Hindustan Times* (February 18, 2006), www.hindustantimes.com/india/india-inspired-first-online-essay-contest/story-ozW6RlcJV3AQkM7ZGnZohN.html, accessed June 6, 2021.

2 Henry Jenkins, *Convergence Culture: Where Old and New Media Collide* (New York: New York University Press, 2006), 15.

3 See Jodi Dean's *Blog Theory: Feedback and Capture in the Circuits of Drive* (Cambridge: Polity Press, 2010) or Geert Lovink, *Zero Comments: Blogging and Critical Internet Culture* (New York: Routledge, 2008). There are many influential scholars, from Katherine Hayles to Sandy Baldwin, who have written on pre-Web 2.0 writing, though they focus predominantly on how digital culture remediates poetry and fiction.

4 Paul Ceruzzi divides the development of the personal computer during the 1970s into two phases: the first, running roughly from 1972 to 1977, saw the rise of miniature computer technology; and the second, from 1977 to 1983, saw microcomputers begin to enter homes and offices nationwide. See Paul Ceruzzi, *A History of Modern Computing* (Cambridge, MA: MIT Press, 1998), 109–206.

5 Instead, the personal aspect of the computer was initially associated more with its size (small enough to be used by a single individual) than with the notion of individual personhood. See Fred Turner's *From Counterculture to Cyberculture: Stewart Brand, the Whole Earth Network, and the Rise of Digital Utopianism* (Chicago: University of Chicago Press, 2006), 105.

6 Kevin Driscoll, "Social Media's Dial-Up Ancestor: The Bulletin Board System." *IEEE Spectrum* 53.11 (November 2016): 54–60, https://spectrum.ieee .org/tech-history/cyberspace/social-medias-dialup-ancestor-the-bulletin-board-system.

7 Turner, *From Counterculture to Cyberculture*, 151.

8 Mark A. Smith, "Voices from the WELL: the Logic of the Virtual Commons," Master's Thesis (University of California-Los Angeles, 1992), 8.

9 British Library, MS Add. 4259, fo. 155. Quoted in Francis Bacon, *The Essayes or Counsels, Civill and Morall* [1625], ed. Michael Kiernan (Oxford University Press, 2000), xlvii.

10 humdog, "Pandora's Vox," in *High Noon on the Electronic Frontier*, ed. Peter Ludlow (Cambridge, MA: MIT Press, 1996), 438.

11 Ibid., 438–439.

12 Ibid., 439–440.

13 Ibid., 439.

14 Georg Lukács, "On the Nature and Form of the Essay," in *Soul and Form* (Columbia University Press, 2010), ed. John T. Sanders and Katie Terezakis, trans. Anna Bostock (1971), 34.

15 Henry Jenkins situates the emergence of viral metaphors in the changing media landscape of the mid-1990s, as companies adapted by engaging new forms of "viral marketing" online, though terms and verbs such as "went viral" or "to go viral" were not widely popularized until the latter half of the 2010s. See Henry Jenkins's *Spreadable Media: Creating Value and Meaning in a Networked Culture* (New York: New York University Press, 2013). The OED online, for instance, cites the earliest use of the phrase "went viral" as appearing in the 2004. See "viral, adj.," *OED Online*, Oxford University Press (June 2021), www.oed.com/view/Entry/223706, accessed July 11, 2021.

16 Peter Ludlow, "A Virtual Life. An Actual Death," *h+ magazine* (September 2, 2009, updated April 23, 2010), https://hplusmagazine.com/2009/09/02/virtual-life-actual-death/, accessed July 10, 2021.

17 *High Noon on the Electronic Frontier*, ed. Peter Ludlow (Cambridge, MA: MIT Press, 1996).

18 humdog, "Pandora's Vox," 444.

19 Scott Herhold, "Net Magazine Salon Epitomizes Fate of Mind over Matter," *Daily Record Newspaper* (February 1, 1998), 57.

20 See Ogi Djuraskovic, "Robot Wisdom and How Jorn Barger Invented Blogging," *firstsideguide.com* (March 20, 2015), https://firstsiteguide.com/robot-wisdom-and-jorn-barger/, accessed July 10, 2021.

21 Two of the earliest online diaries, as they were often called then, are Claudio Pinhanez's Open Diary, hosted by the MIT Media Lab website from 1994 to 1996; and Justin Hall's Links from the Underground, which Hall began in 1994 while interning at the San Francisco-based *Wired* magazine, and kept updating until 2005.

22 danah boyd, "A Blogger's Blog: Exploring the Definition of a Medium," *Reconstruction* 6.4 (2006).

23 Ibid.

24 Ibid.

25 Rebecca Mead, "You've Got Blog: How to Put Your Business, Your Boyfriend, and Your Life Online," *The New Yorker* (November 13, 2000), 102.

26 Ibid.

27 Quoted in Tim Wu, *The Attention Merchants: The Epic Scramble to Get Inside Our Heads* (Penguin Random House, 2017), 269.

28 Josh Marshall, "November 13th, 2000 – 3:37 PM EST," *Talking Points Memo* (November 13, 2000), archived at https://web.archive.org/web/20020401071152/http://talkingpointsmemo.com/nov0003.html, accessed July 21, 2021.

29 Jenkins prefers the metaphor of "spreadability" over that of "virality," arguing that "spreadable media" emphasizes consumers' active role in "spreading" content, whereas "viral media" or "media viruses" frames the circulation of content online as overdetermined and absent of social agency. See Jenkins, *Spreadable Media*.

30 Wu, *The Attention Merchants*, 282.

31 Ibid., 286.

32 William Hazlitt, "On the Periodical Essayists," in *The Selected Writings of William Hazlitt*, ed. Duncan Wu, 9 vols. (1998), V, 87.

33 The authorial status of "nobodies" occupies a central place in both the history of literary publication and online writing. I'm especially indebted to Catherine Gallagher's luminous study *Nobody's Story: The Vanishing Act of Women Writers in the Marketplace, 1670–1920* (Oakland: University of California Press, 1994), which tracks the relationship between the "nobodies" of female authors and fictional personae in the rise of the eighteenth-century novel. On the rise of twenty-first-century writing by and on "nobodies," see G. Thomas Couser's study of the contemporary memoir, whose publication is often enabled by single, one-off essays that gain unexpected popularity: Couser, *Memoir: An Introduction* (Oxford: Oxford University Press, 2012).

34 Eric Gardner, "Gawker's Nick Denton Explains Why Invasion of Privacy is Positive for Society," *The Hollywood Reporter* (May 22, 2013), www.hollywoodreporter.com/business/business-news/gawkers-nick-denton-explains-why-526548/, accessed July 10, 2021.

35 Warren St. John, "A New York State of Blog," *New York Times* (May 18, 2003), www.nytimes.com/2003/05/18/style/a-new-york-state-of-blog.html, accessed July 10, 2021.

36 Carla Blumenkranz, "Gawker: 2002–2007," *n+1* 6 (Winter 2008), https://nplusonemag.com/issue-6/reviews/gawker-2002-2007/, accessed July 10, 2021.

37 Moe Tkacik, "Jezebel Manifesto: The Five Great Lies of Women's Magazines," Jezebel, November 1, 2007, https://jezebel.com/the-five-great-lies-of-womens-magazines-262130, accessed July 10, 2021.

38 Charles Lamb, "Review of the First Volume of Hazlitt's *Table-Talk*, 1821," in *Selected Prose*, ed. Adam Phillips (London, Penguin Books, 2013), 217.

39 Moe Tkacik, "Ten Days In The Life Of A Tampon," Jezebel (May 7, 2008), https://jezebel.com/ten-days-in-the-life-of-a-tampon-388226, accessed July 10, 2021.

40 Phillip Lopate, "Introduction," in *The Art of the Personal Essay* (New York: Random House, 1994), xxiii.

41 Laura Bennett, "The First-Person Industrial Complex," *Slate* (September 14, 2015), www.slate.com/articles/life/technology/2015/09/the_first_person_industrial_complex_how_the_harrowing_personal_essay_took.html, accessed July 10, 2021.

42 Quoted in ibid.

43 Anna Poletti and Julie Rak, "Introduction: Digital Dialogues," in *Identity Technologies: Constructing the Self Online* (Madison: University of Wisconsin Press, 2014), 4–5.

44 Jia Tolentino, "The Personal-Essay Boom is Over," *New Yorker* (May 18, 2017).

45 Tressie McMillan Cottom, "Thick," in *Thick: And Other Essays* (New York: The New Press, 2019), 18.

46 Ibid.

47 Ibid., 19.

48 Katie J. M. Baker, "Here's The Powerful Letter The Stanford Victim Read To Her Attacker," *Buzzfeed* (June 3, 2016), www.buzzfeednews.com/article/katiejmbaker/heres-the-powerful-letter-the-stanford-victim-read-to-her-ra, accessed Jul 10, 2021.

49 Frances Ferguson, "Rape and the Rise of the Novel," *Representations* 20 (Autumn 1987), 97, 100.

50 Baker, "Here's The Powerful Letter."

51 Sharon Cameron, *Impersonality: Seven Essays* (Chicago: University of Chicago Press, 2007), ix.

52 Chanel Miller, *Know My Name: A Memoir* (New York: Penguin Books, 2020), 250.

Theories of the Essay

Adorno, Theodor. "The Essay as Form," *Notes to Literature*. ed. Rolf Tiedemann, trans. Shierry Weber Nicholson. New York: Columbia University Press, 1991.

Aquilina, Mario (ed.). *The Essay at the Limits: Poetics, Politics and Form*. London: Bloomsbury Publishing, 2021.

Atkins, G. Douglas. *On the Familiar Essay: Challenging Academic Orthodoxies*. London: Palgrave Macmillan, 2009.

Atkins, G. Douglas. *Tracing the Essay: Through Experience to Truth*. Athens, GA: University of Georgia Press, 2005.

Atkins, G. Douglas. *Reading Essays: An Invitation*. Athens: University of Georgia Press, 2008.

Basaki, Yota, Subha Mukherji, and Jan-Melissa Schramm. *Fictions of Knowledge: Fact, Evidence, Doubt*. London: Palgrave Macmillan, 2011.

Bensmaïa, Reda. *The Barthes Effect: The Essay as Reflective Text*. Minneapolis: University of Minnesota Press, 1987.

Butler, Cheryl. *The Art of the Black Essay: From Meditation to Transcendence*. New York: Routledge, 2003.

Butrym, Alexander J. (ed.). *Essays on the Essay: Redefining the Genre*. Athens: University of Georgia Press, 1990.

Cruz, María Elena Arenas. *Hacia una teoria general del ensayo. Hacia la construcción del texto ensayístico*. Cuenca: Universidad de Castilla/La Mancha, 1997.

D'Agata, John and Deborah Tall. "The Lyric Essay," *Seneca Review* 27, no. 2 (1997).

De Obaldia, Claire. *The Essayistic Spirit: Literature, Modern Criticism, and the Essay*. Oxford: Clarendon Press, 1995.

Dillon, Brian. *Essayism: On Form, Feeling, and Nonfiction*. London: Fitzcarraldo Editions, 2017.

Forman, Janis (ed.). *What Do I Know? Reading, Writing, and Teaching the Essay*. Portsmouth: Boynton/Cook, 1996.

Gigante, Denise (ed.). "The Essay: An Attempt, a Protean Form," a forum, *Republics of Letters* 4, no. 1 (2014).

Good, Graham. *The Observing Self: Rediscovering the Essay*. London: Routledge, 1988.

Harrison, Thomas. *Essayism: Conrad, Musil, and Pirandello*. Baltimore: Johns Hopkins University Press, 1991.

Joeres, Ruth-Ellen B. and Elizabeth Mittman. *The Politics of the Essay: Feminist Perspectives*. Bloomington: Indiana University Press, 1993.

Klaus, Carl H. *The Made-Up Self: Impersonation and the Personal Essay*. Iowa City: University of Iowa Press, 2010.

Klaus, Carl H. and Ned Stuckey-French (eds.). *Essayists on the Essay: Montaigne to Our Time*. Iowa City: University of Iowa Press, 2012.

Korhonen, Kuisma. *Textual Friendship: The Essay as Impossible Encounter from Plato to Montaigne to Levinas and Derrida*. New York: Prometheus Books, 2006.

Lukács, Georg. "On the Nature and Form of the Essay: A Letter to Leo Popper," *Soul and Form*, trans. Anna Bostock. London: Merlin Press, 1974.

Norman, Brian. *The American Protest Essay and National Belonging: Addressing Division*. Albany: State University of New York Press, 2007.

Olaniyan, Tejumola and Ato Quayson (eds.). *African Literature: An Anthology of Theory and Criticism*. Oxford: Blackwell, 2007.

Plunkett, Erin. *A Philosophy of the Essay: Scepticism, Experience and Style*. London: Bloomsbury Academic, 2018.

Porter, Jeff and Patricia Foster (eds.). *Understanding the Essay*. Peterborough: Broadview Press, 2012.

Retallack, Joan. *The Poethical Wager*. Berkeley and Los Angeles: University of California Press, 2003.

Said, Edward. *The World, the Text, and the Critic*. Cambridge, MA: Harvard University Press, 1983.

Saunders, Max. *Self-Impression: Life-Writing, Autobiographical, and the Forms of Modern Literature*. Oxford: Oxford University Press, 2010.

Singer, Margot and Nicole Walker (eds.). *Bending Genre: Essays on Creative Nonfiction*. London: Bloomsbury Publishing, 2013.

Starobinski, Jean. "Peut-on définer l'essai?", *Pour un temps*. Paris: Centre Georges-Pompidou, 1985.

Wall, Cheryl. *On Freedom and the Will to Adorn: The Art of the African American Essay*. Chapel Hill: University of North Carolina Press, 2018.

Wallack, Nicole B. *Crafting Presence: The American Essay and the Future of Writing Studies*. Logan: Utah State University Press, 2017. Weinberg, Liliana. *Situación del ensayo*. Mexico City: Universidad Nacional Autónoma de México, 2006.

Williams, Orlo. *The Essay*. New York: G. H. Doran, 1914.

Histories and Anthologies of the Essay

Aquilina, Mario, Bob Cowser, and Nicole Wallack (eds.). *The Edinburgh Companion to the Essay*. Edinburgh: Edinburgh University Press, 2022.

Black, Scott. *Of Essays and Reading in Early Modern Britain*. London: Palgrave Macmillan UK, 2006.

Boutcher, Warren. *The School of Montaigne in Early Modern Europe*. Oxford: Oxford University Press, 2017.

Carter, Steven D. (ed.). *The Columbia Anthology of Japanese Essays: Zuihitsu from the Tenth to the Twenty-First Century*. New York: Columbia University Press, 2014.

Chevalier, Tracy (ed.). *Encyclopedia of the Essay*. London and Chicago: Fitzroy Dearborn Publishers, 2012.

Childs, Jason and Denise Gigante, *The Cambridge History of the English Essay*. Cambridge: Cambridge University Press, forthcoming.

Childs, Jason and Christy Wampole, *The Cambridge History of the American Essay*. Cambridge: Cambridge University Press, forthcoming.

D'Agata, John. *The Next American Essay*. Minneapolis: Graywolf Press, 2003.

D'Agata, John. *The Lost Origins of the Essay*. Minneapolis: Graywolf Press, 2009.

D'Agata, John. *The Making of the American Essay*. Minneapolis: Graywolf Press, 2016.

Early, Gerald L. *Speech and Power: The African-American Essay and Its Cultural Context from Polemics to Pulpit, Vols. I and II*. New York: Ecco Press, 1992, 1993.

Ercolino, Stefano. *The Novel-Essay, 1884 to 1947*. London: Palgrave Macmillan, 2014.

Federman, Raymond. *Critifiction: Postmodern Essays*. Albany: State University of New York Press, 1993.

Gigante, Denise. *The Great Age of the English Essay: An Anthology*. New Haven: Yale University Press, 2008.

Gross, John (ed.). *The Oxford Book of Essays*. Oxford: Oxford University Press, 1991.

Landow, George P. *Elegant Jeremiahs: The Sage from Carlyle to Mailer*. Ithaca: Cornell University Press, 1986.

Lopate, Phillip. *The Art of the Personal Essay: An Anthology from the Classical Era to the Present*. New York: Anchor Books/Doubleday, 1994.

Madden, Patrick and David Lazar (eds.). *After Montaigne: Contemporary Essayists Cover the Essays*. Athens: University of Georgia Press, 2015.

McCarthy, John. *Crossing Boundaries: A Theory and History of Essay Writing in German: 1680–1815*. Philadelphia: University of Pennsylvania Press, 1989.

Milnes, Tim. *The Testimony of Sense: Empiricism and the Essay from Hume to Hazlitt*. Oxford: Oxford University Press, 2019.

Murphy, Kathryn and Thomas Karshan (eds.). *On Essays: Montaigne to the Present*. Oxford: Oxford University Press, 2020.

Oates, Joyce C. and Robert Atwan (eds.). *The Best American Essays of the Century*. New York: Houghton Mifflin Company, 2000. eds.

Pollard, David (ed.). *The Chinese Essay*. London: C. Hurst and Co, 2000.

Russell, David. *Tact: Aesthetic Liberalism and the Essay Form in Nineteenth-Century Britain*. Princeton, NJ: Princeton University Press, 2018.

Spinner, Jenny (ed.). *Of Women and the Essay: An Anthology from 1655 to 2000*. Athens: University of Georgia Press, 2018.

Stuckey-French, Ned. *The American Essay in the American Century*. Columbia, MO: University of Missouri Press, 2011.

Waithe, Mark and Michael D. Hurley (eds.). *Thinking Through Style: Non-Fiction Prose of the Long Nineteenth Century*. Oxford: Oxford University Press, 2018.

Walker, Hugh. *The English Essay and Essayists*. London and Toronto: J. M. Dent and Sons, 1915.

Wilkinson, Emily C. *The Miscellaneous: A Poetics of the Mode in British Literature, 1668 to 1759*. Dissertation, Stanford University, 2008.

Theories of the Visual Essay

Alter, Nora. *Projecting History: German Nonfiction Cinema, 1967–2000.* Ann Arbor: University of Michigan Press, 2002.

Alter, Nora. *The Essay Film After Fact and Fiction.* New York: Columbia University Press, 2018.

Alter, Nora and Tim Corrigan (eds.). *Essays on the Essay Film.* New York: Columbia University Press, 2017.

Bacqué, Bertrand, Cyril Neyrat, Clara Schulmann, and Véronique Terrier Hermann (eds.). *Jeux sérieux: Cinéma et art contemporains transformant l'essai.* Geneva: HEAD, 2015.

Barthes, Roland. *Camera Lucida: Reflections on Photography.* Trans. Richard Howard. New York: Farrar, Straus and Giroux, 1981.

Biemann, Ursula (ed). *Stuff It: The Video Essay in the Digital Age.* Zurich: Voldemeer, 2003.

Corrigan, Timothy. *The Essay Film: From Montaigne, After Marker.* Oxford: Oxford University Press, 2011.

Fusco, Coco. *Young, British, and Black: A Monograph on the Work of the Sankofa Film/Video Collective And Black Audio Film Collective.* Buffalo, NY: Contemporary Arts Center, 1988.

Hollweg, Brenda and Igor Krstić (eds.). *World Cinema and the Essay Film: Transnational Perspectives on a Global Practice.* United Kingdom: Edinburgh University Press, 2019.

Jhaveri, Shanay (ed.). *America: Films from Elsewhere.* Mumbai: The Shoestring Publisher, 2019.

Krstić, Igor, Laura Rascaroli, Brenda Hollweg, Roberto Cavallini, Iván Villarmea Àlvarez, and Thomas Elsaesser. "The Essay Film and the City," *Mediapolis: A Journal of Cities and Culture* 3, no. 4 (2018).

Lopate, Phillip. "In Search of The Centaur: The Essay-Film," *Totally, Tenderly, Tragically: Essays and Criticism from a Lifelong Love Affair with the Movies.* New York: Anchor Books, 1998.

Mitchell, W. J. T. *Picture Theory: Essays on Verbal and Visual Representation.* Chicago: University of Chicago Press, 1995.

Montero, David. *Thinking Images: The Essay Film as a Dialogic Form in European Cinema.* Bern: Peter Lang, 2012.

Pines, Jim and Paul Willeman (eds.). *Questions of Third Cinema.* London: British Film Institute, 1989.

Racaroli, Laura. *The Personal Camera: Subjective Cinema and the Essay Film.* New York: Wallflower Press, 2009.

Racaroli, Laura. *How the Essay Film Thinks.* Oxford: Oxford University Press, 2017.

Sontag, Susan. *On Photography.* New York: Farrar, Straus and Giroux, 1977.

Williamson, Glenn G. W. *Eugene Smith and the Photographic Essay.* Cambridge: Cambridge University Press, 1992.

INDEX

Cambridge Companions To ...

AUTHORS

TOPICS

CPSIA information can be obtained
at www.ICGtesting.com
Printed in the USA
BVHW051013031122
651070BV00005B/15